T0169966

OUR MAN IN HAITI

GEORGE DE MOHRENSCHILDT
AND THE CIA
IN THE NIGHTMARE REPUBLIC

JOAN MELLEN

OUR MAN IN HAITI: GEORGE DE MOHRENSCHILDT AND THE CIA IN THE
NIGHTMARE REPUBLIC
COPYRIGHT © 2012. JOAN MELLEN. ALL RIGHTS RESERVED.
PRESENTATION COPYRIGHT © 2012 TRINEDAY

Published by:
Trine Day LLC
PO Box 577
Walterville, OR 97489
1-800-556-2012
www.TrineDay.com
publisher@trineday.net
Library of Congress Control Number: 2012944883

Mellen, Joan.
Our Man in Haiti: George De Mohrenschildt and the CIA in
the Nightmare Republic—1st ed.
p. cm.
Includes bibliography and index.
Epub (ISBN-13) 978-1-936296-53-8 (ISBN-10) 1-936296-53-5
Kindle (ISBN-13) 978-1-936296-54-5 (ISBN-10) 1-936296-57-8
Print (ISBN-13) 978-1-936296-52-1 (ISBN-10) 1-936296-54-3
1. Mohrenschildt, George de. 2. Intelligence service – United
States – History – 20th century. 3. Haiti – Politics and govern-
ment – 20th century. 4. Caribbean Area – Foreign relations
– United States. 5. Oswald, Lee Harvey – Friends and associates.
I. Title

FIRST EDITION
10 9 8 7 6 5 4 3 2 1

Printed in the USA
Distribution to the Trade by:
Independent Publishers Group (IPG)
814 North Franklin Street
Chicago, Illinois 60610
312.337.0747
www.ipgbook.com

ALSO BY JOAN MELLEN

A Farewell To Justice: Jim Garrison, JFK's Assassination And The Case That Should Have Changed History

Jim Garrison: His Life And Times

Hellman And Hammett

Kay Boyle: Author Of Herself

"Modern Times"

"In The Realm Of The Senses"

"Seven Samurai"

Literary Masterpieces: One Hundred Years Of Solitude

Literary Masters: Gabriel García Márquez

Literary Topics: Magic Realism

Bob Knight: His Own Man

Natural Tendencies: A Novel

Privilege: The Enigma Of Sasha Bruce

ed., *The World Of Luis Buñuel*

Big Bad Wolves: Masculinity In The American Film

The Waves At Genji's Door: Japan Through Its Cinema

Women And Their Sexuality In The New Film

Marilyn Monroe

A Film Guide To The Battle Of Algiers

for MALCOLM BLUNT

ACKNOWLEDGEMENTS

I am grateful to all those who helped me bring the story of Dr. François Duvalier's Haiti to life. I am, first and always, indebted to Malcolm Blunt, whose generosity to me knew no bounds. I am very grateful. This book is dedicated to him.

I would also especially like to thank Bruce Adamson, whose indefatigable research into the life and times of George de Mohrenschildt deserves greater recognition. Joseph F. Dryer, Jr. gave generously of his time and memories of Haiti in the 1960s.

Gordon Winslow shared his bountiful research into the life and times of Rolando Masferrer Rojas, and made available a rare photograph of Masferrer in Cuba. Wilfred, thank you!

Howard K. Davis described for me in rich detail an aborted paramilitary invasion of Haiti in which he participated. Donald Deneselya relived for me the months he spent as a CIA infiltrator into the daily life of Anatoliy Golitsyn. Peggy A. Adler shared some of her research into the biography of Clémard Joseph Charles. Gaeton Fonzi was as cordial and helpful as always. James H. Lesar was kind enough to make available to me the AARC files on Clémard Joseph Charles.

I would also like to acknowledge for their kindness in sharing information with me: Anselmo Aliegro Duran; Rolandito Masferrer Betancourt; the late Martin Xavier Casey; John Quirk; Edward Ridgeway ("Jed") Harris; Douglas Valentine; Thomas J. Scully; Nathaniel Heidenheimer; Ed Sherry; John Loftus; and Bernard Diederich. I owe particular thanks to Max Blanchet.

Towards the end, as I was finishing, there was a cohort of long ago, the incomparable historian Larry Haapanen. Larry's methodical work, inquiring mind and dedication are an inspiration to all who are fortunate enough to know him.

I would also like to thank another unsung historian, Alan L. Kent. I am grateful to Alan for his insights and precise research into the Delk Simpson story, not to mention the generosity of spirit that added a sustaining comradely spirit to this project in its final hours. I would also like to thank John Williams for sharing his insights with me. To Peter Lemkin, I owe special thanks.

I am grateful also to Temple University's Sharon Logan for her support.

Much of the research for this book was done at libraries. I would like to acknowledge for their assistance: Carl Van Ness, University of Florida library at Gainesville; Richard Saunders, the Paul Meek Library at the University of Tennessee at Martin; Cynthia Franca, DeGoyler Library, Southern Methodist University; Hope Sudlow, Andrea Merrick and Diane Miller at the Mercer County Library, Hopewell Branch; and the staffs at Princeton University's Selwyn Mudd Library; the LBJ Library in Austin; and the JFK Presidential Library & Museum in Boston. And a special thanks to Tiffany Kelly for her work on the photographs.

My gratitude goes as always to Ralph Schoenman for his unflinching support, generosity and loyalty.

Kris Millegan is the rarest of publishers, sympathetic and welcoming of ideas that do not reside in the mainstream, humble and courageous, a rare combination of qualities. I would also like to thank my editor Margot White for her energetic work on the manuscript, and for her many suggestions as she pushed me, but always gently, to take this story as far as it could possibly go.

A note on usage: "CIA" is commonly referred to throughout this text without the definite article, "the." This stylistic choice is in keeping with the Agency's own practice in referring to itself, both in written and in spoken form. No one with more than a passing acquaintance with CIA is likely to affix the definite article "the" before "CIA."

Larry became involved with proprietaries for a time, legally incorporated businesses actually financed and controlled by CIA. When the Agency wanted to do something interesting in Kurdistan or Yemen, it filed for incorporation in Delaware. It was during this period that he came into contact with a number of Agency assets who had important holdings in sensitive parts of the hemisphere. A man from United Fruit, a man from the Cuban-Venezuelan Oil Trust (it was George de Mohrenschildt as a matter of fact). Merchant banks, sugar companies, arms dealers. A curious convergence of motives and holdings. Hotel interests here, gambling interests there. Men with vivid histories, sometimes including prison. He saw there was a natural kinship between business and intelligence work.

Don DeLillo, *Libra*.

CONTENTS

ONE

An Adoptive Texan with some Intelligence Connections

He was a fey character and an off and on acquaintance over the years as was Clémard Charles and some of the other players in that 'great game' as the Brits are proned [sic] to denote it.

— Edward Browder, solder of fortune, gunrunner, CIA asset

I find out he's also hooked to Army Intelligence. Cuba via Haiti.
— CIA's Laurence Parmenter, a figure apparently modeled on David Atlee Phillips, speaking about George de Mohrenschildt, in *Libra*.

"Our man in Haiti" could be any one of several men. That appellation could refer to George de Mohrenschildt, who enters this narrative fresh from his assignment from CIA to look after the former U.S. Marine Lee Harvey Oswald in Dallas and Fort Worth. De Mohrenschildt is in Haiti on a new project. Our man in Haiti" could be Clémard Joseph Charles, a Haitian banker, who, while working for the dictator François Duvalier ("Papa Doc"), sought CIA's assistance in replacing him. It could even be Papa Doc himself, who became appealing to the U.S. as the Caribbean alternative to Fidel Castro, and so was, finally, tolerated, despite the atrocities he visited upon his already beleaguered people.

"Our man in Haiti" could even be a figure like Isadore Irving (I.I.) Davidson, at the center of intrigue in Haiti, keeping watch for CIA on de Mohrenschildt, Charles, Duvalier and others. This is a story of Haiti in the 1960s. It depicts the collision of military and industrial enterprise, as President Eisenhower put it, along with the increasingly powerful intelligence forces that would prophesy what was to come.

After the 1962 missile crisis, CIA gave up on liberating Cuba and removing Fidel Castro, notwithstanding certain posturing, along with several paramilitary operations designed to fail. Once John F. Kennedy signed his agreement with Nikita Khrushchev not to invade Cuba again, CIA had no alternative but to pull back. Kennedy would be the only president since CIA was founded in 1947 to enter into open conflict with the Agency. At that moment in CIA's history, the Agency was not ready to defy openly the directives of a sitting President, whether in Cuba or in Haiti.

Haiti's finest hour had come at the turn of the nineteenth century when a former slave, Toussaint L'Ouverture, with stunning shrewdness and military savoir-faire, freed the country from both slavery and colonial domination. Tousssaint did not live to witness the Revolution that resulted in Haiti's becoming the first independent republic in the Caribbean, and the first black Republic anywhere. Toussaint had to defeat not only the French colonizers of Haiti, but also the armies of Spain and Great Britain, each with its own interests. The mulattoes, a class as much as they were a race, conspired with the British.

Toussaint perished in one of Napoleon's jails in France seven months before Haiti, in 1804, issued its "Declaration of Independence." Unspeakable bloodshed on the part of Haiti's adversaries had left the country exhausted. Fearing the re-imposition of slavery, the ex-slaves exterminated their enemies.

The new flag of Haiti made clear the minimal expectation of its ex-slave population: "Liberty or Death." As C.L.R. James writes in *The Black Jacobins*, "whites were banished from Haiti for generations, and the unfortunate country, ruined economically, its population lacking in social culture, had its inevitable difficulties doubled by this massacre."

Toussaint would live on in history as the inspiration for Simón Bolívar, who went on to lead the struggle for independence from Spain of five countries in South America. Alexandre Pétion was elected president of Haiti's southern Republic on March 9, 1806. Among Pétion's policies was the prohibition of foreign ownership of the land. When Simón Bolívar sailed into Les Cayes as a political refugee on Christmas Eve, 1815, Pétion nursed him back to health, granted him political asylum, along with military and financial support, and gave him a printing press.

All that Pétion asked in return was that Bolívar emancipate the slaves in the territories he liberated – a promise he did not keep. Bolívar, who was granted sanctuary in Haiti twice, never recognized the country. He refused to invite Haiti to the Congress of American States that he hosted in 1826.

If the Haitian's believed that they were finished with imperialism, James notes, "they were mistaken." Haiti's troubles – the revenge taken upon the former slaves who had led the struggle – resulted in Haiti's becoming and remaining the poorest country in the hemisphere. Its impoverishment was in no small measure the fruit of the colonial powers and the U.S. blockading this first black Republic. There would be no "nation building" by the U.S. here. Toussaint had known that "the guarantee of the liberty of the blacks is the prosperity of agriculture" – Haiti's ability to feed itself rather than relying on commodity production for export. It didn't work out that way.

Haiti has been vulnerable to American investment since the turn of the twentieth century. In 1910, a U.S. entrepreneur built a railroad in Haiti, the better to facilitate his exploitation of the area. Where business went, the U.S. military was not far behind. In 1915, Woodrow Wilson dispatched two companies of Marines to Haiti to protect American investments against growing German competition, .

"Action is evidently necessary," Wilson declared, "and no doubt it would be a mistake to postpone it long." Wilson's pretext will be examined in due course. The military was acting on behalf of empire long before CIA was a gleam in William ('Wild Bill') Donovan's and Allen Dulles' eyes.

On foot, and with fixed bayonets, the Marines visited the Bank of Haiti and "in broad daylight, by use of force, made off with the gold stored there and sent it off to New York." In 1918, the Haitian constitution was revised to permit foreign ownership of land and property, supplanting the revolutionary 1804 document that forbade both. The U.S. Marines remained in Haiti until 1934.

Among the entrepreneurs turning a profit in Haiti in the following years was Brown & Root, who in 1953 signed a $28,000,000 contract to build the Péligre Dam in the Artibonite Valley. Through the Export-Import bank, the U.S. government provided $31,000,000, with Brown & Root entering into its customary "cost plus" arrangement. "Cost plus" meant that an original contract would be amended to meet unexpected costs, which always managed to make their appearance in abundance. Brown & Root were closing up shop when President Paul Eugène Magloire fled the country in 1956.

Preceding Colonel Paul Magloire had been Dumarsais Estimé, who was called "un noir au pouvoir," a black man in power. Estimé had supported rural cooperatives and nationalized the banana industry, and proved too reformist for the elite. He passed a law granting a minimum wage, yet failed to mobilize popular support. A military coup on May 10, 1950, a "bloodless coup" – supported by business, by the Roman Catholic Church, and by mulatto Marxists – ended Estimé's reign and led to the election of Paul Magloire, who had served as commandant of the palace guard under Estimé.

Under Magloire, Haiti's tourism flourished along with its relations with the U.S. as he welcomed foreign investment. Yet Magloire suppressed strikes. He also imposed censorship, shutting down the newspaper *Haiti Démocratique*. He closed down schools that he considered hotbeds of subversion and taxed the population mercilessly.

Magloire's regime was repressive and ridden with corruption, fueled by bribery. He jailed his political opponents and banned political meetings. It wasn't long before yet another military coup was in the offing. A general strike preceded Magloire's flight from Haiti to Jamaica and then on to Brooklyn, New York. Magloire departed from Haiti with twenty million dollars. The Army returned to power, followed by the election of Dr. François Duvalier, "Papa Doc," who had been part of Estimé's government and had opposed Magloire from the start.

Papa Doc was a tiny country doctor, whose notoriety derived from his having battled a typhoid epidemic, for which he earned the nickname. At first glance, he might have seemed an unprepossessing figure, peering out from behind Coke-bottle eyeglasses. He wrapped himself in oversized heavy black wool suits despite Haiti's unforgiving tropical climate. Duvalier, however, was not to be underestimated.

Duvalier ensured his election – the year was 1957 – with a $400,000 bribe to the Army dispensed by his personal banker, Clémard Joseph Charles. Charles tendered his contribution in Duvalier's name. A loyal acolyte of Papa Doc, it certainly seemed, Charles chipped in $46,000 of his own money for soldiers who had not been paid for two months.

A State of Emergency proclaimed at the beginning of 1958 became all but permanent. By April 1961, Duvalier had dissolved the National Assembly and the Senate so that the legislative branch of the government would be a single chamber represented by a single political party. He announced that he would be "president for life."

Duvalier identified himself, as "black," as had Estimé. Robert I. Rotberg writes in *Haiti: The Politics of Squalor* that Duvalier gained wide support by suggesting that mulattoes "could redeem themselves only by thinking black." Duvalier invoked Toussaint L'Ouverture as if he were his moral successor, speaking for the black masses of Haiti. Duvalier also embraced Vodou ("voodoo") as if he were one of the gods himself, dispatched to protect the Haitian people. Duvalier was no friend to foreign-born Roman Catholic priests, whom he persecuted and banished from the country, starting with Monsignor François Poirier, Archbishop of Port-au-Prince.

Freedom of the press soon became a distant memory, as did independent trade unions; in this Duvalier did not differ markedly from his predecessor, Magloire. Duvalier also purged the judiciary and dismissed the president of the highest court, who had urged publicly that Haiti maintain an independent judiciary. Economically, Haiti sank even further, with the balance of trade entirely on the side of its neighbor on the island of Hispaniola, the Dominican Republic.

To ward off opposition, dissent and criticism of any kind, Duvalier did not rely on the Haitian army, which he reduced to 5,000 men. Instead, Papa Doc created a private militia, the *"Tontons Macoutes"* (literally "bogey men"), murderers by reflex and criminals by habit, whose modus operandi was to eliminate entire families.

Uniforms were scarce, but none were required. The *Tontons Macoutes* favored opaque black sunglasses, and, when they could find them, blue jeans. People were gunned down in broad daylight. Many disappeared. Others were tortured and then executed in the basement of the National Palace.

After the Cuban revolution, a nervous Duvalier invited the U.S. Marines back to Haiti to train guerrilla fighters in the event of a Castro invasion. The U.S. obliged. The State Department's William A. Wieland sent an entire rifle company to Haiti, led by a six foot four inch, red headed Marine colonel with a flaming red mustache. Fluent in French, the red-haired colonel brought with him, according to Joseph F. Dryer, Jr., who will be a major character in this narrative, a DC airplane (probably a Super DC-3) and trained four companies of Haitians. (Four companies would amount to about four hundred and thirty-two men). They easily eliminated an invading Castro brigade of six hundred and eighty, who had landed on the south side of the almost impenetrable Haitian jungle, and had begun to move up the island.

CIA did not yet have a station in Haiti. They didn't need one. Toward American business, Duvalier remained benign.

In 1959, the U.S. government sent a $4,300,000 loan for development of the Artibonite Valley, along with a grant of $7,000,000. In 1960, American aid jumped to $21.4 million, while Haiti's sugar quota (the amount of sugar guaranteed by the U.S. for import) rose by twenty-five percent. The Artibonite Valley, through which the Artibonite River flows, is located in Haiti's central plateau. The Valley had been Haiti's main rice growing area, and also featured banana plantations, but the absence of irrigation was a persistent problem.

Over the years, Haitian presidents like Paul Magloire initiated various irrigation schemes. The Péligre dam – 220 feet high and 1,075 feet wide, was to irrigate 80,000 arid acres. When Duvalier came to power, Haiti still owed the Export-Import Bank $25 million on the Artibonite Valley project, which had yet to be productive. In the late 1950s and early 1960s, Haiti was the only Caribbean nation to show a decrease in agricultural production.

Robert and Nancy Heinl write in their history of Haiti that "it was the measure of Duvalier's extraordinary force of character that no nation or agency rendering aid to Haiti ever openly challenged the nonfiscal accounts during his presidency." No one questioned where the aid went. Duvalier announced that his role models were Marx, Lenin, Atatürk, Nkrumah and Mao Tse-Tung. Yet, François Duvalier, whatever his faults and despite his invocation of Communists as his heroes, was, for the United States, preferable to that unpredictable Communist ninety miles from its shores: Fidel Castro.

In exchange for all this largesse, Duvalier was expected to vote with the United States at international meetings. In the Cuban Missile Crisis, Duvalier supported the United States, although before long he was threatening to "bring President Kennedy to his knees." Kennedy held Duvalier at arm's length. Only after Kennedy's assassination was a new investment loan awarded to Haiti, guaranteeing $4,000,000 for an oil refinery. An Inter-American Development Bank loan would improve the water system.

Eighty percent of all this American aid disappeared into the pockets of Duvalier and his minions, just as it had with the presidents who preceded him. Although there were no confiscations of American property, no Castro-style agrarian reform, American businessmen faced repeated shakedowns and harassment from the Duvalier government. Foremost among the entrepreneurs rooted in Haiti was the Texan Clint Murchison, Jr. To be on the safe side, Murchison registered in Washington, D.C. as a lobbyist for Duvalier.

Murchison owned flour mills ("Caribbean Mills"), and a mammoth meatpacking business called HAMPCO, "Haitian-American Meat and Provision Company, S.A." At the flour mills, grey flour was ground for the poor out of imported surplus wheat. In the fiscal year ending June 1962, HAMPCO shipped 1,609,886 pounds of meat; between July 1, 1961 and September 30, 1963, 5,237,242 pounds of meat left Haiti.

Sanitary conditions at HAMPCO were sub-standard. There were no health inspections, and the meat was unfit for the U.S. market. Instead, it was shipped to Puerto Rico where regulation was non-existent.

When "certain deficiencies" finally led to HAMPCO being denied an import certificate even to Puerto Rico,

Senate Majority Leader Lyndon Johnson's secretary, Bobby Baker, made the trouble evaporate – for a commission of one cent per pound. Johnson received his kickback. The scandal was being investigated in late 1963 by Attorney General Robert F. Kennedy, who planned to add this example of Lyndon's malfeasance to his growing list of justifications for removing Lyndon Johnson from the 1964 presidential ticket.

Nor were Lyndon Johnson, Murchison and Bobby Baker the only Texans reaping profits from Haiti. George H.W. Bush's partner in Zapata and Zapata Off-Shore oil, CIA operative Thomas J. Devine, working out of New York, was also doing business in Haiti. By 1985, cheap labor and tax concessions would result in the presence of two hundred and forty factories in Haiti owned by U.S. businessmen. The minimum wage was now only three dollars a day.

Still, American corporations concluded that Duvalier was too blatantly corrupt and unreliable. It was not so much Duvalier's corruption that made the U.S. uneasy. They had dealt with corruption before. Rather, it was the fear of the nationalization of American businesses, along with an unreasonable tax burden, and unpredictable shakedowns for cash, that by 1963 led CIA to enter into serious discussions about how most efficaciously to remove Papa Doc.

* * *

In the spring of 1963, two unlikely companions traveled the eastern corridor of the United States. One was Duvalier's banker and acolyte, Clémard Joseph Charles. The other was George de Mohrenschildt, a White Russian exile living in the United States, and an adoptive

Texan. An indifferent oil geologist who knew little about the subject despite his Master's degree, de Mohrenschildt was charming and unscrupulous. He was a man ready to sell himself to any intelligence service willing to make use of his natural gift for duplicity.

De Mohrenschildt had already entered history as the "friend" of Lee Harvey Oswald, that former U.S. Marine and returned "defector" from the Soviet Union, and his Russian wife, Marina. Behind the transparent mask of a "philanthropist," de Mohrenschildt had shepherded Oswald around Dallas and Fort Worth in 1962 and early 1963. He and his fourth wife, Jeanne, had taken what seemed to be a parental interest in the plight of Marina Oswald, who seemed so restless and uneasy in her new country.

When Oswald moved on to New Orleans in April 1963 – it was now eight months before Oswald would be blamed for the murder of President Kennedy – de Mohrenschildt took up a parallel assignment. His charge was now Clémard Joseph Charles, whom CIA was considering as its replacement for Duvalier. Under the scrutiny of CIA and the 902nd Military Intelligence Group (nicknamed "90 Deuce" for those in the know), and the most powerful component of U.S. military intelligence, de Mohrenschildt and Charles became the Gemini twins of CIA operations in Haiti. That military intelligence and CIA worked hand in hand in the matter of de Mohrenschildt and Charles in Haiti is a given of this story. The common denominator of de Mohrenschildt's relationships with Oswald and Clémard Joseph Charles was CIA.

George de Mohrenschildt was born in oil-rich Baku, in Mozyr, Russia, on April 17, 1911, to a family of oil entrepreneurs. Sometimes he said his birthplace was St.

Petersburg, the more romantic city where both of his parents were born. Sometimes he said he was born in Poland. Sometimes he would claim that he had been born in Sweden of Swedish parents, and that his family had moved to Russia when he was four years old. In all versions, the de Mohrenschildts were aristocrats by birth, courtesy of a title bestowed upon the "Morenskildes" by Queen Christine of Sweden in 1650.

George's father, Sergius, had been governor of the Province of Minsk for the Czar. He was vice-president of the Nobel Oil Company and a "marshal of nobility" in Minsk Province. After Nobel's holdings were confiscated by the Bolsheviks, Sergius von Mohrenschildt developed an interest in agrarian reform and was appointed Deputy Minister of Agriculture for the Beyelorussian Republic, White Russia. He was imprisoned on the pretext that he had protected the Jewish, Greek Orthodox and Catholic religions.

Dramatizing his early life, George de Mohrenschildt would claim that as an eight-year-old he had been hungry, alone, and surviving in the streets by his wits. He had been compelled to beg for food, living like "an animal." So he confided to Igor Voshinin, a Russian friend in Dallas, who reported the conversation to the FBI.

Sergius Alexander von Mohrenschildt was jailed first by the Communist regime in 1920 for criticizing the Bolsheviks. In 1921, he was jailed again and banished to Siberia for life. According to George, his crime had been admitting that he had openly advocated a constitutional monarchy for the Russian people.

Escaping from prison, Sergius von Mohrenschildt moved his family to Vilno, Poland. His wife, Alexandra Zopalsky, of Russian, Polish and Hungarian descent, died of typhoid fever, contracted on the journey from Russia to Poland. In the years to come, George de Mohrenschildt rarely mentioned his mother.

His stories about his father, Sergius, would be numerous, contradictory and unverifiable. Sometimes he said his father was assassinated during the Russian revolution. Sometimes he claimed his father had been prominent in the Bolshevik regime until he disagreed with officials, who threw him into jail. Sometimes he said that he felt sympathy for the Germans because they had been "humane" toward his father when they overran Poland. Sometimes during the war he claimed that his father was languishing in a Nazi concentration camp.

According to former federal prosecutor John Loftus, de Mohrenschildt's father was among Allen Dulles' postwar recruits from the Nazi intelligence services. Loftus does not name his source, except to say that it was a "confidential interview, former agent, OPC (Office of Policy Coordination)," Frank Wisner's clandestine services at CIA. The OPC would soon change its name to DDP (Deputy Director for Plans, both an individual and a CIA component). The word was that the Nazis had assisted the elder de Mohrenschildt in his peripatetic adventures. According to Loftus, Sergius had been a spy reporting on the Bolsheviks for the *Abwehr*, the German intelligence services.

In 1940, de Mohrenschildt and his brother Dimitri, attempted to bring their father, stuck in Vilno, Lithuania, to the United States with a transit visa through Germany. They were unsuccessful. If Sergius had performed some service for the *Abwehr*, apparently the Nazis were ungrateful.

The family could boast of at least one indubitable CIA connection. Dimitri von Mohrenschildt, George's older brother, born in 1902, had arrived in the United States in 1920. An uncle, Peter von Mohrenschildt, was waiting to help him. By 1936, Dimitri possessed not only a Yale degree, but also a Ph.D. in comparative literature from Columbia University.

After serving with OSS, Dimitri became a CIA asset. He joined the Agency officially on April 11, 1950 when he was approved as a contact for foreign intelligence purposes on a limited basis, "not to receive classified information above confidential." Dimitri became a professor at Dartmouth where, as part of his CIA profile, he founded an anti-communist journal called *Russian Review*. He worked closely with CIA's outlet journal, *Reader's Digest*.

Dimitri also helped found CIA's Radio Free Europe. His co-editor at *Russian Review*, Henry Chamberlin, an Allen Dulles intimate, worked for CIA's "AmcomLib," later renamed "Radio Liberty." Dimitri seemed the more conventional of the brothers, yet he too had his non-conformist tendencies, and would live to nearly one hundred years of age on an Ashram in India.

George de Mohrenschildt never assumed so overt a CIA profile. He was a tall, comely man over six feet tall with thick, wavy dark hair, (some remembered it as dark blond). His eyes were light blue – or, as he himself described them, green. He spoke with a pronounced accent that to some sounded German. There was nothing straightforward about him.

Along the dark byways of his continental wanderings, de Mohrenschildt became a solitary drifter. His aristocratic family background bequeathed to him an aversion to work. He would be a desirable intelligence asset because he was – and would remain until his death – under the protection of no one. He was a man easy to discard when his usefulness expired. His life illustrates how CIA treated its assets and contacts when their activities rendered them inconvenient.

From his youth, George de Mohrenschildt had been anarchic, difficult to control. In 1931, when he was twenty, in Antwerp, he had been charged with drunkenness, using a false name, and resisting a police officer. A *Tribunal Correctionel* sentenced him on November 4th, 1931 to eight days imprisonment or a fine of 182 francs. Already clever, he managed to emerge from the incident with a suspended sentence, and was placed on probation for three years.

At twenty, George de Mohrenschildt was already a man without an identity, living as if he had nothing to lose. CIA investigated the incident of his Antwerp arrest from police records when de Mohrenschildt was recruited in 1957 to serve in the ICA, the "International Cooperation Agency" (sic). So explained Richard Helms, CIA's Deputy Director for Plans, to J. Lee Rankin, General Counsel for the President's Commission on the Assassination of President Kennedy, on being asked on June 3, 1964 whether CIA had pertinent files on de Mohrenschildt.

The Antwerp incident also appears in the records of the Office of Security, United States Department of State; this information was passed on to the FBI in March 1964. After the Kennedy assassination, Paul Hartman of the Counterintelligence Research & Analysis section collected some of the 00/CD HH Dallas field office reports on de Mohrenschildt. ("HH" is CIA cablese, a field office designator applied to 00, and CD, the Contact Division, actually the Office of Operations).

CIA's Office of Security claimed that it could locate only one de Mohrenschildt document from 1957 when they checked their files after the assassination – which was laughable. George Mohrenschildt had been a person of interest to the intelligence agencies virtually from the moment he entered the United States.

De Mohrenschildt was educated at a Polish cavalry academy. Later, at the University of Liège in Belgium, he earned the degree of "Doctor of Science of International Commerce." De Mohrenschildt served briefly in the Polish army. From 1934 to 1938, he worked for Sigurd, Inc. a firm manufacturing ski clothes. He had contributed $10,000 to the company, his inheritance from his mother's estate. When he left for the United States, he retrieved some of the money from Sigurd.

On May 13, 1938, with money borrowed from his brother's wife, a loan he later repaid, George de Mohrenschildt sailed alone from Le Havre to New York. Immediately he filed a "Declaration of Intention" to apply for U.S. citizenship. In this new country, he could weave any fabricated web he chose, and no one would know otherwise. A man without a country, he was free to reinvent himself. He changed his name from "von Mohrenschildt" to "de Mohrenschildt" because the "von" made it sound "like a German name." Dimitri retained the "von."

Like the most accomplished, the most proficient of liars, de Mohrenschildt married his lies with half-truths. He boasted that he had been a lieutenant in the Polish cavalry. Sometimes he said he was a "captain." In fact, he was a second lieutenant during his brief army stint.

He claimed to have been on the Polish Olympic Ski team; actually he was a member of a squad that participated in preliminary trials for the Olympics, only to fail to win a single meet. One of his lies had no basis at all:

he invented a brother, a "close associate of Adolf Hitler," who he claimed had been executed by the Nazis.

De Mohrenschildt included on his resume that he had worked for the Polish Press Association, covering the Spanish Civil War; he did write a few articles for the Polish Government Press, but he was never in Spain, let alone in the midst of the Loyalists' bloody ordeal against Franco. He told a young woman acquaintance that he was connected with *Variety* magazine; he had, in fact, written one minor article for them, about the potential of the motion picture industry in Europe. (The woman telephoned *Variety* only to be informed that they had never heard of George de Mohrenschildt.) He claimed to have served with British intelligence during World War II.

Perverse, at social gatherings George de Mohrenschildt was likely to take what would later be called the "politically incorrect" view. He talked of "the virtues of the German form of government under Hitler" and the "disadvantages of democracy." At a restaurant one night – after the Germans had overrun France – someone remarked that the French people were starving.

"No," said von Mohrenschildt, as he then still called himself. "Hitler is taking care of them. They are not starving like they were in the last war."

On another occasion he called Hitler "a smart Austrian," and predicted that the war would end "either by a compromise or a German victory." More than once, he greeted a visitor with his arm raised and the words "*Heil Hitler!*"

On other occasions, de Mohrenschildt affected to be a Bolshevik sympathizer, and many concluded, erroneously, that he had "definite Communistic tendencies." He claimed to have been a member of the Communist Party prior to his entry in 1938 into the United States. Later he

17

denied it. He did brag about being an atheist and once declared, "The Russians don't believe in God, and I don't either. We will all be fertilizer after we die."

Cynicism accompanied his nihilism. His sociopathy – his inability to sympathize or empathize with any other human being – was masked by his abundant charm, quick wit, and continental manners. He traded on his title. The truth was that he believed in nothing.

As one of his landlords noticed, George de Mohrenschildt rarely did a day's work. What he preferred was to consort with the rich. He lived for several months in 1939 in New Orleans, courtesy of friends of his brother.

The FBI recorded the assessment of an informant: George de Mohrenschildt "always seemed to associate with very fine people and moved about in high social circles." Birth and connections mattered greatly to him. He claimed that he was related to President Woodrow Wilson by virtue of the marriage of his uncle, Ferdinand de Mohrenschildt, to Wilson's granddaughter. Ferdinand de Mohrenschildt was First Secretary of the Imperial Russian Embassy in Washington.

In 1939 or 1940, in New York City, shortly after his arrival in the United States, de Mohrenschildt was recruited by Pierre Freyss, the head of French intelligence in the United States (Freyss' cover was the exclusive French fabric company, Schumacher). Freyss worked for French intelligence in 1939 and 1940, prior to the German occupation of France and the installation of the Vichy government.

Freyss was in New York not to sell fancy fabrics to the rich, but to get people to sell large quantities of oil to France rather than to Germany. Freyss recruited de Mohrenschildt to "collect facts on people involved in pro-

German activity," according to a State Department file. Freyss later remembered that he employed de Mohrenschildt as a salesman for Schumacher, selling decorative fabrics – in the late 1930s or early 1940s.

Working for French intelligence, Freyss devoted himself to outbidding Germany for oil. Together with de Mohrenschildt, he traveled to Los Angeles and San Francisco in search of business people sympathetic to France. De Mohrenschildt served Freyss as he would others: he put Freyss in contact with Poles who might help. Freyss later contended that de Mohrenschildt was not paid for his services, although in 1945 de Mohrenschildt told the FBI that his commissions from Schumacher led him to "make a sufficient amount of money."

De Mohrenschildt told the FBI as well that Freyss had him doing work in the "Information and Economics Department of the Intelligence Unit."

De Mohrenschildt's work with Freyss and French intelligence set the paradigm. De Mohrenschildt's talent was as an instrument, a facilitator, a person with a wide circle of acquaintances whom he might bring together for common purposes. He was gifted at serving the agendas of others, and in this function he was aided by his amorality. He had no scruples. In San Francisco, he actually found someone to help Freyss: "Vigario," a Portuguese American, who agreed to monitor the departure of ships bound for Italy carrying oil.

According to de Mohrenschildt, following his meeting with Vigario, he met Freyss at the Rice Hotel in Houston, Texas, and accompanied Freyss through oil country. De Mohrenschildt professed to be amazed by the large number of French people whom Freyss contacted, and who were sympathetic to the French cause. They traveled to Galveston, Corpus Christi, Palestine, and Dallas before driving back to New York where de Mohrenschildt put Freyss in contact with the Polish Consul, who later became the first minister of the Polish government in exile.

Freyss viewed de Mohrenschildt as a man who was not "sympathetic to Communism, Fascism or any subversive ideology," as he told the Civil Service Commission in 1957 when de Mohrenschildt was about to begin his career in U.S. intelligence and the government was scrutinizing both his employment career and his personal life. Freyss liked him well enough to recommend him "for a position critical from the standpoint of the national security." Freyss remained vague about the intelligence work de Mohrenschildt did for him in those years prior to Germany's invasion of France.

After, or perhaps simultaneous with, his work with Pierre Freyss, de Mohrenschildt found himself in Mexico. Women succumbed to his attentions and, more often than not, he solved his financial problems by attaching himself to a rich woman. Among his early conquests was a thrice-married Mexican woman named Lilia Pardo Viuda de Larin. She was thirty-five years old; he was thirty.

Lilia was de Mohrenschildt's type. She was five foot seven inches tall, with dyed auburn hair, blowsy, worldly and glamorously attired. She was a woman with a sixth grade education who socialized with higher-ups in the Mexican government.

One husband, deceased, had been a "chocolate magnate," and had left her a fortune. On this money, she and de Mohrenschildt toured Mexico. Spending about eight months in Mexico, George produced a manuscript titled "The Adventures Of A Young Man." Later he changed the title to "Son of the Revolution." Bawdy and licentious, the story featured at its center a "Mexican Mae West."

De Mohrenschildt's written English was sub-standard, and the book was never published. That didn't stop de Mohrenschildt from telling the FBI that it had been published – by Ernest Hemingway's publisher, Charles Scribner's Sons. The Bureau checked: Scribner had never heard of the book, or of de Mohrenschildt.

One day in 1941, in the company of Lilia, de Mohrenschildt photographed and sketched the Coast Guard station and ship channel near Port Aransas, Texas. A rootless cosmopolite like de Mohrenschildt, with his Teutonic accent, photographing a military installation attracted the attention of the authorities. Two thousand dollars was in his pocket.

Lilia Pardo de Larin and de Mohrenschildt had remained in this outpost of civilization for between six and eight days, Lilia admitted. First denying to Inspectors from the Immigration and Naturalization Service that George had a movie camera, Lilia amended her statement on the next day, April 20th; he had a small Kodak, she said. They were at the Coast Guard facility at Corpus Christi, Lilia claimed, because "the fishing...was good," and they wanted "to bathe on the beach and fish." George had made drawings of two persons who were fishing from the dock, and painted sailboats in watercolors. When anyone asked now, he said he was Swedish and French.

To the INS inspectors, de Mohrenschildt produced papers including his Declaration of Intention to become a United States citizen, and a Certificate of Entry into the United States to become a permanent resident, dated May 13, 1938. He also had a re-entry permit, an Alien Registration Receipt and a Notice of Classification from

Local Draft Board number 44, stating that he was 4F. Among his effects was a zipper briefcase filled with papers that he did not volunteer to show to the inspectors.

From that moment on, de Mohrenschildt lived under the radar of several U.S. intelligence agencies. U.S. Customs was brought into the case, as was the office of the Attorney General in Corpus Christi, Texas. The FBI was not far behind.

Military intelligence took an interest in de Mohrenschildt's activities and whereabouts, and noted that he claimed that he was trying to get a position with Nelson Rockefeller's Inter-American Affairs organization. That did him no service. The Office of Naval Intelligence opened a file on George de Mohrenschildt. The FBI would remain on his case for the rest of de Mohrenschildt's life.

At first glance, George de Mohrenschildt appeared to be a Nazi agent. He had expressed pro-Nazi, anti-American views. He had detailed photographs of the harbor defense at Corpus Christi. He was running around with a woman of dubious morality, who was not his wife. Lilia's politics did not particularly concern the authorities in that era when morality and politics were viewed as one and the same.

The Mexican government informed him that he was persona non grata in Mexico and ordered him to leave the country. De Mohrenschildt, unperturbed, claimed that the expulsion was prompted by General Maximino Ávila Camacho, who was jealous of de Mohrenschildt's relationship with Lilia Larin.

In 1942, de Mohrenschildt applied to the State Department for permission to leave the United States to visit Mexico and return. As an alien, he was required to obtain this. Permission was denied. Already de Mohrenschildt had a "refusal" or "lookout" on his file at the Department of State passport office, imposed on October 8, 1942. Such a "lookout" suggested that the person posed a security threat or had made false statements to the government. De Mohrenschildt pleaded that "his attitude toward the war was a proper one. He had done nothing to warrant any other view of his case by anyone."

It was early in the career of this international trickster, but already his word meant nothing to anyone. The State Department took a dim view of his need to go to Mexico to be with his "fiancée." He was "in a ticklish position," de Mohrenschildt wrote on his "Application for Permission To Depart From The United States," "as to how I shall come back if I am reclassified and called to the U.S. Army, very peculiar situation."

Why not help in the war effort? he was asked. Besides, didn't he know that he was "not the only suitor that Mrs. Larin has?" The State Department then asked him a "confidential" question: could he name the man "who offered to send an airplane to Cuba recently to bring Mrs. Larin back to Mexico?" Lilia had alighted in Havana at the time.

De Mohrenschildt, who had no intention of serving in the U.S. Army, stiffened, but then gave up the name. It was Maximino Camacho, the Minister of Communications, the brother of the President of Mexico, and the leader of the Fascists in Mexico. Camacho, de Mohrenschildt added, was "the real power behind the government."

Her association with Camacho accounts for Lilia's having been denied entry to the United States in 1942, although she had obtained a visa. The ground had been that "her presence in the United States might be prejudicial to the interest of the nation." Eventually Lilia was granted a permit to enter the United States, where her children were at school, "on the condition that she does not contact Mohrenschildt while she is here."

De Mohrenschildt was told by the State Department that his being allowed to remain in the United States should be vindication enough, given the incident at Corpus Christi.

When he was denied a re-entry permit, he demanded a hearing from an Interdepartmental Committee of Members of the State Department, the War Department, The FBI, the USIS (United States Information Agency), and the Office of Naval Intelligence. The hearing was held on February 12, 1943. De Mohrenschildt's appeal was denied and he was granted no visa. Before the brouhaha had concluded, he had involved an Assistant Secretary of State, A.A. Berle, Jr.; a Brigadier General; the Director of the FBI; high-level Navy officers, and others.

Between 1941 and 1948 the FBI, out of virtually every field office in the country, watched de Mohrenschildt. They kept a record of his every lie, every contradiction. Collecting money Lilia had forwarded to him, he wrote in a letter to his bank: "I'll probably be very soon in the armed forces." The FBI registered the lie, aware that de Mohrenschildt had already secured 4-F classification on the ground of a supposed heart condition, and would never be sent off to war.

When Bureau agents opened his trunk and suitcases, they discovered that he was a painter of no small accomplishment. Later the Newton Gallery on 57th Street in New York City exhibited seventy of his watercolors of Mexico. The reviews were outstanding.

De Mohrenschildt's tumultuous relationship with Lilia continued into the 1940s. At one point, Lilia's Algerian-born husband, Jorge Guasco, showed up in New

York and threatened to shoot both of them on sight. De Mohrenschildt managed to have Guasco thrown into jail for six months. When the lovers were separated by national borders, Lilia sent George passionate letters, claiming that she couldn't live without him. "I cannot physically stand your absence," she wrote.

Agonizing over the visa denial that prevented them from meeting while she remained in Mexico, Lilia chose to overlook George De Mohrenschildt's flaws and defended him against the authorities that were keeping them apart. "Nor is it their business, if your income is from practicing the noble profession of gigolo or hiring yourself as a sodomist," Lilia wrote. In the same letter, she addressed him as "My Adored Turrocckka," among other endearments. De Mohrenscildt promised, vaguely, to marry her "should she perfect her divorce [she was still married to husband number three] and make certain financial settlements which he had in mind."

When things fell apart, Lilia was bitter. She called de Mohrenschildt a "blackmailer" and a man "capable of anything and for his useless and vicious life needs large sums of money and so naturally sells himself to the highest bidder." He was a "dangerous snake." Now Lilia wondered why the U.S. would even consider granting such a man citizenship. (De Mohrenschildt would become a U.S. citizen in 1947).

Learning of the Lilia-de Mohrenschildt saga, on October 30, 1944, FBI Director J. Edgar Hoover suggested to future CIA operative Birch D. O'Neal, then serving at the American Embassy in Mexico City, that he should interview Lilia Pardo.

In the 1940s in New York, George de Mohrenschildt went through the motions of being employed without actually doing any work. Hired by the Equitable Life Assurance Society, he never sold any insurance. (In 1940 he had failed, "by about five points," he told the FBI, to pass the examination for Casualty Brokers Insurance agent).

FBI records indicate that on July 30, 1942 de Mohrenschildt acted on behalf of a New York-based company called "Film Facts, Inc." that had been organized by Pierpont Morgan Hamilton, a grandson of J. Pierpont Morgan. Film Facts was being run by a "fifth cousin" of de Mohrenschildt named Konstantin Maydell, who in fact was no relation at all.

Maydell's archives contained "many films of a pro-Nazi nature." One of the films, *Spain In Arms*, was decidedly pro-Franco. De Mohrenschildt met Maydell through Maydell's showing of *Spain In Arms* at the Ritz-Carleton Hotel.

Pro-Franco or not, de Mohrenschildt professed that it was the best documentary he had ever seen, and contacted Maydell. Opportunistic from the start, de Mohrenschildt then contacted the Polish Consulate and proposed that they sponsor a documentary about Poland, to be called *Poland Forever*. In addition to the producers' financial difficulties, *Poland Forever* depended on the arrival of footage from Germany, which was seized en route by the British and held up for too long to make the film feasible.

That Maydell's sympathies were with Germany did not bother de Mohrenschildt; he told the FBI that Maydell was "nothing but a soldier of fortune interested in making money" and who "didn't give a darn" about one country over another. In short, Maydell seems to have been a mirror image of de Mohrenschildt himself. De Mohrenschildt added that "Maydell's outstanding characteristic was his anti-Semitism."

Listening to all this, the FBI wondered whether de Mohrenschildt himself was a "German propagandist." Maydell was soon interned as a "dangerous enemy alien." De Mohrenschildt would tell the Warren Commission that Maydell was a White Russian who thought he could get the return of his Russian estate with the help of the Germans.

There is one other appearance of a film company in de Mohrenschildt's convoluted history. In de Mohrenschildt's CIA file there is a memo dated July 30, 1942, written by an Ensign Horrigan. It was addressed to Commander Vanderbilt of the Office of Strategic Services (OSS) and stated that de Mohrenschildt claimed to have represented an Irish film company that had taken pictures during the Spanish Civil War. Horrigan had also discovered that de Mohrenschildt's uncle Ferdinand's apartment had been raided and that many films of a pro-Nazi nature were discovered.

* * *

About the war years, de Mohrenschildt lied profusely. He claimed that from 1941 to 1943 he had been employed by the Economic Resources French Military Mission in Washington, D.C. Yet there was no record at the French consulate of a "George de Mohrenschildt." Vichy government personnel were interned in Hershey, Pennsylvania from November 1942 to February 1943, with the French mission buildings in Washington, D.C. under seal. All French government personnel who remained in Washington were either members of the military or typists.

When Dimitri von Mohrenschildt joined OSS in 1943, the Office of the Coordinator of Information (COI)

– precursor of the OSS and still operating at home – wondered whether Dimitri's brother George might not also be "good material." OSS officer William Vanderbilt recommended that George become an "OSS non-citizen agent," based in Mexico. George, in Washington, D.C., filled out an application, only for OSS to reject him because of the Corpus Christi caper. The record states that George de Mohrenschildt "was not hired because he was alleged to be a Nazi espionage agent."

Not yet having given up on marrying George de Mohrenschildt, Lilia seethed, plotted and pouted, using every political contact at her disposal to gain entry into the United States. But de Mohrenschildt thought better of marrying a woman five years his senior, who was fantasizing about bearing him a son. On a trip to Palm Beach, George met Dorothy Pierson, the eighteen-year-old daughter of a millionaire who was already in possession of her healthy trust fund. Soon Dorothy was pregnant and shortly after she and George were married and living on her family's money.

During the summer of 1943, de Mohrenschildt rented a chauffeur's cottage for them out on Long Island. His landlord would later call him "a proficient liar and apparently shiftless," but that wasn't the worst of it. George taunted Dorothy with tales of his successes with other women. There was well-documented marital violence. Once he kicked her in the abdomen. He struck her on the head with a hammer. During a Christmas party, with Dorothy now heavily pregnant, George "was kissing and pawing other women," right before her eyes.

He tortured Dorothy by declaring that, in view of the type of people she and her parents were, the child would probably be born without arms or legs. (Those words would bear an ironic consequence: the two children de Mohrenschildt would have with his third wife, Wynne Sharples, would be afflicted with fatal cystic fibrosis).

De Mohrenschildt's sexual proclivities were "abnormal," Dorothy said, her final word as she fled to Europe after their eight month long nightmare of a marriage was finally over.

Their daughter, Alexandra, would be raised in Arizona by Dorothy's cousin, Nancy Pierson Sands, with whom Dorothy shared a grandfather, and Franklin Clark. Alexandra de Mohrenschildt grew up as "Donna Clark."

Dorothy's mother was relieved that the marriage had ended: she had concluded that George de Mohrenschildt was a homosexual. Later, de Mohrenschildt would claim that the marriage failed because Dorothy had objected to the stenographer he had hired to help him write his book, and was even jealous of his affection for his dog.

In February 1945, the FBI finally sat George de Mohrenschildt down for an interview. Even facing domestic intelligence, de Mohrenschildt could not prevent himself from speaking against his own interest. The "Communistic form of Government of Soviet Russia is the better form of government on the European continent," de Mohrenschildt said, not for the last time. He admitted that he was "prone to exaggerate some on recounting activities in which he had participated." His instinct for self-preservation kicked in only when he denied that he had taken photographs of the Coast Guard installations at Corpus Christi.

Like those nineteenth century people down on their luck and pursued by creditors or the law, people who scrawled G.G.T. –"Gone to Texas" – on their abandoned hovels, de Mohrenschildt found his way in 1945 to that former Republic. In Texas, he would be employed by several of the most successful of Texas entrepreneurs, from Clint Murchison to D.H. Byrd, to Herman and George Brown. Many of these corporate moguls enjoyed strong CIA connections.

Even before he moved to Texas, de Mohrenschildt had been employed by Humble Oil for three months in 1939. He went to Louisiana to work as a rotary helper, only to be laid off because his "services were poor." He claimed he had a deep cut on his arm, as well as amoebic dysentery, and fled the arduous oil fields. One informant would tell the FBI that George de Mohrenschildt "would rather live by his wits than do an honest day's work."

As soon as he took up formal residence in Texas, de Mohrenschildt went back to school, earning a Master's degree in petroleum geology from the University of Texas at Austin. He financed his studies with a grant from the "Russian Student Fund" that also supported his brother's anti-Communist journal, *Russian Review.* De Mohrenschildt's amorality reasserted itself and he cheated on his examinations with "ponies" that he carried blatantly into the exam room. (Ponies are crib sheets, a risky form of cheating).

Everyone cheats, de Mohrenschildt argued when he was caught. Out of his abiding narcissism he viewed the world in his own image, always confident that charm trumped morality. Indeed the University of Texas hired him as a tutor in the romance languages department. On occasion, de Mohrenschildt boasted that he spoke every European language – except German. Sometimes he included Hungarian, at other times not.

At the University of Texas, young women called him the "Mad Russian," and one said that he could undress a woman just by looking at her. His behavior remained that of a man who lived as if he had nothing to lose. He'd rush up to an embarrassed girl, click his heels, bow from the waist, and kiss her hand. That was nothing compared to how he humiliated a Czech language professor by attacking him in front of his students for speaking Russian with a Czech accent.

1946 found de Mohrenschildt in Rangely, Colorado. He was employed by the Rangely Field Engineering Committee, not as a "petroleum engineer," but to gather data and documents charting the production of the various oil companies developing the Rangely oil field. First hired as an assistant to the chairman of the committee, de Mohrenschildt became chairman himself, only to neglect his duties as long as he could get away with it.

His secretary would report that he "neglected his job and was quite irresponsible in his personal affairs." No matter that he had risen to a position of authority, he spent his time in nearby Aspen skiing, while the secretary did his work. De Mohrenschildt, she concluded, had "the temperament and habits of a bon vivant continental European," a man who thought that America was a "rich place" where he was destined to live well. He was "somewhat unprincipled and quite independent."

Although the FBI had written "closed" on his file in 1945, in fact they were still monitoring de Mohrenschildt's mail, making a list of his Rangely correspondents and their addresses.

Serial monogamy suited George de Mohrenschildt, although no woman could abide him for long. Joining him in Colorado was his second wife, Phyllis Washington, whom he married in July 1948. Nicknamed "Fifi," Phyllis was a playgirl, and the stepdaughter of foreign service officer and CIA asset Samuel Walter Washington.

In snowy Aspen where the skiing was good, de Mohrenschildt put up at the best hotel. He placed Phyllis on the payroll as a "janitress taking care of the engineering building" in Rangely, a duty "Fifi," of course, never performed. He also put his personal charges on his expense account, which was expected to run $100 a month, but which amounted to ten times that. George was "quite sure no one would seriously examine his expense accounts."

De Mohrenschildt's marriage to Phyllis Washington replayed the Dorothy Pierson scenario. The woman was rich, there was abundant physical abuse, and the marriage lasted less than a year. Once George struck Phyllis so hard that her face had to be sewn up. On another occasion, she grabbed a knife and, retaliating, went after him.

Yet "Fifi's" rich investment banker uncle, William Stix Wasserman, who would remain friendly with de Mohrenschildt, concluded that she was impossible to live with, ran her husband into debt and was irresponsible. Phyllis Washington's later life was characterized by frequent bouts of mental illness. In 1964, she was committed to D.C. General Hospital, in Washington, D.C.

De Mohrenschildt stole the household furnishings his bosses lent to him for his home in Aspen. Returning to Rangely with a trailer full of furniture, he wrecked his car. Soon he received a letter marked "very personal." An audit followed. His being fired from his job at Rangely in 1950 had been inevitable. At this moment, de Mohrenschildt established a life-long pattern, leaving behind unpaid bills. This time there was one lawsuit pending against him, at Denver, for $100.

Before long, de Mohrenschildt found himself a third wife, a woman richer than either Phyllis Washington or Dorothy Pierson. Wynne Sharples was well on her way to becoming a medical doctor. More to the point, her father was a successful oilman.

Some said Wynne Sharples married de Mohrenschildt, whom she had known only briefly, because his title appealed to her. Sharples herself would later admit that she was captivated by his "royal background," and that George de Mohrenschildt was a man attractive to most women. In an outright lie, he had told her that his parents were killed by the "revolutionists" in Russia, a story that lent an aura of adventure to their relationship.

What appealed to de Mohrenschildt was that Wynne Sharples was rich, and they could live off her family's money, which they did. The best man at their wedding was de Mohrenschildt's old colleague from French intelligence, Pierre Freyss, who would also be godfather to their son.

"Didi," as Wynne Sharples was known, learned soon enough that George de Mohrenschildt was a man who "doesn't know right from wrong," but could "entertain a king" and "charm a bird off a tree." With Sharples, de Mohrenschildt had two children afflicted with cystic fibrosis, both of whom would die before they reached adulthood.

Physical abuse defined this marriage as well. De Mohrenschildt struck Sharples and once nearly ran her over with his car. She noted that he was universally violent toward women. Once, at a dinner party, he slapped an elderly, heavy-set woman so hard that she fell forward into her soup. When she dropped her glasses, and her false teeth became dislodged, De Mohrenschildt laughed.

He was also a classic snob. Looking over his fellow guests at a party, the one-time baron said, "The most distinguished person here is the butler."

He resented the rich and successful, since he was neither, and periodically professed sympathy with Marxism. "Comes the revolution," de Mohrenschildt told Sharples, "you and your family will be first to go." Mannered, sly, he pretended to be sympathetic toward the poor and the marginalized. "The best people are the Negroes," he said. "They are simple and good and not rich." As if he were Levin in Tolstoy's *Anna Karenina*, he said, "All we need is nature and the peasants." Yet on occasion he slapped the servants.

He was a handsome man who used his sexuality as a weapon to dominate and degrade people. Lying on a bed with a nine-year-old child, he said, "Are you going to grow up to be a sexy girl?" He remarked to a little boy, "You look like a pansy to me." One day Wynne asked him whether there was any truth to the rumors that he was homosexual.

It isn't true, de Mohrenschildt said. Then he added, "Anyway, in Europe we look at those things differently." That he was unfaithful to all his wives was a given. When Sharples was away, he entertained women in their home, a fact reported by the maid.

And always he would steal, so that Sharples never gave him access to the funds of the National Cystic Fibrosis Research Foundation, which she founded (with George) in 1955, and of which she was president; "Didi" devoted herself to this foundation exclusively. Nor would she trust de Mohrenschildt with confidential information.

He "played at" the business of developing oil properties, Wynne said, increasingly irritated. After a while, she told him that he was getting on her nerves staying home all day with nothing to do. On September 3, 1954, de Mohrenschildt rented an office at the Republic National

Bank Building in Dallas for $194 a month so that Wynne didn't have to deal with him, during the day at least.

Samuel Butler, the President of Sharples Oil, later told the FBI that the Sharples family "was forced to spend considerable sums of money on occasion to bail de Mohrenschildt out of various oil deals."

After five years of marriage, Wynne Sharples was relieved to be rid of this man who was "irresponsible, unreliable, childish, temperamental and foolish." He fought their April 1956 divorce until she threatened to accuse him of being a homosexual; he did not deny it. Community property included one hundred shares of the Sharples Oil Corporation; all of de Mohrenschildt's assets at that point derived from his connection to Wynne Sharples.

When their son Sergius died in 1960, de Mohrenschildt sued for his share in the trust fund set up for Sergius by Sharples' father, who preferred that the money be transferred to the trust of their daughter, Nadejda. De Mohrenschildt objected. Both parents were beneficiaries of Sergius' trust, he argued. De Mohrenschildt only received $13,577 of his half of the $40,000 because he had not paid the child support he had owed.

Just as de Mohrenschildt retained his contact with Fifi's uncle, William Stix Wasserman after they were no longer together, he repeated the pattern with relatives of Wynne Sharples. At their wedding, de Mohrenschildt had met Wynne's uncle Edward J. Walz. De Mohrenschildt cultivated this contact, and in 1961 he persuaded Walz to go into business with him.

De Mohrenschildt's role was to arrange oil leases with money raised by Walz. Their company was called "Waldem." De Mohrenschildt did not produce any oil leases, however, and the partnership ended abruptly. He was "an excellent petroleum engineer, but was not a competent or aggressive business partner," Walz said, with considerable generosity, after he dissolved their partnership and the company.

Then, just as he was about to leave for Haiti in 1963, de Mohrenschildt brought suit against Wynne Sharples, who was now married to a doctor, for permanent custody of Nadejda. He told the child that in Haiti she wouldn't have to sleep in a plastic tent or go to school, and she wouldn't even have to wear clothes. To retain custody of her daughter, to defeat her former husband in court, Sharples had to invoke the pornographic murals in de Mohrenschildt's bathroom. She emerged victorious.

In Texas during the fifties, de Mohrenschildt worked for CIA-connected oilmen like William Buckley, Sr., at Pantepec Oil (Venezuela); Buckley's son William was a CIA asset. Clint Murchison was a partner. He went into business with his step-nephew, Edward Hooker, who had been George H.W. Bush's roommate at Phillips Academy at Andover (Massachusetts). Dimitri had married Edward Hooker's mother, Betty. With Edward Hooker based in New York, de Mohrenschildt moved to Abilene, Texas, where he worked out of his hotel room and traveled around, again with the objective of buying up oil leases.

This business also failed. Hooker blamed de Mohrenschildt's "inability to respect confidences," "general unreliability" and "lack of a sense of responsibility." George de Mohrenschildt, Hooker said when he was questioned by the U.S. Civil Service Commission, "cannot be trusted implicitly with any type of secrets, let alone government secrets."

Among de Mohrenschildt's CIA-connected Texas employers was Brown & Root. Another was the Schlumberger Oil Well Drilling Company. As a Texan CIA asset remarked dryly, it was difficult to discern where Schlumberger "began and CIA left off." In 1968, under pressure, CIA admitted to "extensive traces on this company" and acknowledged "current contacts with the main Schlumberger office in Houston and with three or four subsidiaries elsewhere." Schlumberger's relationship with CIA dated at least from the mid-fifties.

In June 1955, according to one CIA document, "there had been occasional but circumspect contact with the main Schlumberger office in Houston for an extended but unspecified period. Such contact continues." Another document states that there are "extensive CIA traces on this company, and on various persons connected with it. Because of French control, DCS [Domestic Contact Service] admits, dealings with the firm have been circumspect." The Garrison investigation, in the late 1960s, into the Kennedy assassination provoked CIA to release information about its longstanding relationship with the Schlumberger Well Surveying Corporation of Houston.

Yet another CIA-de Mohrenschildt connection was with ARAMCO oil's James "Terry" Duce, whose name appears in de Mohrenschildt's address book for the early 1950's. Duce's career parallels that of de Mohrenschildt; he would become Aramco's chief contact with the State Department and CIA, among their all-important oil connections.

Author Bruce Adamson was to discover at least ten CIA assets or employees in de Mohrenschildt's 1954-1955 address book. Adamson also points out that among de Mohrenschildt's fellow tenants at the Republic National

Bank Building was CIA-connected Dresser Industries. Heading Dresser, was H. Neil Mallon, who became an intimate of Allen Dulles. It was Neil Mallon who would found the Dallas Council On World Affairs, an outlet for CIA's political point of view.

Still another CIA connection in de Mohrenschildt's history, Adamson discovered, was Samuel Walter Washington, "Fifi's" stepfather. Washington, although he was officially a foreign service officer, was on loan to CIA in the years preceding the 1954 coup when he supervised more than two hundred and fifty employees in Guatemala, although he was not the coordinator of the coup. Higher level CIA officers can claim that distinction. As Adamson points out, Samuel Washington had been evaluated by so highly placed a CIA officer as Frank Wisner, who ran the clandestine services. Washington had been assigned to CIA from the Foreign Service in September 1950.

In Dallas, de Mohrenschildt, along with other White Russians of his acquaintance, was monitored not only by CIA, but by the 66th Military Intelligence Group (MIG), reporting to "90 Deuce," the 902nd MIG, a highly secretive organization. CIA classified its de Mohrenschildt file as "Secret."

A Texas oil and gas executive named Samuel Ballen became one of de Mohrenschildt's few friends. Forgiving, Ballen saw de Mohrenschildt as a "wonderful, undisciplined creature of nature," although "the economics and realities of life have given him much trouble." Ballen concluded that this was "a man who owes allegiance to mankind and not [to] any particular country."

Others were less charitable. De Mohrenschildt's fecklessness, his amorality, invited speculation. An oil man named Dimitri Djordjadze thought that George was "still trying to get even with the world for what he consider[ed] his loss, the wealth and position taken from him by the Russian Revolution."

It is no wonder that the reviews on de Mohrenschildt's character were mixed, and that acquaintances were given to pondering his character and motives. De Mohrenschildt's long intelligence history suggests that this was a man forever concealing who he was, throwing people off the scent of what he was really about. In the late 1950s, when de Mohrenschildt began to serve U.S. intelligence, he put to good use his slippery, self-contradictory personae.

De Mohrenschildt retained his identity as a sometime Nazi-sympathizer. One evening he invited Jewish friends to the Dallas "Bohemian Club" where he launched into a long rant on the virtues of Heinrich Himmler. Sometimes de Mohrenschildt professed to be an admirer of Bolshevism, only, on another occasion, to grant that he couldn't live in Russia because he would be killed. He continued to assume the persona of a man who could not be defined. By 1957, he was a CIA operative, so that his affectations as Nazi or Bolshevik sympathizer seem designed to ensure that his cover would remain intact.

Some dismissed him as a perpetual adolescent, immature and irresponsible. That, too, was part of the façade. He was a man perfectly placed to be used – an empty shell waiting to be filled, and, as always, a practiced liar.

In 1954, CIA beckoned de Mohrenschildt directly through its commercial front, the International Cooperation Administration (ICA). ICA was a forerunner of the Agency For International Development (AID), itself to be frequently utilized as a CIA front. That ICA and CIA were often interchangeable is suggested in a 1956 CIA document on the subject of a "Soviet Repatriation Campaign." CIA and ICA are described as dual entities, both taking "special action" on the issue of asylum for refugees: "Special action by ICA and CIA has been undertaken."

De Mohrenschildt's entrance into government service surprised many, including Phyllis Washington's uncle, William Stix Wasserman. Wasserman believed that de Mohrenschildt was not "politically minded," but was "frivolous in nature," and lacked "any profound sense of responsibility " – that frequently heard complaint among de Mohrenschildt's acquaintances. At best he was a "semi-serious Russian playboy."

His Dallas neighbor Igor Voshinin remarked that, "de Mohrenschildt does not believe in anything, either religious or political." This was profoundly true. CIA had long known that de Mohrenschildt had failed to "establish good moral character." The Agency drew de Mohrenschildt into its fold nonetheless. Once you were part of CIA, its values and behavior became yours anyway. CIA wanted people who were pliant, people who would make no distinction between the truth and their interpretation of it.

What may have attracted ICA/CIA, in addition to the de Mohrenschildt family intelligence history, was precisely that George de Mohrenschildt was a man who didn't believe in anything. Despite, or because of, his unsavory past and reports of his dishonesty and indiscretions, CIA's Office of Security granted him the approvals required for intelligence work. Wooing Yugoslavia and

Tito had long been a particular ambition of Allen Dulles. According to Dulles' wartime lover Mary Bancroft, he so loved that country that he knew "the name of every city, town, river, bridge, railway line and personality in the entire country."

The cover story was that the government of Yugoslavia was hiring de Mohrenschildt as a "consultant in oil resources." De Mohrenschildt explained to the press: "Yugoslavia now buys both oil and oil machinery from Russia and the Soviet bloc. Our State Department would like to see Marshal Tito's nation become self-sufficient in oil." George de Mohrenschildt was to advise the Yugoslavs "on ways to increase oil production." He was now telling anyone who asked that he was "of Swedish extraction."

De Mohrenschildt described his work in Yugoslavia as follows: "Supervised drilling and completion methods in the whole country. Set up pattern for bottom-pressure surveys. Introduced new methods in the field of reservoir engineering and production. Supervised surface geological work on the Adriatic coast, resulting in the discovery of Povinj Field, Istria." He was said to be among "the first of a group of specialists who would be doing this type of work there."

The International Cooperation Administration cleared de Mohrenschildt and in 1957 he was sent off to Yugoslavia. He was to spend one month in each of five Republics where oil or wildcatting operations were in progress to assist in locating oil. Then he was to devote three months to exploration work on the Dalmatian coast of the Adriatic between Trieste and Albania. That was the official story. This was a man who was singularly incompetent at the oil business. If de Mohrenschildt managed to make himself useful in Yugoslavia, or elsewhere, his efforts had little to do with petroleum engineering.

After eight months, de Mohrenschildt was accused of drawing secret military fortifications and invited to leave Yugoslavia. His partner, George D. Mitchell, Jr., a geo-physical consultant, who also went to Yugoslavia on behalf of the International Cooperation Administration, but who aroused no suspicion, was invited to remain. Mitchell later gave out the story that de Mohrenschildt was not asked to remain "as there seemed to be some dissatisfaction with his work on the part of the Yugoslavian officials."

Back in Dallas in December 1957, de Mohrenschildt sat down with J. Walton Moore, the officer in charge of the CIA field office. De Mohrenschildt generated at least ten separate reports of his European trip, reports forwarded by Moore to other federal agencies (see Appendix). By now George de Mohrenschildt's CIA connection was an "open secret" in Texas, oilman George Kitchel told Bruce Adamson.

From Yugoslavia, de Mohrenschildt was sent to Ghana "to do some surveying work to assist in the development of the oil industry there." His May and June 1958 trip to Ghana was sponsored by an "American-Swedish syndicate." His assignment was to lay out plans for "preliminary work and cooperation with the *Institut français du pétrole* on geophysical work"; he advised clients on the terms of the concession, or so he said. Under CIA auspices, he traveled to France, Switzerland, Italy, England, West Germany and Belgium.

CIA must have been satisfied because in 1958 de Mohrenschildt went off to Hungary, this time under the auspices of AID. Full use of de Mohrenschildt was being made by CIA, not only during these foreign trips, but also apparently at home where he was among the Agency contacts of a lawyer named Herbert Itkin, as we will see later. An August 13, 1958 document from the Personal Security Division of the Office of Security, directed to the Domestic Contact Division, refers to CIA's being in the process of "determining the extent and level of use of Subject."

De Mohrenschildt returned to Yugoslavia in 1958 on behalf of oilman John Mecom, whose private foundation would later be exposed as a CIA proprietary front. A "proprietary" was a corporation organized or utilized by CIA as a cover to conceal its operations. In Miami, for example, CIA had at least fifty-four dummy corporations that it used as fronts for its operations against Cuba. These included boat shops, real-estate firms, detective agencies, travel companies, airlines, gun shops and more.

By 1958, it no longer mattered that CIA's informants were calling de Mohrenschildt "eccentric, irresponsible, conceited, an adventurer fond of exaggeration and overly aggressive." Some noted that he associated "with persons of questionable loyalty, reputation and moral character." As always, George was sometimes flush with cash, at other times stone broke. He was a typical example of "HUMINT," the human intelligence operative who was flawed, his ethics deeply questionable and, for those very reasons, suited to CIA service.

In November 1959, de Mohrenschildt found himself back in Mexico, closing a deal for George Brown's subsidiary company, Texas Eastern, with PEMEX, the national oil company whose partners included George H.W. Bush. In town was Anastas Mikoyan meeting with the Cubans, and offering them advice on how to structure and organize a police state, Soviet style. Later de Mohrenschildt told the Warren Commission that he had reluctantly passed up an opportunity in Mexico City to dine with Mikoyan for fear of irritating his Texas oil friends.

De Mohrenschildt had married wife number four, Jeanne Le Gon, in June 1959. Jeanne was an acerbic, aggressive woman of Russian extraction. She had been born in Harbin, China in Manchuria. Sometimes now de Mohrenschildt used the alias "Philip Harbin," a typical de Mohrenschildt joke. It was the "Philip Harbin" alias that he used in the late fifties in relation to Haiti operations. Sometimes de Mohrenschildt called himself "P. Forestier."

Most of his acquaintances in Texas, observing his minimal living standard, concluded that he had very little money. Yet, as often as he requested loans and borrowed from friends, he always paid them back, suggesting an unacknowledged financial source. Sun Oil geologist Ilya A. Mamantov noted that de Mohrenschildt "seems to get along well financially and travels extensively." Having friends in high places paid off; at one point, he borrowed $600 from Thomas J. Attridge, the Deputy Manager of the Equitable Life Assurance Society of the United States.

An anomaly of de Mohrenschildt's life was that his financial circumstances fluctuated wildly. As his former son-in-law Gary Taylor would say of George and Jeanne, sometimes they "scrimped and saved" and sometimes they "had enough money to do as they pleased." The truth was that George de Mohrenschildt never worked steadily, not even for CIA.

As if to conceal whatever source of money he had, de Mohrenschildt lived off yet another wife. For a while, Jeanne Le Gon took a job selling hats in a department store to pay the bills. In addition to his financial fluctuations, he continued to display his characteristic unreliability and amorality in other areas. One of de Mohrenschildt's acquaintances later reported to the FBI that, "he was very interested sexually in the daughter of one of his wives." That had to be Christiana Le Gon, who worked for him for a while as a receptionist.

Among the de Mohrenschildts' adventures was a fourteen-month "walking tour" of Mexico and Central America in the company of a donkey and a dog. In their equipage were two pistols and a shotgun, which were confiscated at the Panama border. The source of funds for this expedition puzzled their friends. Coincidentally or not, in Guatemala they happened upon the CIA training camp for Brigade 2506, bound for disaster at the Bay of Pigs. De Mohrenschildt's final destination was Haiti where he would meet with banker Clémard Joseph Charles.

Upon his return from the "walking tour," de Mohrenschildt wrote to Ambassador George C. McGhee whom he had met at that CIA redoubt, the Dallas Council on World Affairs. Would McGhee help him by showing the manuscript he wrote of his trip, along with the maps and photos he made, to someone in the State Department? To spike McGhee's interest, de Mohrenschildt suggested that friends in Europe were urging him to send his manuscript to a contact in the Soviet Union. Surely someone in the State Department was "interested in the situation existing in the interior of these seething countries."

De Mohrenschildt closed his letter to McGhee awash in false modesty: "My simple report may give some useful ideas to the policy-forming bodies of the State Department." Under his name, he wrote "Ph.D.," a degree he had never earned. McGhee replied that he remembered de Mohrenschildt from his participation in the Dallas Council on World Affairs. He would forward the manuscript to "Latin American experts."

That manuscript never surfaced, either in published or in unpublished form. It certainly seems as if de Mohrenschildt was concealing his real motive and intentions – which were focused on that first black Republic, Haiti.

De Mohrenschildt had first visited Haiti in 1956, remaining from April 5 to May 12th. On behalf of the Sinclair Oil Company, he had worked on a project that was abandoned when no oil was discovered. That de Mohrenschildt had developed powerful contacts in Haiti is obvious. From 1959 on, he would be the recipient of seven loans from the Bank of Haiti, the government's bank.

In 1961, on the final stop of his "walking tour" of Mexico and Central America, de Mohrenschildt spent two or three months in Haiti. During this visit, he and Clémard Joseph Charles persuaded Haitian officials that the country was in need of a geographical survey and mapping project. On September 8, 1961, the Secretary of State of the Government of Haiti made de Mohrenschildt an official offer, inviting him to submit an estimate of the cost of an initial survey.

"It is understood that you will act under the auspices of the *Banque Commerciale d'Haiti*," the letter read, "and by virtue of an agreement with them." De Mohrenschildt was to "make the necessary financial arrangements of the exploitation of the petroleum and mineral resources which would be technically and economically justifiable."

Soon de Mohrenschildt and Charles were drawing up a contract with the Government of Haiti for "petroleum and mineral research in the regions of the Republic that seem promising to you."

De Mohrenschildt concocted a grand scheme for a "Haitian Holding Company." It would reconstitute the entire economy of Haiti, he claimed. As his partner, he named Clémard Joseph Charles, Duvalier's acolyte and the president of the first private bank in Haiti, the *Banque Commerciale d'Haiti.* "I received offers of a similar nature," Charles wrote to de Mohrenschildt on July 31, 1962 in his somewhat fractured English, "but I chose you and Texas so I am convinced that the goal desired will be attained."

Charles obviously viewed Texas and CIA as one and the same, not surprisingly since so many of CIA's corporate assets – not least, Herman and George Brown of Brown & Root – were headquartered in Texas. A host of CIA-infected tax-exempt foundations, conduits to channel money for clandestine purposes, were also located in Texas. Many of their proprietors, from John Mecom to George Brown, were connected to George de Mohrenschildt.

The Hoblitzelle Foundation of Dallas, which CIA held in trust, was based in the Republic National Bank of Dallas building, where George de Mohrenschildt had maintained an office. Between 1959 and 1965, the Hoblitzelle Foundation received contributions of $505,700, of which $250,000 was listed on IRS Form 990-A as having arrived from "anonymous donors." The rest came from other foundations. The Hoblitzelle Foundation then disbursed money to CIA operations, CIA-funded groups, and CIA asset propagandists. The name for these traveling funds was "pass through money."

In Dallas, de Mohrenschildt moved among CIA assets and contacts, ranging from the Dallas Council On

World Affairs, to the foundations. His one-time employer, John Mecom, had incorporated the San Jacinto Fund, a conduit for CIA money, Richard Harwood wrote in the *Los Angeles Times* and *Houston Chronicle*. The San Jacinto Fund enabled CIA "to penetrate financially, the structure of private institutions here and abroad without public knowledge of what was going on."

In Texas, some others of George de Mohrenschildt's CIA connections were among those running the CIA-sponsored foundations. Oveta Culp Hobby, President Eisenhower's Secretary of Health, Education and Welfare, for one, became the only woman tolerated by Herman Brown at the cigar-smoke-filled Suite 8F at the Lamar Hotel in Houston where Herman held court. Oveta's CIA clearances covered the years from 1959 to 1966.

These CIA-connected Foundations were themselves intertwined. William A. Smith, a director at Brown & Root's Texas Eastern, was a founder and trustee of the San Jacinto Fund. This fund in turn sponsored the National Student Association, a CIA front; among CIA's defenders in its financing of the National Student Association was General Philip H. Bethune, an eminence at the Dallas Council on World Affairs. As reporter Richard Harwood described it,

> The Americans thus involved made it possible for the CIA to penetrate, financially, the structure of private institutions here and abroad without public knowledge of what was going on. And they made it possible for the beneficiaries of this secret money to accept it without suspicion of taint.

Not surprisingly, CIA opened a file on Harwood.

"I am persuaded that with you and Texas," Clémard Joseph Charles repeated as he signed on to George de Mohrenschildt's ambitious holding company, "such a job does not surpass our capacities." A third partner would be B. Gindine-Tardieu, who held the monopoly on the export of bananas from Haiti to the United States.

Gindine-Tardieu had migrated to Haiti in 1935 on behalf of an English Syndicate of Investment to organize the export of wood and to build starch factories in the Caribbean. Now he owned a chocolate paste factory in Port-au-Prince. Among his assets were considerable real estate holdings. Gindine-Tardieu had invested for years in the development of cooperatives in Haiti, and was adviser to Clémard Joseph Charles' bank. Charles called Gindine-Tardieu his "spiritual father."

As outlined in a document generated in Dallas on de Mohrenschildt's letterhead and dated August 1, 1962, the Haitian Holding Company would be incorporated in the state of Texas. It would provide the following to Haiti: increased tobacco planting; a new cigar factory; cheap housing; a new wharf; and a hydroelectric plant "in conjunction with the dam that had already been built in 1953 by Brown & Root." It promised projects that included: canning lobster tails; marketing coconut candy; building a cotton wool plant; organizing a local insurance company (Papa Doc had already granted Charles a monopoly on automobile insurance on the island); operating a sisal plantation; hemp factories; several sugar plantations; a casino; a film production company – and more.

De Mohrenschildt's prospectus concludes with a veiled endorsement of François Duvalier as the hemisphere's non-communist alternative to Fidel Castro: "One should not forget the...geographical position of Haiti." On the resume that accompanied this prospectus, de Mohrenschildt added an eccentric category – his own "Special Connections":

> ...in government circles in Venezuela, Mexico, Haiti, Dominican Republic, Cuba, Colombia, Argentina, Ghana, Nigeria, South Africa, Middle East, especially Iran, France, Yugoslavia, Sweden, Poland, Belgium, and Austria.

This category may well have been the most honest on an otherwise inflated resume.

De Mohrenschildt was grandiose in his descriptions of his Haiti project. He would be in charge of the "Haitian Government Development Projects," he claimed, including the construction of a large airfield. He had been in contact with and had "the approval of high government officials in Washington, D.C."

In quest of investors, de Mohrenschildt tried some of his Texan, CIA-connected cronies. One was Jean de Menil, a Schlumberger son-in-law and managing director of the company. His spouse, Dominique, as de Menil's widow, would become a leading patron of the arts in Houston.

De Mohrenschildt assured de Menil that the projects outlined for his holding company were agreeable "to Washington and Haiti," and would proceed "under the auspices of the Alliance for Progress" with the Inter-American Development Bank "willing to contribute substantially to our program." AID would protect their interests.

So de Mohrenschildt signaled that CIA was behind the scheme. According to author Edward J. Epstein, de Mohrenschildt assumed that his "American connections" were appreciative and would further his interests when his contract with Duvalier was finally executed in the spring of 1963. De Menil, nonetheless, turned him down.

Soliciting funds for his use in Haiti, de Mohrenschildt invited oilmen of his acquaintance for lunch at the Dallas Petroleum Club. None put up any money for his Haitian Government Development Project. He also asked Russian friend Paul M. Raigorodsky for a $100,000 investment. Like de Menil, Raigorodsky turned him down. Raigorodsky had concluded that de Mohrenschildt's "primary interest is women." For a while in 1955, they had gone in on some oil speculation together, but all the drilled holes turned out to be dry.

In August 1962, de Mohrenschildt returned to Port-au-Prince, advising his correspondents that they should write to him in care of Clémard Joseph Charles, President of the *Banque Commerciale d'Haiti*. Clémard Joseph Charles had returned to Port-au-Prince, according to a Haitian newspaper story, following a trip to New York "accompanied by Mr. James R. Greene, vice-president of the Manufacturers Hanover Trust Company. In Port-au-Prince, Greene visited Clémard's bank, with which he hoped "to do business."

Now George de Mohrenschildt returned to Dallas to fulfill one more assignment for CIA.

J. Walton Moore invited George de Mohrenschildt for lunch at the CIA field office in Dallas where the subject was the former Marine and ostensible Soviet "defector" Lee Harvey Oswald, who had returned to the United States in June. In fact, Oswald had been a participant in the false defector program run by CIA Counter Intelligence chief, James Angleton. Now, in the summer of 1962, in the midst of all their plans for moving to Haiti, and from no motive of their own, George and Jeanne de Mohrenschildt suddenly took an enthusiastic interest in Lee Oswald and his Russian wife, Marina, niece of a Soviet intelligence officer.

That George de Mohrenschildt, social climber, and perpetual seeker of contacts with the rich and well connected, should take up socially with the lowly Oswald of his own choice and volition strains credulity. It was an unlikely acquaintance – this half-educated, surly ex-Marine, a supposed defector of no social provenance, and the snob de Mohrenschildt. In his many social forays with and on behalf of Oswald, de Mohrenschildt had to have been on assignment. As author Harold Weisberg would remark years later, "if there was any meaning in de Mohrenschildt's association with [Oswald], it had to be related to framing him."

De Mohrenschildt arrived at his first meeting with Oswald in the company of a CIA informant named Colonel Laurence Orlov. As J. Walton Moore related in a memo of May 1, 1964, Orlov was Moore's frequent handball partner. It seems apparent that J. Walton Moore, head of the Dallas CIA field office, had set up the meeting between de Mohrenschildt and Oswald.

On October 1, 1962, the de Mohrenschildts escorted Marina Oswald to the home of retired Navy Admiral Chester Bruton, with whom de Mohrenschildt professed that he and his wife were close. Unexpectedly, Oswald turned up. When Bruton asked Oswald about his service in the Marine Corps, according to de Mohrenschildt, he received such a negative response from Oswald that the conversation ended abruptly.

Soon, despite Oswald's lack of acquaintance with the social graces, the de Mohrenschildts were inviting Lee and Marina Oswald to parties. De Mohrenschildt hosted a dinner in honor of Oswald on February 13, 1963. The guests included the son of a director of CIA's Radio Free Europe.

For the Oswald's, de Mohrenschildt performed small services. De Mohrenschildt paid an outstanding Oswald bill at the YMCA. When Marina sought respite from her surly, nervous husband, de Mohrenschildt enlisted his now-grown daughter, Alexandra, and son-in-law to welcome Marina to their home. It was an act of philanthropy, de Mohrenschildt later claimed. He and his wife liked to help the poor, he said.

Among the forensic evidence of de Mohrenschildt's relationship with Oswald was an original photograph of Oswald in his backyard holding a gun along with copies of *The Militant* and *The Worker*. It was inscribed in Oswald's handwriting, "To my friend George." There was also a partial manuscript de Mohrenschildt wrote titled, "I Am a Patsy, I Am a Patsy," about his relationship with Oswald.

De Mohrenschildt's friend Sam Ballen, a financial consultant for High Plains Natural Gas and Electrical Log Services, one day escorted Oswald to a job interview at a company located in the Republic National Bank Building. Ballen later revealed to the Warren Commission that he had spent two hours with Oswald in his office outlining Oswald's employment options. For the rest of his life, the normally affable and forthcoming Ballen refused to reveal to whose office he accompanied Oswald. No government investigator could pry this information from him, one of many hints of how power in the U.S. was shifting away from elected officials.

Later de Mohrenschildt said J. Walton Moore had "assured him that it was safe" for him to assist Oswald. Following the protocol set for CIA by Allen Dulles – that agents or assets or employees are not obliged to tell anyone anything, let alone the truth, that CIA need be loyal only to its own culture – Moore would deny he had ever discussed Oswald with de Mohrenschildt. Moore lied too obviously. He insisted that he had met with de Mohrenschildt on only two occasions. One was in the spring of 1958 when the subject was "China."

Soon Moore was forced to correct himself. He had interviewed de Mohrenschildt in 1957 after his return from Yugoslavia and had "periodic contact" with him over the years for "debriefing" purposes, Moore later admitted. This was standard CIA-speak, the same formulation CIA used for its New Orleans employee Clay Shaw, as CIA's history section finally acknowledged in the 1990's. No one was a CIA asset; businessmen in contact with the Agency were innocent travelers being "routinely" debriefed. "Routinely" was another CIA buzz word.

The Shaw example is worth pondering. In 1992, CIA's history component, a section of the Agency devoted to chronicling CIA's own history, would reveal – after years of denials, and obfuscation by CIA assets – that Shaw was not merely a businessman being "debriefed" after his travels by CIA. This document declares that Shaw had been a "highly paid" CIA asset. Issuing from CIA's "PRO-JFILES," it adds: "Our survey found nothing in these records that indicates any CIA role in the Kennedy assassination or assassination conspiracy (if there was one), or any CIA involvement with Oswald."

Then comes the extraordinary admission: "These records do reveal, however, that Clay Shaw was a highly paid CIA contract source until 1956." (In many CIA documents, the end date of service is more often than not standard disinformation, so that the 1956 date has to be treated skeptically). In Shaw's case, it was certainly not accurate.

In 1964, after the Kennedy assassination, just to be on the safe side, CIA destroyed de Mohrenschildt's personnel file.

"I would never have contacted Oswald in a million years if Moore had not sanctioned it," de Mohrenschildt told author Edward J. Epstein years later, and this rings true. J. Walton Moore had requested that de Mohrenschildt "keep tabs on Oswald." Later de Mohrenschildt claimed that Moore had assigned him to "find out about Oswald's time in the USSR."

In a quid pro quo, Epstein suggests, Moore would assist de Mohrenschildt in setting up an oil survey contract with Papa Doc.

There is no direct evidence of CIA's role in implementing de Mohrenschildt's deal with François Duvalier. Nonetheless, the contract was executed in March 1963, a month before Oswald left Texas for New Orleans. CIA had another assignment in mind now for de Mohrenschildt.

Lest there be any lingering doubt that George de Mohrenschildt played for CIA in Dallas and Fort Worth the same role Clay Shaw did in New Orleans – that of handling and shepherding and monitoring Lee Harvey Oswald in his daily life – a further piece of evidence has emerged. Two large CIA Office of Security (OS) files reside at the National Archives. They date from 1967, the time of Jim Garrison's investigation and indictment of Clay Shaw in a conspiracy to assassinate President Kennedy involving Lee Harvey Oswald.

These OS files, brimming over with more than two hundred documents and photocopies of clippings pertaining to the Garrison case and Shaw, are not marked "Garrison" or "Shaw." Rather, the file jackets read: "George de Mohrenschildt."

With Oswald set on the path that would lead to his being framed for killing President Kennedy, his "friend" George de Mohrenschildt was given another charge on whom to keep an eye – Clémard Joseph Charles. The contract with Duvalier was cover for de Mohrenschildt's presence in Haiti; there had never been any intention of paying de Mohrenschildt. Before long, de Mohrenschildt was given to know that he would not be paid in cash by the Government of Haiti, but was to take his fee out of the profits of a sisal plantation he was expected to run, but never would.

In March 1963, de Mohrenschildt signed two contracts. One was with the government of Haiti for an oil survey. It was worth $285,380. The other was with the bank of Clémard Joseph Charles. At the Republic National Bank in Dallas, de Mohrenschildt applied for a letter of introduction to a bank in Port-au-Prince.

In April, de Mohrenschildt wrote a letter almost as preposterous as his friendship with Lee Harvey Oswald. It was to President John F. Kennedy and requested that Kennedy write the introduction to the book de Mohrenschildt would never write about his Central American walking tour. He had been acquainted with Kennedy's mother-in-law, Janet Auchincloss, de Mohrenschildt confided. The predictable reply, in the negative, came from a Kennedy aide.

By 1964, the agencies that held files on George de Mohrenschildt, in addition to the FBI and CIA, included the Office of Naval Intelligence; the Assistant Chief of Staff, Intelligence, Department of the Army; the Department of State; and the Civil Service Commission.

TWO

Clémard Joseph Charles Teams Up With George De Mohrenschildt

[Thomas J. Devine] a "cleared and witting commercial asset under Project WUBRINY."

— CIA Directorate of Operations document

De Mohrenschildt's putative Haitian partner, Clémard Joseph Charles, was born in Gonaives, in the north of Haiti, on April 21, 1923, making him twelve years younger than George de Mohrenschildt. He was the son of a professor father and a peasant mother. Later he would claim to be a "simple peasant," and "100 percent black," a political profile well suited to the churning racial politics of Papa Doc's Haiti where mulattoes remained the enemy. Clémard Joseph Charles was a dark-skinned man, short of stature at five foot seven inches tall. He was neither prepossessing nor an imposing figure, but pleasant of mien and affable.

Before he went to work for Duvalier, Charles, a self-made man, had compiled a variegated resume: he had been a teacher in rural schools; a pathologist; an upholsterer; a timekeeper; a plantation supervisor; and a freelance journalist. Banking came later.

His success and access to Duvalier led to Charles' becoming Controller General of the Haitian Southern banana industry (he was already a manufacturers' representative in an import-export business). In 1953, Charles went to London as a member of the economic mission of the Haitian government. Back home, he became exclusive agent in Haiti for General Electric (UK), for Siemens Schukerwerke, and for Toyota Motors. Along the way, he picked up a share of Haiti's cocoa industry. Allying himself with Duvalier afforded him diplomatic status; he traveled abroad as Duvalier's emissary.

In 1958, Duvalier dispatched Clémard Joseph Charles to Cuba to make a deal with an enterprising American businessman named Joseph F. Dryer, Jr., who was running a "kenaf" business. Growing like a hibiscus plant, kenaf was a substitute for jute. From kenaf, you could make paper; carpet-backing; rope; curtains; twine; upholstery; vegetable oil; army camouflage; linoleum backing; and, of course, bags to transport sugar and coffee.

Kenaf was to be the Western Hemisphere's alternative to jute, a commodity monopolized on the world market by India and Pakistan. The world production of jute was 4.5 billion pounds a year. Cuba alone purchased $100 million a year of jute from India, while India purchased nothing from Cuba. Cuban kenaf operations were designed to provide the West with an alternative to jute, should India or Pakistan or both fall to the Communists.

Dryer's company was called "North Atlantic Kenaf Fiber Corporation." No fool, Duvalier learned that kenaf, which grew to be ten feet tall in just six months, would do as well in Haiti as it did in Cuba.

Joe Dryer was a very handsome, very rich entrepreneur, a man of boundless confidence who had survived a sniper attack on Iwo Jima that blew out the center of his chest. After that, Dryer was inclined to assume risks. He was witty, filled with intellectual curiosity and *joie de vivre*. Dryer enjoyed strong connections with the U.S. government that derived from his having worked with Marine intelligence in the late forties on Cold War related missions of a highly secret nature.

In 1951, Dryer was a member of the Munitions Board in Washington, D.C., a connection that inspired the government to help Dryer and his brother, Peter, finance their kenaf business in Cuba the following year. Their plan was to develop a kenaf seed supply to produce sandbags and other items for the U.S. military.

Such were Joe Dryer's social connections that, as a result of one of his sons befriending one of Ernest Hemingway's sons at Dartmouth, Hemingway became a close friend. (Dryer would wind up with one of Hemingway's hunting rifles). When Joe married his Cuban wife Nancy in 1956, Hemingway served as a *testigo* at their wedding, which meant that he "represented" their families and sat with them at the church services. Hemingway appeared in a dark suit, white shirt and tie.

"Papa got all dressed up for you!" Mary Hemingway said. Joe Dryer's wedding was the only time in Cuba that Hemingway had gotten dressed up for any occasion. Once the legendary bullfighter Luis Miguel Dominguin came to spend a week in Cuba with Hemingway. Pondering the death of Manolete in the bull ring, Dominguin wondered whether to take up another career.

Hemingway told him stories of people he had known who had moved on to other careers, but he never gave Dominguin any advice about what he should do. Meanwhile Hemingway asked Joe Dryer to show Dominguin around Havana, which he did. Hemingway spoke a slow, meticulous Spanish, not fluent, and not rapid fire, but he made himself understood.

In Cuba, during the dictatorship of Fulgencio Batista, Dryer moved among the most substantial of business owners with strong CIA connections. Yet, Dryer had a foreign competitor growing kenaf in Cuba. He was a long-time CIA asset named Michael J.P. Malone, who ran the "Kenaf Corporation," a subsidiary of the formidable Czarnikow-Rionda sugar brokerage, of which Malone was a vice-president. Malone soon offered to buy Dryer out.

Like everyone else, Dryer was much taken with Malone, a "good soul" who, alas, walked with that terrible limp. The fact that Malone, who had once been aide to Francis, Cardinal Spellman, talked like a New Yorker appealed to Dryer. They also shared a Sullivan & Cromwell lawyer. Malone came replete with at least five CIA handlers.

"From all we know of Joe Dryer," Malone wrote to Alfie Fanjul, the head of Cuba Trading, a Czarnikow subsidiary, "he is a very good man." Still, business was business. Dryer refused Malone's offer to buy him out.

In 1958, Dryer requested a $50,000 investment in his kenaf business from Czarnikow. Robert J. Kleberg, Jr., CEO of King Ranch in South Texas – and who had established a satellite King Ranch in Cuba in partnership with George A. Braga, the head of Czarnikow – was brought into the discussion; it was Malone who ran Kleberg's Cuban ranch. Dryer met Kleberg only once. Kleberg stayed in the "big house" at Manati, among the group of Czarnikow sugar subsidiaries, and it seemed to Dryer that he didn't spend all that much time outdoors, but liked parties. Kleberg, however, whose story will be told elsewhere, was not a man accessible to anyone outside the sphere of King Ranch, its needs and concerns.

Malone now suggested a partnership between Dryer's company (North Atlantic Kenaf Fiber Corporation) and Manati Sugar, with Dryer renting a thousand acres from Czarnikow, and the use of their equipment. A Czarnikow representative would serve on his board. Czarnikow's Cuba Trading figured in the deal as well, with the Fanjuls trying to control the kenaf seed. This deal was completed.

Kenaf is important to this story because it was kenaf that brought Joe Dryer to Haiti. It will be, in part, through Joe Dryer's eyes that the story of George de Mohrenschildt and Clémard Joseph Charles and the dangerous game they played in Haiti, will emerge.

It was in 1958 that Dryer, who had loved Haiti since his first visit there with his family in 1937, first entertained Clémard Joseph Charles, visiting from Haiti. Dryer found Charles open and honest and forthright.

"I'd like to invite you to Haiti to consider growing this fiber," Charles said. "I'll introduce you to people in the government and I'll find you land that you can rent."

In Haiti, Dryer looked over land in the Artibonite Valley where Brown & Root had built their hydroelectric dam. "We might build a bag mill some day," Charles had said, according to Dryer, "but for now we're interested in your growing fiber for hard cash." Charles continued to hope that someday he and Dryer might develop a coffee and sugar bag industry in Haiti.

"I want ten percent of your company for helping," Charles said. Dryer thought this was fair for someone with the government influence that Charles enjoyed. He could easily have requested twenty-five or thirty percent. Charles was a just man, and a kind one, a man easily approachable. Later Dryer discovered that if a family were suffering hard times and went to Charles, he would quietly help them out.

Meanwhile Dryer held on in Cuba. When Batista's air force strafed his plantation, Dryer turned to the American Embassy for help. When the rebels captured him one day, he held his ground, his *sang froid* another legacy of his having survived Iwo Jima. No, being dressed in camouflage did not mean he was part of Batista's army, Dryer told the armed guerrilla fighters who were holding him captive. Like the majority of people of his generation, Dryer says, he sympathized with Fidel Castro.

Surmising that his days of doing business in Cuba might be numbered, in the autumn of 1958 Dryer flew to Washington in search of funding to expand his kenaf operation. He approached Nelson Rockefeller's International Basic Economy Corporation (IBEC) as well as the International Cooperation Administration (ICA) for which George de Mohrenschildt had ventured to Yugoslavia.

Where should his new company, the Inter-American Investment Corporation, be incorporated? Dryer inquired of ICA officials. They suggested Panama. Ultimately Dryer's new Panamanian corporation would take over the Cuban operation as a "wholly-owned subsidiary." Dryer hoped to have a kenaf bag factory operating in Haiti by January 1, 1961. Part of this story involves how American businessmen functioned in Haiti, and how CIA, sensitive to their needs, attempted to destabilize the Duvalier regime.

Back in Cuba in November 1958, Dryer greeted a Haitian delegation that included H. Marc Charles, the Secretary of State for Agriculture and Clémard's cousin. Clémard Joseph Charles himself acted as Dryer's agent as they hammered out a contract. Papa Doc knew well how to make Haiti hospitable to American business. Dryer was offered five years to operate his kenaf business, free of any revenue tax; there would be no exportation duties on his kenaf.

For the next five years, taxes would be paid on a fifty percent basis. Upon signing the agreement, Dryer was required to deposit in the National Bank of the Republic of Haiti $20,000 as guaranty for the execution of the contract. This money supposedly would be returned after the amount of the deposit had been spent in Haiti in the work of land preparation.

Duvalier also guaranteed to Dryer "the free movement of the capital invested during the length of the contract." Beginning in 1960, Dryer promised to produce 1.5 million pounds of fiber a year. Dryer would gain "exclusive rights to the development of kenaf, sesame and ramie for twenty-five years."

Dryer was sanguine. He believed that within five years he could sell two hundred million pounds of kenaf in the United States. Dryer set up a company called Haitian NAKORE, SA, which was to grow into one of the largest concerns in Haiti. He grew kenaf on a thousand acres producing seed for export. The future for business in Haiti seemed promising.

Dryer later reflected that he would never have been accepted by the Haitian government had Clémard Joseph Charles not introduced him to the government by arranging a meeting of himself and his wife with the *Grande Conseil de techniques* in the Presidential Palace. This consisted of twelve elderly white-haired black gentlemen dressed in dark suits, white shirts and ties.

Before this group, Dryer had to make a presentation. Because he had only schoolboy French, his wife Nancy did the translating. His talk was designed to thwart the heavy French competition. Dryer succeeded and, as he recalls, none of it would have been possible had it not been for the assistance of Clémard Joseph Charles.

Dryer's presentation was followed by an elaborate dinner hosted by the Commander of the Palace Guard and including, as fellow guests, the Minister of Development and the Minister of Tourism, along with their wives. Charles had felt that for Joe Dryer to be protected, this event was mandatory.

As for the Cuban operation, still in business, Dryer was worried. Castro had not yet taken power, but Dryer was already looking beyond Cuba. He requested that Czarnikow-Rionda invest in his new kenaf business in Haiti. Discussions between Dryer and Czarnikow continued after the 26th of July movement was victorious on January 1, 1959 and Fidel Castro took power. Michael J. P. Malone wasn't overly alarmed. He insisted that, "the situation in Cuba seems to be more eased." Dryer wasn't so sure.

Haiti has "honored all concessions during the past fifty years," Dryer argued in a February 1959 "preliminary report" on the "Investment Potential of the Kenaf Industry in Haiti" that he forwarded to Michael J. P. Malone. Labor was cheap, and Duvalier would protect American investments. Dryer anticipated a 15% return on Czarnikow's investment, beginning in 1960. He predicteded that Castro, who had made agrarian reform the cornerstone of the revolution, would confiscate his kenaf plantation; the absence of available kenaf coming from Cuba should make an investment in Haiti all the more appealing and lucrative.

Malone considered Dryer's proposal. Then, unwisely, Czarnikow turned him down.

For the next year and a half, Dryer continued to grow kenaf in Cuba. Soon the Castro government placed a representative in Dryer's office. His company couldn't write a check without its being initialed by one of Castro's officers. Then Castro confiscated everything and Dryer returned to the United States.

As he sought to finance his Haitian kenaf plantation, Dryer turned to highly placed connections. It wasn't difficult for his new investors to see that with Cuban kenaf no longer available, Haiti would become an important source. He was able to enlist in his new business: Kidder Peabody; Billy Bloomingdale; the Phipps family through Bessemer Securities; and Continental Grain, the largest grain trading company in the world.

In the years to come, Dryer would express his displeasure with Castro; indeed, none of the businessmen whose property was confiscated in Cuba ever forgave him. Foremost among them would be Robert J. Kleberg, Jr., and his right hand man, Michael J. P. Malone. In 1963, Dryer invited into his Palm Beach mansion twelve men who had been captured and imprisoned in Cuba following the Bay of Pigs invasion. In ill health, they had just been released and needed somewhere to regain their strength.

* * *

Clémard Joseph Charles had become a banker in 1959 when he founded the "Haitian Industrial Mortgage Bank," depositing $100,000 in the Marathon State Bank in Marathon, Florida. His partners were two Miami citizens, Jackson D. Rains and Robert H. Slatko. The opening ceremonies on October 27, 1959 in Port-au-Prince were attended by Papa Doc himself.

Music blared, flags were unfurled, and the Presidential Guard was on parade. Charles addressed the crowd. The bank expects "to interest large American firms in building assembly plants in Haiti," he said. When one of the Miami partners was indicted in the United States for using the mails to defraud, the bank quickly failed.

A year later, Charles again tried his hand at banking. With the renewed blessing of Papa Doc, he founded the *Banque Commerciale d'Haiti,* the country's first private bank. The official photograph of Clémard Joseph Charles that hangs in the bank shows an already balding, dark-skinned, dignified man in a heavily starched white shirt. Gold cuff links sparkle at his wrists. He is smiling broadly, but his eyes are wary.

Clémard Joseph Charles was now a prominent public figure in Port-au-Prince. On August 24, 1962, a Haitian newspaper profile by Emanuel C. Paul described Charles as "proud of his peasant origins...dark, average in size, quick and prematurely balding under a broad forehead." He has a "progressive mind and strongly believes in the value of effort...and is never discouraged by obstacles."

"Whenever you happen to meet him," Paul writes admiringly of Clémard Joseph Charles, "he speaks of new projects for the development of the country. The waiting room of his bank is always full of people, some asking for credit, others with less obvious motives." Charles is "a new type of businessman we did not know before," Paul adds, "one who is interested more in the well-being of his homeland than in his own profit. He is a man who wants to help the 'less fortunate ones' and a model of honesty, discipline and tenacity." Paul informs his readers that already Charles has turned down a number of political appointments offered to him by President Duvalier.

Papa Doc showered Charles with honors: "Commander of the Order of Civil Merit"; the "Order of Work"; the "Order of Agricultural Merit." Charles was a godfather to one of Duvalier's children. In 1962, as Duvalier's emissary, Charles received the key to the City of New York as an honored visitor. Charles was rising to prominence even though he wasn't a good-looking man and lacked charisma.

His alliance with Papa Doc resulted in Charles' becoming a figure of considerable interest to the American intelligence services. CIA and military intelligence placed Charles under close surveillance. Their assessment of the man was not always sanguine. In August 1962, the 902nd Military Intelligence Group, "90 Deuce," requested that the FBI check on Charles' business activities in Miami.

* * *

The instability of the government of Haiti had been of CIA interest even before Duvalier came to power in 1957. Testifying about his CIA and FBI affiliations, in a host of venues including New York Federal District Court, New York lawyer Herbert Itkin revealed he had met in July of 1954 in Philadelphia with Allen Dulles to discuss the political future of Haiti. Three years later, with his CIA handler Mario Brod, Itkin had discussed the possibility that he might organize Mafia hit men to accomplish the assassination of Papa Doc. Itkin's story was that the Mafia would carry out the assassination in return for a commitment that the gangsters behind the assassination would receive the gambling concession in Haiti.

What is intriguing is that, along the way, Itkin named as one of his CIA contacts, "a man who identified himself as Philip Harbin." Harbin did not mention CIA – any

CIA asset, employee, officer or contact knew enough not to do that. Harbin said only that he was "from that man in Philadelphia." Itkin described "Philip Harbin" as a man who "could have been of Polish or Russian family background." He was a man who "had an affluent, professorial air." He was well dressed.

The man Itkin described seems shorter than de Mohrenschildt, but other details suggest that it was indeed he. If it is difficult to locate examples of George de Mohrenschildt using his other alias, "P. Forestier," here we have an example of de Mohrenschildt as – Philip Harbin.

Itkin photostated his law firm's correspondence and passed it to "Harbin." When he opened his own firm, Itkin explained his financial predicament to Harbin, who advanced him $5,000, a loan he never repaid. Harbin had other functions: "in an attempt to develop material, Harbin asked Itkin whether he knew anyone else who could work for him."

According to Itkin, he was never given any means of contacting Harbin. Harbin would call him from time to time and ask what there was to report. Harbin emerges as a vivid figure. He tells Itkin to "stay close to Brod and everyone would be happy." This sounds, indeed, like the cynic de Mohrenschildt.

Brod encouraged Itkin to pay $20,000 to a Haitian group, including one "Luis des Joies." When a Provisional Haitian Government in Exile was formed in San Juan on May 12, 1963, Itkin was hired by the group as its attorney. On June 10th, he registered with the Department of State as a Foreign Agent on this group's behalf. They met with Forrest K. Abbuhl of the Haitian Affairs desk at State. We will soon encounter Abbuhl offering his perspective on Clémard Joseph Charles as a suitable successor to Papa Doc.

Yet another aspect of Itkin's and Brod's plotting in 1963 was to "harass Cuba, if not invade it, from the northwest part of Haiti." Another priority for CIA was to see that Juan Bosch was not elected president of the Dominican Republic, the better for the Agency to use that northern area of the island of Hispaniola for its own purposes. Itkin and Brod were also involved in recruiting and financing Haitians to invade Haiti. Over and over, we learn in the CIA documents about Itkin that the Mafia was involved in the plans to "knock off DUVALIER." Itkin referred to the mob as "hoodlums."

De Mohrenschildt's choice of the alias "Philip Harbin," as we know, derived from "Harbin" (China) being the birthplace of his wife Jeanne. Among the many lies de Mohrenschildt would tell was his statement to Warren Commission lawyer Albert Jenner that he had never "been in any respect an agent." None of his foreign ventures had ever involved any political activity, de Mohrenschildt lied.

Eventually "Harbin" passed Itkin over to a CIA officer named "Bernard H. Moncure," a "CIA Staff Agent." According to the CIA documents, Moncure "rode piggyback on Itkin's contacts with the Haitians to make his own operational contacts within the group." As the documents admit, there was "high-level governmental interest in removing Duvalier from office in 1963."

CIA admits that, in March 1963, Moncure had recruited Itkin for the FBI for domestic issues while maintaining for CIA the use of Itkin for "foreign intelligence matters." By 1968, Itkin would be a witness in a series of criminal indictments for the U.S. Attorney for the Southern District of New York starting with New York City Water Commissioner Marcus. As a matter of course, the Agency denied that Itkin had ever met with Allen Dulles.

For the record, CIA also insisted that, "there is no agency record of Phillip [sic] Harbin." They had to have known otherwise.

From the moment Duvalier took power, CIA began to dispatch paramilitary operations designed to destabilize his regime. An eight-man incursion, comprised of an American deputy sheriff and some Haitian exiles, was among the earliest to arrive. Duvalier ignored them.

American businessmen kept up the pressure on CIA to remove Duvalier. One such investor wrote to Allen Dulles in October 1960. He had viewed a television documentary called "Paradise in Chains," depicting Duvalier as a "terrorist and dictator worse than Batista." Surely U.S. investment would be better served by a more reliable and stable head of state.

The U.S. government was irritated by Duvalier's style of blackmail. At the 1961 Punta del Este conference of the Organization of American States, Duvalier had bartered his vote for the expulsion of Castro from the organization in exchange for U.S. financing of a new international airport in Port-au-Prince. The U.S. had no alternative but to comply. But it rankled: Haiti had been over the years the recipient of millions of dollars in loans, either directly from the U.S. or from agencies where the U.S. exerted no small amount of influence.

A month after John F. Kennedy was inaugurated, in February 1961, his Special Assistant Arthur Schlesinger suggested an incursion into Haiti. Three months before the Bay of Pigs disaster, Schlesinger proposed what he termed a "black operation." Haiti would lure Castro into sending a few boatloads of men onto a Haitian beach in what would be portrayed as a *Cuban* effort to overthrow Duvalier.

If Castro could be induced to commit an offensive act, Schlesinger fantasized, the moral issue would be clouded, and any anti-U.S. campaign in Haiti "would be hobbled from the start." Yet in March, 1961 there seemed "no one on the scene now who gives any promise of being able or willing to establish a decent constructive government." It was that vacuum that Clémard Joseph Charles hoped to fill.

The Bay of Pigs defeat on April 17, 1961 made an overt operation into Haiti impossible. "Whatever is done will be attributed to the United States," said John McCone, Dulles' successor as Director of Central Intelligence, in a paper on "Haiti." Not that McCone opposed the overthrow of Duvalier. He cautioned only that whoever arrives to take Papa Doc's place "will require external assistance."

In 1962, CIA continued to search for "a viable alternative to Duvalier." That summer, Edwin Martin, the Assistant Secretary of State for Inter-American Affairs, suggested to President Kennedy that CIA should be "entrusted to continue with the evaluation of personalities and possibilities" preparatory to removing Duvalier, and "replacing him with something we can live with."

Gun-shy after a botched invasion of Cuba that was not his idea, and which he regretted not having canceled, Kennedy was ambivalent about an operation into Haiti with CIA playing "an active covert role," as Edwin Martin suggested. Kennedy did not object to overthrowing Duvalier, or even to CIA's leading the charge, so long as the U.S. role was concealed. His concern was that if the plan backfired, the "Communists" would become Duvalier's "heirs."

On August 9, 1962, Kennedy discussed Haiti with Richard Helms, the Deputy Director for Plans, which was then the name of CIA's clandestine services – today it is known more benignly as the "National Clandestine Service." McCone had granted CIA approval to provide weapons to a group working against Duvalier, Helms reported. Unfortunately, CIA's efforts had met with opposition from Duvalier's "goon squads," the *Tontons Macoutes*, "a repressive force of no mean substance." Operations in Haiti were "a dangerous business." CIA's best local agent, a former chief of the Haitian Coast Guard, was getting nowhere, Helms admitted to the President.

"Another coup really doesn't do any good if you don't have anybody to work with," Kennedy said.

Helms complained about Duvalier's "shakedown of the business community," protecting the corporations being always a high, even the highest, priority for CIA. But Kennedy refused to consent to an "active effort" to remove Duvalier even as he sought the "means to secure a change" in Haiti's leadership. When Secretary of State Dean Rusk suggested that we should be prepared to move into Haiti, and General Maxwell Taylor promised he could deliver U.S. Marines ashore in Haiti "within fifty-one hours," Kennedy "reacted sharply."

"This is too long," Kennedy said.

In January 1963, Kennedy suspended shipments of war materiel to Haiti, and cut off a highway loan. Construction of the new jet airport in Port-au-Prince proceeded since it might be useful later "to meet a United States military requirement." As he would in Vietnam, Kennedy preferred using Special Forces rather than ground troops for these incursions. The above conversations reveal that he had no problem with the removal of Duvalier. The issues were the means and the aftermath.

Kennedy remained convinced that although it was "hopeless to try to work with Duvalier," under no circumstances should the U.S. "try to dislodge Duvalier without a fairly clear idea of who would replace him." Together, CIA, FBI and INR (the State Department Bureau of Intelligence and Research) compiled a dossier of "promising Haitian exiles and visible resistance figures from which we are trying to select those most likely to be capable of heading a successor government."

In this last year of Kennedy's life, CIA was "involved in discussions with an exile group which had the objective of overthrowing President Duvalier," Director of Central Intelligence William Colby admitted to the Church Committee more than a decade later. The result was "a couple of efforts to send people into Haiti...a paramilitary operation...sort of like the Bay of Pigs, that kind of invasion." One plan involved General Léon Cantave, who in 1963 received "a heavy shipment of large arms from a U.S. Government agency in Washington." More than eight such invasions would follow.

In February 1963, Clémard Joseph Charles, a rich man by Haitian standards, with business interests valued at $500,000, paid a personal visit to the U.S. Embassy in Port-au-Prince as part of his campaign to be chosen by CIA as Duvalier's successor. Charles talked about "the participation of American venture capital" in Haiti. He reiterated that he had "favorable relations with well-placed Duvalier regime figures" and "a line into the palace."

He mentioned that Duvalier had granted him a monopoly on automobile insurance in Haiti so that each year every Haitian was compelled to purchase $67 worth of liability insurance from him. Charles also had an interest in the government franchise granting a Canadian the right to handle all public transportation of merchandise and passengers. Then he distributed a brochure about his bank, along with a biographical data sheet about himself.

The first Embassy official to be suspicious of Clémard Joseph Charles was David R. Thomas, who observed that Charles "does not enjoy the best of business reputations." Another Embassy officer, Phil Williams, called Charles "a common crook, more promoter than businessman, and should be avoided." While some found Charles appealing (This "negro strikes the well-dressed figure of a banker"), CIA was wary. The Agency continued to monitor the activities of Charles very carefully.

CIA's informants discovered that some of the notes of the *Banque Commerciale d'Haiti* had been guaranteed by dubious political personalities. Some mortgages were in arrears, so that the president had to ask the holders of the mortgages not to foreclose "in order to avoid a scandal." The CIA asset who reported this information believed that Charles was "dishonest" and knew nothing about banking.

There had also been a Byzantine scandal connected with the Haitian-American Society for Agricultural Development (SHADA), which owned the land of Charles' sisal plantation. In 1952, the Export-Import Bank had granted a loan of $2,500,000 to buy the shares of SHADA's American investors. The new SHADA administrators were former officers of the National Bank of Haiti, with SHADA controlling the sale of sisal through an entity created on April 8, 1963, the "Hewlett Bay Agriculture and Economic Development Corporation, S.A."

In 1963, Duvalier turned SHADA over to Clémard Joseph Charles' *Banque Commerciale d'Haiti* in return for which the bank would cover the expenses of George de Mohrenschildt's geological survey. Well aware that Haiti was the target of U.S. paramilitary efforts, Duvalier planned to use Charles and his bank for the purchase of weapons and airplanes from the United States. Rumors abounded that Charles was a bagman for Duvalier, providing pay-offs to U.S. politicians.

In the spring of 1963, Clémard Joseph Charles flew to the United States for a series of high-level meetings to be held in the company of George de Mohrenschildt. 90 Deuce at once checked on de Mohrenschildt's character. They learned that he had an aunt who was a prominent New York socialite and that, under the Czars, his family was "high in diplomatic and military circles." That was just the beginning.

It was in April 1963 that Charles accelerated his efforts to persuade CIA to back him. He enlisted George de Mohrenschildt to introduce him to U.S. government officials and CIA people. CIA kept military intelligence in the dark, so that 90 Deuce found itself wondering whether CIA wanted to talk with Charles only about his business enterprises.

Outside of Haiti, Charles was not shy about revealing the motive for this trip to the United States. He was playing a double game for the good of his country, he told the CIA operatives with whom he had dealings. No matter that Papa Doc had served as his patron and supporter, Charles hoped to persuade CIA to overthrow Duvalier and install *him* as the new President of the Republic of Haiti.

Charles brought with him to the U.S. a nine-page document spelling out why he should be CIA's choice. He had no doubt that CIA hoped to overthrow Duvalier, and he was correct in that supposition. The remaining issue was whom they would choose to take his place.

His goal, Charles wrote, was to put an "end to the leonine privileges of a minority whose personal interest stands against all honest and impartial government." He described himself as a fervent supporter of democracy and a "broader representation of the interest of the people." What Haiti needs, Charles insisted, is the "development of industry and exploitation of our natural resources so as to promote an improvement of living conditions."

Financing obtained from abroad, in particular from "the specialized agencies of the United States government," was crucial to the well being of Haiti, Charles wrote. Should the U.S. support him, Charles promised, he would maintain an environment hospitable to U.S. business.

* * *

Having returned, temporarily, to Dallas, George de Mohrenschildt sent a thank you note to Colonel Roy J. Batterton, Jr., Chief of the U.S. Naval Mission in Port-au-Prince. It reveals that de Mohrenschildt had already promoted the cause of Clémard Joseph Charles with the Colonel. After a "pleasant afternoon" with de Mohrenschildt, Batterton assured the army that Clémard Joseph Charles seemed to be an "intelligent, sincere businessman."

From his perch in Dallas, de Mohrenschildt dedicated himself to promoting the cause of Clémard Joseph Charles with U.S. government officials, an assignment similar to his CIA-authorized handling of Lee Harvey Oswald. On April 17, 1963, de Mohrenschildt wrote to Vice President Lyndon Johnson requesting an appointment "to talk to you about an important strategic country." He wished to introduce Lyndon Johnson to "a Haitian businessman and banker, president of the only private bank in Haiti, Mr. Clémard Joseph Charles."

Those connected to Haiti had identified Lyndon Johnson as someone with interests in the first black Republic at least two years earlier. Victor Nevers Constant, Duvalier's Secretary of State, had written to Vice President Johnson on November 25, 1961. He hoped, Constant wrote, that Johnson might help the tourist industry of Haiti "within the spirit of the Alliance For Progress."

De Mohrenschildt described himself as a Texan since 1939 when he had worked, briefly, for Humble Oil. Knowing that Lyndon Johnson had long been the recipient of financial support from Herman and George Brown of Brown & Root, de Mohrenschildt in this letter dropped the name of "the late Herman Brown, an old friend and customer of mine," which was not exactly the case.

He and Charles, de Mohrenschildt wrote, have "a crazy idea of improving the social and economic condition of this small but important country so close to Cuba." The reply from Lyndon Johnson's office arrived the very next day, April 18th, an astonishingly swift response, as Bruce Adamson has noticed. On this day de Mohrenschildt deposited a check for $1,200 in his Dallas savings account, its origins unknown. De Mohrenschildt had not been gainfully employed since his return from Yugoslavia and Hungary, and since his trip to Iran for John Mecom when he facilitated Mecom's relationship with the Shah.

In March 1963, the powerful 902nd Military Intelligence Group referred to George de Mohrenschildt as "a business associate of Vice-President Lyndon Johnson."

On April 19th, the de Mohrenschildts left for New York.

When he found his way to Washington, D.C., de Mohrenschildt met, not with Lyndon Johnson, but with Johnson's assistant for National Security Affairs, Air Force Colonel Howard Burris. A native Texan, Burris was an intelligence officer who had been involved in CIA's 1953 coup against Iranian president Mohammed Mossadegh. He was an intimate of Richard Helms and of General Charles Cabell, right hand man of Allen Dulles, and brother of Dallas mayor Earle Cabell, who was to be in office at the time of the assassination of President Kennedy later in the year. An oilman by profession, Burris had created the Cuban-Venezuelan Oil Voting Trust Company, only to have his Cuban oil properties to be confiscated by Fidel Castro.

Clémard Joseph Charles departed from Haiti for New York on April 23. Upon his arrival, he was interviewed by a CIA informant who is identified in the CIA document describing their meeting only as a "former journalist." With no fear that his words would get back to Papa Doc, Charles confided to the informant that he was in a strong position to become head of a provisional government once Duvalier was removed. Duvalier was likely to unleash a reign of terror and had to be stopped before he liquidated his opposition, Charles volunteered.

Speaking as if he were aware that this "journalist" was a direct pipeline to CIA, and that CIA was motivated by fear that Haiti might become a second Cuba, Charles added that Duvalier was about to accept aid from the Soviet bloc. In contrast, he would establish a democratic Haiti, one "friendly toward the United States, and save the country from a Castro-type Communist takeover."

Charles then boasted of his "wide range of support among the peasantry, anti-Duvalier army officers, intellectuals, journalists and businessmen." Should he not be appointed provisional president, Charles said, he might accept the post of Secretary of Finance and Economic Affairs.

In New York, Charles met with his kenaf partner, Joe Dryer. Charles had sent a limousine to the hotel to pick up Dryer and his partner, Clark Cassidy. Dryer recounts that he and Cassidy both were fond of Charles. Charles had a secretary with him, a woman who, as Dryer knew through his own intelligence connections, had been planted on Charles by CIA.

In the late 1970s, Dryer told the House Select Committee on Assassinations that Charles had "many connections" with the Central Intelligence Agency. He added that George de Mohrenschildt had "some intelligence connection," although he professed not to know with which country. It seems clear that CIA held both Clémard Joseph Charles and George de Mohrenschildt within its radar, destined for some role in Haiti's political future.

When Dryer assessed Charles and his ambitions years later, Dryer said he had approved of Charles' goal of becoming president of Haiti. He'd be as good as anyone we know based on how he treated us in Haiti, Dryer thought. Charles was interested in building Haiti and had the good of Haiti at heart. Dryer did not believe that Charles had offshore bank accounts of the type people like him customarily favored. Charles had never asked Dryer to do anything underhanded. To assist him in his kenaf operation, Charles had introduced Dryer to Analous Barthelemy, an old agronome of the highest competence and reliability, for which Dryer was grateful.

To Dryer now, in 1963, Charles described George de Mohrenschildt as his "business associate," adding that de Mohrenschildt had an appointment with Vice President Johnson.

A generous man, Dryer supplied Clémard Joseph Charles with some useful letters of introduction, testaments to his character. One was to Senator Kenneth Keating of New York, a long-time friend of Dryer's father. Another was to Democratic Congressman Paul Rogers of Florida. He hoped, Charles confided, to talk with "well-informed U.S. sources" without running "unnecessary risks" of Duvalier discovering that he was plotting with CIA against him; this would have been treasonous by any definition. Charles said that he intended, for the moment, to remain in Duvalier's favor.

Dryer had his own bank conduct a credit check on George de Mohrenschildt, with the understanding that the name of the client initiating the inquiry "remain confidential." The bank official, however, reported to Special Agent William W. Hamilton of the New York FBI field office. He described the person checking on de Mohrenschildt only as "a firm dealing in the import and export of fibers."

Dryer denies that he arranged for a credit check on de Mohrenschildt, but given his concern for Charles, and his doubts about de Mohrenschildt, it seems that it could only have been he, a businessman "dealing in the import and export of fibers."

The ensuing credit report, issuing from the Republic National Bank in Dallas, arrived on June 14th. It was "favorable concerning de Mohrenschildt's credit." The evidence suggests that, along the way, Dryer had confided what he knew about Clémard Joseph Charles and George de Mohrenschildt to Army intelligence. Dryer's views, as outlined above, appear, almost verbatim, in the released files of 90 Deuce.

* * *

It is April 25, 1963 at the Knickerbocker Club at 2 East 62nd Street, immediately east of Fifth Avenue in New York City. Two CIA operatives are conferring in the club's library: C. Frank Stone, III, who is responsible for CIA's WUBRINY operations, and Thomas J. Devine, CIA's principal asset on the project. Devine had been a CIA staff employee, who ostensibly "resigned" in 1953 to "go into private business." He is situated now at a company called "Train, Cabot and Associates." Devine's partner, John Train, a long-time CIA asset, was a founder of the CIA-sponsored *Paris Review*. Devine was well liked at CIA. Gale Allen, his clandestine services case officer at the Directorate of Operations, had recommended Devine as "the most discreet and security conscious business contact" he had ever met.

WUBRINY, which has never been explained in any detail, was a CIA proprietary operation in Haiti run out of the office of the DD/P, the Deputy Director for Plans, Richard Helms. In his report of the Knickerbocker meeting, Stone would refer to Devine as WUBRINY/1. The clues as to what WUBRINY was about are scant. CIA's "WU" digraph reflects a generic CIA proprietary relationship, unlike "AM," which always designated "Cuba."

An example: CIA's E. Howard Hunt, the future Watergate mastermind, worked under the "WU" digraph to conceal his activities in New York behind a book-publishing/research entity called JPRS (Joint Publications Research Service), which produced in this particular section propaganda tracts destined for Latin American consumption. There were CIA-JPRS sponsored propaganda projects for the entire globe: Middle Eastern; East European; South Asia; Western Europe; and other components. Other commercial enterprises under the aegis of CIA were designated as WUPUNDIT, WURAISIN and WUSENDER. If CIA was gifted at anything, it was creating all manner of covers for its operatives.

Having taken a phoney "early retirement," Hunt was about to move to Europe as head of covert action operations in Spain, a trajectory that CIA did not wish to be exposed. Joining Hunt under similar covers were two figures associated with Lee Harvey Oswald: Priscilla Johnson McMillan, one of two people to interview Oswald in Moscow; and Richard E. Snyder, the consular official at the U.S. Embassy in Moscow who met Oswald there. Snyder was a CIA employee under cover, and had been for years.

A digression: Richard E. Snyder has entered history as the officer at the American Embassy in Moscow who dealt with Lee Harvey Oswald when he arrived to renounce his American citizenship in October 1959. Snyder, questioned by Allen Dulles on behalf of the Warren Commission, stated that he was "a Foreign Service Officer of the Department of State." Indeed, Snyder's official roles at the Moscow Embassy were as Second Secretary and American Consul.

Snyder's relationship with CIA is best described as an informal operative; he was utilized "off the books" by Nelson Brickham, Chief of SR6, in 1956-57. However, in April 1959, he was security cleared by CIA for liaison prior to his State Department placement in Moscow. No doubt Dulles had kept a straight face as he interrogated one of his own.

When Lee Harvey Oswald arrived in Moscow and encountered Richard E. Snyder, he was speaking to someone "owned by" the Central Intelligence Agency. When the House Select Committee on Assassinations considered Snyder, they found that his CIA file "had been red-flagged" by the Agency and "maintained on a segregated basis," despite Snyder's insistence to the Committee that he had left the service of CIA in 1950. That was an outright lie.

Prior to his departure for Moscow, CIA documents reveal, Snyder had been a CIA recruiter or "spotter" at Harvard where he was studying. Snyder's counterpart at Princeton as CIA recruiter was pipe-smoking Dean of Students William ("Bill") Lippincott.

In 1956, Snyder attempted to recruit a subject to whom he described "operational tasks ... recruitment inside, letter drops inside, dead drops and casing for dead drops," among other assignments. They would use the "letter pouch," sending letters to "a CIA controlled address" so that "technical people can give us definitive opinions as to whether the Soviets are getting into this channel." Among those with whom Snyder initiated contact for possible CIA employment was a young professor who had received his Ph.D. from Harvard, Zbigniew Brzezinski.

CIA was delighted with its "spotter" Snyder's suggestion. Brzezinski, CIA thought, was a person of "undoubted integrity and courage," and was "highly motivated in an anti-Soviet sense," as he would continue to be in his time with Jimmy Carter, and beyond. He knew "his Communism inside and out." All that remained to be cleared up for CIA before they planned to send Brzezinski on a

"Russian tour" during the coming summer of 1957 was "the man's possible loyalties." CIA hesitated only because Brzezinski held passports from both Canada and Poland: "Would the Agency be able to control him?"

Another connection to Devine in this story is that Herbert Itkin – who had been working for CIA in planning the assassination of François Duvalier – or an associate of Itkin's, was being considered by the Agency to participate in WUBRINY operations. The extant document associating Itkin with WUBRINY suggests that he was not so enlisted, but it isn't clear. There was, however, as we shall see, a WUBRINY/2, who has yet to be identified.

In his contact report about his April 25th meeting with WUBRINY/1 at the Knickerbocker, Stone refers several times to "a second meeting with banker Charles...scheduled for Friday, 26 April." WUBRINY/1 knew that Charles would be accompanied by a "Texan" named "deMOHRENSCHILDT, George; DOB: 1911; POB: USSR; CIT: U.S.A. (?); Businessman." That Devine did in fact meet with Charles and de Mohrenschildt the following day makes it abundantly clear that Devine enjoyed the CIA cryptonym of WUBRINY/1.

Thomas J. Devine began as a Texas wildcatter, someone who drills wells in areas not yet known to be oil fields on the hunch that they might be. He was not only a commercial asset of CIA, but was also a close associate of George H.W. Bush. Devine had invested heavily in Bush's Zapata Oil and his name appears on the incorporation papers of Bush's company, Zapata Offshore. So close were they that Bush called Devine by the nickname "T."

Although his resumé may claim otherwise, Devine continued to participate in CIA operations. Far from having resigned from CIA, within two months, on June

12, 1963, he will be granted "a Covert Security Approval by the Directorate of Operations...for use of subject in Project WUBRINY operations." So in his report of this April meeting, Stone refers to Devine not by name, but repeatedly as WUBRINY/1, while CIA redacts the name of the Ambassador being discussed.

Today, at the Knickerbocker Club meeting with his CIA handler, Devine is a "cleared and witting contact" at Train, Cabot which houses and manages a CIA proprietary corporation concealed under the cryptonym WU-SALINE. Among Devine's CIA duties as WUBRINY/1 are "mortgage arrangements for businesses in Haiti."

April 25, 1963 had already been a busy day for Thomas J. Devine. Before arriving at the Knickerbocker Club to confer with Frank Stone, he met with the American Ambassador to Haiti, and with Clémard Joseph Charles. The principal topic was mortgages on real estate in Haiti, as well as the desire of the American Ambassador to Haiti to raise money to build a home for rental on a three-acre plot that he had recently purchased in Haiti. Charles acceded eagerly to CIA's requests. He promised that his bank would offer a first mortgage to the American Ambassador.

Devine informed Frank Stone that on the following day, he expected Charles to visit his office in the company of a "Texan" businessman to discuss mineral concessions in Haiti. CIA was aware that Manufacturers Trust, Empire Trust and Irving Trust in New York were already doing business with Clémard Joseph Charles.

From the April 25th meeting at the Knickerbocker between Stone and Devine, it seems clear that Charles' bank was involved in providing mortgages for CIA-friendly people. Devine recounted that Charles had promised to provide for him "an up-to-date balance sheet on his bank," which was to issue a first mortgage with WUSALINE, that CIA entity operating out of Devine's office, and, "to come in for a second mortgage of $5,000."

Much time was devoted to CIA's use of Charles' bank on behalf of its employees and assets in Haiti. Devine told Stone that Charles was "offering [the Ambassador] "overdraught facilities in his bank, which means, in effect, unsecured personal loans to enable the Ambassador to draw checks while awaiting the receipt of his salary allowance." CIA was testing Charles, determining whether he would comply with its demands, and place his bank at its disposal.

There was a down side, however. Devine speculated "as to whether or not Mr. Charles is trying to put the Ambassador "under operational control through finances in the same way we would be doing should we complete the mortgage arrangements." Using Charles and his bank for such a favor would grant him power over CIA. The Agency would be putting itself in his debt.

On Project WUBRINY, Devine would remain a "cleared and witting commercial asset" of CIA until at least 1968. Devine served the important CIA mandate, as journalist Kirkpatrick Sale put it, of "meshing with and protecting the interests of major American businesses, especially of the multinational corporations."

"Get as much information as you can!" Stone instructed Devine regarding his meeting the next day with Clémard Joseph Charles and George de Mohrenschildt.

* * *

There is something more to be said about George H.W. Bush and his connection to CIA and Thomas J. Devine.

WUBRINY in Haiti wasn't the only project in which they were mutually engaged. Devine and George H.W. Bush were also working together on a CIA-sponsored business venture under the cryptonym WUBRINY/ LPDICTUM. LPDICTUM was a cryptonym that denoted being "involved in proprietary commercial operations."

According to retired Marine Corps lieutenant colonel turned author William Corson, LPDICTUM indicated that George H.W. Bush had been assigned the task of searching for "people who could be targeted for recruitment by the Agency as business assets." Throughout the 1960s, Devine and Bush traveled the world together, Devine armed with a "standing TS [Top Secret] clearance" from CIA.

In his confirmation hearing for Director of Central Intelligence, Bush would lie, insisting he had no prior connection with CIA. Yet CIA's Cover & Commercial Staff, reviewing CIA's association with Bush in a 1975 document released under the JFK Act, admitted that Bush had "prior knowledge" of the "now-terminated project WUBRINY/LPDICTUM."

An older document, dated November 29, 1963, initiated by J. Edgar Hoover, refers to Hoover's having debriefed "Mr. George Bush of the Central Intelligence Agency" on the Kennedy assassination. It was an unusual Hoover locution, adding the name of the agency to which an individual was connected. Certainly it was uncharacteristic of Hoover to blow the cover of a CIA operative in an official document, but in this case he did. At the very least, it suggested a strong dislike of George H.W. Bush, if not outright personal hostility.

Confronted by this inconvenient revelation of his connection to CIA, one he had already denied, Bush lied, again. He claimed that Hoover was referring to a "George William Bush," a CIA photographic analyst, and not himself, George Herbert *Walker* Bush. So Bush inadvertently revealed that he was a CIA insider, despite his denial to the contrary. Had he not been, he would not have known, of course, of the existence of his CIA namesake.

In the ensuing furor that erupted when the Hoover document became public on September 21, 1988, George William Bush, a lowly CIA employee, swore under oath before the United States District Court for the District of Columbia that he had never been debriefed by Hoover or anyone else in the FBI.

Reporters demanding an explanation from CIA were told by CIA's press flack that he would "neither confirm nor deny" that Hoover was referring to George H.W. Bush. The name of the CIA spokesman was – Bill Devine.

In the murky universe of CIA's involvement with U.S. businesses, some of Bush's other CIA associations surfaced. They include CIA assets helping Bush structure the foundation for an illegal oil drilling partnership in Mexico through PEMEX, a CIA-connected oil monopoly. Bush was aided by Neil Mallon's Dresser Industries, which had long provided cover jobs for CIA employees. Agents under cover were disguised as Dresser salesmen and dispatched overseas where Dresser sold its drilling equipment. Dresser's CEO Mallon, was, of course, well known to Allen Dulles.

Bush collaborated with Mexican government officials, who worked closely with the Mexico City CIA Chief of Station. Bush then created PERMARGO, of which Zapata owned a 50% interest. PERMARGO was made to appear as if it was entirely owned by the Mexican government because Mexican law required all drilling contracts to be held by Mexican nationals. Bush's partner, Jorge Díaz Serrano, would be convicted of defrauding the Mexican government of $58 million. It was H. Neil Mallon who had recommended that Bush become involved in the scheme. Bush got away with the deception.

Zapata Offshore served as a conduit through which CIA disbursed money for operations. Sources in CIA's Directorate of Operations told *Wall Street Journal* reporter Anthony Kimery that Bush "personally served as a conduit through which the Agency disbursed money for contracted services." As a "part-time purchasing front for CIA," Zapata provided supplies for the Bay of Pigs operation, leasing cargo vessels and shipping CIA cargo disguised as oil drilling equipment.

That Kimery was the son of a CIA employee facilitated his access to CIA officers, whose testimony allowed him uncompromisingly to break this important story. In his article, one that has been often cited, Kimery does not expose their names.

Despite all this, during his confirmation hearings for Director of Central Intelligence, Bush asserted, under oath, that he had only a "general knowledge" of how CIA operated, no more than any informed citizen. He was not challenged, and was duly confirmed.

* * *

On Friday morning, April 26, 1963, George de Mohrenschildt and Clémard Joseph Charles appear on schedule at Devine's office. De Mohrenschildt does most of the talking, promoting his "Haitian Holding Company," which "cooperates with Charles' bank in an effort to rework and create certain industries and enterprises in Haiti." A reflexive name-dropper, de Mohrenschildt elaborates on the official connections enjoyed by Clémard Joseph Charles.

He will be returning to Haiti on May 24th, de Mohrenschildt confides, adding that in the past two years he has made several trips to Haiti. He plans to open an office in Charles' bank to handle the car insurance business. He has also done geological work for the "Meek Company."

De Mohrenschildt claims that he obtained his sisal concession, not from Duvalier, but from Haiti's Minister of Finance, Hervé Boyer, "a splendid person" and "likely to survive any change in the regime." If Devine registered the implication – de Mohrenschildt suggesting that Duvalier's days in office were numbered – he did not let on.

Charles adds that de Mohrenschildt's contract with the Government of Haiti for an oil exploration survey was for $280,380, along with a ten-year option on the sisal concession. The contract had been drawn up on March 13th, and announced in *Le Moniteur*, the official newsletter of the Haitian government. Charles handed Devine a copy of the issue of *Le Moniteur* in question.

To begin operations, de Mohrenschildt was awarded $20,000, drawn on Charles' bank. The sisal plantation in question would turn out to be, HSCA investigator Gaeton Fonzi discovered, "a derelict operation they never went near."

Slowly, surreptitiously, the real subject of the meeting snakes to the surface – politics, the overthrow of Duvalier and his being replaced by Clémard Joseph Charles. Glancing around the room, and over his shoulder, de Mohrenschildt murmurs that he and Charles are awaiting the fall of Papa Doc. "My connection with this is, of course, confidential," de Mohrenschildt whispers. Then he strolls around collecting every handout in Devine's office.

To his surprise, Devine discovers that there is a third partner, B. Gindine-Tardieu, who will be arriving in New

York on Sunday. He will be a financial conduit, Charles explains, since "it is not appropriate for a banker to ask for money," an "amazing statement," CIA's C. Frank Stone would reflect when Devine conveyed the remark to him late that afternoon. Devine arranges an appointment to meet Tardieu on Monday, indicating that he is on board with the Charles-de Mohrenschildt scheme.

Haiti is wrapped in political turmoil. On this very day, April 26, 1963, assassins fire upon Duvalier's limousine. Inside are his children and their bodyguards. The children escape unharmed.

Meanwhile de Mohrenschildt is in New York. He finds his way to the exclusive Racquet and Tennis Club where he pilfers some of their stationery, intended for members. He writes a letter to his Dallas acquaintance Paul Raigorodsky. It is now that he suggests that Raigorodsky invest in his "Holding Company."

At five that afternoon, on the "sterile line" they had set up, Devine telephoned Frank Stone with his report of the visit of Clémard Joseph Charles and George de Mohrenschildt. Neither man impressed him, Devine said. De Mohrenschildt was "a typical international financier and wheeler and dealer," as well as an irritating "paper grabber." Both men "showed an element of bluff in their presentation." Devine noted that they spoke "deprecatingly" of President Duvalier, yet "glowingly" of investment possibilities in Haiti. CIA was operating on a "need to know" basis, and neither Devine nor Gale Allen seem to have been aware of de Mohrenschildt's history with CIA.

I never heard of the "Meek Company," Stone said, questioning de Mohrenschildt's oral resumé. CIA's interest in Clémard Joseph Charles meant, inevitably, that they would inquire into the bona fides of his traveling companion. Gale Allen of the Directorate of Operations at once requested an "expedite check of George de Mohrenschildt, exact reasons unknown."

On April 29th, three days later, CIA's Office of Security sent the Domestic Contact Division a copy of a 1958 report they had on George de Mohrenschildt.

* * *

In New York, and later in Washington, D.C., de Mohrenschildt and Charles were tracked by both CIA and 90 Deuce. Supervising the military intelligence surveillance was Dorothe Matlack, Assistant Director of the Office of the Domestic Exploitation Section, Army Chief of Staff for Intelligence, "OACSI." Matlack was Army intelligence's chief liaison with the Central Intelligence Agency, which had awarded her its own "Top Secret" clearance. She did not carry a military rank.

Colonel L. Fletcher Prouty was then the Pentagon's logistics liaison with CIA within the Office of Special Operations. He has described Matlack as coming "from a real black intelligence arm of the Pentagon." In a draft of a March 6, 1990 letter to former New Orleans district attorney, Judge Jim Garrison, who continued to investigate the Kennedy assassination until the end of his life, Prouty terms Dorothe Matlack "one of [Edward] Lansdale's special 'black' intelligence associates in the Pentagon."

It was Matlack who would meet de Mohrenschildt at National Airport when he flew from Haiti to Washington to testify before the Warren Commission, linking de Mohrenschildt with both the military and CIA. He was a person of interest to both, with the military, as always, taking second place.

90 Deuce learned that Charles' bank rated a poor third among the three Port-au-Prince banks. V.E. Blacque, for a time the commercial officer at the U.S. Embassy in Port-au-Prince, had warned de Mohrenschildt, whom he had known since before World War II. De Mohrenschildt should not have anything to do with the sisal plant that the Haitian government was dangling before him.

To assist her in assessing the character of Clémard Joseph Charles, Matlack enlisted a long-time CIA asset under military cover, Colonel Sam Goodhue Kail. In Cuba, Kail had been assigned from June 3, 1958 to January 4, 1961 to report on the Cuban army. Among those he handled was future Alpha 66 terrorist Antonio Veciana. It should surprise no one that Joe Dryer had known Kail in Cuba.

In Cuba, CIA agents would assume the names of Embassy military personnel, while the military would assume the identities of the agents. Agency operatives, not only in Cuba, but elsewhere, would often be awarded full military personnel files, including false dates of birth. They would be given military rank that remained with them all their lives. But they belonged to CIA.

A notorious example was Colonel Edward Lansdale, Graham Greene's "Quiet American," but hardly "quiet" to those in the know. In Lansdale's case, he enjoyed a full military career before the creation of CIA. From 1954 on, he was theirs. Even his military promotions were odd, not done the way the military customarily operates. Lansdale's promotion to General was driven by Allen Dulles. Dulles wrote to Curtis Le May, who did not know Lansdale at all; Lansdale duly got his promotion - at the behest of the DCI.

"Hey! You're not Colonel Kail!" a Cuban had shouted one day at Kail; he had known Kail only under his cover name. At the moment Kail enters the Clémard Joseph Charles/George de Mohrenschildt story, he is in Florida, on loan from the Joint Chiefs of Staff to CIA in a clear example of the symbiotic relationship between CIA and the military.

Kail now worked for Justin F. Gleichauf, who had opened a CIA field office of the Domestic Contact Division, part of the Directorate of Intelligence, for the purpose of interrogating recent Cuban refugees. Gleichauf and Kail operated out of an abandoned World War II Marine air base in Opa-Locka, Florida. Kail conducted debriefings at the "Caribbean Admission Center."

When Kail garnered a "live one," he would turn him over to CIA's Miami station, JMWAVE. He reported both to the Chief of Army Intelligence in Washington, D.C. and to CIA. Another of Kail's frequent contacts was E.M. Ashcraft, chief of CIA's Domestic Contact Division.

Applying for access to CIA headquarters at Langley in February 1962, Kail had no trouble. His security file reveals that CIA had granted him "Top Secret" clearance as of 1957. That Dorothe Matlack would enlist so powerful a figure as Kail suggests how seriously CIA and Army Intelligence were taking Clémard Joseph Charles as a replacement for Duvalier.

Before she could contact Kail and put him in touch with Joe Dryer, Matlack had to proceed through the chain of command and clear the interview with two Generals. One was General Alva Revista Fitch, Assistant Chief of Intelligence for the Army. Once Fitch was on board, Major General Roland Haddaway Del Mar, formerly of the Antilles Command, and director of the Inter-American Defense College, had to be consulted.

On April 29, 1963, General Fitch replied to Matlack. Cautiously, she suggested that Charles might indeed be a "potential source on Haiti." By now, Dryer had himself written to Fitch, recommending Charles as a man "of great interest to the U.S. government in view of the events in Haiti." Charles was "in President Duvalier's favor," Dryer had added. Shrewdly, Dryer added this detail: Charles was no oppositionist, which would have made acquaintance with him on the part of U.S. officials embarrassing had it been discovered by Papa Doc. Meeting with Charles might easily be explained away should such an explanation prove necessary. He was close to the seat of power in Haiti.

Matlack assessed Kail as "a very smooth operator." She had now been given the green light to set up a meeting between him and Dryer for the purpose of clearing Clémard Joseph Charles to meet with both military intelligence and CIA. If all went well, Kail was to ask Clémard Joseph Charles to contact her directly.

All this Matlack conveyed to her CIA contact Anthony Czajkowski, of the Domestic Contact Division (00). She believed that April 29th was the day de Mohrenschildt had scheduled a meeting to discuss Clémard Joseph Charles and his future with Vice President Lyndon Johnson, Senator Kenneth Keating, and Congressman Rogers. Matlack recognized that Clémard Joseph Charles' making contact with elected officials at the highest level represented a step toward his being chosen as the person to replace Papa Doc. CIA would be making the decisions. Government officers were recruited in advance to endorse the coup that would catapult Clémard Joseph Charles into the Presidency of Haiti.

On the morning of May 1, 1963, at 10:45, Kail arrived at Dryer's Palm Beach home. He asked Dryer for any background he had on Clémard Joseph Charles, and discovered that Charles was a director of Dryer's Haiti kenaf operation. Charles was also the owner of at least eight other enterprises.

Dryer recommended Clémard Joseph Charles wholeheartedly for Haiti's presidency. He praised Charles for his "honesty" and "ability" and "his adroitness in being in everybody's good graces in Haiti," qualities that would serve him well as Haiti's new president. In Haiti, Charles had always been "apolitical," attached to no faction, although of late he had manifested "some political inclinations," and might even be dreaming of "some day becoming president." Also in Charles' favor was that a cousin was a former Haitian ambassador to the United States.

A fount of information, Dryer added that Charles had started his first bank with two American partners, contributing $100,000 to their $400,000. When the Americans had made off with some of the money, Charles paid off all the losses. "He is connected with everything and everybody," Dryer said, and is a "good friend" of President Duvalier, and close to both the army and the *Tontons Macoutes*. Duvalier had appointed Charles to head SHADA, under whose auspices the government of Haiti sponsored oil exploration, rubber exports and the exploitation of forest resources.

Charles was now traveling with "a Texan geologist named de Mohrenschildt," Dryer informed Kail. De Mohrenschildt was trying to arrange a meeting for Charles with Vice President Johnson.

Dryer had encountered de Mohrenschildt in Haiti a year or two earlier. Shortly after they met, ever on the lookout for wealthy, influential people with whom to connect, de Mohrenschildt had invited Dryer to dinner in New York.

At the time, de Mohrenschildt was ensconced in a modest apartment on the Upper East Side. Hardly the abode of a person of substance, it had a few bedrooms and a living room and was likely to have belonged to de Mohrenschildt's brother, Dimitri. The décor was tasteful and subtle; there were Russian icons and other antiques. Dryer remembered George's wife as "an elderly low-class lady." This was not how Jeanne Le Gon de Mohrenschildt would have liked to be described – she who was filmed swimming in the nude during their Central American walking tour. The dinner was a good one, Dryer remembered.

Taking note that Charles' connection with Lyndon Johnson was through de Mohrenschildt, Kail perked up. He wanted to know more about de Mohrenschildt, just as Frank Stone did. Dryer suggested that Kail contact "Mr. Ted Black," the Commercial Officer at the American Embassy in Port-au-Prince, and obviously a CIA asset.

As this meeting drew to a close, Dryer telephoned Charles, who was staying at the Park Sheraton Hotel in New York. Then he handed the phone over to Kail, who suggested to Charles that he travel to Washington, D.C. to meet Mrs. Dorothe Matlack. Kail provided Charles with Matlack's telephone number. At this moment Clémard Joseph Charles was moving within the highest U.S. military and intelligence circles, at the point where CIA and the Pentagon intersect.

Kail was not troubled by Charles' having posed as "a good friend of President Duvalier," or by his being Duvalier's principal distributor of largesse to American politicians. Kail thought that both Duvalier and Charles might prove to be useful to CIA's implementation of Operation Mongoose, its renewed war against Fidel Castro.

It is no small matter for CIA to select a candidate to run a foreign country. Intrigue will characterize all the events that follow in this narrative.

On May 2, 1963, at 8:15 in the morning, Matlack is at her desk at the Pentagon conferring with CIA's Anthony Czajkowski.

Together they hatch a plan to send a Captain Rogers, the Defense Intelligence Agency Haitian desk officer, to New York, to confer with James Balog of the CIA's New York field office. The subject of their meeting will be Clémard Joseph Charles. Matlack hands over all the information she has collected on Charles to Czajkowski so that he can transmit it to Balog. A few last minute tidbits are sent to Rogers to pass on to Balog.

The plan is for Rogers and Balog to interview Clémard Joseph Charles at 1:30 this afternoon at the Park Sheraton. Balog is not to reveal his CIA connection. Instead, he will present himself under his Army intelligence cover.

Rogers, Balog and Clémard Joseph Charles spend four hours together. Duvalier would "kill my family if he learned of this meeting," Charles says. No fool, Duvalier would immediately recognize, judging from the cast of characters present, that a coup against his government is in the offing and that Clémard Joseph Charles has some role in it.

Charles reveals that he has met with James R. Greene, a vice-president at the Manufacturers Hanover Trust Company, to "attract U.S. capital for the development of the Haitian economy."

The real purpose of the meeting, of course, is politics, not economics, "what the United States should do in the current Haitian situation." Charles hopes that "President Kennedy and other high U.S. government officials will give him an opportunity to present his plan to save Haiti from Duvalier and Communism." He would confer with them "most discreetly," he promises.

As the meeting dwindles toward its conclusion, Charles suggests to the intelligence officers that they meet his "good American friend and business partner, George de Mohrenschildt." Without guile, he invites Balog to visit him in Port-au-Prince "as soon as the Duvalier crisis is resolved."

That night, Captain Rogers flies to Washington. From New York, Balog phones Czajkowski with his report of the meeting. He has established "good rapport" with Charles, Balog says. Both he and Rogers are pleased that Charles has "never been tied up with any political party, an advantage he holds over other Haitian politicians." Balog also reports to Matlack, to CIA's Western Hemisphere Division, and to CIA's "Latin American Branch."

On May 4th, Clémard Joseph Charles attends yet another meeting with his military and CIA contacts. This time he meets with Anthony Czajkowski, Jim Balog and Mayo Stuntz of the Operational Support Branch. They had the Counter Intelligence function within 00/ the Domestic Contact Division. "Counter Intelligence," in addition to the operational intelligence it may collect for its own use, entails measures and operations required to negate intelligence activities of the opposition.

Encouraged by such high level interest, Clémard becomes more open and forthcoming. He remarks that, "if possible," he prefers "to deal with U.S. government officials without his Texan friend and business partner, George de Mohrenschildt." He has sensed that de Mohrenschildt has not been making a good impression, that people are wary of him.

Charles reveals that Jerry W. Johnston at the Chase Manhattan Bank has promised him a two million dollar loan for the construction of new housing in Haiti, a loan contingent on "the return of political stability to Haiti." The Agency for International Development (AID) would cover 90% of the loan, with Charles handling the remaining ten percent.

About the role the U.S. government would play, Charles is quite specific. He would like the U.S. once more to send the Marines into Haiti, in the manner that the U.S. entered Lebanon. A provisional government would be set up to ensure law and order and to protect American residents and businesses in Haiti.

Two days later, on May 6th, Mayo Stuntz confers with Jim Balog. The Western Hemisphere Division of CIA is now willing to meet with Clémard Joseph Charles. Balog is to arrange the appointment.

Balog and Rogers now circulate a report of their contacts with Charles, and formulate questions that remain to be answered. So far, Charles seems well on his way to accomplishing his mission of enlisting CIA and the U.S. military in overthrowing Duvalier and installing himself in Duvalier's place.

At 4:30 p.m. on May 6th, 1963, Jeanne de Mohrenschildt telephones Captain Rogers in Washington. Clémard, George – and herself – are able to meet with him at noon the next day, if Captain Rogers would be so kind as to "get them a hotel." It is Charles who is worried, who does not want to be embarrassed by being refused a hotel room in segregated Washington, D.C.

Rogers turns the task of locating a hotel that will accept a black man over to Dorothe Matlack.

Jeanne de Mohrenschildt is a singularly unpleasant woman. She insists that either she or Mr. Charles must have a confirmation of the meeting with CIA by 6:30 that evening or they will not journey to Washington. In a peremptory manner, she demands that Matlack confirm within two hours that hotel rooms have been reserved. Although Jeanne de Mohrenschildt has no political role in this or any of the events that follow, she has, not for the last time, inserted herself into the mix.

As for Matlack, she is involved in the Clémard Joseph Charles-de Mohrenschildt saga as the liaison between CIA and Military Intelligence, although she has not expected that to include finding hotel rooms. It is too important an effort for CIA not to have enlisted Military Intelligence, although CIA is in the driver's seat.

Jeanne de Mohrenschildt's inappropriate, indiscreet reference to CIA leads Matlack to phone Czajkowski. No such meeting with CIA has been set up, he says quickly. The hotel problem remains unresolved.

Matlack requests that Czajkowski find them a hotel "in view of the color problem and their [CIA's] long range interest." Czajkowski insists that he is in no position to make hotel reservations and urges that Matlack do it. Matlack suggests that he call Balog.

In this strange parody of musical chairs, Matlack next contacts the Intelligence Division of the State Department. Deputy Chief of Protocol William Tonesk is assigned to find "suitable hotel accommodations for Mr. Charles in view of color problem." But it's Matlack who finally makes the reservations, one at the Mayflower, another at the Albion Towers. Then she phones Charles, whose English is so halting that he hands the telephone over to Jeanne de Mohrenschildt.

A luncheon is arranged for noon the next day, May 7th, at the stately Willard Hotel. But is CIA on board? Balog telephones Czajkowski and requests that he "iron out any conflict."

Czajkowski's first impulse is to exclude Matlack from the luncheon, but Matlack objects. She is, after all, the point of contact with Charles, and Charles believes that the "someone" he is meeting for lunch is Matlack. Matlack states her case: Charles "expressed initial reluctance to be interviewed unless she was present and vouched for any other personnel."

Matlack adheres to a military culture. Her bosses authorized her to meet Charles for lunch and, if only for that reason, she cannot withdraw. Yet, Matlack wants CIA to send a representative to the luncheon because, after all, she has "absolutely nothing to see Charles about."

At 8:40 on May 7th, the morning of the luncheon at the Willard, Czajkowski conveys a message to Matlack. Balog has informed him that the CIA ops people are interested in meeting Charles, but "CIA wanted Charles alone." Matlack and army intelligence are not welcome. Should that not be possible, CIA will "make other arrangements." For CIA to reveal its plans in the presence of the military, which was subordinate to CIA, is unthinkable.

The distribution of power throughout these events reveals the larger structural configuration. The Pentagon gives way to CIA – and by implication, behind the scenes, so would the president, the supposed "Commander in Chief." In the decades to come, this hierarchy – already manifest in Ronald Reagan's "endorsement" of Iran-Contra – would become more apparent: Barack Obama would participate in a charade suggesting that he is making the decision to send a "surge" of 30,000 additional troops to Afghanistan, to cite but one example. CIA fought that war openly in the field, its new normal. The interactions between Matlack and CIA reveal how subordinate the Pentagon was already to CIA.

Never one to act unilaterally, Matlack consults Colonel Kail. Kail advises her to meet Charles because of "Charles' relationship to President Duvalier...and Haiti's strategic position relative to Castro's Cuba." The military has an interest, although it is not as primary decision maker in these events.

She will meet Charles, Matlack decides, introduce CIA's operations man, make her excuses about another commitment, and depart. Czajkowski agrees, so long as Matlack understands that "CIA should have Charles."

Czajkowski promises to call her back with the identity of the "interested CIA man." When he does call, it's to tell her that the DD/P (Deputy Director for Plans, Helms) refuses to attend if Matlack is there at all. CIA would be represented, but not by anyone from the clandestine services. Mayo Stuntz has weighed in and decided that CIA would meet privately with Charles, later in the afternoon.

At the Willard Hotel luncheon, CIA would be present, but only in the person of Anthony Czajkowski of the Domestic Contact Division. Czajkowski would be introduced to Clémard Joseph Charles as a Professor from George Washington University. It's a long and thorny road upon which Clémard Joseph Charles, an idealistic man in his prime, has embarked in his effort to become CIA's replacement for Papa Doc. This man who is "never discouraged by obstacles" has entered into a world of duplicity, secrecy and deceit.

THREE

Has CIA Abandoned Clémard Joseph Charles? George De Mohrenschildt In Haiti

Come on down to Haiti. The CIA will protect you.

– George de Mohrenschildt

On the morning of May 7, 1963, Clémard Joseph Charles and George and Jeanne de Mohrenschildt fly to Washington, D.C. Shortly before noon, CIA's Anthony Czajkowski strolls into the dark wood-paneled lobby of the Willard Hotel. Dorothe Matlack is already waiting for him. When Charles arrives, Matlack introduces Czajkowski as a professor from George Washington University, as planned.

Matlack is surprised that Charles has brought along George de Mohrenschildt of whose ambiguous history she is now in full possession. From Matlack's perspective, and she is nothing if not shrewd, Charles seems "frantic and frightened," while de Mohrenschildt dominates him in some way. That Charles is already a full-fledged CIA asset is reflected in the fact that his name – and only his

– would be redacted from CIA's memorandum of that lunch at the Willard.

As is his wont, de Mohrenschildt monopolizes the conversation. He recounts his life story: how he was born in Baku, Russia (or "Mozyrz" or "Mozyr" or "Mozyt"); how he worked for the International Cooperation Administration in Yugoslavia in 1957; and how he met "President" Gomulka, who was so impressed that he invited him to Poland. It didn't matter who the higher-up was – Stalinist or capitalist – de Mohrenschildt likes him. Gomulka and Charles are partners "in a sisal business in Haiti," de Mohrenschildt adds.

As for Charles, "frantic" or "frightened" as he first appeared to Matlack, he is not shy about his ambitions. He suggests directly and without subtlety that the U.S. send the Marines to Haiti, supported by Haitian army officers. Before Matlack can make her getaway, de Mohrenschildt and Charles attempt to enlist her help in setting up meetings for them with government officials. Charles requests an appointment with Mr. Edmund Wise of the Agency for International Development (AID) about a loan.

It was Vice-President Lyndon Johnson, Charles confides, who provided him with Wise's name – obviously the fruit of George de Mohrenschildt's meeting with Howard Burris, Johnson's Air Force Intelligence and perhaps CIA-connected security advisor. De Mohrenschildt had not succeeded in meeting with wily Lyndon Johnson after all.

According to historian Larry Haapanen, among those de Mohrenschildt did meet in Washington D.C. that May of 1963 was a CIA officer named Nicholas M. Anikeeff, who had known de Mohrenschildt back in the thirties, before World War II. For CIA's Soviet Russia division, Anikeeff had liaised with the Gehlen group, Allen Dulles' prize Nazi intelligence recruits. Anikeeff had been involved in operations behind the iron curtain.

CIA contacts were, however, nothing unusual for de Mohrenschildt by now. Anikeeff sets up an appointment for de Mohrenschildt in Washington, D.C. with Senator Claiborne Pell: CIA officer to CIA asset. There is no record of whether de Mohrenschildt kept that appointment or what transpired if they did in fact meet.

At lunch as well, Charles requests that Matlack do some secretarial tasks for him. Would she make some copies for him of a letter of introduction written on his behalf and directed to Senator Hubert Humphrey?

This letter was written by Phyllis Washington's uncle, William Stix Wasserman. The effusive letter praises Charles for advancing in Haiti "liberal notions in regard to cooperatives, the welfare of labor, and the necessity of creating a new relationship between capital and labor through profit sharing." Charles' ideas will go a long way to "nullify to some extent the siren song of Communist propaganda," Wasserman adds. His suggestion is that the U.S. government should "look for men with Mr. Charles' ability and attitudes to see what can constructively be done to bring some hope to that unfortunate island."

Cordially, Charles invites Matlack and Czajkowski to dinner on May 9th, in two days time. Neither accepts. Matlack is particularly suspicious of de Mohrenschildt. "I knew the Texan wasn't there to sell hemp," she was to tell the FBI later.

As Matlack and the de Mohrenschildts depart, Czajkowski takes Charles aside. "Mr. Green," a CIA Western Hemisphere operative, will meet him in the lobby at 2:15, Czajkowski tells Charles. This is a meeting about which

CIA has released no descriptive document for the benefit of history.

Back at her desk, Matlack attempts to arrange a meeting for Charles with Edmund Wise of AID. She reaches Forrest K. Abbuhl, the Haitian Desk man at the Intelligence Division of the State Department. Abbuhl expresses his "extreme displeasure" at the very idea that anyone in the United States government should be in contact with Clémard Joseph Charles.

Charles is close to the Duvalier government, Abbuhl objects, and has been in "several shady financial dealings." Charles is "bad medicine," Abbuhl says angrily, a "cheap two-bit crook," "unreliable," and "mixed up in a variety of unsavory business deals."

Despite Abbuhl's hostility, he reveals that the U.S. government is not yet done with Clémard Joseph Charles. Although the State Department has concluded that Charles is "an undesirable character," he might still be of use, if only because he has a "pipeline to the Palace." On this day, a "Mr. Zagovsky" warns Matlack not to sponsor Charles in any appointment with AID. Things have taken a nasty turn for poor Clémard.

At 4:45 on that afternoon of May 7, 1963 Anthony Czajkowski telephones Matlack. CIA has "NO" further plans to contact Charles, he announces. As part of the Domestic Contact Service, Czajkowski now falls out of the loop, with CIA's far more powerful clandestine services taking over the relationship with Clémard Joseph Charles.

Czajkowski is left to voice the official CIA line, one that bears only a slim relationship to reality. The only reason CIA had even met with Charles was because of the "political information" he could impart about what was going on in Haiti – this will be the cover story with respect to Clémard Joseph Charles that those in the Agency without a "need-to-know" will be given. The official version of these events – given to CIA components not in on the operation regarding Charles – is that Charles was never going to be at the center of a CIA effort to remove Papa Doc.

"Our interest seems to have been satisfied," Czajkowski adds. CIA now plans to "disengage ourselves as gracefully as possible." Copies of this seemingly final decision are sent to the Chief of Operations; to the Support Branch (Stuntz); to the Latin American Branch; to the Index (Control); and to the Dep/Coll chrono. The message is contrary to the actual fact. CIA, other documents reveal, continued its interest in Clémard Joseph Charles.

Privately, Czajkowski is perplexed. Equally dismayed is Colonel Roth of the Operations Branch of military intelligence, who wants to know from the clandestine services why CIA seems to have dropped Charles so abruptly. It is CIA at its most convoluted, with one component concealing its goals from the others.

A miasma now settles over military intelligence, miring the Charles project in a fog of uncertainty. The next day, May 8th, Charles leaves several frantic telephone messages for Matlack in an effort to figure out what is going on. Colonel Roth requests further information. A Colonel Reinhard and a Colonel Albro are debriefed at two that afternoon, so 90 Deuce learns that "CIA/DDP stated they had no reason to drop him [Charles] because of derogatory information." What then, if anything, has gone wrong?

The two colonels request, for the moment, that Matlack call Charles back and explain that she had been unable to set up an appointment for him with Mr. Wise of AID because of "the press of business." Colonel Roth, of the Operations Branch, Military Intelligence, attempts to obtain from CIA/DDP the reason for the abrupt dropping of Charles.

Pretending to "search its records" to respond to the inquiries of military intelligence's Support Branch, CIA claims to entertain "no record of a current operational interest in subject," which is not the case. The Pentagon knows this is not realistic since CIA had been "listening" since 2 May on a daily basis. This renders specious CIA's official view that "after contact of 7 May" their interest had been "satisfied."

Matlack phones Czajkowski and tells him that the Operational Branch of her office is still discussing Charles with CIA's clandestine services to determine a future course of action. Czajkowski is wary. Charles' role is now up to the State Department or the Army, he says. Confused, Matlack attempts to gather what intelligence she can. She hears a rumor that one of Charles' cousins had been mentioned as Duvalier's successor.

Matlack believes that the "U.S. government should continue to 'play ball' with Charles as a future asset in Haitian affairs." She also fears that "charges might later be made that ACSI [herself] had interfered or had obstructed CIA contact with Charles." She is concerned that CIA and the Army "not be working at cross purposes."

Matlack evades Charles, but she is not dismissive. Tactfully, she turns him down when he reissues his May 9th dinner invitation. Placated, he promises to call her again on May 13th to see if she has made the appointment for him with Wise or another AID representative. Charles confides that he has an appointment with Senator Kenneth Keating at 4 o'clock on May 14th, a meeting that will not take place. Close to CIA, Keating – who would be the first Senator to expose the presence of Soviet missiles in Cuba – obviously is in the loop.

On May 9th, CIA's Frank Stone receives a response to his April 26th request for traces on George de Mohrenschildt from the CIA operations component. It turns out that there is a considerable de Mohrenschildt file, with many records residing in the Western Hemisphere office in Mexico City. There are references dating back to de Mohrenschildt's attempt to join the Office of Strategic Services. There are records of Office of Naval Intelligence investigations of de Mohrenschildt in 1942 and 1943 having to do with de Mohrenschildt's taking pictures of the coast guard installations outside Corpus Christi, Texas. There is an FBI file dating from 1941 to 1948.

From the military intelligence and CIA documents, and from the negative reports on George de Mohrenschildt, one might now conclude that CIA has no further interest in Clémard Joseph Charles as the successor to a deposed Papa Doc. Yet that is not the case.

Far from being done with Clémard Joseph Charles, CIA maintains its interest and surveillance of both Charles and de Mohrenschildt. On that same May 9th, Clémard's CIA shadow, someone clearly known to him, encounters Charles at Washington's National Airport. Charles, the agent reports to his superiors, is dressed "nattily" in a grey silk suit. Traveling with him is – George de Mohrenschildt.

"What in the world is going on now in Haiti?" the CIA man says, seemingly without guile.

"We're going to bring down Papa Doc," Charles says.

As Charles and de Mohrenschildt fly off to Chicago, CIA is consolidating its records on de Mohrenschildt.

Anna Panor at headquarters of the Directorate of Operations, finds three reference cards pointing to a de Mohrenschildt file at the Office of Security; an OSS file; and a 201 file. One document states: "De Mohrenschildt was of interest to CIA in 1958," which was the year he went to Hungary. It is now May 9, 1963 as Panor forwards these documents to Frank Stone.

In its summary of its 1963 contacts with Clémard Joseph Charles, Military Intelligence notes that he had arrived "with an unspecified amount of money which he wanted to invest in the U.S." His "much broader non-commercial objective" was one that "would require cooperation from many departments and agencies of the U.S. government." This, of course, refers to the overthrow of Duvalier.

Yet Charles has met with no high officials. Instead, he has been shuffled off onto "medium rank people." No meetings "were physically held at the Pentagon." Shrewdly, the analysts at Military Intelligence write into the file that de Mohrenschildt had been "introducer, interpreter, and general foot-rubber." He "did not appear to have a substantive role in Charles' project," which was "fomenting some type of overthrow of the Duvalier government."

A lieutenant colonel named T.H. Selecman reports to the Army on May 10th that de Mohrenschildt would be returning to Haiti on May 24th, when he and his wife would take up permanent residence in Port-au-Prince. Selecman requests of his superiors "whatever data is available to you concerning these personalities." Selecman tells the Army that the State Department Haitian Desk officer, Mr. Abbuhl, doubts the advisability of dealing with Charles. It may well be, as Charles feared, that his association with de Mohrenschildt has brought him into disrepute and threatens to undermine his effort to replace Papa Doc.

On May 15, 1963, in New York, Thomas J. Devine and Frank Stone confer once more, this time at the Sheraton East Hotel. In attendance, in addition to the two, is a CIA colleague of Devine's whom CIA designated as WU-BRINY/2. The documents do not identify this figure, but the context makes clear that his presence is related to the fact that the primary subject of the meeting is George de Mohrenschildt. The meeting begins at 10:30 in the morning and continues until 5:20 in the afternoon.

Stone reports to Devine that CIA has now completed an exhaustive trace on de Mohrenschildt, coming up with "a large amount of derogatory information regarding the USA." They know that in 1945 de Mohrenschildt had told the FBI that "Communism was best for Europe," if not for the U.S. They know de Mohrenschildt is not a Communist, and that he worked for CIA in Yugoslavia and Hungary.

The ongoing interest of Stone and Devine in de Mohrenschildt at least suggests that Clémard Joseph Charles continued to figure in CIA's efforts to depose Duvalier. I am briefing you, Stone told Devine, so that in the event that you ever encounter de Mohrenschildt again, you will know the facts and "handle yourself accordingly."

From the context, this suggests that Stone was making certain that Devine divulge nothing to de Mohrenschildt. He needn't have worried. Devine was a seasoned CIA employee and knew well how to maintain his silence, as indicated by his never having revealed over the years anything about WUBRINY, or any other CIA operations in which he was involved, to scholars and historians who came calling.

Sure enough, a week later, on May 21ˢᵗ, George de Mohrenschildt shows up at Devine's office unannounced. Clémard Joseph Charles returned to Haiti on May 18ᵗʰ, de Mohrenschildt reports. He is "being seriously considered as the next President of Haiti." Charles would "make an excellent President of Haiti as soon as Duvalier can be gotten out." Again de Mohrenschildt sounds the theme that Charles "has never been tied up with any political party."

De Mohrenschildt confides that he has obtained "some Texas financial backing" for his Haitian operations, without specifying from whom. He has also visited "interested people in Washington regarding M. Charles' candidacy."

At 4:30 that afternoon, using the "sterile line," Devine reports to C. Frank Stone on de Mohrenschildt's surprise visit. The document recording this call is titled: "WU-BRINY – George DE MOHRENSCHILDT," leaving no doubt that Devine was, indeed, WUBRINY.

With respect to Haiti, John F. Kennedy attempted to tie the hands of CIA, his adversaries throughout his brief tenure in office. In a Security Action Memorandum dated March 23, 1963, Kennedy decreed that, "involvement in any program to unseat Duvalier should be limited, for the present at least, to encouraging and helping fund an effort by Haitians." While seeming to retreat from any open effort to remove Duvalier, the U.S. continued to search for his successor. By June 1ˢᵗ, they still had not located "a leader that could be trusted and who seemed able" to serve that function.

Renewed pressure on Kennedy to give CIA free reign in Haiti arrived from U.S. Ambassador Raymond Thurston. On June 18, 1963, Thurston warned that unless we change the regime in Haiti within two to three years, "the danger of communist activity was substantial." Taking Thurston's warning seriously, Kennedy then gave his ally, Dominican Republic President Juan Bosch, "a complete green light on building up a Haitian force."

Money and equipment would flow into that country occupying the northern half of the island of Hispaniola. Thurston was confident that "five hundred well-trained Haitians could remove Duvalier" with "not more than a battalion of United States forces sitting off shore as back-up just in case."

Late in May 1963, the de Mohrenschildts drove back to Dallas where they spent two days packing up every-thing they owned. According to de Mohrenschildt in his quasi-biography of Lee Harvey Oswald, they deposited their belongings at "Southwestern Warehouses" and paid for four years of storage. They departed with their rent in arrears for one month and drove to Miami, from where they would send their automobile to Haiti. His hair now streaked with gray, de Mohrenschildt behaved as if he was leaving the United States for good, his bridges burn-ing behind him.

In Port-au-Prince, the de Mohrenschildts moved into a house that hugged the side of a steep hill. Part of a com-plex called "Lyle Estates," their "little house on the side of a mountain" was named "Villa Valbrune." Residing in this compound was Papa Doc himself. To gain entrance, you had to pass through heavily guarded gates. Wherever the higher-ups lived, you could find George de Mohrenschildt.

A Philadelphia acquaintance, a lawyer named Thom-as P. Mikell had asked de Mohrenschildt how he could do business with a man like Duvalier. He was doing business with Duvalier "on a man to man basis to make money and the political actions and philosophy of Duvalier are of no interest to me," de Mohrenschildt said.

The rest of Haiti was in shambles. The rivers ran brown, the hillsides having been denuded of trees by the poor, who needed the wood to make charcoal for cooking. Not that Haiti's wrenching poverty troubled George de Mohrenschildt, who enjoyed the life of the rich and privileged. He threw elaborate and frequent dinner parties and joined a country club in leafy green Pétionville, the suburb of Port-au-Prince in the hills, luxuriant with flowers, where the rich mulattoes resided. De Mohrenschildt lived like the British expatriates in Kenya before independence, manifesting no guilt about exploiting the poor to support a decadent life style.

"Come on down to Haiti," de Mohrenschildt invited a New York friend named Thomas Josten. "The CIA will protect you!"

Much given to bragging, de Mohrenschildt described his business plan as costing out at $500,000,000. Among his boasts was the dubious claim that he was working for Clint Murchison, and that Vice President Johnson of the United States was interested in his investments in Haiti through Murchison.

De Mohrenschildt established an office in the building of the *Service de Géodésie et de Cartographie,* but he created no new maps. In fact, his "oil exploration" contract with the government of Haiti was bogus. It had been conceived to allow certain Haitian government officials, for their personal benefit, the right to exploit the sisal operation at Montrovis, a "gold mine."

Later, Clémard Joseph Charles confided to U.S. Embassy officials that previous petroleum surveys had not yielded encouraging results. Rather than create new maps, de Mohrenschildt had borrowed existing surveys and aerial photographs taken several years earlier by the American government's geodetic service. As had always been the case with de Mohrenschildt, hard work was not an option.

By June 12th, de Mohrenschildt had filled out a passport renewal application in Port-au-Prince, stating he intended to return to the U.S. within 12 months. The same day he executed an application for registration for residency in Port-au-Prince, to expire on June 9, 1965.

In August 1963, a U.S.-sponsored invasion of Haiti was launched. Anti-Castro soldiers of fortune, among them Loran Hall, joined in the hope of securing a base in Haiti, from which to launch operations into Cuba, just forty miles away at the closest point. The operation was led by General Léon Cantave, Lieutenant Colonel René Léon, Pierre Paret, and Emile Wooley. Among those involved were also American CIA-connected soldiers of fortune like Robert Emmett Johnson, a paramilitary expert and sometime journalist who had worked for Dominican dictator Rafael Trujillo.

Starting out from a border town of the Dominican Republic, the generals planned to march to a fortress that would serve as their headquarters. On the way, they were ambushed. Behind the scenes lurked former president Paul Magloire. The failed scenario had included the assassination of Duvalier.

In the wake of this particular CIA-inspired invasion, Papa Doc unleashed the *Tontons Macoutes,* who zeroed in on anyone even rumored to have helped Cantave. Severed heads impaled on pikes were paraded through the streets of Port-au-Prince.

"CIA had a commitment to the failure of this effort," admitted McGeorge Bundy, still President Kennedy's National Security adviser. "The whole 1963 operation was so fascinatingly inept," Robert Emmett Johnson wrote in 1968, following yet another CIA invasion, "that I suppose the Central Intelligence Agency simply could not resist the temptation to show what professionals can do." Even as CIA operations in Haiti seemed futile, with no possibility of succeeding, they served to enhance CIA power, and could be utilized as justifications for what would become CIA's bloated, and finally incalculable, budget. Success would have meant the assassination of Duvalier and/or the overthrow of his government. But such success was not necessary.

In October 1963, images of President Kennedy were placed under lighted candles in the Vodou temples of Haiti. A pin was stuck in the middle of Kennedy's neck. Addressing assembled troops in a port city, Papa Doc complained about the hostile relationship between the United States and Haiti. "The big man in the White House isn't going to be there much longer," Duvalier predicted. His fury over the U.S.-financed August invasion continued unabated. Later Duvalier would claim that he had willed President Kennedy's death by Vodou magic.

In Haiti, intimations of murder, including Papa Doc's, were perpetually in the air. A cable from CIA's Mexico City station chief to the Director of Central Intelligence, dated November 4, 1963, stated that Haiti's Minister of Tourism, visiting Mexico City, had claimed that he was "going to be next President of Haiti, that he will have present president killed."

According to de Mohrenschildt, he heard "the story of the [Kennedy] assassination" while driving from a reception at the Syrian Embassy in Port-au-Prince to the "house of this friend of ours who works at the [American] Embassy." Arriving, they supposedly heard on the radio that the accused assassin was named "something Lee."

"Could it be Lee Oswald?" de Mohrenschildt told the Warren Commission he had said.

His disingenuousness would not stand up well for long. Soon, his former son-in-law Gary Taylor would tell the FBI that he knew of no other person who had more influence over Oswald than George de Mohrenschildt.

"Don't we know someone by that name?" Jeanne de Mohrenschildt murmured. "He used to come to our house regularly and you gave him money...."

The day after the Kennedy assassination, among dinner guests at the de Mohrenschildt's "luxurious hillside villa," as novelist Herbert Gold described their house, George confided to his guests that he knew both Jackie Kennedy and Lee Oswald. Oswald, de Mohrenschildt had said, "turned out to be rather disturbed, didn't he?" De Mohrenschildt served rum-sodas, "the best thing for the heat and the bites – you forget about them." To Herbert Gold, "he seemed proud of his peculiar place in history."

De Mohrenschildt attempted to cover his tracks, to conceal the origin of his contacts with Oswald which, after all, were highly public in certain Dallas circles. In a personal letter dated December 9, 1963 to his friend Thomas J. Attridge, reacting to the assassination, de Mohrenschildt fabricated the story that Oswald had been "discovered" by some friends of his in Fort Worth. De Mohrenschildt named lawyer Max Clark as the person who had introduced him to Lee Harvey Oswald. De Mohrenschildt deliberately misspelled the name as "Osval" and "Osvald."

Before the Warren Commission had convened, De Mohrenschildt expressed his certainty that Oswald was guilty of the assassination of President Kennedy. "Osvald" was a "crackpot," a "crazy lunatic," who acted "for some crazy, psychopathic reason none of us will ever understand," de Mohrenschildt wrote, predicting the language of the Warren Report to come – with its jargon about Oswald having been a sociopath. It was a perspective that by the end of his life de Mohrenschildt would renounce entirely.

Narcissist that de Mohrenschildt was, he wrote Attridge that when he and his wife had taken Marina and the child away from Oswald, they too "might easily have been shot also."

It was part of de Mohrenschildt's persona to avoid consistency.

To Colonel Lawrence Orlov, to whom he could not claim credibly that it had been Max Clark who introduced him to Oswald – since he had visited Oswald for the first time in Orlov's company – de Mohrenschildt wrote that Oswald was too intelligent a person to have assassinated President Kennedy. It was his "hunch," de Mohrenschildt said, that there was someone else behind Oswald.

Marina Oswald reported to the FBI that "a few days after" April 10, 1963, de Mohrenschildt had asked Oswald, "How is it that you missed General Walker?" This inspired the State Department to instruct the U.S. Embassy in Port-au-Prince to re-interview the de Mohrenschildts, and to "establish from them and through examination [of] their passports when they arrived in Haiti and whether or not they have returned [to U.S.] since their original arrival in Haiti from Dallas."

On December 17, 1963, the de Mohrenschildt's were located in Cayes, Haiti and "urged" to return to Port-au-

Prince to be interviewed again. Two days later, on December 19, they were reinterviewed at the U.S. Embassy. They showed Embassy First Secretary Norman E. Warner their passports, which revealed no stamps of re-entry into Haiti.

On January 15, 1964, de Mohrenschildt, a man incapable of self-restraint, sent an indiscreet letter to his friend Everett D. Glover with respect to his relationship with Oswald. "It's interesting," de Mohrenschildt wrote, "but before we began to help Marina and the child we asked the FBI man in Dallas or in Fort Worth about Lee and he told us he was completely harmless." De Mohrenschildt had to have known that this was a charge – one easily exposed – that would enrage the FBI, and J. Edgar Hoover in particular, should it be repeated to anyone in the Bureau.

Sure enough, Glover showed de Mohrenschildt's letter to the FBI, now in charge of investigating the Kennedy assassination for the Warren Commission. Hoover was incensed that anyone in the FBI should be accused of calling Oswald "harmless." At once Hoover was up in arms. It's entirely false, he barked.

A Renaissance-style over-reacher, de Mohrenschildt, whose connection to Oswald derived entirely from CIA, had gone too far in attempting to implicate the FBI. Hoover decided to dispatch Special Agent W. James Wood to Haiti to set de Mohrenschildt straight.

In the year of his death, George de Mohrenschildt would tell Dutch journalist Willem H. Oltmans that "a Mr. Parker of the FBI" had come to see him in Haiti within twenty-four hours of the Kennedy assassination and "intimidated him" by referring to "interests who don't want the story to come out." Neither to Oltmans nor to anyone else did de Mohrenschildt tell the truth, that there was no "Mr. Parker." Rather, it was Wood who interviewed de Mohrenschildt in Port-au-Prince – in March 1964, not on the weekend of the assassination.

In January 1964, de Mohrenschildt remained optimistic about his prospects in Haiti. "The sisal deal works out fine," he wrote Everett Glover. He affected to be relieved to have left Texas behind for good: "Boy! I can assure you it is a pleasure not to be in Texas with decent people here and forget all the hatred and discriminations. Our relations here are so honest and pleasant...."

Into 1964, de Mohrenschildt's Dallas scams pursued him. In absentia, he was the subject of court litigation. It was alleged that he had leased oil land to another person without holding a valid lease on the property. The false representation had occurred on October 27, 1962. Now de Mohrenschildt owed $1,000 to Dabney A. Austin. It was yet another scam. De Mohrenschildt did not have legal access to that land.

Austin had paid de Mohrenschildt the second $500 at a dinner at the de Mohrenschildt home on October 27, 1962. While their business was being transacted, an unexpected visitor knocked at the door. It was Lee Harvey Oswald. Together the group watched de Mohrenschildt's home movie of his walking tour of Central America. Austin Dabney filed his petition against de Mohrenschildt in Dallas County District Court on March 6, 1963.

Duvalier might have become hostile to the United States government, but American business continued to flourish in Haiti during Lyndon Johnson's administration. Former Ambassador Raymond Thurston had been Kennedy's man. The new Ambassador, Benson E.L. (Ellison Lane) Timmons, noted on December 18, 1963: "Murchison/Davidson interest in Haiti has been source of encouragement to Duvalier."

"Davidson" referred to Isadore Irving (I.I.) Davidson, an international arms dealer and go-between based in Washington, D.C. and among Duvalier's registered U.S. representatives/lobbyists.

It was through Davidson that Carlos Marcello, the Louisiana crime boss, did business with Murchison – that oilman who was a great friend of J. Edgar Hoover – and who ran meatpacking and flour operations in Haiti. Famously, Murchison entertained Hoover, gratis, at his Hotel Del Charro in La Jolla, California. Another frequent guest was I.I. Davidson.

Davidson was also the go-between, facilitating a cash payoff from the Murchison family to Bobby Baker, the Secretary for the Majority Leader of the U.S. Senate, Lyndon Johnson.

When the Bobby Baker scandal broke, exposing how Baker was splitting fees with Lyndon Johnson from the Murchison Haitian meat business, testimony was taken from Thomas D. Webb, a Murchison representative/lobbyist in Washington. From that testimony it emerged that a Murchison Construction Company was among I.I. Davidson's clients. In Haiti, I.I. clearly was on Clint Murchison's payroll.

In 1961, I.I. Davidson arranged that the spoiled HAMPCO meat produced by the Murchison brothers operation no longer be sold to Puerto Rico, but to Davidson's friend, William Kentor, president of Packers Provision Company, a Chicago meat wholesale outfit. In a deal brokered by I.I. Davidson, Kentor agreed to continue to pay the one-half cent a pound commission previously arranged to go to Bobby Baker. The other half cent went to the Webb law firm representing the Murchisons in Washington D.C.

In addition to I.I. Davidson, the hidden beneficiary of the scam remained Lyndon Johnson. It was Johnson, who had arranged that the Agriculture Department license Murchison's inferior meat after it had been denied an export license because of poor sanitary conditions at the plant.

In 1963, Kentor's Packers Provision Company paid out $9,800 in commissions to Tucker & Baker, Bobby Baker's law firm, which was their fee on two million pounds of meat. The meat that went to market in Chicago for American consumers was no better in quality than the rotting meat sent to Puerto Rico. To disguise its quality, this meat was "ground up to make sausages, frankfurters, bologna, and some hamburgers."

The Senate committee investigating Baker remained baffled about why Bobby Baker, whose nickname on Capitol Hill was "Lyndon Junior," continued to receive his finder's fee. The entire I.I. Davidson/Clint Murchison/Bobby Baker/Lyndon Johnson configuration epitomized entrepreneurial life in the nightmare republic. Anything went. The Kennedy assassination, of course, rescued President Lyndon Johnson from the Bobby Baker scandal.

I.I. Davidson was born in Pittsburgh in 1921. By 1941, he was in Washington working for the War Production Board. In 1955, I.I. was selling machine guns in quantity "to various Middle Eastern countries." In 1958, he shipped 30,000 weapons to the Philippines.

Davidson termed himself a "five percenter, out to make a fast buck." He was affable, witty and ironic. Sharp and quick-witted, he knew how to be good company, a choice dinner party partner. There were few you would rather sit beside.

Not least among Davidson's clients was CIA, for whom Davidson often functioned as a lobbyist on Capitol Hill. Like George de Mohrenschildt, I.I. had worked for that CIA spin-off, the International Cooperation Administration. The FBI defined I.I. as "well known to CIA."

Davidson's business card read: Occupation: "Door Opener and Arranger," and he served a wide clientele in that capacity. He spied for Papa Doc on Haitian exiles, and covered himself always by telling the FBI what he knew.

Israel was his passion, and by 1958 "I. Irving," as he referred to himself, was a registered agent for the state of Israel. The *Wall Street Journal* reported that I.I. had "persuaded some responsible persons in the U.S. Army to purchase a machine gun manufactured in Israel called the "Uzi." I.I. Davidson worked hard for Israeli military industries, and persuaded NATO to "grant Israeli companies concessions and contracts for a jet airplane." It was reputed that Davidson's best friend was Shimon Peres.

Another of Davidson's clients was Anastasio Somoza of Nicaragua, for whom he tried to obtain bullet proof vests from the FBI. In Cuba, during the last hurrah of the dictatorship, he sold Batista thirty T-17 tanks, delivered from Nicaragua. I.I. also bought automatic weapons from Israel for Batista's war against Fidel Castro.

1959 found Davidson, registered as an agent for Nicaragua and the "Israeli Military Industry," spying on the Cuban revolution for the FBI with the aid of his own paid informants, whose names he refused to register as foreign agents. A report of June 11, 1959, sent by I.I. to the

Bureau quotes, "a U.S. intelligence Agency" stating of Ernesto Guevara that, "if he is not a Communist, he will do for one until another comes along." I.I. was not beyond passing peddled CIA information to the FBI.

Among I.I. Davidson's most flamboyant political efforts was his organizing a busload of anti-Castro pickets bound for Washington, D.C. The date was April 6, 1959, the purpose of the demonstration to harass Fidel Castro, who was visiting the United States. "They are really going to give it to him," Davidson exulted. Castro is going to be "most unhappy when he arrives in Washington," I.I. predicted.

I.I. hired two Cubans to supervise the picketing. They were "advised on all their activities by Irving Davidson," reads an FBI account of the event. I.I. paid for all the handbills and placards, not to mention the bus, out of his own pocket.

Davidson visited Batista in Portugal in February 1960, having collected $12,500,000 for bribes to ensure safe haven in the United States for the Cuban dictator. It was a rare Davidson defeat. That Batista did not settle in the United States was, in part, owing to CIA irritation. In the final days of the Batista dictatorship, a Belgian ship loaded with weapons sailed into Havana harbor. That night CIA's crack divers slid into the water and planted explosives to blow the ship up, as if they wished to see Batista depart – an act they would soon regret.

According to John H. Davis in *Mafia Kingfish*, Davidson was close to J. Edgar Hoover, to Lyndon Johnson, and to Richard Nixon. In Washington, D.C., Davidson shared an office with muckraking journalist, Jack Anderson.

Contradictions notwithstanding, Davidson also did business with Carlos Marcello. When in 1961 Marcello, on orders from Bobby Kennedy, was kidnapped and deported from New Orleans, I.I. Davidson was among the few who had Marcello's telephone number in Guatemala.

Davidson assisted Marcello in his immigration troubles via the criminal division of the Justice Department and an Immigration and Naturalization Service official. This was Mario Noto, whom Davidson promised a job with Coca-Cola, a company Davidson represented as a lobbyist. In compensation, Davidson quipped, his reward would be "a free cup of coffee."

It was Davidson who introduced a swindler named Joseph Hauser to Carlos Marcello, a move that led to Marcello's arrest and conviction in the BRILAB case. Davidson was arrested as well.

Not least, I.I. Davidson was a long-time supplier of arms and ammunition to CIA for its various paramilitary operations. For CIA, Davidson traded in information as well as in weaponry. He remained so close to CIA that he forged no deals that did not conform to Agency policy. One among several international profiteers swarming in and out of Haiti in the 1960s, I.I. had registered with the United States Department of State Office of Munitions Control, as an exporter and importer of rifles and surplus vehicles.

For the record, J. Edgar Hoover said he disapproved of I.I. Davidson. Yet, when the FBI was searching for exiled Cuban sugar czar Julio Lobo, they turned for assistance to Lobo's friend and fellow Jew, Davidson.

In 1974, CIA was to purchase from I.I. Davidson 25,000,000 rounds of ammunition at a cost of $3,125,000 "provid[ing] the Agency with a five-year supply." After discussions with the Defense Department, William Colby, then-Director of Central Intelligence, decided that CIA would itself bear the burden of securing arms.

I.I. Davidson first met with Papa Doc at the Presidential palace in early December 1963. A copy of the Fulbright committee's Senate investigation of foreign lobbying sat on Papa Doc's desk. Davidson had testified that the United States had been shaking hands with our enemies and kicking our friends in the teeth, a view that appealed immediately to Duvalier, who felt that as an anti-Communist in the Caribbean, he had not been sufficiently appreciated. That month, at the palace, I.I. Davidson met Clémard Joseph Charles. Charles, I.I. reported later, was attempting to explain to a Haitian woman what had become of one of her relatives in prison.

Later Davidson remarked that he been hired as a public relations man for Duvalier "because of the way I stuck up for my clients during the Senate foreign lobbying investigation." Duvalier hired him on December 12, 1963 and Davidson filed his registration statement with the Justice Department on December 19, only for it to be returned as unacceptable because Davidson had failed to translate Duvalier's authorization statement from French into English – and, no doubt not accidentally, hadn't given enough detail on what his services would be to Haiti.

Davidson's nemesis at the Justice Department was the prickly Assistant Attorney General J. Walter Yeagley, whom his boss Ramsay Clark didn't like any better than I.I. Davidson did. In 1963, when Davidson signed on with Duvalier, he was already registered as an agent for Nicaragua, Panama, Ecuador, and Indonesia.

By January 3, 1964, Davidson was registered by the Justice Department as a "public relations adviser and commercial agent" for Papa Doc. But even before being registered, Davidson had asked Edwin M. Martin, now former Assistant Secretary of State for Inter-American Affairs, "what could be done to improve Poppa Duvalier's image in the United States."

Brashly, Davidson recounted that he told President Duvalier that, "I would be his dollar-a-year man until I decided on a price tag for my services." Davidson had emphasized to Duvalier his contacts with such Washington, D.C. newspapermen as Jack Anderson. Later, Davidson would claim that he had been able to create a warmer feeling toward Haiti on the part of the American government.

One day in 1964, in his capacity as go-between, I.I. Davidson visited the U.S. Embassy in Port-au-Prince, carrying a letter from Dr. François Duvalier. The dictator demanded the transfer of four Embassy officers for conspiring against the Government of Haiti. U.S. Ambassador Timmons, new on the job, had already made a bad impression on Duvalier. Now Duvalier wanted him gone.

I.I. Davidson was able to move about freely, purchasing arms and war materiel for Duvalier in 1963 and 1964 because he was a CIA asset and an FBI informant. To U.S. intelligence, he sold Duvalier as the "not Castro."

Among the few who challenged Davidson's arms deals was Senator Wayne Morse of Oregon, one of two Senators who opposed the war in Vietnam at that time. Morse described I.I. Davidson as "an agent of the FBI and CIA who, for many years, had represented in Washington the interests of Central American dictatorial regimes, including Trujillo's." Senator Morse observed that Davidson acted "in concert with the policy-making of the State Department and the U.S. Central Intelligence Agency." Later Davidson's daughter Lynne would work for CIA, in keeping with the Agency's practice of employing family members of its agents and assets.

From the moment of President Kennedy's death, CIA had been keeping George de Mohrenschildt under surveillance. He was a man who knew too much and a man who was expendable. Despite his collection of influential acquaintances, de Mohrenschildt was very much alone. There was no one available and willing to rise to his defense should he find himself in harm's way.

It wasn't difficult to spy on de Mohrenschildt because he ran a salon. In Haiti, he gathered at his dinner table foreign traders, informants, gunrunners, Euro-trash and hangers-on of specious provenance, a veritable ship of fools. No one knew who was working for whom.

One evening de Mohrenschildt displayed for his guests an official-seeming card splashed with illegible handwriting. It was signed by President Duvalier and granted de Mohrenschildt the right "to travel anywhere he wished within Haiti without any difficulties."

Port-au-Prince CIA station chief Joseph G. Benson appointed the pseudonymous "Conrad V. Rubricius" to spy on de Mohrenschildt. Rubricius would report directly to the Chief of CIA's Western Hemisphere Division, Desmond Fitzgerald, suggesting that de Mohrenschildt remained of the highest interest to the Agency. CIA's focus remained on de Mohrenschildt's relationship with Clémard Joseph Charles, who apparently continued as a candidate to replace Duvalier should CIA find the means to overthrow him.

Rubricius befriended de Mohrenschildt, a man perverse enough to welcome someone who was obviously spying on him. Both were members of the Pétionville country club where they swam in the pool, played tennis, and sailed out to sea when the opportunity presented itself.

At a de Mohrenschildt dinner party on February 4, 1964 the guests included: the Mexican Ambassador to Haiti; a member of the (outlawed) Haitian Communist Party; and a de Mohrenschildt employee and Texas geology student named Austin Boyd. Also at the table was de Mohrenschildt's son-in-law Ragnar ("Rags") Kearton, who was married to Jeanne's daughter Christiana. Ragnar's father was vice-president and manager of the Space Systems Division of the Lockheed Missile and Research Company. This would later become the weapons behemoth, Lockheed-Martin, a company that, in another context, will shortly enter this narrative.

The entertainment that evening was yet another screening of the two-hour home movie of the de Mohrenschildt's Central American tour.

De Mohrenschildt enjoyed mixing people of contradictory political persuasions. Among those favored with his invitations was Roger Gaillard, member of Haiti's PPLN (*Parti populaire de libération nationale)* and, according to CIA, "a well-known, self-avowed Communist." Gaillard's wife was Bulgarian and worked with Wlodzimierz Galicki, the Polish Commercial attaché, who was to become de Mohrenschildt's closest cohort in Haiti.

Occasionally Joseph F. Dryer Jr. was invited to these dinners. By now, Dryer found de Mohrenschildt distasteful, a name-dropper, perpetually boasting "of the wealthy and aristocratic people he knew in New York." He seemed to have attached himself to Clémard Joseph Charles as his "unofficial adviser." Dryer, who liked Charles, was still uneasy about the relationship.

Dryer continued to believe that de Mohrenschildt had "some intelligence connection," he later told House Select Committee investigator Gaeton Fonzi. Dryer conveyed all of this to CIA and to army intelligence, as well. "I could never figure out what he [de Mohrenschildt] did," Dryer said.

Now whenever Dryer ran into de Mohrenschildt, Charles was there as well. It seemed that de Mohrenschildt, despite Charles' close connection to Papa Doc, feared for Charles' life. One evening after dinner de Mohrenschildt followed Charles home in his car "to provide him security." It was a dangerous gambit Clémard Joseph Charles had undertaken, working for Duvalier while plotting to overthrow him.

Sometimes de Mohrenschildt, Dryer and Charles met at *Le Picardie,* a Pétionville restaurant owned by a "beautiful mulatto" named Jacqueline Lancelot, who is forty or forty-one years old when she enters this story. Her family was highly placed; her father owned the one "essential oil" (for cosmetics) factory in Haiti.

Jacqueline seemed to be an octoroon, only one-eighth African; she was so very pale that she seemed to be French. She was small boned, yet at least five foot six, and wore her hair in a French twist. Educated in France, Jacqueline spoke perfect French, never Creole, and wore chic clothing, Chanel style. In the evening she might be found in pearls, silk blouses and skirts, and very high heels. In the daytime, she favored sundresses, but of a quality that bespoke Yves Saint Laurent.

Jacqueline Lancelot was so stunning that many men exclaimed that she was the most beautiful woman they had ever seen. She was so exquisite, Joe Dryer thought, that she could have appeared on the cover of *Paris Match.*

One day Joe asked Jacqueline Lancelot for her photograph. A woman without vanity, all she had was one taken when she was eighteen years old. "Give me that!" Joe said, and Jacqueline did. (Journalist Bernard Diederich, less susceptible, was not so sanguine; he remembers Jacqueline Lancelot as "thin as a stick").

Jacqueline had married an energetic young French chef from Burgundy. Together they had run *Le Picardie* until one day the Frenchman sailed off on his yacht accompanied by his black mistress, leaving Jacqueline and their two children to fend for themselves. Jacqueline, who had never worked a day in her life, took over the restaurant, which became the finest in Haiti. Escargots cost sixty cents a dozen. The filet mignon was exceptional, as was the French style roast chicken. If you ordered lobster for lunch, Jacqueline Lancelot might send over a bottle of champagne and drink a glass with you, her attention focused entirely on your husband. She was that kind of Frenchwoman.

Le Picardie was located in a white stucco chateau high on a cliff complete with battlements, so that you felt secure and protected as you sat at one of the tables outside looking down on the city of Port-au-Prince. Inside, where Jacqueline lived, were old, very elegant rooms decorated with antique French furniture. Outside, you sat under the stars, and you could hear merengue music or Vodou drums beating in the distance.

Lancelot's conversation was always political and *au courant,* although she never went too far; when all was said and done she seemed in favor of the status quo and had not broken with the Duvaliers. There were rumors too that Jacqueline Lancelot was a spy, adding to her allure. At times when she was absent, there was talk of her running around the French-speaking African countries that she visited too frequently for it not to be noticed. The name *"Mata Hari"* came to mind.

Once a month, an eclectic group gathered at *Le Picardie*: Dryer; the Naval Attaché from the American embassy who may or may not have worked for the Office of Naval Intelligence and was a former fighter pilot who had distinguished himself in Korea; the head of CARE; the Dominican representative to Haiti; and the Haitian representative of Bernie Cornfield – who ran the largest investment fund in the world, the "Fund of Funds."

There were also three women in the group: a divorced mulatto and friend of Jacqueline's; a woman who had been a model in France and had been born deaf, yet learned to speak English, French and Spanish; and the secretary of the German *Chargé d'affairs.*

If *Le Picardie* wasn't the place to be, it was the Hotel Oloffson where the rooms were named for celebrities: the "John Gielgud," the "Marlon Brando" casita out by the pool, the "Mick Jagger." (For a time, George de Mohrenschildt resided at the Oloffson's "John Barrymore Suite"). All the fruits and vegetables served at the Oloffson were doused first in a vat of Chlorox, then in a rinsing vat, then in another vat – this one of purified water with a drop or two of iodine in it.

The Oloffson began as the French Victorian-style mansion of dictator Jean Vilbrun Guillaume Sam, the fifth president in five years. Son of a former president, this Sam reigned for five months, between March and July of 1915. His repression culminated in the executions of 167 political prisoners, including a former president. The mulattoes were Sam's particular targets; after the executions, the mulatto population rose up against him.

Sam fled to the French embassy, where the enraged populace discovered him hiding in a toilet. First, he was beaten. Then his body was thrown over the embassy's iron fence, where he was impaled. As if this wasn't enough, the mob ripped his corpse to pieces. Then he was beheaded, and the head paraded around town on a pike.

Woodrow Wilson, discovering a suitable pretext, sent in the U.S. Marines. The Marines requisitioned the three-story mansion, creating a hospital wing-clinic. When the Marines at last departed from Haiti in 1934, the gingerbread mansion was leased to a Swedish woman named Oloffson; it was opened as a hotel in 1935. The lease passed to a former New York stockbroker named Maurice de Young, who was part of the Caribbean Legion, a group of liberals out to "topple tyrants," as author Hugh Thomas put it. This loosely organized confederation was formed in March 1948.

Juan Perón enlisted the Legion, which at its height consisted of only several hundred exiles and 5,000 rifles. Among its members were Fidel Castro and Che Guevara, as well as their political opponent Rolando Masferrer. Among their targets was Rafael Trujillo, dictator of the Dominican Republic. The Caribbean Legion also cast its sights on the dictatorships in Nicaragua and Costa Rica. Its influence was among the Central American and Caribbean countries.

CIA notes in a document, "The Caribbean Legion": "Haiti's traditional rivalry with the Dominican Republic makes its attempts to remain neutral difficult." CIA calls the Caribbean Legion a "clandestine and important instrument through which the 'democracies' are pursuing their 'anti-dictatorship' policy." Its influence was more ideological than military. It was the sort of group that would meet at such a place as the Oloffson.

During de Young's tenure running the Grand Hotel Oloffson, he became notorious for serving such specialties as soup made of caiman ("alligatorid crocodilian"), a fierce breed of crocodilian reptile with an elongated snout that de Young raised in the hotel swimming pool. Over the years, the Oloffson fell into disrepair, and was more about intrigue and mystery than luxury living. Even the telephones fell silent.

Once during the Duvalier years the telephone rang at the Hotel Oloffson and the waiters were so surprised that they dropped their trays. The phone hadn't worked in months. It was the telephone company checking on the line. That telephone never worked again.

Every night at the bar of the Oloffson, you could meet Aubelin Jolicoeur, the gossip columnist for *Le Nouvelliste*. Jolicoeur was the model for "Petit Pierre," the police informant in Graham Greene's *The Comedians*. "A tiny figure of a man," as Greene put it, his trademark was his gold-topped cane. Jolicoeur worked for Duvalier's intelligence; he had known Duvalier since their boyhoods in Jacmel. Jolicoeur was a mulatto, son of a French father and a Haitian mother.

Jolicoeur would meet every plane that landed at Port-au-Prince airport with the line, *"Bonsoir, cheri.* Mr. Haiti at your service." Jolicoeur would call on people at their hotel on their first night in Haiti if he thought they were interesting. He and Joe Dryer became good friends. Joe called him, affectionately, "Aubie."

"I don't know who you are," Jacqueline Lancelot told Joe Dryer one day.

"What do you mean?" Dryer said.

"What's a Marine doing here? You're very close to the Marines." She knew that Dryer was a Marine veteran of Iwo Jima, and member of the Marine reserves still, and that he was friendly with the red-headed Marine Colonel who had come to Haiti to train guerrilla fighters.

"If I were you," Jacqueline Lancelot told Dryer, "I would not be talking to that person." She was referring to George de Mohrenschildt. "I don't understand how you could put up with that man, how you can stand to see him.

"You wait and see," Jacqueline said. "De Mohrenschildt is up to no good. I know he's trying to get on the board of directors of Clémard Joseph Charles' bank. I know you and Charles are in business together, but I don't like de Mohrenschildt. I'm scared of him. There's something bad about him. He follows me around." Jacqueline confessed that de Mohrenschildt had tried to take her to dinner, but she had refused.

During these years, Jacqueline Lancelot enjoyed the company of a variety of men. Once her dinner date roared up to the restaurant on a motorcycle, and he turned out to be a Polish count. She liked men, but she hated and distrusted de Mohrenschildt. Seemingly anti-Duvalier, Jacqueline Lancelot was a woman of multiple loyalties, not so different from de Mohrenschildt himself.

Intelligence people frequented *Le Picardie,* and CIA agents would head from the airport to Jacqueline's restaurant even before they checked in at the U.S. Embassy. Among Jacqueline Lancelot's informants in Port-au-Prince was a Pan American Airlines employee who was working for CIA; Pan American was used in Haiti for CIA cover. Jacqueline's Haitian contacts also included the head of tourism and his brother, the Commander of the Palace Guard. To the CIA agents who frequented her restaurant, Jacqueline passed information about the Duvalier government.

Soon Jacqueline Lancelot confided even stranger news to Dryer. It was on a night at *Le Picardie*, some time after the Kennedy assassination, that she conveyed this information. A bank acquaintance who had "handled the funds" had told her that a "substantial" sum of money, between $200,000 and $250,000, had been deposited in de Mohrenschildt's Port-au-Prince bank account, which was not the bank of Clémard Joseph Charles.

The check had been drawn on a Bahamian bank. The money had been paid out quickly in a swift turnaround, and transferred somewhere else. Over the years, this figure of $250,000 has been frequently repeated. (Joe Dryer, in September 2011, was certain that the figure was misinterpreted by the House Select Committee on Assassinations.) In fact, the probable figure, $50,000, worth about $350,000 in today's money, was certainly a large enough amount in Haiti in those years to attract notice.

Apparently, de Mohrenschildt was still serving his once and future masters. As for how Jacqueline Lancelot came upon this information, Joe Dryer was given to understand that she knew the bank teller who had handled the transaction.

In the same conversation, Jacqueline had even more startling news for Dryer: "You're going to find out that de Mohrenschildt had something to do with the Kennedy assassination," Jacqueline said.

"Come on!" Joe said. The very idea seemed preposterous.

"You're going to find that the Warren Report will have his name all over it," Jacqueline Lancelot insisted. It was one of those candlelit romantic nights at *Le Picardie* when you didn't believe anything anyone told you. Then, lo and behold, there were pages and pages in the Warren Report about de Mohrenschildt. Dryer had no idea that de Mohrenschildt had been acquainted with Lee Harvey Oswald, but Jacqueline Lancelot, from her many CIA contacts, had known it.

Everyone was connected: George de Mohrenschildt and Howard Burris; Haiti and Martin Marietta; Delk Simpson and the Kennedy assassination. These associations do not rise to the level of either legal or historical evidence. Mere wisps, they collide in mid-air and are reflected in this italicized section: speculations, they bespeak the impossible, the illogical, the real.

It was perpetual scoundrel time in Papa Doc's Haiti, with a parade of rogues marching in and out of Port-au-Prince airport. We can follow George de Mohrenschildt and Clémard Joseph Charles through the military intelligence reports of "90 Deuce," and through the reports of CIA spies keeping these two under constant surveillance. Yet as we sit, awash in paper – even with Counter Intelligence chief James Angleton's "twenty-nine page epic" cataloguing de Mohrenschildt's mail to assist us – the story is only partially available. The dots march diagonally across the page, but they refuse to intersect. Yet they also refuse to dissolve away.

Beyond all that good paper, all those "documents," there is yet another scent of intrigue in Haiti involving George de Mohrenschildt and the Kennedy assassination, the burden of the second half of George's life. It is not yet a narrative; it is certainly not evidence, if only because no investigative body chose to take notice of it. Yet the story of Colonel Delk Simpson and his possible role in implementing the Kennedy assassination intrudes into Haiti during its scoundrel time.

O'Wighton Delk Simpson's involvement in Haiti begins with a hard fact. In the personal telephone book de Mohrenschildt kept, beginning in 1954 and continuing to the end of his life, there is a cryptic entry. Amid the cross-outs and strike-outs, amid the nooks and crannies of de Mohrenschildt's looping handwriting, is the odd entry: "Martin-Marietta/Haiti." Nearby is the name of the company's president, "George Bunker." George de Mohrenschildt was a social climber and opportunist, and he was forever collecting the names of those whom he might use. Yet Martin-Marietta, an aviation defense contractor, enjoyed no presence in Haiti during the Duvalier years.

And there appear certain other connections in de Mohrenschildt's phone book, dots that search each other

out across the pages. There are at least two entries for How-
ard Burris, former Air Force intelligence officer and Vice
President Johnson's security advisor. Burris, as we know,
was the man de Mohrenschildt met in Washington, D.C.
when he had hoped to put the case of Clémard Joseph
Charles before Lyndon Johnson himself.

Burris, in turn, was close to another former Air Force
Intelligence officer, Colonel (Lt. Colonel) O'Wighton Delk
Simpson. And Simpson in 1963, the year in question, was
employed by Martin-Marietta.

Burris and Simpson had served together on Johnson's
Inauguration Parade Committee. Both intersected with
the intelligence community. Simpson, who wound up in the
protocol department of Martin-Marietta, was an Air Force
officer who never learned how to fly a plane. He was close
enough to CIA that he would later serve on the board of
the Association of Retired Intelligence Officers, founded by
David Atlee Phillips and Gordon McClendon.

None of this would be of particular moment but for the
fact that in the late 1970s, at the time of the House Select
Committee's re-investigation of the Kennedy assassination,
Colonel Delk's son, Delk Junior, came forward to talk about
how his father had been a "bagman" in the Kennedy assas-
sination and had brought money out of – or into– the Re-
public of Haiti – for that purpose. Delk Junior had walked
into a room where his father was in the midst of count-
ing the money that he had brought back from Haiti in the
summer of 1963, money that his father admitted was going
to be used in the assassination.

Delk Junior then telephoned the Inspector General of the
Central Intelligence Agency. Even acknowledging that he was
a troubled young man, Delk's rambling conversation included
the stark assertion, "Father paid the hit man in Haiti."

Delk Senior himself seems to have considered the possibility of coming forward, provided of course that he would be granted immunity, but he never did so. Nor was he investigated by the HSCA, although his son and his son's girlfriend, whose name was Diane "Didi" Hess, requested that the Committee inquire into the story. The personal invaded the political. Had Delk Junior not assaulted Didi, who called the police, the concerned Delk Senior might not have confided some truths of all this to her, as he apparently did.

From Didi Hess, we learn the Colonel's words: "It's all true.... Whatever I did, it was because I had to do it." The Colonel told Didi that he had become involved in loose strands of the Kennedy killing "for the greater good...I did it because it was necessary," he said, "and I got myself involved." The Colonel had made contact in Haiti with someone involved in the assassination to whom he transferred money.

Didi signed affidavits affixed to interviews she granted, swearing to the truth of these assertions. Over the years, she never embellished or changed her story. She never sought notoriety. She has lived the life of a respectable citizen; she has worked for the United States government both at the White House and at the Pentagon where she was denied security clearance for a Top Secret position because she had given testimony on the matter of Colonel Simpson before the HSCA.

We do not spot the Colonel in the available records, neither in the summer of 1963 nor in 1964 – but it was easy to slide in and out of Haiti unnoticed in those years. Among the transients invading the nightmare republic were disreputables like Herbert Itkin, one of whose handlers, 'Philip Harbin,' is known to the readers of this story as 'George de Mohrenschildt.' There's CIA paper on that.

Colonel Simpson's name belongs in this story of Haiti because it seems fitting that even fragments be granted a hearing in the strange saga of George de Mohrenschildt, Lee Harvey Oswald, and Clémard Joseph Charles. Life hung in the balance every day in terror-ridden Haiti where, forty-eight years later, in October 2011, 450,000 people in a nation of ten million would be suffering from cholera. It was a place where "bagmen" might make their pay-offs. It was a time when a troubled young man might notice too much cash in his father's possession and search for an explanation. It was a time when the truth seemed to be its own reward.

"Martin-Marietta/ Haiti."

FOUR

Philippe Thyraud De Vosjoli: Everyone Is Connected

He's writing a book.

— Jacqueline Lancelot

"I have a friend in the United States, and you and he would get along," Jacqueline told Joe Dryer one day. "Call him up when you get there."

Now Jacqueline Lancelot drew Joseph Dryer into her intelligence network. The telephone number she handed to him belonged to Philippe de Vosjoli, an officer high in the French clandestine services, the SDECE (*Service de Documentation Extérieure et de Contre-Espionage*). It had been from de Vosjoli that Jacqueline had learned of George de Mohrenschildt's connection to the Kennedy assassination, and it had been on de Vosjoli's behalf that she had enlisted one of her many sources to monitor de Mohrenschildt's bank account. Jacqueline Lancelot was de Vosjoli's favorite, his most astute and reliable Haitian informant.

Having served in the French services during World War II, in 1951 de Vosjoli became Charles de Gaulle's liaison between French intelligence and CIA's counter intelligence branch. De Vosjoli had known James Angleton since the early post-war years, and been instrumental in Angleton's receiving the *Légion d'honneur*.

Among de Vosjoli's assignments after he moved to the United States and was based at the French Embassy in Washington, D. C., was to monitor the activities of the French Communist Party in the Caribbean. In particular, he focused on a group of agitators active from Guadeloupe to Cuba, working among "the colored population." De Vosjoli focused on the operatives who had led Castro's abortive 1959 invasion of Haiti.

"From Haiti," de Vosjoli writes in his memoir, *Lamia*, "I had received information about the work of agitators from Guadeloupe, all members of the Communist Party." This information came from Jacqueline Lancelot, whose means of penetrating the Communist Party in Haiti she did not reveal to Joe Dryer.

It became a habit. Dryer would disembark from the Sunday night Pan American flight to West Palm Beach and call de Vosjoli to deliver Jacqueline's message. The first time he dialed the number he had no idea that he was calling the French Embassy.

From the U.S. mainland, Dryer would mail letters from Jacqueline Lancelot to de Vosjoli. One day, she said, "You two really ought to get together. He's writing a book. He's going to be blowing the lid on France." She did not elaborate, but Joe Dryer, being the curious fellow that he was, soon discovered what that meant, as would the entire world via a film directed by Alfred Hitchcock.

Philippe Thyraud de Vosjoli was a textbook spy, an intelligence mastermind, although in appearance he bore no resemblance to James Bond in any of his incarnations. He was a short, balding Frenchman, rather stocky, and wore horn-rimmed reading glasses. Yet women were attracted to him, perhaps because he had "a way with his eyes," as Jacqueline Lancelot put it.

De Vosjoli affected Raybans and wore well-tailored suits. Good taste was natural to him. He was in his forties when he arrived in the United States, a figure exuding consummate self-confidence.

Upon arriving in the United States, de Vosjoli tackled a particular assignment, one he fulfilled with aplomb. In exchange for American war materiel to fight its war in Indochina, France would provide the Americans with intelligence. So de Vosjoli saw to it that CIA financed the French war in Indochina.

Another of de Vosjoli's early tasks was not so easy to fulfill. CIA's Director of Central Intelligence, Walter Bedell Smith, requested in 1952 that he confer the French Legion of Honor posthumously on Joe Kennedy Jr., the better to help his brother, John Fitzgerald Kennedy, in his campaign for the U.S. Senate. The request had come from their father, Joseph P. Kennedy, who had been serving on Dwight Eisenhower's President's Foreign Intelligence Advisory Board.

French Ambassador Henri Bonnet promptly vetoed the idea. The elder Kennedy had not endeared himself to the French with his friendly attitude toward Hitler and his lobbying that the U.S. not assist the Loyalists in Spain. Worse, Joe Kennedy had been critical of France after its defeat at the hands of the Germans in 1940.

Ambassador Bonnet was overruled by higher authority – the power of CIA already trumped that of mere diplomats. The issue became moot when John F. Kennedy became a U.S. Senator without the award having been conferred upon his brother.

Before long, de Vosjoli was reporting as often to James Angleton at CIA as he was to his superiors at home. De Vosjoli learned from the Cuban Consul General in

New York that Senator Homer E. Capehard, an Indiana Republican, had taken a bribe of $20,000, with $40,000 forthcoming should he succeed in effecting the asylum of Fulgencio Batista in the United States. At once de Vosjoli reported this to Angleton. So I.I. Davidson was trumped.

De Vosjoli was a man who took risks. Narrow escapes from the Germans before he was twenty-one years old instilled in him fortitude and courage. He was a man who acted on his principles regardless of the personal consequences he might suffer.

Among the most controversial of his positions was his support of his wartime mentor, now Algerian Governor General Jacques Soustelle, a former professor at the *École pratique des hautes études.* Soustelle was now the political eminence of the Organization of the Secret Army (OAS), which was determined that Algeria remain in French hands, even if it took the assassination of President de Gaulle to accomplish this end.

The French settlement of Algeria began in the middle of the 19th century. By the time the FLN (Algeria's National Liberation Front) was set up in 1954, there were a million French people living in Algeria. For de Vosjoli, as for the many longtime French settlers of Algeria, the threat of Algeria's falling under Communist/Arab rule was sufficient cause for him to support the *Organisation de l'armée secrète*, a terrorist group that would be responsible for at least thirty assassination plots against de Gaulle. During one period, famously, de Gaulle was able to reside at the *Elysée* Palace only two or three days a week, returning by air to *Colombey-les-Deux-Églises* where he could enjoy some measure of security.

De Vosjoli had admired Soustelle since he was a young man in his twenties and Soustelle was his superior in the forces of the Free French. "Even his worst enemies couldn't deny his extraordinary intellectual capacities," de Vosjoli writes of Soustelle. If he faults Soustelle for anything, it is for his not having opposed de Gaulle politically. Soustelle, de Vosjoli believed, "easily could have become chief of the government, but his deep and sentimental loyalty to de Gaulle made him step aside." That loyalty was born of their having worked together when de Gaulle was Soustelle's superior with the Free French during World War II.

Soustelle, de Vosjoli insists, was "undoubtedly beyond reproach. I would vouch for him any time and welcome him in my home." His public endorsements of Soustelle alone would have inspired the wrath of the President of the Republic.

During the period of the Algerian struggle for independence, Soustelle was not shy about advocating publicly the overthrow of de Gaulle. He had openly suggested that the assassination of de Gaulle would be a small price to pay for keeping Algeria French. Like so many French, Soustelle saw Algeria as an integral part of France. Always, Soustelle condoned OAS, whose terrorism rendered it among the "most notorious fascist organizations in French history." Soustelle's politics had hardened since that egalitarian moment when he had supported the Resistance to the Nazis.

On December 7, 1960, Philippe de Vosjoli hosted a luncheon in Washington D.C. The guest of honor was Jacques Soustelle. At the table sat Richard M. Bissell, Jr., CIA's DD/P, and Bissell's soon-to-be successor, Richard Helms. The de Vosjoli-hosted luncheon lasted long into the afternoon and contributed to de Gaulle's fury at CIA and his disillusionment with de Vosjoli. What was discussed specifically at this luncheon has never been disclosed. What was important was the very existence of such an event – CIA meeting with de Gaulle's profoundest enemies.

Secret as de Vosjoli hoped the event would remain, it was reported in France's leading newspaper, *Le Monde*. "It now seems established that some American agents more or less encouraged Maurice Challe," *Le Monde* wrote. Challe was the leader of the revolt of the French generals. Rumors circulated that CIA officer John Philipsborn met with OAS leader *Général* Raoul Salan in Algeria in April 1961. So author Douglas Valentine has reported in *The Strength of the Wolf*. (Philipsborn was a "political officer" or Foreign Service Officer, a CIA operative using State Department cover, a not infrequent practice.)

Nor was *Le Monde* alone in exposing CIA's alliance with OAS. In the *New York Times* of April 29, 1961, James Reston wrote that CIA "was involved in an embarrassing liaison with the anti-Gaullist officers who staged last week's insurrection in Algeria." *Time* magazine on May 12th reported that Maurice Challe had been "encouraged by the CIA."

John F. Kennedy now asked his press secretary, Pierre Salinger, to telephone Allen Dulles and request a briefing on the Algerian generals. A few hours later, Richard Helms arrived at the White House where he "denied categorically that CIA at any time had sided with the rebel generals." He couldn't deny the fact of the luncheon and so he admitted that CIA "had conversations with people around the generals on a kind of fact-finding mission."

Helms insisted that "no promises were made to anybody." Cloaked in plausible deniability, CIA could claim that "there was no contact with the generals themselves." Kennedy might summon Helms, but he couldn't oblige him to tell the truth. No one could – in any branch of the government.

CIA filtered funds to the OAS through its fronts, among them PERMINDEX and the *Centro Mondiale Comerciale,* based in Rome. Six years later, both organizations would be exposed in *Paese Sera,* an Italian newspaper, for "illegal political espionage activities." The French called PERMINDEX "a subsidiary of the CIA." Among its leaders was Ferenc Nagy, a long-time CIA asset dating back to the time of Frank Wisner. Nagy was "a munificent contributor to the movement of Jacques Soustelle."

As Andrew Tully writes in his history of CIA, "the evidence indicates that there were CIA operatives who let their own politics show and by doing so led the Challe rebels to believe that the United States looked with favor on their adventure." CIA officer Paul Sakwa, demoted and sent home from France to be stashed as a "Special Assistant" to Bissell, and soon to resign from the Agency, told author Douglas Valentine that CIA definitely supported Soustelle's putsch.

The infatuation between CIA and OAS would be yet another example of CIA's pre-empting a President and making policy as the Agency saw fit. Sakwa came to believe that "what began as an effort to promote and defend democracy" on CIA's part had "evolved into operations designed to thwart real, incipient or imagined Communist threats at the expense of democracy itself." For the twenty-first century, the term "terrorist" could easily be substituted for "Communist," in Sakwa's assessment.

The question of for whom de Vosjoli worked had blurred. Assignments began to come to him directly from CIA. In August 1962, at a time when Americans could no longer travel to Cuba, Allen Dulles, that "retired" CIA eminence, suggested that de Vosjoli go to Cuba on CIA's behalf. De Vosjoli directed an intelligence mission to Cuba to determine whether the Soviet Union had placed offensive nuclear weapons on the island.

"I decided to fly to Havana and check up on things myself," de Vosjoli writes in a memoir published in *Life* magazine. From his Cuban sources, he claims, he received "as many as 50 or 100 separate reports a day." With his own eyes, he witnessed "huge multi-wheeled tractors transporting Russian rockets under canvas covers."

Diligently, de Vosjoli reported to both of his masters. "What I learned," he was to write, "I passed on to Paris and shared with the American intelligence authorities." He delivered photographs of MRBM missiles, offensive nuclear missiles, and SAM anti-aircraft rockets to John McCone at CIA. How he had obtained these photographs he did not say, but there is no doubt that he left Cuba with photographic evidence and that there were operatives at his disposal on the island. After the Bay of Pigs, de Vosjoli had made many trips to Havana, setting up "new dead drops" to improve his "communications," as he puts it in *Lamia*.

Among his sources was Fidel Castro's sister, Juanita. Among those who assisted him was an agent who took photographs that revealed a large hole being drilled into the ceiling of a cavern through to the pasture fifty feet above, a hole large enough to hold a missile; it was oriented in the direction of the United States. Another of his informants was a young man who had served in the French army in Germany as a noncommissioned officer and was now vacationing in Cuba. De Vosjoli was nothing if not enterprising in matters of espionage.

Later the French government would accuse de Vosjoli of having "acted without instructions in supplying French-gathered intelligence to the Americans." More grateful, John McCone, de Vosjoli acknowledges, thanked him "in private." There is no reason to doubt him on this.

De Vosjoli carried a second set of the photographs of Soviet nuclear war materiel in Cuba to Senator Kenneth Keating of New York. CIA informed Keating about the situation in Cuba even before they reported to President Kennedy. Keating took de Vosjoli's photographs to the United States Senate.

On August 31, 1962, on the floor of the Senate, Keating revealed intelligence on the Soviet offensive missiles in Cuba of which even John F. Kennedy was unaware. He had been "reliably informed," Keating said, that 1,200 troops wearing Soviet army fatigue uniforms had arrived in Cuba. The President of the United States was the last to know.

"Those CIA bastards!" Kennedy fumed, according to journalist Sander Vanocur. "I'm going to get those bastards if it's the last thing I ever do." It was one more skirmish in the battle between Kennedy and CIA with Keating functioning as a shill for the Agency.

De Vosjoli, too, served Kennedy's adversaries. For so sophisticated an operative as Philippe de Vosjoli, nothing he did could have been unwitting. Later Bobby Kennedy, "getting even," as he put it, moved to New York and ran against Keating for his Senate seat – and beat him.

Under the cover of French intelligence, de Vosjoli became a CIA agent. Walt Elder, a special assistant to John McCone, revealed to James Angleton's biographer, Tom Mangold, that "De Vosjoli was recruited and worked for us. It was a CI (Counter Intelligence) operation run by Angleton. De Vosjoli was waiting to be asked, and perfectly willing. In effect, he asked us, 'What kept you?'"

CIA had a term for its relationship with Philippe de Vosjoli: de Vosjoli was a "recruitment-in-place." Another agent termed de Vosjoli a "willing walk-in."

De Vosjoli remained at his post at the French Embassy working for Charles de Gaulle while at the same time he provided CIA with classified information. CIA officer Newton ("Scotty") Miler confirmed Walt Elder's statements. "De Vosjoli was Jim's [Angleton's] operation, but it was carried out with the knowledge of the DCI."

Among the operations with which de Vosjoli assisted the Agency was providing CIA with France's code books. It was de Vosjoli from inside the French Embassy who opened the door for the FBI black-bag team that photographed the papers with Minox cameras. Walt Elder told Mangold that de Vosjoli was paid by CIA.

* * *

The OAS scandal and the mission to Cuba for CIA were preludes to de Vosjoli's final confrontation with de Gaulle and his superiors in the French intelligence services. Through a Soviet defector named Anatoliy Golitsyn, a KGB officer who had worked in the Reports section in Moscow, the U.S. learned that the KGB had infiltrated the leadership of both NATO and the French government. President Kennedy wrote a personal letter to French president Charles de Gaulle informing him that from his source, Golitsyn, he had learned that the French intelligence services, and even De Gaulle's own cabinet, had been penetrated by Soviet agents.

CIA provided Golitsyn with a $200,000 tax-free signing bonus. With it, he bought a house in McLean, Virginia, for $40,000, not far from CIA headquarters, and he went to work. French counter intelligence people arrived from Paris to assist in the questioning. They received quite a turn, de Vosjoli later wrote, when Golitsyn exhibited "an all but encyclopedic knowledge of the secret workings of the French intelligence services."

Soon CIA and de Vosjoli learned from Golitsyn that in the 1950s the KGB had penetrated the French SDECE as well as NATO. During the intense questioning of Golitsyn, de Vosjoli himself was "kept fully abreast of what he was saying," he writes in *Lamia*

To assist in the vetting of Golitsyn, CIA dispatched to his house a twenty-three year old member of SR6 (Soviet Realities), a counter intelligence component of the Soviet Russia division. For several months, CIA translator Donald Deneselya, a Russian-speaking operative of Russian descent, worked as Golitsyn's administrative assistant. Deneselya told Golitsyn that he was a Georgetown student who had studied Russian. He used an alias, " Donald Denison," and concealed that he was reporting back to CIA.

Golitsyn was a small man, five feet six inches tall, with dark hair combed back from a high forehead and penetrating eyes. He gave young Deneselya the run of his refrigerator, which was stocked with pickled herring, sardines, and Russian black bread. Even while he lived under the protection of CIA, Golitsyn remained his own man.

Careless about preserving his cover, Golitsyn once attended a Russian show where he was spotted by a Soviet diplomat. He had no desire to meet other Soviet defectors, not least the notorious Yuri Nosenko, whom he believed was not bona fide. Golitsyn had predicted that the KGB would dispatch a false defector to determine the damage of Golitsyn's betrayal and that was Nosenko.

CIA sent over TOP SECRET documents for Golitsyn to peruse, so as to determine who the infiltrating KGB agents were. They presented him with lists of all the personnel at Soviet Embassies around the world and asked him to identify which individuals were KGB and which were actual diplomats. The documents Golitsyn indicated as not being recognizable to him were always the forgeries CIA had sent over to test his credibility. Ninety-nine percent of what Golitsyn said was subsequently verified.

CIA shared the fruits of its interrogations of Golitsyn with de Vosjoli, not least the shocking discovery that de Gaulle's own cabinet had been penetrated by Soviet agents, and that a KGB network with the code name "SAPPHIRE" had been working within the SDECE itself.

French counterintelligence teams followed the Americans in questioning Golitsyn. As de Vosjoli writes: "The French counterintelligence teams were thorough. They sat down with the Russian day after long day. They pressed him hard. Everything he said was recorded on tapes. The tapes were run back at the end of the day, the leads were separated out, and every night a long coded summary went out to SDECE headquarters in Paris."

De Vosjoli was the person most affected by Golitsyn's revelations. An abundance of KGB agents apparently had infiltrated the government circles closest to de Gaulle, and within NATO. De Gaulle and his advisers were not pleased when de Vosjoli named some of his own direct superiors in de Gaulle's government as KGB agents. For de Gaulle, this amounted to an embarrassment of monumental proportions. De Vosjoli was recalled to France.

"We no longer consider America our ally, our friend," de Vosjoli was told. De Gaulle and his cabinet were concerned over de Vosjoli's close connection to James Angleton, noting that, "all the talk of someone [KGB] in high places came via the CIA." The French view in Paris was that "we could never be sure it was Golitsyn talking or the CIA."

De Vosjoli was outraged that the French did not act on Golitsyn's evidence. De Gaulle apparently preferred to keep KGB agents in high places in the government of France to avoid a scandal. Unwilling to face the negative publicity attendant upon his firing de Vosjoli, de Gaulle sprang a trap.

De Vosjoli was assigned to organize a "scientific and military spy ring," to create an intelligence network in the United States to determine the Americans' nuclear capabilities. Golitsyn had predicted that just such an assignment would be dangled before de Vosjoli, and there it was. De Vosjoli feared that whatever he learned might fall into the hands of the KGB.

De Vosjoli refused the assignment. On October 18, 1963, he resigned from the SDECE. On the evening of his resignation, CIA threw de Vosjoli a party at an Italian restaurant in Washington, D.C. In return for his service to CIA came gifts: an antique clock from Richard Helms, and an antique coffeepot from James Angleton. "I am probably the only French intelligence officer in history to defect to the United States," de Vosjoli said with his customary irony. Angleton personally helped arrange de Vosjoli's permanent residence in America.

Accusing him of having supplied intelligence to the Americans without permission, de Gaulle denounced de Vosjoli for being a "defector to the CIA." It seemed to de Vosjoli that his very life was in danger. "I was in hiding from paid killers," he would write. Exile would be his portion.

Joe Dryer was intrigued by having been put in contact with one of the Western world's premier spies, Philippe de Vosjoli. Some time after 1968, driven by his insatiable curiosity, Dryer contacted an acquaintance named George P. Hunt, who was Henry Luce's right-hand man and managing editor at *Life* magazine.

"What can you tell me about Philippe de Vosjoli?" Dryer said.

"I wrote an article in *Life* about his book, *Topaz*," Hunt said.

Ostensibly the work of Leon Uris, author of *Exodus*, *Topaz* was actually the story of de Vosjoli's life. The hero is named Andre Devereaux, and his "real love" is his chief operative in Cuba, Juanita de Córdoba, a thinly disguised portrait of Jacqueline Lancelot. Like Jacqueline, Juanita has been left alone to raise two children. Like Jacqueline, "she was a woman who made a man feel good." Juanita pours Deveraux's drinks, lights his cigars, and dances with him until dawn.

Through the depiction of Devereaux's relationship with Juanita, *Topaz* reveals the role Jacqueline Lancelot played for CIA in Haiti. She is a "woman of prominence, above suspicion, and highly placed in inner circles," perfectly placed to serve as a "source for information." In *Topaz*, it is Juanita's espionage ring that provides Devereaux with hard evidence of Soviet offensive missiles in Cuba. Juanita arranges dead-letter drops in secret places and passes messages for Devereaux to the French Ambassador at cocktail parties, formal dinners and in broad daylight.

The real-life Juanita's "excellent eye," of course, was not in Cuba but in Haiti. Wistfully, Joe Dryer remembers that he enjoyed no intimate relationship with Jacqueline Lancelot. Apparently her heart belonged to the head of French intelligence in the United States.

Charles de Gaulle appears in *Topaz* as "La Croix," an arrogant man who sacrifices the truth and the security of

France by concealing that among his closest advisers is a KGB agent. All La Croix cares about is that his place in history not be tarnished. La Croix has "his grip on the throat of the country," Uris/de Vosjoli writes. At the close of the novel, Devereaux is rescued by his closest ally, "Michael Nordstrom," a figure obviously based on James Angleton.

Dryer discovered that de Vosjoli hadn't wanted to put his name on the manuscript of *Topaz*, which was published in 1967. Given his still-precarious situation, it was a prudent decision. Determined to make his story known, he searched for a writer who already enjoyed a wide following – hence, Leon Uris. Uris was paid, Dryer suggests, merely to sign the contract, and perhaps to polish the book a bit. It was a rare case of the ghostwriter taking sole credit as author.

When Uris failed to honor their financial arrangement, de Vosjoli sued him in a California court. He was awarded $352,350, plus interest, as well as half the future earnings from both the novel and the Alfred Hitchcock film adaptation.

After *Topaz* was published in the U.S., a wave of suicides swept through government circles in France, suggesting that Golitsyn had been more than accurate. On April 26, 1968, Philippe de Vosjoli was depicted on the cover of *Life* magazine. His photograph, by the distinguished photographer Alfred Eisenstaedt, reveals a man wearing dark glasses and a homburg. His face is concealed; all we see is de Vosjoli's black-clad back.

On May 9, 1978 de Vosjoli, now a permanent resident in the United States, was interviewed at his home in Lighthouse Point, Florida by the House Select Committee on Assassinations. Only a three-page summary of the interview has been made public. It bears an ambiguous hand-written annotation: *"Reviewed by CIA: No Comment required or appropriate."*

The summary reveals that de Vosjoli was proud to have "developed a number of agents inside Cuba," and to have been "instrumental in informing Director John McCone about the placement of Russian offensive missiles inside Cuba." De Vosjoli claims to have provided the first real information the United States had on this subject. De Vosjoli also reveals how the French SDECE developed an "executive action" or assassination program, as had CIA.

Between 1959 and 1961, de Vosjoli says, the SDECE brought representatives of French intelligence to Washington, D.C. where they "met with their counterparts in CIA." Among the topics on the agenda was the assassination of Fidel Castro. SDECE volunteered its own "action" group to carry out the assignment.

"Look, why don't you let us handle this for you?" the French offered. "We have experts who can kill Castro without it being traced back to you and your problems with him will be over." The French chancery in Havana was only two doors from the home of Celia Sánchez, Castro's sometime mistress. "Fidel used to come there alone in his jeep to see her," de Vosjoli told his interviewers. "It would have been easy!"

CIA declined the French offer. When de Vosjoli later learned that CIA had enlisted the Mafia in its attempted assassinations of Castro, "he was appalled at the stupidity and amateurishness of it." The only logic he could discern in a CIA-Mafia connection "was if the CIA had 'other' dealings of a sinister nature with the same Mafia types which they were looking to conceal."

De Vosjoli produced another bombshell for the HSCA. He had been in New York a month after he resigned from the SDECE. It was November 19, 1963 and he was picking up mail at 535 Fifth Avenue, an old mail drop. Nearby, he spotted the French chief of station, a Monsieur Hervé, walking along Fifth Avenue with Colonel George de Lannurien, the chief of counter intelligence for SDECE and its third in command.

De Lannurien had been de Vosjoli's fiercest adversary in the SDECE, challenging Golitsyn's revelations. De Lannurien himself was among those named by Golitsyn as suspected KGB infiltrators. Colonel de Lannurien had "a history of contacts with the Soviets which dated back to the period after World War II when the Soviets had arranged his escape from Slovakia," de Vosjoli told his American interrogators.

Why, de Vosjoli wondered, was Colonel de Lannurien meeting with the SDECE in New York? Why was the Colonel even *in* the United States at that moment?

De Vosjoli recounted to the government investigators that he had followed Colonel de Lannurien to the Harvard Club. There, according to de Vosjoli, the Colonel "had lunch with a group of right-wing extremists from Texas." He believed that the meeting had something to do with the Kennedy assassination, which was to take place four days later.

The summary does not reveal how de Vosjoli figured out that the Colonel's luncheon companions were right-wing Texans, or that they were talking about the Kennedy assassination. The National Archives claims that it cannot locate a copy of the full transcript of the interview with de Vosjoli.

De Vosjoli continued his contacts with Jacqueline Lancelot after his resignation from the French services. The information he received now could only have been

161

destined for CIA. He made several trips to Haiti for the Agency. Jacqueline Lancelot's messages to Philippe de Vosjoli, as conveyed by Joe Dryer – who continued to carry her intelligence from Haiti to the United States – always concluded with her sending her love.

FIVE

A Sheikh From Kuwait

Friendly and evil at the same time."
— Conrad V. Rubricius, CIA employee

Despite the absence of overt encouragement from CIA, Clémard Joseph Charles kept stoking the fire of his ambition to become president of the Republic of Haiti. He enlisted Joe Dryer to contact people in Washington on his behalf, one of whom, as before, was the Pentagon's Dorothe Matlack. Another was CIA-connected William Avery Hyde, father of Ruth Paine, who had sheltered Marina Oswald, and with whom Marina was living at the time of the Kennedy assassination.

Ruth Paine's own CIA contacts included her brother-in-law John Hoke who, for a time, was on loan to CIA from AID; her sister, Sylvia, who was a CIA employee; and Talbot Bielefeldt, Chief of the Soviet Section of the Foreign Documents Division.

In Haiti, Dryer cultivated his own nest of informants, among them a long-time CIA asset named Jack Cogswell. Cogswell was a "businessman" who had served the Agency in Cuba where he reported to David Atlee Phillips. Phillips would admit to their acquaintance in his testimony on April 25, 1978 before the House Select Committee on Assassinations. Cogswell was an amiable, well-educated man with a propensity to "drink in the morning," Phillips recalled.

"I did some favors," Cogswell admitted, referring to his CIA history. CIA documents reveal that Cogswell was utilized by both the Agency and the FBI. In New York, he reported to the FBI operative people trusted most during those years, Frank O'Brien.

Cogswell became a source of intelligence for Joe Dryer. In particular, Cogswell kept an eye on de Mohrenschildt. He informed Dryer that de Mohrenschildt acted "strange" in Port-au-Prince. It had been Cogswell who had observed de Mohrenschildt following Clémard Joseph Charles in his automobile. Dryer was not certain whether CIA placed Cogswell in Haiti or whether he had gone there voluntarily, but it was obvious that he was working for someone. "He was doing fun and games with the CIA," Dryer adds.

Dryer says he himself avoided CIA, while remaining close to AID and to the Office of Naval Intelligence, as well as to Marine Intelligence. "I stayed as far away from the CIA as possible," he says. During his time there, two CIA-employed brothers surfaced in Haiti and were responsible for several "unnecessary deaths," as Dryer puts it. Dryer wanted nothing to do with them. That CIA was deeply embedded in Haiti, there was no doubt. As for whom Joe Dryer worked, he laughs and says, "The Marine Corps. Once a Marine always a Marine." For this period of time, he says, he was a "farmer." Joe Dryer was a very unusual farmer indeed.

You were never safe in Haiti. Someone shot a colonel, and Joe Dryer thought he'd better leave for a while. Sitting next to him on the Pan American flight to Miami was his friend, the young naval attaché, with whom he shared those monthly dinners at *Le Picardie*. On the opposite side, across from him, was the Pole who represented the Soviets. The plane was diverted from its normal route – Jamaica and then on to Miami – to the Cayman Islands, which was in the opposite direction.

The naval attaché leaned over and asked the Polish Communist agent, "what do you think of the market for Polish hams here?" referring to the Cayman Islands. Boxes of Communist literature had been discovered in a warehouse, precipitating the furor that led to their having to get out of Port-au-Prince for a while.

The reign of terror that accompanied the presidency of Papa Doc proved to be too much for Joe Dryer, who finally moved his kenaf business out of Haiti. For three years, Dryer had navigated the shoals of the Duvalier dictatorship. He had been able to run his kenaf plantation without interference from Papa Doc, in keeping with Duvalier's policy of hospitality toward American business in Haiti and, of course, his garnering a share of their profits.

Then – in 1963 – investment in Haiti became no longer safe. One day, Dryer sat behind a card table on an open field. It was payday. Stacks of gourdes (worth twenty cents each) were piled in front of him as his workers lined up to be paid. Dryer's manager had hired four soldiers from the Haitian army to serve as guards.

Suddenly, thirteen or fourteen of the *Tontons Macoutes* materialized out of nowhere in their blue dungarees and sunglasses. They were armed with rifles. Standing at first on the perimeter, they circled the area. Then they began to inch forward, their rifles pointed inward. Slowly they closed the circle. Dryer quickly dispatched his brother Peter to the army garrison at St. Marc for assistance.

Soon the *Tontons Macoutes* had kidnapped the four soldiers Dryer had hired for protection. Silence descended over the crowd as an army truck drove up before the *Tontons Macoutes* could escape with their prey. The captain demanded the return of the soldiers and the *Tontons Macoutes* disappeared.

It was a pyrrhic victory. The *Tontons Macoutes* soon gained sway over the Haitian army. Now security for American business in Haiti became a distant memory.

In 1963, Dryer closed his kenaf operation for good. Three of his best machine operators had been kidnapped, never to be seen again. Dryer had to stage an operation worthy of a Graham Greene novel.

The German freighter scheduled to pick up Dryer's kenaf fiber arrived at night and tied up at the dock at St. Marc. Some of Dryer's men got the port captain drunk, while others drove the kenaf equipment from the Artibonite Valley to St. Marc and loaded it onto the freighter, which sailed away safely. Dryer took his equipment because, had he not, it would surely have been confiscated by Papa Doc's people. It was worth too much to be left behind – and could not easily be replaced.

So as not to excite suspicion, Dryer stayed behind for a day or two. Following that brief wait, Dryer hopped a Pan American flight to the United States, thereby avoiding reprisals attendant upon his having spirited valuable agricultural machinery out of Haiti. Before long, he would be back.

On February 12, 1964, J. Lee Rankin, the Warren Commission's general counsel, requested that the FBI provide a "full-scale background intelligence type report of the de Mohrenschildts." On the 18th, Hoover wrote back, his pen dripping with sarcasm: "For your information," he told Rankin, "investigation has been conducted by this Bureau concerning George de Mohrenschildt based on his alleged pro-German sympathies and activities...."

Among the field offices that had monitored de Mohrenschildt under "Security Matter-Registration Act" were: New York, Albany, Newark, Cincinnati, El Paso, Dallas, Philadelphia, San Diego, Miami, Phoenix, Denver San Francisco, Los Angeles, Washington, D.C., Houston, and New Orleans. Everyone was watching George de Mohrenschildt.

In the course of its investigation for the Warren Commission, the FBI asked CIA directly whether de Mohrenschildt was one of theirs. The reply came from the head of the clandestine services, Richard Helms. "George de Mohrenschildt is not and has not been an employee of CIA, nor is he a contract employee of CIA," Helms wrote. Then, he added, coyly, he "may possibly be a contact of that Agency."

This was boilerplate. CIA admitted that de Mohrenschildt was the source of "a few reports in 1957," with contact continuing until 1961. This was yet another example of how CIA, more often than not, in admitting contact with people, fabricated the ending date of their service. Helms lied to Hoover when he said that CIA had not heard anything of de Mohrenschildt since 1961.

From the FBI's extensive interviews of de Mohrenschildt's friends and acquaintances in Texas, further de Mohrenschildt connections emerged. George Kitchel, a close friend of George H.W. Bush, said that de Mohrenschildt was a close acquaintance of Texas oil entrepreneurs H.L. Hunt, the Clint Murchisons, and Sid Richardson. There were three Murchison family names in de Mohrenschildt's phone book of 1954-1955.

Another person who knew de Mohrenschildt well was oilman John Mecom, who had flown him to Iran. As a personal acquaintance of the Shah, Mecom had considered de Mohrenschildt the perfect contact to present the Shah with a business proposition concerning oil.

Unanimously, everyone who knew George de Mohrenschildt commented now on how assiduously he cultivated the rich, famous and well connected. One acquaintance stated baldly that de Mohrenschildt "seemed to seek out wealthy people for friends." Even de Mohrenschildt's untruths were designed "to give the listener the impression that he had high-level connections and influence in government and business circles." All this testimony more than amplifies the reality that de Mohrenschildt's "friendship" with Lee Harvey Oswald was motivated by something more than the "philanthropy" that de Mohrenschildt claimed was his purpose.

That de Mohrenschildt was self-destructive and could not help but undermine his own interests also emerged during the FBI's investigation on behalf of the Warren Commission. An insurance man told the FBI that George "will probably get kicked out of Haiti as it probably will not be long before he finds something to start bitching about in connection with business dealings in Haiti."

While the Warren Commission wrestled with how to define the relationship between George de Mohrenschildt and the "lone assassin," CIA continued to track Clémard Joseph Charles. Wherever he traveled, CIA was at the airport, literally. When Charles surfaced in a foreign country, CIA penetrated his business.

CIA tracked Charles to Mexico City. Charles claimed that he was refinancing a loan for his bank in order "to purchase cheap sisal cordage machinery from the Yucatan." It didn't take CIA long to figure out that Charles was actually in Mexico City to locate 30 surplus T-28 fighter aircraft and 24 U.S. surplus naval craft. This was another of Charles' missions for Papa Doc, locating military hardware to defend Haiti against "sporadic attacks by anti-government rebels." Duvalier would make a down payment on the planes with a letter of credit for $210,000 drawn on Charles' bank.

From Mexico City, on February 24, 1964 Charles flew to Los Angeles. The U.S. State Department, for the record, was now dismissing him as simply "a controversial figure here [in Haiti] with political ambitions."

On March 7, James Wood of the FBI finally made his Hoover-authorized special trip to Port-au-Prince to interview George de Mohrenschildt. Wood's intention was to challenge De Mohrenschildt's claim that he had checked with the FBI before pursuing his acquaintance with Oswald, only to have been assured that Oswald was "harmless." With whom at the FBI had de Mohrenschildt spoken? Wood wanted to know.

De Mohrenschildt again named "Max Clark." In fact, Clark had never been employed by the FBI. He was a lawyer who had been Director of Security at the Convair Division of General Dynamics, a Texas-based defense contractor. There was a slight connection to Oswald, however. Clark was married to a woman who was half-Russian, and who was telephoned at one point by Oswald.

You can imagine de Mohrenschildt squirming during the interview with Wood. He had told so many lies that he had no choice but to invent new ones. He denied that he had ever said anyone had told him Oswald was "harmless." When Wood produced the letter to Everett Glover in Dallas in which de Mohrenschildt states that someone in the FBI had reassured him that Oswald was harmless, de Mohrenschildt retracted his denial. It had been a stupid lie: why would anyone have talked about Oswald being "harmless" before Oswald had been accused of committing a crime?

Trapped in an obvious fabrication – that the FBI had cleared his acquaintance with Oswald – de Mohrenschildt then identified J. Walton Moore as an FBI agent, knowing full well that Moore was CIA. The last time he had talked with a Special Agent of the FBI was in 1957, de Mohrenschildt now claimed. It was just after his return from Yugoslavia, when he was interviewed by J. Walton Moore in Dallas.

The Bureau was well aware that Moore ran the CIA field office in Dallas, and so was de Mohrenschildt. The lie was so transparent that one might well conclude that de Mohrenschildt the risk taker was taunting the Bureau, waiting to see what would happen when this lie was exposed. What seems apparent is that de Mohrenschildt was doing his inadequate best to keep CIA out of the discussion of the Kennedy assassination. He tried desperately to conceal that it was CIA that had sent him to look after Oswald in the first place. Like any agency contact, asset or employee, he was following CIA protocol – that you never so much as mention "CIA" to any outsider.

With James Wood and Norman E. Warner, First Secretary of the American Embassy, as witnesses, de Mohrenschildt wrote a retraction of his false statements implicating the Bureau in the actions of CIA. Yet even his retraction was replete with statements contrary to fact.

He claimed that he believed that J. Walton Moore was an FBI agent, which he knew was not the case. He blamed a White Russian acquaintance, George Bouhe, not only for having introduced him to Oswald, but for telling him that Max Clark was in charge of the FBI for the Southwestern United States. He affected not to remember that he had written to Glover telling him he had checked with the FBI, who had told him Oswald was "harmless."

Caught in two Bureau-infuriating lies – that Moore was FBI rather than a CIA agent, and that someone in the FBI had told him Oswald was harmless – de Mohrenschildt backtracked. "I have never talked with anyone in the FBI before today about Lee Harvey Oswald, to the best of my memory," he now said. This of course was true: it was with CIA that he had discussed Oswald.

By the close of this embarrassing interview with Wood, De Mohrenschildt was compelled to issue a promise: "I will also be certain not to make any statements or inferences to the effect that I have any contacts or friends within the FBI."

J. Lee Rankin forwarded the report of the de Mohrenschildt interview in Haiti to J. Edgar Hoover personally. Infuriated that de Mohrenschildt had again identified Moore as an FBI agent, Hoover told Rankin, "Go ask the Central Intelligence Agency!" Then, incensed, Hoover himself wrote to the Director of Central Intelligence: "Our Dallas office has advised that Mr. Moore is an employee of your Agency in Dallas." Behind Hoover's anger, of course, was his protection of the FBI as an institution. Certainly he did not want the Bureau named or involved in the setting up of the accused murderer of the head of state.

Hoover decided not to close de Mohrenschildt's case. Instead, he placed de Mohrenschildt on a "Reserve Index, Section B," making it possible for the Dallas Office to conduct a further review should action be "deemed warranted." De Mohrenschildt's FBI file would in fact never be "closed."

In March 1964 CIA officer Jim Balog reported to Anthony Czajkowski that "previously the de Mohrenschildt couple indicated their desire to get in touch with us."

In Port-au-Prince, rumors and innuendos about de Mohrenschildt and his wife swirled. "They are pushy, arrogant and heavily addicted to name-dropping," Ambassador Timmons observed. The State Department wondered whether CIA "had had a hand in ruining de Mohrenschildt's relations with Duvalier." CIA denied it.

In April 1964, a "Haitian friend" told de Mohrenschildt that Papa Doc had received an "official letter" from Washington denouncing him as a "Polish communist." A cabinet minister, likely to have been Minister of Finance Dr. Hervé Boyer, confirmed that there had been such a letter, and advised de Mohrenschildt to get himself a "clean bill of health from the United States government."

That same April, the de Mohrenschildts prepared to fly to Washington, D.C. to testify before the Warren Commission. Jeanne requested, preposterously, that the Warren Commission compensate her husband for his time at "his usual consulting fee" of $150 a day, and insisted that they be allowed to bring their two dogs to Washington.

George contacted his old acquaintance Janet Auchincloss, who invited him to dinner. Mrs. Auchincloss' daughter, Jacqueline Kennedy, declined to attend. Maintaining his connections to the higher-ups was important enough to de Mohrenschildt to ignore issues of tact. He remained a man who lived as if he had nothing to lose; if Mrs. Kennedy had agreed to attend the dinner so much the better for his credibility.

Historian Larry Haapanen discovered that Mrs. Auchincloss turned over George de Mohrenschildt's letter to her to Allen Dulles, which was how it became a Warren Commission exhibit.

From within the bowels of its contending components, CIA circulated documents about de Mohrenschildt. Paul

Hartman of the Counter Intelligence Staff sent R.S. Travis of the Support Branch, Contact Division, a list of the reports Counter Intelligence had received from de Mohrenschildt, case number 43259. These had been forwarded by J. Walton Moore from the Dallas field office. Ten reports are listed, but only by number, beginning with 00-B-3,094,376. They reflect de Mohrenschildt's activities for CIA beginning in 1957 with his assignment from the International Cooperation Administration that had taken him to Yugoslavia.

On April 21, 1964, Paul Hartman sent a memo to Raymond Rocca, saying that a Mr. Dahlgren, C/WH/6, had called to say that George de Mohrenschildt had walked into the U.S. Embassy in Port-au-Prince and complained that the U.S. had ruined his business relations with Duvalier. Hartman wrote: "Judging by the papers I have seen, we have had no hand in black-balling him. Rather, I thought that the extensive FBI inquiry might have caused the problem."

De Mohrenschildt was dangerous to CIA because he knew that CIA had an interest in Oswald at least a year before the Kennedy assassination. Army intelligence, given its relationship with de Mohrenschildt – tracking him with regard to his relationship with Clémard Joseph Charles – was sufficiently worried about what de Mohrenschildt might say to the Warren Commission that Dorothe Matlack herself met his April 21st flight from Haiti at National Airport. The Warren Commission put them up at the Willard. Among other tidbits, de Mohrenschildt told the Warren Commission that Marina Oswald had "lied [to them] on several points."

He had brought with him to Washington a file of newspaper articles about Clémard Joseph Charles. One identified Charles as having entered into a multimillion dollar housing project deal with the financial assistance of American banking interests. His own efforts in Haiti were purely commercial, de Mohrenschildt told people, with "no other purpose or intent." He continued to promote the political ambitions of Clémard Joseph Charles.

In Washington, de Mohrenschildt seemed to be more interested in countering the "official" letter denouncing him as a "Polish Communist" than in the Warren Commission proceedings. The letter – its author apparently unknown to him – posed a serious problem, and prompted de Mohrenschildt to make a personal appearance at the State Department; whether it was unannounced or by appointment is not clear. His objective was to inquire whether an official letter had been sent to the Government of Haiti exonerating him.

The State Department denied knowledge of any letter calling him a "dangerous Communist." They denied having sent any official communication about him to the Government of Haiti.

Someone at CIA might have sent it and not informed the State Department, a State Department official suggested. Ambassador Timmons, the U.S. Ambassador to Haiti, attributed the letter to "some business competitor," to which de Mohrenschildt remarked melodramatically that, "he always had lots of enemies." His history is that of a man ever in search of fresh enemies.

When de Mohrenschildt was asked by the State Department's John R. Wineberg how he could do business with such a person as Duvalier, he repeated what he had told Philadelphia lawyer Mikell: he was dealing with Duvalier on a man-to-man basis rather than on the basis of Duvalier's political philosophy. Duvalier's political actions are of no interest to me, de Mohrenschildt said. Political or moral scruples had never been luxuries he could afford.

To the State Department functionaries whom he encountered during his visit to their offices on April 24, 1964 – among them Elizabeth von Thurn of the Caribbean desk – de Mohrenschildt presented a rosy picture of his successes in Haiti. He revealed that he had discovered a deposit of between 2 and 2.5 million tons of coal. He had also discovered bauxite deposits.

He said he hoped to interest AID in financing a processing plant. He was told, coldly, that the Agency for International Development chooses projects "on a very selective basis."

De Mohrenschildt claimed to these lower level State Department functionaries that he and Clémard Joseph Charles were making $200,000 a year from their sisal plantation. With his customary bravado, de Mohrenschildt told the State Department that he didn't believe that the U.S. government should give any more aid to Haiti. Haiti could "get along just fine by itself."

"When the government of Haiti wants to do something, it always finds the money," he said, "and if A.I.D. ever did want to do anything, it should find a good, interesting project, like my coal project, and invest in it." George de Mohrenschildt may not have been a successful businessman, but he knew better than to reveal weakness or need.

He was doing "quite well" in Haiti, de Mohrenschildt claimed to everyone he met and to his correspondents. In a letter to his Dallas friend Thomas J. Attridge, he had written shortly after his arrival in Haiti: "The work is advancing in a cheerful atmosphere." He admitted that, "we are concentrating so much on the survey that nothing is being done with Mohrenschildt & Co., Inc. But we will become active in 1964." He does not mention Clémard Joseph Charles by name. "The total production is OK," he wrote, "and my friend, the banker, is behaving well."

To Dorothy Pierson's cousin, Nancy Pierson Sands, who had raised his daughter Alexandra, de Mohrenschildt announced that he had found oil "near the Santo Domingo border" and was beginning drilling operations with Brazilian and Argentine partners. This was an entire fabrication.

In May, CIA followed Clémard Joseph Charles aboard a flight bound for Miami where he met with M. Baboun, the Haitian consul. Once more, Charles was on a quest for war materiel for Duvalier. This time Charles hoped to procure cannon-armed PT boats with radar and sonar and diesel engines and airplanes. CIA tracked him to Dallas where he visited an arms merchant named Fred Orleans.

During these years, one of the thugs whom Papa Doc had ordered to terrorize the neighborhood of Carrefour-Feuilles in Port-au-Prince was Justin Bertrand, owner of the Carnival (Mardi Gras) band, Zobolo. Bertrand had served for a time as general foreman of the Department of Public Works. For safekeeping, Bertrand handed over to Clémard Joseph Charles two or three hundred thousand dollars. Charles offered Bertrand no receipt for the money. After a while, Bertrand began to ask himself how he could recover it. He "swore to get his money back, even if it meant eliminating the banker and his entire family." This was the world in which Clémard Joseph Charles moved.

Whether Charles was acting on behalf of Papa Doc in holding onto Bertrand's money, or whether it was on his own behalf, it is impossible at this late date to say. Clearly at least some of Charles' business activities were shrouded in mystery. The incident suggests why journalists like Bernard Diederich remember Clémard Joseph Charles as an "operator."

On June 3, 1964, as the Warren Report was being readied, Richard Helms wrote a letter to J. Lee Rankin, Warren Commission General Counsel. Helms was offering yet another lie for the record. Helms stated that – until after the murder of President Kennedy – CIA had "no information establishing a link between the de Mohrenschildts and Lee Harvey Oswald or his family."

Helms wrote: "At CIA headquarters, the association between the de MOHRENSCHILDTs and the OSWALDs was noted for the first time in December 1963 when it was reported from Haiti that the DE MOHRENSCHILDTs had appeared at the Embassy and volunteered information about their relationship with the OSWALDS."

What was important for CIA was to date their knowledge of de Mohrenschildt's relationship with Oswald, now an open matter, *after* the assassination of President Kennedy. CIA could not, by this argument, have suspected Oswald, could not have done anything to prevent the assassination.

J. Walter Moore knew better. Two weeks before the Warren Commission released its report, the U.S. government would destroy de Mohrenschildt's federal employment file – which would have linked de Mohrenschildt with CIA dating from 1957, at least.

After de Mohrenschildt testified before the Warren Commission, CIA tightened its surveillance of him in Haiti. For the rest of his life he would be a man from whom Clémard Joseph Charles would have done well to have distanced himself.

Whether de Mohrenschildt knew that "Conrad V. Rubricius" was a CIA spy or not, de Mohrenschildt continued to solicit his company. On June 8, 1964 de Mohrenschildt invited Rubricius to dinner "to meet two very interesting Belgian priests." One of them, Father Stockman, turned out to be a Dutch priest whose parish was on the Haitian-Dominican border. He had arrived in Haiti in the 1950s. Rubricius attempted to smoke him out.

"Present conditions in Haiti are very bad," Rubricius said.

"The political situation in the area covered by my parish, like most areas of Haiti, is very tense," Stockman said.

Suggesting that he suspected that his remarks would be reported elsewhere, de Mohrenschildt defended Duvalier's Haiti. "These conditions are not unusual," de Mohrenschildt said. "They've existed throughout Haitian history."

"All Haitians of all classes now live in a state of terror," said Father Stockman, an honest priest. "This condition did not exist when I first arrived in Haiti."

De Mohrenschildt considered it to be in his best interests to praise Haiti, not only at social functions in Port-au-Prince, but also in his letters home. They were "safe and secure and loved Haiti," he wrote to Lyndon Johnson intimate, lawyer Morris I. Jaffe. The reality was that in 1963, the year George de Mohrenschildt moved to Haiti, the annual per capita income was $75.00; the average for Latin America was $307.00. Ninety percent of the Haitian population was illiterate; infant mortality was approximately fifty percent.

Even John F. Kennedy's bellicose Secretary of State, Dean Rusk, was obliged to cast a discerning eye on Haiti. In 1961, in a statement to the State Department, the ordinarily hard-eyed Rusk allowed himself a flicker of sympathy for the suffering people of Haiti: "Haiti is the cesspool of the Western Hemisphere, under a dictator whom we abhor. If Haiti went the way of Cuba, we ourselves cannot, in good conscience, say that this could be worse for the Haitians."

It wasn't long before De Mohrenschildt was running out of money. A Texas geology student who had come to assist him was going home because de Mohrenschildt could no longer afford his services. This was Austen Boyd, and the June 8th dinner would be his farewell to Haiti.

Inevitably, in June 1964 the Kennedy assassination was a particular topic of dinner table conversation. He and his wife "were friends of Mr. and Mrs. Lee Harvey Oswald," de Mohrenschildt said. He called Oswald "a very confused and disturbed young man," the line the Warren Commission would adopt in its not-yet-public Report.

Both George and Jeanne de Mohrenschildt disparaged Marina Oswald. She's "a very vicious and evil woman," de Mohrenschildt said. Jeanne added that Mrs. Oswald discussed her marital sex life openly and complained about her husband's sexual inadequacy. De Mohrenschildt's message was that sexual ambivalence had provoked Oswald into "doing what he did," the issue being not Oswald's sexuality, but de Mohrenschildt's acceptance of the official version of the assassination. His intention, apparently, was that Rubricius report that he had accepted the government's position that Oswald was guilty.

Rubricius attempted to keep the de Mohrenschildts talking about Oswald. Was there any substance to the view expressed in foreign periodicals like *L'Express*, the Paris weekly, that the Kennedy assassination "was a plot organized by Dallas millionaires?" Rubricius wanted to know.

"President Kennedy was hated by the Dallas elite," de Mohrenschildt said smoothly. It is "very likely that certain reactionary elements in Dallas...organized a plot to get rid of Kennedy and used a disturbed person like Oswald to achieve their ends." Jeanne de Mohrenschildt quickly proffered her agreement.

Gossip leavened their days. On June 18, 1964, Rubricius spotted Mrs. de Mohrenschildt at the Pétionville Club. She needed to speak to him privately "on a very urgent matter," Jeanne told the CIA man. She and George had been to see President Duvalier, who had inquired about the divorce of Ambassador Benson E. L. Timmons. Timmons was doing a good job, Duvalier had said. He regretted that any personal development might interfere with Timmons' mission in Haiti.

It was most unusual for the President to take an interest in personal matters, Jeanne said. Duvalier had offered his services to bring about a reconciliation between the Ambassador and his wife. He had requested that Mrs. de Mohrenschildt locate Mrs. Timmons and persuade her to return to Haiti.

"What should I do?" Jeanne asked Rubricius.

"Bring the whole thing to the personal attention of the Ambassador," Rubricius said.

From one of his informants, Kermit V. Salahub, Rubricius heard that the story of $250,000 having been deposited in de Mohrenschildt's bank account after the Kennedy assassination was false – which itself was false, except perhaps with respect to the amount. Rubricius reported this news to the CIA station chief in Port-au-Prince, Joseph G. Benson. Ambassador Timmons then conveyed the information to the Chief of the Western Hemisphere Division, Desmond Fitzgerald. CIA interest in de Mohrenschildt remained as healthy as ever. What role CIA had in the arrival and departure of those funds would remain a mystery into the next millennium.

Gunrunners and arms dealers moved freely in and out of Papa Doc's Haiti. Among them was a San Antonio lawyer named Carl Raymond Crites. Clémard Joseph Charles met him at the airport. Crites' cover was that he was representing pharmaceutical firms. The local newspaper, *Le Nouvelliste,* described Crites as an associate of that other Texan Charles has hosted, Fred Orleans.

In June of 1964, a "Mexican" mission, entirely unofficial, of course, arrived in Port-au-Prince. It was led by a Victor Blanchett. Fred Orleans, who purported to have investments in Mexico, was in the group. De Mohrenschildt was enlisted as Blanchett's interpreter. The Mexican group agreed to lend Clémard Joseph Charles' bank $250,000 at seven or eight percent interest. Then the deal stalled. Clémard Joseph Charles was not a lucky man.

While Blanchett haggled with Papa Doc regarding what these Mexicans and other foreigners would bring to Haiti, on June 10th, "two Jews from Dallas," as *Time/Life* stringer Will Lang would describe them, arrived in Port-au-Prince. Their names were Henry Klepak and Sidney Schine. They had come to Haiti, Klepak and Schine insisted, to make a deal with the Caribbean Cordage Mill.

In fact, their business was to offer Duvalier surplus T-28 airplanes, "free of charge."

In 1952, Schine had set up American Aircraft Supply Company, Inc., a Texas company brokering airplanes and airplane parts. In the fifties, he had served as a lawyer for nightclub owner Jack Ruby, a client awaiting notoriety as the future assassin of Lee Harvey Oswald. A decade later, in February 1962, Schine and attorney Henry Klepak formed Empire Trading Corporation, which was involved in the "export and import trade with foreign governments in cash and goods." Empire Trading exported aircraft and other heavy machinery and equipment, always on a cash basis. Klepak's hobby was collecting information on con men. It takes one to know one.

When Klepak and Schine arrived in Haiti, they were already being investigated by the U.S. government for fraud involving the smuggling of several hundred thousand dollars of gold bullion out of the United States, via Mexico. The final destination of the gold was – Switzerland. CIA had tracked Schine to Karachi, Pakistan and to the Congo, familiar trajectories of the professional gunrunner.

Some time in 1964, Schine submitted an application to the State Department for an export license to sell 36 T-28 jet fighter planes to the Government of Haiti. Later James Angleton requested that the FBI "query the Department of State for information on the activities in Haiti of Sidney Schine and Henry Klepak." It was difficult even for CIA to keep up with Schine and Klepak.

The Klepak/Schine "free of charge" offer seemed too good to pass up. Clémard Joseph Charles discovered that $25,000 was needed to "recondition" the engines of the "free" airplanes. Desperate, Duvalier agreed anyway.

Then the deal fell apart because, as CIA recounted, someone in ZRMETAL [Washington, D.C.], but not

ODACID [State Department], learned about it and canceled the export licenses. At the same time, the Mexican investment in the bank of Clémard Joseph Charles fell through for good.

Duvalier blamed Clémard Joseph Charles for these two strokes of ill fortune. Their relationship began to fray.

* * *

By June 20, 1964 George de Mohrenschildt had expanded his entourage. At his table for dinner that evening in a place of prominence sat the Polish commercial attaché, Wlodzimierz Galicki, who represented the Soviet bloc in Haiti. Philippe Pallas, a Frenchman who worked for the United Nations, had also been invited, along with a young American technician named Robert Taylor. Taylor worked with the United States-sponsored malaria eradication program. Rubricius described him and his wife as a PBPRIME [United States] couple. Among the guests was also – Clémard Joseph Charles.

Rubricius took a long hard look at Clémard Joseph Charles. He is "coal black," Rubricius would report. Rubricius' assessment was that Duvalier's sponsorship of Charles reflected his determination to undermine the political power of the mulattoes, who had long dominated the political environment in Haiti.

Rubricius also noted that both de Mohrenschildts were "extremely friendly and solicitous" toward Charles. During the drinks portion of their dinner party, Charles remarked that he had just returned from Denver, Colorado and Dallas. That very day, he said, he had met with Colonel Georges Danache of the Haitian Air Corps. Danache had agreed to accompany him to inspect some airplanes. Rubricius knew that Charles' trip had something to do with transporting two T-28 airplanes to Haiti.

Charles introduced the subject of racism. He deplored the racial situation in the United States, he said, as his sensitivity to racial segregation in Washington, D.C. made clear.

"Steps are being taken to ameliorate this situation," Rubricius said. "And, besides, the United States is not the only country where racial problems exist." Charles stared at Rubricius, perceiving that the reference was to Haiti. Rubricius dropped the subject. He was there, after all, not to voice his political opinions, but to observe.

Mid-way through the meal, Charles rose from his seat and departed without a word. "He has taken ill and has been forced to leave," de Mohrenschildt explained to his guests. President Duvalier has been keeping Charles "very busy" lately and this "has had an adverse effect on his health."

His dual loyalties were taking their toll on Clémard Joseph Charles.

With Charles gone from the party, there was an opportunity for Rubricius to focus on another of de Mohrenschildt's guests. This was a round-faced, thirty-five year old man with dark curly hair and finely carved features, thin lips and flashing dark eyes. A mustache graced his upper lip. Tinted eyeglasses added to his mystery. He was new to Haiti, said this short, strikingly handsome man, who had arrived only on June 12th.

De Mohrenschildt introduced him to his guests as "Sheikh Mohamed Fayed," an "oil businessman from Kuwait."

"I'm an official guest of the Haitian government," the "Sheikh" said. His English was excellent, his French, to which he turned only when absolutely necessary, merely passable. With his "slightly Negroid features," Rubricius thought, this man might easily pass as a member of the Haitian mulatto elite.

"Sheikh Mohamed Fayed" had not arrived at George de Mohrenschildt's dinner party unaccompanied. By his side was a member of Duvalier's Presidential Guard, Lieutenant Woolley Gaillard. Dressed in civilian attire, Gaillard remained silent throughout the dinner. Later he would be observed with Fayed at local nightclubs. When Fayed had first arrived in Haiti, Aubelin Jolicoeur reported, he had moved into the best suite at the best hotel, El Rancho, in Pétionville. "Papa Doc was spellbound, blinded by Fayed," Jolicoeur later remembered.

Fayed claimed that, like de Mohrenschildt, he was keenly interested in exploring oil possibilities in Haiti. If oil exists in the Dominican Republic, there must be oil in Haiti too, he believed.

He is not here for pleasure, de Mohrenschildt perceived at once.

In this land of deception and intrigue, crawling with CIA spies and informants, where arms dealers came and went at will, Fayed fit right in. He was, of course, neither a Sheikh nor from Kuwait. Mohamed Abdel Moneim Ali Fayed was born in Alexandria, Egypt on January 27, 1929, the son of a schoolteacher.

Mohamed Fayed grew up to be a gifted salesman, as he peddled everything from Singer sewing machines to Coca-Cola. His fortunes changed when he was rescued from oblivion by Adnan Khashoggi, arms dealer and future billionaire, who would be implicated in the Iran-Contra scandal. Khashoggi's father was the personal physician to King Abdul-Aziz ibn Saud, the founder of modern Saudi Arabia.

Khashoggi hired Mohamed Fayed at his company, Al-Nasir, ostensibly to make "furniture deliveries." Soon Fayed was making "side deals." Based in Saudi Arabia, Al-Nasir publicly was a rice and cotton brokerage. In 1960, CIA recorded that Al-Nasir was a "cover firm for the Egyptian Intelligence Service."

Mohamed Fayed had become a senior Egyptian intelligence officer, as the Egyptian services mirrored CIA. Just as CIA co-opted commercial enterprises as covers through which to maneuver and conceal its activities, as well as to plant its agents, the United Arab Republic used Al-Nasir for its own illegal transactions, particularly those with France.

Al-Nasir's profits were "transferred to a special government fund for financing clandestine operations for the United Arab Republic's military intelligence." These were operations not covered by the country's public budget. Among Al-Nasir's "trading company" projects was the shipment of arms through Suez Canal ports to South Africa for distribution in African countries for use by "anti-European" (anti-colonial) insurgents.

Al-Nasir Trading Company was directed by a Lt. Colonel Muhammad Ghanim of the counter-espionage branch of Egyptian military intelligence. His salary was paid by the military, rather than by Al-Nasir. Earlier, Ghanim had managed the "Niel Company" in Beirut. Under the pseudonym "Muhammad al-Maari," Ghanim had organized an uprising in Beirut. In 1959, in one more example of the globalization of intelligence, CIA tracked Ghanim through Geneva, Paris and Brussels. CIA was assisted in this effort by the Israeli Ministry of Defense.

Along the way, Fayed married Khashoggi's sister, Samira, a marriage that endured for two years, from 1954 to 1956. Later Khashoggi was forthright in his distaste for his former brother-in-law: "Mohamed always had the image of lying and making up stories." What Khashoggi meant, but was not willing explicitly to state, was that Mohamed presented not the "image," but the reality, and that he was indeed a liar.

This man is friendly and yet evil at the same time, Rubricius, a sophisticated professional intelligence agent, realized at once.

His relationship with Khashoggi in tatters, Fayed came to Haiti with a letter of introduction to Papa Doc, courtesy of a Geneva-based Croatian arms dealer named Bozo Dabinovic. Bozo described himself as a Monaco-based shipping agent. A few years earlier, the French Navy had suspected him of running guns to the Algerian FLN.

In Haiti, CIA at once investigated Fayed. They consulted the Kuwaiti Embassy to check on whether the company Fayed claimed he ran, the "General Commerce and Navigation Company of Kuwait," was actually registered in Haiti. It wasn't. Fayed's bank accounts resided in Geneva, CIA soon learned.

It was still June 1964 in Port-au-Prince when Mohamed Fayed burst abruptly into the world of George de Mohrenschildt and Clémard Joseph Charles.

Fayed's social debut occurred at de Mohrenschildt's dinner table on June 20, 1964. On that same day, a force of between thirty and fifty rebels landed at Saltrou, on Haiti's southern coast. It was one more singularly unsuccessful paramilitary invasion of Haiti.

The next day, June 21, 1964, Rubricius, Galicki and George de Mohrenschildt met up at the Pétionville Country Club swimming pool.

"Even in the country, living conditions in Mexico are vastly superior to those in Haiti," Rubricius remarked. Galicki could only agree.

"Conditions in Haiti are nowhere near as bad as some people believe," de Mohrenschildt insisted.

The T-28 plane deal remained on everyone's mind. "It's the work of Clémard Joseph Charles," de Mohrenschildt confided. He added that Charles' recent trip had nothing to do with Mexico making investments in Haiti. "That deal has received so much erroneous publicity lately in the American press," de Mohrenschildt complained.

Rubricius remained silent. He knew the planes would not be coming to Haiti, at least not legally, because the U.S. government was closing in on Papa Doc, and had no intention of granting an export license for the 30 T-28A aircraft that Charles had located.

Yet the Johnson administration had been generous to Duvalier. In 1964, U.S. investment in Haiti amounted to more than sixty million dollars. The debt owed to the U.S. by the Haitian government grew. U.S. policy toward Haiti was about business, the "long-term cost to our economy."

Mohamed Fayed joined the de Mohrenschildt circle. On June 22nd, he attended a pizza dinner at the home of Philippe Pallas. While everyone was eating, Fayed suddenly got up from the table. He must be at his hotel to receive an urgent overseas telephone call, he explained. An hour later, he returned.

On July 8th, there was yet another paramilitary invasion of Haiti by Haitian exiles, with CIA foreknowledge. It failed, seeming to have been more a form of harassment of Duvalier than a serious attempt to remove him.

"If I'm forced to flee the country," Duvalier promised, "I'll level Port-au-Prince first!"

Whether through lack of will, or policy, CIA was finding it as difficult to dislodge Duvalier as it was to remove Fidel Castro. Or, perhaps, CIA was ambivalent about going through with assassinations in both cases.

Papa Doc had not given up on securing those T-28 airplanes. In August, from his office at Empire Trading, Sidney Schine made many toll calls to Clémard Joseph Charles. The calls were registered to an alias, "Carlos Climer."

In September, Schine and Clémard Joseph Charles were observed traveling together from Miami to Port-au-Prince. The U.S. government had turned down Schine's application to sell jet fighters to Haiti, despite his possession of a letter of credit from the Haitian government and a promise that they would purchase the planes. Schine was in daily contact with members of the Haitian government.

"Why is the U.S. blocking the T-28 plane deal?" Jeanne de Mohrenschildt asked Rubricius. "Why not let the Haitians buy a few planes? They won't be able to do anything with them." She remarked that she had spotted Sidney Schine at the Ministry of Finance.

"Such matters are not my responsibility," Rubricius said. He believed that Mrs. de Mohrenschildt was satisfied with this reply, which was not the case.

Everyone in Port-au-Prince dined out on stories about the "plane deal." At a diplomatic reception hosted by de Mohrenschildt's new best friend, Wlodizmierz Galicki, de Mohrenschildt introduced Rubricius to a "Mr. Carol Roussier," a thirtyish, well-dressed businessman from Texas.

"Roussier has just arrived in Haiti in connection with the plane deal," de Mohrenschildt joked in his cynical way. Later Roussier remarked to Rubricius that it was most unfortunate that the U.S. government canceled the plane deal. Duvalier was, after all, a strong anti-Communist. If the United States puts obstacles in his way, he will be forced to look elsewhere to protect himself.

Rubricius concluded that Roussier was in Haiti "in connection with some underhanded business deal."

During this summer of 1964, Rubricius was busy. He was assigned to spy not only on de Mohrenschildt, but also on Galicki. Reinforcements arrived in the person of an agent who was awarded the cryptonym EVLEMON-1.

EVLEMON-1 reported to Rubricius on meetings between Galicki and the de Mohrenschildts. CIA also spied on Galicki when he was not in the company of either de Mohrenschildt or Charles. Galicki was, after all, the reigning member of the Communist bloc in Port-au-Prince.

CIA recorded an outing Galicki made to the movies with his mistress, a tall, brown-skinned Haitian teenager between fifteen and eighteen years old. When she visited, Rubricius reported to the CIA chief of station, "she and Galicki go upstairs to the bedroom." Two English-speaking Jamaicans visited Galicki, as did a black government deputy and two "unidentified white men."

De Mohrenschildt was happily enjoying a carefree life that summer. Unburdened by work, he chipped in with the local manager of Pan American Airways, Robert McElhannon, to purchase a 25-foot motorboat. On August 9th, de Mohrenschildt cast off for Isle Cabrit in the Arcadin Islands, ten miles north of Port-au-Prince.

On board were Galicki and a new member of their set, Wojciech Stawinski, a Polish national. Rubricius too was present. Soon CIA uncovered that Stawinski was a member of the Polish state marketing organization, arranging exhibitions of home wares. This, of course, might easily be his cover.

A cloud hovered to spoil de Mohrenschildt's day. Papa Doc, de Mohrenschildt confided, had concluded that he had been involved "in some way" with the assassination of President Kennedy and had been considering expelling him from Haiti, contract or no contract. De Mohrenschildt pleaded his case directly to Papa Doc, insisting that he was not an assassin hiding out in Haiti. Duvalier had relented and permitted him to remain. Still, de Mohrenschildt was uneasy, fearing that Duvalier would cancel his oil exploration contract.

In the car on the way home, de Mohrenschildt opened up for Rubricius the grab bag of his political opinions.

"Communism has something to offer the underdeveloped world," de Mohrenschildt said. "Capitalism…has nothing to offer except a continuation of the status quo." (It was comments like this that had led an acquaintance to threaten de Mohrenschildt angrily, "if the United States ever goes to war with Russia, I'll get a gun and take care of you." But de Mohrenschildt had only laughed).

De Mohrenschildt told Rubricius that he opposed the U.S. dispensing foreign aid.

"The United States should permit the countries of Latin America to choose the form of government they desire," he asserted. "If they wish to go Communist, they should be permitted to do so. They have got to find their way by themselves. The United States position in Latin America is completely lost because the U.S. has nothing to offer the Latins."

"It is better to be a Negro in Russia and in the satellite countries than in the United States because Negroes get a much better treatment in Communist countries," de Mohrenschildt added. He pointed to Stawinski as "a good example of the beneficent effects of the Polish Communist system."

Rubricius noted that de Mohrenschildt became "very emotional" when he talked about Communism. That he was in the presence of a CIA man, if he knew it, would not have bothered de Mohrenschildt. He had, after all, expressed such views openly from the day he arrived in the United States in 1938.

De Mohrenschildt confided to this CIA man that Clémard Joseph Charles was his business partner in all his dealings with the Haitian government. Charles owns 20% of the sisal mill, de Mohrenschildt said. He believed he had been cheated by Charles, de Mohrenschildt added, but he preferred being a minority stockholder anyway. He didn't want the headache of running day-to-day operations. George de Mohrenschildt once more revealed his antipathy to hard work. As the wife of Igor Voshinin had told the FBI, de Mohrenschildt could never work for more than two hours a day without getting headaches.

De Mohrenschildt boasted that he and Charles were promoting "all sorts of business deals with Americans, particularly Texans, and the Haitian government." San Antonio lawyer Carl Raymond Crites was one of their principals. It was a typical de Mohrenschildt tactic: mentioning the involvement of respectable or quasi-respectable people to add legitimacy to his schemes.

In mid-August, the de Mohrenschildts entertained a writer named George Edwin McMillan. His wife was Priscilla Johnson, who had interviewed Oswald in Moscow for the North American Newspaper Alliance (NANA). Priscilla Johnson had applied for employment with CIA in 1952, only to be turned down. But the Agency retained an interest in her.

NANA had been established in 1922 as a union of fifty major newspapers. In its glory days, NANA had sent Ernest Hemingway to report on the Spanish Civil War, and became part of a distinguished history indeed. When NANA was purchased in 1951 by Ernest Cuneo, a former OSS operative, its image changed and it was seen as a front for espionage. Under Cuneo, NANA published CIA-connected reporters like Victor Lasky, and Virginia Prewett, whose husband worked for CIA.

George McMillan had been employed "within the U.S. Embassy in Moscow during two periods of residence." De Mohrenschildt described him as a "good friend."

McMillan had come to Port-au-Prince to persuade the de Mohrenschildts to appear on a television documentary to discuss Oswald. You will be paid "very handsomely," McMillan promised.

De Mohrenschildt informed Rubricius that he had declined the invitation, claiming that he desired "no further publicity" on the Oswald question. Nonetheless, in September, the de Mohrenschildts flew to New York ostensibly to appear on the program.

It seemed that almost everyone who visited de Mohrenschildt was connected to CIA. Paul Johnson, co-director of the Haitian-American Institute, which was attached to the U.S. Embassy, arrived on September 12, 1964. As Johnson reported to his CIA handler, he was shocked to hear both de Mohrenschildts speak in a "pejorative sense" about America.

Johnson was particularly irritated when de Mohrenschildt offered an anecdote about an American Negro, departing from Haiti, who had protested, "Where do you want me to go, Birmingham?"

"The aforementioned Negro might help his race by going to Birmingham," Johnson had said indignantly.

George de Mohrenschildt was too worldly not to perceive when he was crossing swords with a CIA asset. "What do you know about the CIA?" he asked Johnson suddenly.

"Maybe I am and maybe I'm not with the CIA," Johnson said, flushed with anger. "But in any event I wouldn't say I was if I were, and I wouldn't say I was or wasn't if I wasn't." This, Johnson thought, should put an end to de Mohrenschildt's prying.

In his report of this encounter to CIA, Johnson wrote that de Mohrenschildt was attempting to "popularize Duvalier to the guests." Then he added, "Of course, he works for the Duvalier government." Johnson decided that de Mohrenschildt and his friends were "unstable and possibly dangerous. They seem to want to destroy the true American image and are biting the hand that feeds them."

CIA rebuked Johnson for his indiscretions. He was ordered "in any future situation like this" to "deny categorically any CIA connection and all knowledge of the organization." He should say that the very nature of his work was "such that he could not consider any association with CIA." The Port-au-Prince station chief then reported the Johnson-de Mohrenschildt encounter to Desmond Fitzgerald.

Radford W. Herbert was now Assistant Chief of the Western Hemisphere Division. Herbert forbad Johnson [EVMINCE-2] from maintaining "even light social contact with de Mohrenschildt." John Whitten, Chief of Western Hemisphere/2, agreed. EVMINCE's operational use was never to be mentioned to "non-KUBARK [CIA] personnel." With de Mohrenschildt the subject of interest of "many agencies," CIA issued a "blanket restriction" on associating with him.

Soon after, CIA reconsidered. The ban on association with de Mohrenschildt was not "believed consistent with ODYOKE [United States Government] interest." CIA dispatched yet another asset, EVMINOR-1, to spy on de Mohrenschildt.

September 1964: George de Mohrenschildt and Clémard Joseph Charles remained hopeful that the U.S. would come to Clémard's aid. De Mohrenschildt wrote a letter to Howard Burris. De Mohrenschildt had known Burris' wife Barbara Jester, daughter of former Texas Governor Beauford Jester, at the University of Texas, a connection de Mohrenschildt cultivated. Would Burris request a meeting for Clémard Joseph Charles with the president of the United States, Burris' former boss, Lyndon Johnson? Burris complied, and honored de Mohrenschildt's request.

On September 22, 1964, his chief assistant and factotum, Walter Jenkins, replied for Lyndon Johnson. "We have sent a letter to him after discussing it with the Department of State," Jenkins wrote to Howard L. Burris. It was not possible for the President "to see him now." Yet Johnson did not close the door entirely. "We will keep your comments on him in mind," Jenkins added.

Paul M. Popple, Johnson's Correspondence Assistant, wrote to Clémard Joseph Charles that, should he be visiting Washington later in the year, he was to contact "the office of the President's Special Assistant, Mr. Thomas C. Mann, Assistant Secretary of State for Inter-American Affairs." For the moment, however, there would be no audience for Clémard Joseph Charles with the President of the United States – or anyone on his staff.

In September 1964, Mohamed Fayed moved into a house provided to him by Papa Doc. It had been the residence of Clement Barbot, chief of Haiti's secret police and a former leader of the *Tontons Macoutes.* Before long, Duvalier turned on Barbot and ordered him jailed, and then murdered. Barbot's house came with servants and a swimming pool.

Here Fayed lived with his bodyguard Gaillard. On Sundays, you could observe the two swimming in the pool. George de Mohrenschildt visited on occasion, but Fayed's more frequent guest was Clémard Joseph Charles.

Fayed had promised Papa Doc that he would build an oil refinery and a wharf to develop the Port-au-Prince harbor. Mohamed was so persuasive that Duvalier canceled his prior contract with Charles Valentine of Valentine Petroleum – a contract signed in November 1962 and guaranteed for ten years for $327,304 by the U.S. Agency for International Development. Valentine had deposited $50,000 in a Port-au-Prince bank account as a gesture of his good will. Valentine's partner was an old cohort of George de Mohrenschildt, the Texas oilman John Mecom.

While Papa Doc was structuring his contract with Mohamed Fayed, Valentine continued working, unaware that his own contract, and therefore his time in Haiti, was coming to an end. Eight weeks passed. Suddenly and without warning, Valentine and two of his associates were arrested at the luxury El Rancho Hotel in Pétionville. They were allowed three hours to pack up and leave the country. Duvalier kept AID's $327,304.

Later, in a court of law Valentine demanded that the money be returned to him. His damages, he claimed, amounted to $817,000. He was offered a settlement that he called "so small, it's ridiculous." It was incidents like this that encouraged CIA in the belief that Papa Doc had to be removed.

Duvalier's contract with Mohamed Fayed for the new wharf was announced in *Le Moniteur* on September 19, 1964. It was actually granted to two people: Fayed and Clémard Joseph Charles. Fayed was to invest five million dollars for "consolidating, enlarging and modernizing its facilities" within thirty years. In exchange, Fayed would collect all fees for the docking, piloting, and loading and unloading of vessels, a privilege worth hundreds of thousands of dollars a year.

Fayed would also collect five percent of the freight charges on all merchandise moving in and out of Haiti; he would be the exclusive agent for all the shipping companies operating out of Port-au-Prince. Duvalier also offered Fayed the exclusive right to import and sell petroleum products. Unlike Valentine, Fayed was not required to deposit any money in advance. His contract would run not for ten years, as Valentine's did, but for fifty years.

Mohamed Fayed now opened an office in the same building as Clémard Joseph Charles' bank. Heavy red velvet carpeting adorned its floors. At once Fayed began to transfer money from the Port Authority into his personal account at the Port-au-Prince branch of the Royal Bank of Canada, a bank with which, among others, George de Mohrenschildt had been doing business in Dallas.

SIX

George De Mohrenschildt Under CIA Surveillance

De Mohrenschildt is of extreme interest to the Federal Bureau of Investigation.

— John Whitten, CIA officer

In the late summer and early autumn of 1964, gold smuggler and airplane broker Sidney Schine toured the region of Haiti bordering the Dominican Republic, that area from which raids by Haitian rebels were emanating at a ferocious clip. He had heard that "American CIA agents were stirring up the trouble," Schine said. He also took a penetrating look at the Murchison businesses in Haiti.

"The Murchisons are making a lot of money on the Bobby Baker-inspired meat deal," Schine observed, noting that they also had "an unpublicized flour business operating that represents substantial profits."

On October 8th, safely back in Dallas, Schine gave an interview to "that *Life* magazine stringer," Will Lang, who had been following his activities in Haiti. Lang reported directly to Holland McCombs, a CIA-connected journalist employed by *Time/Life*.

Schine told Lang that he had signed a contract with the Duvalier government for the sale of fifteen T-28's —

but the State Department had blocked the sale. Schine had managed nonetheless to move some planes to Haiti via Co olidge, Arizona, Baja California, and Mexico. As he was negotiating these maneuvers, Schine had corresponded with George de Mohrenschildt.

Acquaintances were kept on a need-to-know basis, so Schine was surprised when he received a letter from de Mohrenschildt with the U.S. Embassy in Port-au-Prince as his return address. Schine had not viewed de Mohrenschildt's interests as being synonymous with those of the U.S. government. De Mohrenschildt had confided to Schine that he was "extremely aggravated about the publication of his friendship with Lee Harvey Oswald." Schine also knew that the U.S. Treasury Department was attempting to establish whether Dallas was the base for subversive operations into Latin America, only to have been denied the use of wiretaps.

Later, reporter Lang slyly asked de Mohrenschildt whether he knew Sidney Schine. He did, de Mohrenschildt admitted, and "promptly terminated the conversation."

The efforts of Klepak and Schine to arm Papa Doc were aided by I.I. Davidson, whose associations included the ARAMCO Corporation, yet another CIA cover company. I.I. fully expected Papa Doc to depart for exile in Switzerland. If Duvalier did not comply, Davidson predicted: "the U.S. govt will try to find ways to depose him."

Davidson was aware that the U.S. government now saw Duvalier as unreliable; he could not be counted on to support the United States at foreign meetings, such as those of the Organization of American States. The treatment of Charles Valentine also did not sit well with the government; it portended similar arbitrary moves against other American businesses. CIA and the State Department saw eye to eye on this matter.

By the mid-sixties, it was an open secret: CIA was out to dethrone Papa Doc. Years later, on trial in federal court, I.I. Davidson admitted that he had engaged in activities "in the interest of the United States" involving "Haitian matters." The details are "of a sensitive nature." I.I. behaved as if he were an intelligence operative; you did not spell out for anybody, whether or not you were under oath, the details of what you were up to.

So it should not be surprising that by 1964, when Papa Doc was desperate for weaponry, airplanes and ammunition, he would turn to I.I. Davidson. Not only was Davidson already working for Duvalier, but he was also among the most savvy, the most clever and well-connected arms dealers in the world. In March 1964, Davidson had been observed in Port-au-Prince in the presence of Klepak and Schine.

On September 29, 1964 the *Washington Post* reported that Papa Doc had received two T-28 fighter planes that had been flown to Haiti from Dallas – illegally. Duvalier had made a down payment with a letter of credit for $210,000 drawn on the *Banque Commerciale d'Haiti,* the bank of Clémard Joseph Charles. Duvalier had also managed to procure some U.S. Navy gunboats through Charles.

Assisting in transporting these planes to Haiti was a CIA-connected soldier of fortune, ace pilot and smuggler named Edward Browder. An aviator of legendary competence, Browder had tested planes for Lockheed and flown for Pan American Airways – that redoubt of CIA assets in Haiti, as the files of CIA Counter Intelligence reveal. Browder is notable for his political adventurism.

In 1948, he had been sentenced to eighteen months for conspiracy to organize a military expedition against Venezuela and to bomb Caracas. He said he had participated in CIA's 1954 "ouster" (Browder's term) of Jacobo Arbenz Guzman of Guatemala. Browder also admitted that he knew "Dr. Duvalier of Haiti."

That same year, Browder was imprisoned by Mexico's secret service authorities for "immigration violations." During one interrogation, a .45 caliber revolver was discharged next to Browder's ear, rupturing his eardrum. Browder wrote to Director of Central Intelligence Allen Dulles, and asked Dulles to get him out in exchange for information about a plot against President Figueroa of Costa Rica. Had he not already established relations with CIA, Browder could never have written Allen Dulles such a letter with any hope of receiving a reply.

In its documents referring to Browder, CIA dissociates itself from his activities. He had made "false claims... in reporting procurement of aircraft and arms for the liberation forces in Guatemala," the Agency writes. CIA adds that Browder's criminal record in the U.S. dated from 1949 and included his violating the Neutrality Act and organizing a military force against a friendly power (Venezuela), for which he had been convicted.

Among Browder's scams was an attempt to induce Henry Luce to send *Time/Life* reporters to film a coup from a Costa Rican base. Frank Wisner himself had dictated the reply, which was to be signed by C.D. Jackson, an agency asset embedded at *Time/Life*.

By 1954, CIA was calling Browder an "unscrupulous adventurer, who is willing to sell his services to the highest bidder." CIA's F.F. Holcomb writes: "He is also a facile liar and apparently enjoys inflating his reputation as a soldier of fortune."

Browder also claimed he had worked for Dominican Republic dictator Trujillo for years – with CIA support. Later, arrested with stolen securities in his possession, he let his son speak for him. His father, Browder's son said, had securities and bonds from Fidel Castro. They were payment for war supplies.

On April 17, 1962, Browder was arrested for "illegally exporting military aircraft; conspiracy to steal government property; conspiracy to aid revolution in a foreign country" and assorted crimes like passing worthless checks and auto theft. Browder termed himself a "soldier of fortune" and admitted that his business was selling arms and ammunition.

Edward Browder was a sandy-haired, graying man, when he enters the Haiti story in 1964, only five foot eight or nine inches tall, 165 to 170 pounds. Sporting a small mustache, he favored grey Western-style sport jackets, and was noticeably bow-legged. As far as his appearance went, he was a man at whom no one would look twice.

Along the way, Browder had made the acquaintance of both George de Mohrenschildt and Clémard Joseph Charles, "on and off" in the "great game," as Browder put it, enlisting the British euphemism for the intelligence services. He found de Mohrenschildt a "fey character," a more benign description than that of CIA's Russ Holmes, who in his "draft biography" would call de Mohrenschildt a "sodomite."

By October 1964, Browder was partnering with Henry Klepak and Sidney Schine as they struggled to supply Papa Doc with those airplanes he wanted so desperately. There is a record of Schine handing Browder $1,000. For what service, Schine would never say, but there is little doubt that Schine needed Browder to carry out his lucrative contract with Papa Doc.

In the name of a phantom company, Browder leased an airplane in November 1964 and flew it to Port-au-Prince, where he promptly abandoned it. It was an operation layered in intrigue. The person from whom he rented the plane – and to whom he was introduced by Sidney Schine – was one James D. Owens, who was involved in the exporting and importing of oil and gas, and was based in Dallas.

Browder rented the plane under the name "Timothy de Jong" of the "Ace Research Company." His purpose, "de Jong" told anyone who asked, was to recover "certain treasures in old Mexico."

Browder never returned the plane to Owens. If Owens reported to the authorities that his plane was missing, Schine warned, "both of them will be in trouble." Owens went to the FBI anyway.

"De Jong" now reported that Owens' plane had turned up in the Grand Bahamas Islands, having been flown there by one "Jack Browder." Browder's luggage had been filled with carved mahogany statues, obviously obtained in Haiti, along with hemp (kenaf) baskets. He planned to leave the plane there for a week, and then take the statues to a Cessna dealer in West Palm Beach named James B. Tilford, Jr.

When Owens retrieved his plane in West Palm, Tilford told him that the man who had been flying it was Edward Browder. Browder had filed a flight plan for Rock Sound, Grand Bahamas Islands, for a 1962 Cessna Skyknight plane. It was "a common practice for persons flying to Cuba, Haiti, or other points where they did not want their exact destination to be known, to check out to Rock Sound." More often than not, they provided false names. Browder had once charged gasoline at the Tilford Flying Service in the name of "L. Martin." That day he had been flying an old Continental Airlines DC-3 NI8945.

Owens discovered that there was "a Dallas group" that was working with "Timothy De Jong supplying President François Duvalier with planes and arms."

The FBI pondered an October 1, 1964 *Houston Chronicle* article headlined "U.S. Fighter Planes Smuggled Into Haiti." It described a preliminary investigation of two T-28 planes delivered to Haiti by American "adventure pilots" to be used as fighter-bombing training aircraft against guerrillas in South Viet Nam and the Congo where CIA was already embedded. Duvalier had wanted the planes "to fight guerrillas in the Haitian mountains," the article said.

Schine had promised Owens, who owned a DC-3, that he could provide him with a T-28 parked in Dallas. It was a web of intrigue worthy of the pen of John le Carré or, to use Joe Dryer's locution, CIA "fun and games." Browder – who sometimes used the alias John D. McCormick, among others – was, by his own admission to the House Select Committee on Assassinations, an "off and on Company man."

Soon Browder was spotted cashing a check for $24,000 signed by Clémard Joseph Charles through his account at the Manufacturers Hanover Trust Bank in New York. It was yet another example of Clémard Joseph Charles violating the law on behalf of Papa Doc, the man whom he hoped to replace as president of Haiti. It was as well another instance of how Papa Doc so compromised Charles as to make it less than likely that Charles would ever succeed in the quicksand of Haitian politics.

In the *Washington Post* article describing Duvalier's purchase of the T-28 aircraft, I.I. Davidson was named, as was Clémard Joseph Charles. Davidson at once demanded a retraction – and got it. He told the State Department that a Texas lawyer named Fred Orleans, who was involved in the sale of the T-28s, had remarked that there was no need to worry about export licenses because "the White House will overrule the State Department."

The State Department and CIA worked together to forestall prosecution of those responsible for violating the ban on importing the planes to Haiti. An Opa-Locka, Florida witness reported that State and CIA were "unwilling to let a key witness testify." Illegal wiretaps led to the conviction of four men.

However, the higher-ups – Klepak, Schine, Davidson and Browder – escaped without being charged. Observers concluded that Haiti had been able to arrange arms sales because Duvalier had the cooperation of "at least one segment of the American intelligence agencies or the military," even as they were attempting simultaneously to overthrow him.

Everything in Haiti, as with CIA, remained on a need-to-know basis. One day in 1965 Papa Doc asked I.I. Davidson: "who is George de Mohrenschildt, really?" The question is reported in a CIA Office of Security memorandum of January 7, 1976, reported to CIA by Davidson himself. In this memorandum, I.I. Davidson does not include his reply to Duvalier.

In the fall and early winter of 1964, while Clémard Joseph Charles and various CIA adventurers were working on the airplane deals, George de Mohrenschildt spent much of his time with the Polish commercial attaché, Galicki. Between October 30th and December 29th, they met at least twenty times – for chats, tea, cocktails, dinners, or just impromptu visits.

CIA struggled to keep track of all these encounters. They registered that Clémard Joseph Charles did not attend these meetings between de Mohrenschildt and Galicki. For the identities of de Mohrenschildt's other guests, CIA consulted Pan American flight manifests. A perpetual question within CIA was whether George de

Mohrenschildt was a double agent, or even a triple agent, serving not only CIA, but others as well.

His history as a man for sale was well known: his intelligence records, dating from the 1940s, ponder whether he was working for the Nazis and later, whether he was even in the pay of the Bolsheviks. That de Morhenschildt spent so much time with the leading Communist in Haiti, Galicki, was alarming.

The records of de Mohrenschildt's social life were now being forwarded to CIA Counter Intelligence chief, James Angleton.

In Port-au-Prince, the de Mohrenschildts had begun to behave without personal restraint. One day at the American Embassy, in an uproar over her dog's misbehavior, Jeanne de Mohrenschildt pursued the receptionist into the toilet and slapped her in the face. On her way out, cursing the receptionist, Jeanne also shouted a few insults at the U.S. Marine Guard.

The de Mohrenschildts "muscled in on" the Embassy Commissary, which they were not entitled to visit, and this was duly noted. Ambassador Timmons disapproved of the de Mohrenschildts, who, he remarked, "have been in touch with almost all the adventurers and carpetbaggers who have visited Port-au-Prince this year, including Mohamed Fayed and Fred Orleans."

Unless you have arrangements in advance involving a business matter, an official told the de Mohrenschildts, you are not to set foot in the American Embassy. Ambassador Timmons had already been made aware of the de Mohrenschildts' "disparaging remarks against Americans here, American institutions and American policy." No Americans in Haiti had ever voiced such anti-American views.

CIA also informed Timmons about the inordinate amount of time de Mohrenschildt was spending with Galicki. CIA described Galicki as the only "Soviet bloc official stationed in Haiti, and a channel of instructions to the local Communist parties."

Having been presented with a bottle containing a black liquid that had seeped from the ground at a location outside Port-au-Prince – without any drilling needed – Mohamed Fayed flew three British oil experts to Haiti. Their assignment was to assess the possibility of refining the country's oil deposits. In the company of Fayed and his bodyguard Gaillard, the group drove out of Port-au-Prince. Every ten miles they were stopped by *Tontons Macoutes,* "in rags but carrying machine guns."

The "oil" turned out to be the residue of low-grade molasses sitting at the bottom of an old bonfire site on a French sugar plantation. The experts informed Fayed that a full seismic study of Haiti to determine whether there was oil present would take seven years and cost $250 million. And that, for the moment, was that, although speculation about Haiti's oil reserves, particularly its off-shore capability, would continue into the next century.

As for Mohamed Fayed, when he wasn't scheming, he courted two women. One was de Mohrenschildt's beautiful, blonde and married daughter, Alexandra. The other was Duvalier's daughter, Marie-Denise. Rumors circulated that Fayed and Marie-Denise were soon to be married. Every day, Fayed had flowers delivered to the National Palace, even when he was traveling outside the country.

Fayed was a domineering man, Alexandra discovered. He chastised her for "lateness," and expressed his irritation when at a nightclub they frequented she danced with another man. A CIA informant summed it up: their fling reflected no more than "beautiful married woman attracted to available wealthy handsome male." Alexandra never trusted Fayed, and the dalliance soon evaporated.

De Mohrenschildt knew that Fayed had stolen some of his maps of Haiti's oil reserves, maps that were not his to begin with. He didn't like Fayed, although all de Mohrenschildt would say publicly was that he was "withholding judgment with respect to the Egyptian." Together they frequented the local nightclubs, both drinking "cognac straight." De Mohrenschildt's association with Fayed was "professionally necessary but dangerous," CIA concluded. They watched the two men closely.

Fayed began to move money from his account at the Royal Bank of Canada and send it out of Haiti.

In late November 1964, CIA Counter Intelligence followed Fayed as he traveled to Europe and the Middle East, expanding the surveillance of Fayed that the Agency had established in Haiti. The Chief of the Special Projects Group reported to the Western Hemisphere Chief that Mohamed was "negotiating an arms deal with President Duvalier." Fayed had "connections with Fidel Castro, and in the past was involved with Trujillo."

On December 1, 1964 CIA inserted a document into George de Mohrenschildt's "201 file." It read, "in contact with Muhammad Fa'Id [sic]." It was accompanied by Fayed's own "201" number.

CIA opened thousands of "201," or "personality files." The subject could be anyone in whom there was sufficient intelligence interest. Influential critics of the Agency immediately earned "201 files." The process was handled by the Record Integration Division (R.I.D.), created in 1952.

If you were mentioned on five documents, someone could open a "201" on you, although, on occasion, a single, telling document would suffice. People in the field filled out an "831," a file-opening request, attaching the relevant documents on the subject. The Record Integration Division itself did not operate as an independent entity, and did not open 201s unless they were requested by another component, such as the Soviet Russia Division. R.I.D. could not open 201s on their own volition; they had to receive requests, either from Headquarters or from the field.

CIA often opened 201 files on "persons of interest" to them as well as on their own employees, assets and contacts. To be the subject of a 201 file did not mean that you worked for the Agency; Jim Garrison, the New Orleans district attorney, and an Agency adversary, had a 201 file, as did Clay Shaw, a man who worked for CIA and whom Garrison indicted for conspiring to murder President Kennedy. It was also possible to be the subject of two 201 files – an "overt" and a "covert" one.

CIA tracked Mohamed Fayed to the Waldorf Astoria Hotel in New York, noting that he was maintaining "contact with a certain George de Mohrenschildt, apparently of Texas," a disingenuous entry given how well CIA knew George de Mohrenschildt. De Mohrenschildt is described as having been "mentioned in the Warren Commission Report."

Fayed's deals with Duvalier were now of interest to: the Chief of the Western Hemisphere Division; the Deputy Director for Plans (Helms); and J. Edgar Hoover. Helms discovered that "Muhammed" Fayed had earlier been an "Ops Contact" for CIA, a fact revealed on a marginalia stamp affixed to a message from Helms to Hoover.

("Marginalia stamps" were informal comments placed on a document by either the sender or the recipient.) Just as CIA had apparently used, distrusted and discarded Fayed, so it would with many of its assets from George de Mohrenschildt to Manuel Noriega and Saddam Hussein. As a CIA asset, Saddam was deployed first in 1959, and then, successfully, on February 8, 1963, in the assassination of Prime Minister Abdul al-Karim Qasim; later Saddam would become an enemy to be demonized.

Further intelligence about Fayed arrived at the clandestine services through "a friendly Western service," obviously Britain's MI6. The British had tracked Fayed in Haiti and learned that he had become a naturalized Haitian citizen in November 1964, although he had not lived in Haiti for the ten years required for citizenship. Fayed was now carrying a Haitian diplomatic passport.

At the close of 1964, the Port-au-Prince shipping agents were in an uproar over Fayed's having taken over their business. International shippers threatened to boycott Haiti if Fayed remained the exclusive agent. Their loss of revenue would be substantial because Fayed had exclusive rights. Some of these agents were likely to go out of business.

Local shippers promised they would make money for Haiti, as they had in the past, whereas Fayed was unreliable and likely to disappear. They sweetened the deal for Duvalier by offering to charge a further tax on shipping arrangements, money that would wind up in his pocket – or in Swiss bank accounts.

U.S. Ambassador Timmons was dubious about the chances for success of the shipping agents in their efforts against Fayed. Timmons needn't have worried. CIA joined the effort to separate Duvalier from Fayed, enlisting one of its most favored allies, W.R. Grace & Co., long a firm providing CIA with covers for its people.

W.R. Grace sent a representative to "get [a] first-hand view of the situation." An emergency meeting of the local shipping companies was scheduled for early January 1965.

At this moment, Duvalier himself decided to test his new best friend, Fayed. Duvalier told Fayed he urgently needed $30,000 in cash. Fayed turned him down, either because he didn't have the cash, or because he surmised that his days in Haiti were numbered. At once Duvalier removed Gaillard from duty as Fayed's bodyguard. This was a threat to Fayed's life if ever there was one. Duvalier's meaning was unmistakable.

Mohamed Fayed took the hint and hopped the next plane out of Port-au-Prince. The Port Authority found itself short of money, sufficient for Duvalier to appoint a three-person commission of inquiry, headed by Paul Isaac, an accountant in Haiti's Department of Justice. When Duvalier discovered that Fayed had embezzled $153,440 from Haiti's Port Authority, he was so angry that he deported the British manager of the Royal Bank of Canada, although the manager had taken no part in Fayed's scam.

Mohamed Fayed today, as canny as the day he sat behind his dark glasses at George de Mohrenschildt's dinner table, is a prosperous, dignified man, still handsome and self-possessed if now in early old age. Having owned London's flagship department store, Harrods, for twenty-five years, in 2010 Fayed sold it to the Sovereign Wealth Fund of the emirate of Qatar for one and a half billion pounds, of which six hundred twenty five million pounds would go to satisfying bank debts.

Among Al Fayed's holdings remained a football team, Fulham, F. C. Fayed was desperate to be accepted by the British establishment, but they always held him at arm's length. At one time he purchased a "Royal Warrant" on Harrods, for which he paid a good deal of money to the Royal Family so that he could use the Royal Coat of Arms on his stationery..

In 2011, Fayed financed, to the tune of four million dollars, a documentary suggesting that the death of his son Dodi al Fayed, in the company of Princess Diana, was not the result of an accident. There had been a cover-up, and Fayed was willing to pay to uncover the truth, which was an "unlawful killing." His son's death had not been an "accident."

Directed by actor Keith Allen, the documentary, *Unlawful Killing*, suggests that the driver of the white Fiat Uno, seen speeding away from the scene of the crash, had ties to MI6. At the inquest into Diana's death, the car had been identified only as a "following [vehicle]" not connected to the paparazzi.

Premiered at Cannes, *Unlawful Killing* was at once banned in Britain – unless eighty-seven cuts were made. The uproar over this film, in and of itself, suggests that it contains more truth than the British establishment was willing to acknowledge.

In August 1965, with Mohamed Fayed gone forever from Haiti, Clémard Joseph Charles was still in Duvalier's good graces. Charles assumed the concession for the development of the Port-au-Prince wharf. In search of an American company for backing, he chose W.C. Langley, brokers, of 115 Broadway, New York City. Clémard's U.S. connections remained intact.

One day in 1965, Clémard Joseph Charles asked Joe Dryer, back in Haiti, regarding de Mohrenschildt: "Should I make him a director of my bank?"

Dryer was a man who didn't say "no" without a reason. He was not going to repeat what Jacqueline Lancelot had said, which was that de Mohrenschildt was "slimy."

"I'm not comfortable," Dryer said, "because I don't know who he is." He still didn't know exactly for whom de Mohrenschildt worked, but he was certain that the man was a manipulator.

Clémard had invited Dryer to be a director of his bank. Dryer had said, in effect, thank you, but no thank you. He did not want to be involved in politics in Haiti, and he knew that Clémard had his eye on the presidency. Dryer was aware, too, that Clémard Joseph Charles had an agenda: he wanted to have white people on his board, and foreigners who were well respected.

In March 1964, FBI's Sam Papich, the Bureau's long-time liaison with CIA, had provided the Agency with the FBI's fact sheet on "Baron George de Mohrenschildt, George Von Mohrenschildt." The document describes George's brother Dimitri as being close to Allen Dulles, now officially *former* Director of Central Intelligence, and Warren Commission member. The Haiti narrative reveals considerable inter-agency collaboration. Hoover may have been testy with CIA officers, but the FBI and CIA worked harmoniously on any number of occasions.

Years earlier, a 1948 memo from Frank Wisner to Hoover had declared that the FBI would be subservient to CIA in any number of areas, making clear there would be as much cooperation between CIA and FBI as there was rivalry. Now, in Haiti, CIA requested that the FBI investigate the activities of Sidney Schine and Henry Klepak. CIA would "appreciate receiving any information which your Bureau may receive on their activities." This was just the beginning of CIA-FBI collaboration as CIA sought to unravel the activities of George de Mohrenschildt and Clémard Joseph Charles in Haiti.

CIA was so uneasy with George de Mohrenschildt, and what he might say about the Kennedy assassination and J. Walton Moore's role in sending him to befriend Oswald, that they had begun to open every piece of de Mohrenschildt's mail. Noting the name and address of each correspondent, CIA then requested that the FBI investigate every one of them. This project was supervised by Counter Intelligence chief James Angleton, reporting to the Deputy Director for Plans.

Assisting Angleton in this obsessive (and illegal) spying on de Mohrenschildt was John M. Whitten (CIA pseudonym "John Scelso"). Whitten remained the Chief of Western Hemisphere/2. He worked closely with Angleton's assistant, Jane Roman, on the de Mohrenschildt surveillance.

In handing over the mail, CIA station chief Joseph G. Benson reported directly either to Whitten or to the chief of WH/4, the Western Hemisphere division that encompassed Cuba. (The different numerical sections of "WH" denoted the geographical area for which each was responsible within the structure of CIA's Western Hemisphere division.)

It was John Whitten who sent the names of the people who corresponded with de Mohrenschildt to the FBI for file checks. Through Sam Papich, Hoover demanded a separate file check sheet for each name. Whitten obliged, beginning with twenty-six names.

Angleton trained a counter intelligence officer named "Leoussis" in "flaps and seals and appropriate equipment," which CIA pouched down to Port-au-Prince. De Mohrenschildt's mail was to be opened, the instructions said, but the tampering must never be attributable to

U.S. officials. If anyone noticed that the mail had been opened, CIA was to blame the local post office.

In April 1965, Angleton himself sent the FBI a 29-page memorandum listing de Mohrenschildt's correspondents. He requested "any possible derogatory information available" on any of the names, in addition to those who had already been investigated. It was rare for Angleton to have signed off personally on so long and revealing a document, but he did so in this case.

Angleton explained to the FBI that George and Jeanne de Mohrenschildt had "been of interest to your Bureau and to the President's Commission on the Assassination of President Kennedy." Another reference read: "De Mohrenschildt connected Lee Harvey Oswald and accordingly of extreme interest."

Many of the names, Angleton writes, "have intelligence connections, whether US or foreign." Sometimes they had, as CIA liked to put it, connections with "a predecessor organization of this Agency." That was OSS. Under Angleton's signature on this long document is the line: CSCI-316/01306-65. CSCI stood for "Clandestine Services Current Information/Intelligence."

True to his character, Angleton went too far. He said, if anyone should ask, they were to be told that the monitoring of de Mohrenschildt's correspondents was being done at the request of Hoover himself. CIA's explanation for the surveillance of de Mohrenschildt was "De Mohrenschildt connected Lee Harvey Oswald and accordingly of extreme interest KUBARK [CIA] and ODENVY [FBI]."

Hoover was not amused at Angleton's suggestion that the FBI was the instigator of the surveillance of de Mohrenschildt and his correspondents in Haiti. It still rankled that de Mohrenschildt had lied about his own

CIA case officer, J. Walton Moore, calling him an FBI agent! Still, the FBI cooperated.

Each of de Mohrenschildt's correspondents was investigated as to date of birth, nationality, business interests, military records – and whether they had an intelligence history. Among them was Marcus Joseph Brandel, on whom CIA had opened a 201 file. Brandel "was either in British or Dutch intelligence." Having served in the Dutch military, he became a director of the Dutch electronics firm, Phillips NV. Now he was living quietly in Neuilly-sur-Seine, outside Paris.

There was no probable cause for Brandel's rights being violated and his being subjected to an FBI investigation, apart from his having written a letter to George de Mohrenschildt. Brandel had entered de Mohrenschildt's sphere purely because he was the husband of de Mohrenschildt's first wife, Dorothy Pierson. But CIA observed no strictures with regard to the privacy of anyone, then or later.

Another of de Mohrenschildt's Haiti correspondents was Fedor A. Garanin, who had been a member of the "Soviet State Security Service" since the mid-1940s, Richard Helms calculated. CIA suspected Garanin, now attached to the Soviet Embassy in Washington, D.C., of having been an agent of Stalin's OGPU (Joint State Political-cal Directorate), and later of the KGB. Garanin had been posted to Cuba in 1943, which was the year U.S. intelligence began to track him. He became a Second Secretary of the Soviet Legation in Havana.

After World War II, Garanin served in the United States, Hungary and Finland. In 1953, an American exchange professor in Helsinki would describe Garanin's efforts "to cultivate & recruit him as an agent." Still, CIA had to conclude that Garanin's contact with de Mohren-schildt was "one-time and casual."

On October 1, 1964, Colonel Lawrence Orlov, J. Walton Moore's handball partner, wrote to de Mohrenschildt. It had been in Orlov's company that de Mohrenschildt had visited Oswald for the first time. This correspondent at least was no stranger to CIA.

After Hoover's protests, in October 1964 CIA resumed its surveillance of de Mohrenschildt on some occasions with "no checking with ODENVY." Other figures in CIA Counter Intelligence became involved in CIA's de Mohrenschildt-Haiti spying operation. Paul Hartman, a Riga-born officer, conferred with Raymond Rocca, head of Counter Intelligence's Research & Analysis division. Was de Mohrenschildt linked to any "subversive or extremist organization?" Hartman asked.

De Mohrenschildt's mail yielded no smoking guns. A gossipy letter from Sam Ballen was all about Marina Oswald who "feels all men want to go to bed with her." Marina, Ballen wrote, felt that Jeanne de Mohrenschildt was jealous of her because "George has carnal feelings for Marina."

In fact, it was Marina who apparently nurtured carnal feelings for de Mohrenschildt. In March 1964, she asked her friend Mrs. Katherine Ford if she thought George de Mohrenschildt was a "normal person." Ford interpreted the question to mean that Marina was sexually attracted to George.

"I've never heard how George de Mohrenschildt was in bed," Mrs. Ford said.

Pierre Freyss, that French intelligence officer for whom de Mohrenschildt had worked in the late 1930s or early 1940s in New York, and who had been best man at de Mohrenschildt's wedding to Wynne Sharples, wrote a letter to de Mohrenschildt. ODENVY reported that Freyss was "French intel," who had been recruited by OSS, but had been dropped following his November 1943 training for "talking."

This was enough for JMWAVE, the CIA station in Miami, to request that the CIA chief of station in Port-au-Prince "attempt open" mail from Schumacher, that purveyor of luxury fabrics for whom Pierre Freyss still worked. Freyss remained of importance in de Mohrenschildt's history as an officer of the intelligence services of another country who had been able easily to recruit de Mohrenschildt. In the intervening years, might not other countries also have enlisted this man whose history reveals him to have been for sale to any number of bidders?

F. Schumacher & Co., a family owned company founded in 1889, remained a leading purveyor of luxury textiles, hand-printed wall papers and decorative fabrics. Their textiles would adorn the White House, the Chambers of the United States Supreme Court and the Metropolitan Opera House at Lincoln Center in New York City. One line of fabrics had been designed by Frank Lloyd Wright. A man of consummate good taste, de Mohrenschildt had to have felt at home among Schumacher fabrics.

In November 1964, a postcard arrived addressed to de Mohrenschildt from someone named Erik E. Lehmann. It was postmarked "Ceylon." It contained the line: "Has there been any progress in our matters?" This, the FBI could not decipher.

Other letters were equally impenetrable. In January 1965, a letter arrived from a Mexican address that was connected with Oswald. CIA headquarters cabled its

Mexico City station for traces, identities. They were going to considerable trouble for meager results.

A letter arrived in early February from a female "Polish citizen." Who was this woman? Both CIA's Western
Hemisphere Division and the FBI sought her identity.

When a letter arrived with the return address of a
Swiss post office box, John Whitten again enlisted Paul
Hartman, who then contacted the CIA station in Switzerland to check on the identity of that box holder. It turned
out to belong to Bozo Dabinovic, the Yugoslav who had
provided Mohamed Fayed with his introduction to Duvalier. James Angleton did his homework on Dabinovic:

> Bozo was formerly employed by the *Société*
> *Générale de Surveillance, S.A.*, where his em-
> ployment was terminated because he allegedly
> engaged in undescribed unethical practices. Fol-
> lowing this termination, he entered into business
> for himself. He has been described as a highly
> capable, unscrupulous operator who would be
> more successful if he took few[er] changes [sic].

Early in 1965, CIA informed the FBI that de Mohrenschildt was known to have had "connections with two foreign intelligence services." He consorted with KGB operatives like Garanin and he had worked for the French. There
was also that old rumor that he had been with British intelligence. De Mohrenschildt remained "of extreme interest" to
the Federal Bureau of Investigation," Whitten reminded the
FBI, because he had been "an acquaintance of Lee Harvey
Oswald, the accused assassin of President John F. Kennedy."

An interesting letter came in February 1965 from a
"former Kubarker," as CIA put it. This was Nicholas M.

Anikeeff, who had been with the Soviet Russia division. Counter Intelligence released the names of most of de Mohrenschildt's Haiti correspondents, but not that of its own former officer in the Agency's Soviet Russia division.

The FBI was not requested to do a file check on this particular de Mohrenschildt correspondent, Anikeeff, about whose career CIA knew more than anyone else. Anikeeff had left the Agency only recently, either in 1963 or 1964, and abruptly, reasons unknown; he had not served his full twenty years. That de Mohrenschildt had people writing to him who had been highly ranked CIA officers was best kept quiet.

The Port-au-Prince station chief was now ordered to "attempt effect entry of all letters to and from this individual." The order was signed by Radford Herbert, Raymond Rocca and John Whitten.

"In view of fact many agencies have interest in Iden," Whitten writes – the word 'Iden' referring to the "identity" of the subject of the document, de Mohrenschildt – "the making of such a ruling applicable to you is believed consistent with ODYOKE [U.S. government] interests." The heavy surveillance of de Mohrenschildt was explained as KUBARK [CIA] continuing "to discharge its responsibilities to ODYOKE."

"Request you not repeat not mention proposed operational use of EVMINCE [Paul Johnson] to non-Kubark personnel," Whitten added. Johnson had left CIA, rendering him a dangerous, suspicious figure.

Early in 1965, attempting to lure Hoover into its net, CIA asked "if the Bureau was interested in having CIA conduct any investigation." Hoover stepped back from his previous belligerence. "If the Agency developed or received any information of obvious interest to the Bureau, we would like to be informed," the FBI said.

Even when Galicki was absent from Port-au-Prince, de Mohrenschildt frequented his office. One day a CIA informant spotted de Mohrenschildt chatting with Galicki's replacement, Casimir Salacinski. A short, fat, graying American was also present. CIA had no idea who he was, an irritating development.

Another figure of ambiguous loyalties who bedeviled CIA in Port-au-Prince was a former Pan American Airways employee named Jean K. Saurel, now director of the Haitian Tourist Bureau in New York City. CIA wondered if Saurel was "an agent of President Duvalier," communicating with the Americans on Duvalier's behalf. Late in November 1963, Saurel had provided a CIA asset with inaccurate information about de Mohrenschildt – that he was "of Polish descent or citizenship."

Saurel had also "demanded and received things from members of the *Tontons Macoutes*." A member of the *Tontons Macoutes* had rescued him when he was prevented one day from leaving the palace grounds. CIA suspected that Saurel might even himself be a member of the *Tontons Macoutes*, a suspicion sufficient for Paul Hartman to tell J. Edgar Hoover what he knew about Saurel. More than in most places, in Haiti you never knew who was working for whom. Clémard Joseph Charles himself would be mentioned in a CIA document as a member of the *Tontons Macoutes.*

In their compulsive talk of how they had known Oswald and had testified before the Warren Commission, the de Mohrenschildts did not aid their cause. At a cocktail buffet, Jeanne complained to U.S. Embassy official V.E. Blacque that "personal data" about herself and her husband had been published in the Warren Report, including their multiple divorces. She claimed they had been promised that such personal information would not be made public.

In fact, Hoover said, he did try to protect "considerable information of a highly personal nature which was furnished to our Agents during the investigation" of Michael and Ruth Paine and George and Jeanne de Mohrenschildt. It was Warren Commission lawyer J. Lee Rankin who insisted on making everything public.

The Warren Report was not complete, Mrs. de Mohrenschildt said. Then she attacked the Report's conclusion. "A sinister plot could have triggered the assassination," she said, given that Oswald held no personal grudge against the president. Oswald's anger was directed entirely towards Governor John Connally. And hadn't Oswald in Dealey Plaza been "watching to his right," focusing on another shooter?

With his *sang froid* intact, at the U.S. Embassy, V. Blacque reported to Ambassador Timmons that tears had sprung to Jeanne de Mohrenschildt's eyes as she invoked the "great love" she had felt for President Kennedy.

George de Mohrenschildt chafed under the social restrictions imposed on him by the American ambassador. He resented been "slighted" and barred from contact with his old Embassy acquaintances. It was all based on a "personal incident," he said, referring to Jeanne having slapped the receptionist. He hoped that the incident did not damage his reputation. That incident had occurred in December 1964, two months earlier.

Then another side of de Mohrenschildt surfaced. If he continued to be barred from contact or association with Embassy personnel, he said, he "would have to take drastic measures." He could be a bully, threatening, and unpleasant, as his third ex-wife Dr. Wynne Sharples had told the

223

Civil Service Commission. No "drastic measures" were taken by de Mohrenschildt, however. It was all bluff.

George de Mohrenschildt was not entirely idle in Haiti. February 1, 1965 found him near Postel, exploring a source for fresh water in southern Haiti. It was in that area that he had discovered that deposit of bauxite that would turn out to contain fourteen million tons. It was a discovery, Paul Johnson/EVMINCE-1 had believed, that "could have a substantial influence on the economy of the country." Of course, the Reynolds Mining Corporation was already mining bauxite in Haiti, rendering de Mohrenschildt's discovery less important.

CIA wondered whether de Mohrenschildt would reveal his bauxite discovery before he was assured of his own percentage. He had "not told anyone else of his discovery," EVMINCE-1 informed his superiors. CIA had to be cautious. If news of de Mohrenschildt's discovery of bauxite were leaked, it would be traceable to CIA informant Paul Johnson, EVMINCE-1.

In a dispatch entitled "Possible Economic Standing of George de Mohrenschildt," CIA's Chester D. Dainold (a pseudonym for Desmond Fitzgerald) urged that CIA be discreet so as to keep EVMINCE-1 "perfectly clean." EVMINCE-1 had "expressed his intense dislike of men he cannot completely trust and a slip at this time would affect the presently good operational relationship with him." In Haiti, as elsewhere, a reliable operative was hard to find.

One night in February 1965 EVMINCE-1 was pawing through Galicki's garbage when he came upon "torn up drafts of letters," including the draft of a letter to Clémard Joseph Charles indicating that de Mohrenschildt

Dr. François Duvalier, President for Life of Haiti: "The big man in the White House isn't going to be there much longer." (Getty Images).

Papa Doc and his son and successor, Jean-Claude (Baby Doc), who offered the beleaguered people of Haiti more of the same.

George de Mohrenschildt with his fourth wife Jeanne: " I have never talked with anyone in the FBI before today about Lee Harvey Oswald, to the best of my memory." (Courtesy of Bruce Adamson).

Clemard Joseph Charles at center: "We're going to bring down Papa Doc." At the right is the secretary CIA planted on Charles. (Courtesy of Joseph F. Dryer Jr.).

Clémard Joseph Charles
&
Joseph F. Dryer,
Président
Thomas Preston,
Ingénieur en Chef
&
Peter D. Rowntree,
Agent
de la
North Atlantic Kenaf Corporation

ont le plaisir de vous inviter à une demonstration d'un Décortiqueur
aliments à la main pour ... les ... petites

Joseph F. Dryer Jr. and Clemard Joseph Charles go into the Kenaf business together in Haiti. (Courtesy of Joseph F. Dryer Jr.).

le Samedi 27 Juin en cours, à 9:00 heures du matin.

Port-au-Prince, le 20 Juin 1959

George H.W. Bush: Under LPDICTUM, Bush searched for "people who could be targeted for recruitment by the Agency as business assets." (Courtesy of Bruce Adamson).

Joseph F. Dryer, Jr.: "Dryer had to stage an operation worthy of a Graham Greene "entertainment." (Courtesy of Joseph F. Dryer, Jr.).

From left to right: Allen Dulles, General Edward Lansdale, General Charles Cabell and General Nathan F. Twining. Lansdale's promotion to General was driven by Allen Dulles.

Joseph F. Dryer, Jr.: "What is a Marine doing here? You're very close to the Marines." (Courtesy of Joseph F. Dryer, Jr.).

Air Force Colonel Howard Burris had been involved in CIA's 1953 coup against Iranian president Mohammed Mossadegh.

Jacqueline Lancelot at the age of eighteen, the only photograph she had of herself: "If I were you, I would not be talking to that person." (Courtesy of Joseph F. Dryer Jr.).

Joseph F. Dryer, Jr. with Aubelin Jolicoeur at the Hotel Oloffson: "*Bonsoir cheri*. Mr. Haiti at your service!" (Courtesy of Joseph F. Dryer, Jr.).

Le Picardie restaurant in Pétionville: Outside you sat under the stars, and you could hear meringue music or Vodou drums beating in the background.

At *Le Picardie*: Jacqueline Lancelot is at the extreme right, partially obscured. The name "Mata Hari" comes to mind.

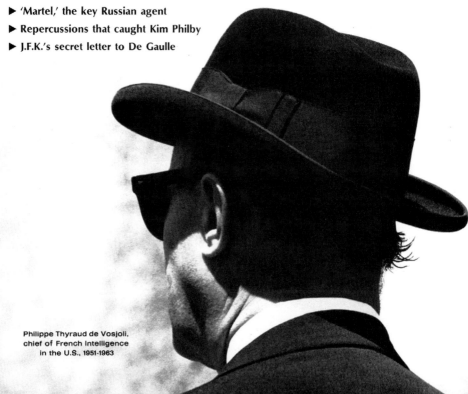

LIFE

THE
FRENCH
SPY SCANDAL

The former chief of French Intelligence in the U.S. reveals the fantastic story of Soviet espionage that penetrated De Gaulle's official family

▶ 'Martel,' the key Russian agent
▶ Repercussions that caught Kim Philby
▶ J.F.K.'s secret letter to De Gaulle

Philippe Thyraud de Vosjoli,
chief of French Intelligence
in the U.S., 1951-1963

Philippe Thyraud de Vosjoli graces the cover of Life magazine: "He's going to blow the lid on France." (Getty Images).

APRIL 26 · 1968 · 35¢

Isadore Irving Davidson: "Murchinson/Davidson interest in Haiti has been source of encouragement to Duvalier." (AP/Worldwide).

Rolando Masferrer Rojas in Cuba: "You have to fight for your principles." (Courtesy of Gordon Winslow).

Martin Xavier Casey: "Men in white jackets were sent by CIA to examine them."

George de Mohrenschildt teaching at Bishop College which, Gaeton Fonzi discovered, had "all along been funded by the CIA."

Joseph F. Dryer, Jr. with business associates.
(Courtesy of Joseph F. Dryer, Jr.).

Isadore Irving Davidson in New Orleans during the Brilab trial: "If I get knocked out of the box, it's going to hurt this country." (AP/Worldwide).

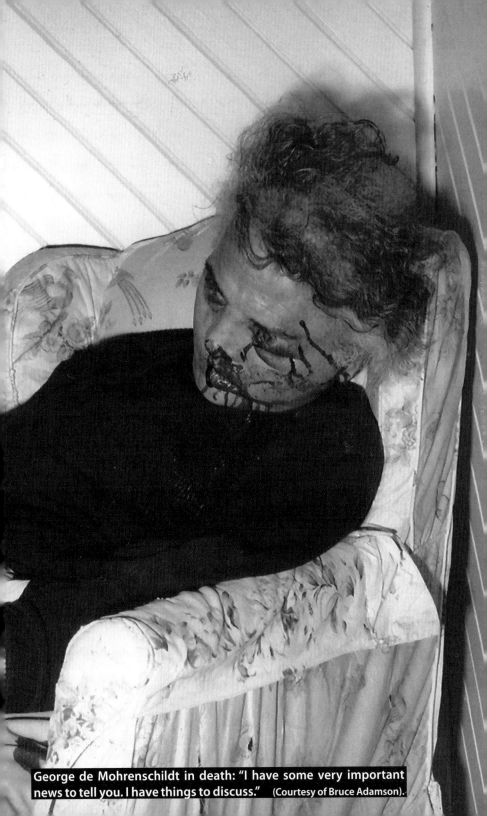

George de Mohrenschildt in death: "I have some very important news to tell you. I have things to discuss." (Courtesy of Bruce Adamson).

Jean-Claude (Baby Doc) returned to Haiti in 2011

Paul Rothermel: Everyone's favorite uncle

W. Herbert Hunt and Nelson Bunker Hunt:
Philip Hirschkop: "The government may have been trying to cover up the infiltration of the Hunt Oil Company by the Central Intelligence Agency."

N B HUNT

H. L. Hunt: "I was simply trying to help Lyndon."

had agreed to the sale to Galicki of sixty tons of grades "x" and "y" sisal. Had de Mohrenschildt become an agent of the Polish government? For whom de Mohrenschildt was actually working perplexed everyone who made his acquaintance in Haiti, from Joe Dryer to CIA itself. That he served more than one master seemed a distinct possibility, given his chequered history.

It was a given that CIA monitored all significant business transactions in Haiti. News of the sisal sale was passed orally to the FBI on February 26, 1965. The information moved from John Whitten to Jane Roman and then to Sam Papich. It included the detail that one day around this time Clémard Joseph Charles had been spotted in Galicki's offices. In March, Desmond Fitzgerald sent that dispatch to the chief of station in Port-au-Prince inquiring as to de Mohrenschildt's finances.

In May, CIA sent the FBI a report on its surveillance of de Mohrenschildt's mail, as if the entire operation had originated with the Bureau. This report is obviously an example of CIA papering the written record. Counter Intelligence writes that they had queried the FBI and had been informed that the FBI had "no further interest" in de Mohrenschildt. In fact, the FBI never had any motive for investigating de Mohrenschildt in Haiti in the first place. It had all been a CIA effort.

On November 22, 1965, CIA, from Headquarters, thanked formally its Port-au-Prince station for its efforts in intercepting and monitoring de Mohrenschildt's mail. The illegal surveillance now ceased.

At the close of 1965, George de Mohrenschildt decided to abandon his vanishing prospects in Haiti. CIA and the Army had not yet facilitated the overthrow of Papa

Doc. Clémard Joseph Charles seemed no closer to the presidency of Haiti than he had been in 1963.

De Mohrenschildt thought he might leave Haiti in February or March 1966, after extracting from the government at least $100,000 for his services. In lieu of payment, he declared himself willing to accept Haitian real estate: property on the coast with tourist or commercial potential.

CIA had not quite let George de Mohrenschildt out of its sights, however. They noted in late December 1965, as they reported on his planned departure from Haiti, that he had added a suspected Soviet agent named Nicolas Roude to his entourage.

SEVEN

The Paramilitary Game

"We have the green light from the CIA."
Rolando Masferrer Rojas

"There will be no Cuba and no Bay of Pigs here."
Doctor Magiot in Graham Greene's *The Comedians*.

I n the spring of 1965, CIA sponsored a cornucopia
of invasions of Haiti. If Joe Dryer's abandonment of
his kenaf business hadn't been reason enough, the
Valentine-Fayed affair had persuaded the Agency that
American business was not secure under Papa Doc. Haiti
had been overrun by weapons dealers and various unsa-
voury characters, many of whom, as CIA noted, graced
George de Mohrenschildt's dinner table. Behind the
scenes lurked drug smuggling, with Haiti as a station in
a triangular smuggling operation that brought heroin to
the U.S. Once more CIA assumed the uneasy role of providing resources for the downfall of Papa Doc without
implicating ODYOKE, the U.S. Government.

Records reveal that in these paramilitary invasions,
which seem designed more to destabilize Duvalier's
government than actually to overthrow it, the U.S. was
unanimously on board. Lyndon Johnson's national security adviser McGeorge Bundy arranged that the State

Department and CIA "coordinate on investigating alternate sources of political power in Haiti."

The President's "303 Covert Action Committee" now authorized CIA to make "an intensive survey of Haitian individuals of influence, both inside and outside the country," who would best serve "U.S. interests." Candidates would be assessed according to their "responsiveness to U.S. direction." Only a national leader under the domination of the U.S. and close to CIA was acceptable to rule over what Graham Greene had termed in his novel *The Comedians*, the "nightmare Republic."

By June 1965, the Joint Chiefs had compiled a list of four "potentially useful" Haitian officers; the military was again serving CIA's policy. Desmond Fitzgerald "took these under advisement." One officer was already known to CIA, having proven himself to be "of some use in a covert role on another continent." The name "Clémard Joseph Charles" does not appear on these declassified lists.

The minutes of the June 10, 1965 meeting of the 303 Committee include a section entitled "Haiti – The Threat and Possible Pre-Emptive Measures," foreshadowing the far more costly pre-emptive wars of the twenty-first century.

The "303 Committee" was a direct descendant of the 5412 Committee, a vehicle for the authorization of covert action, chaired by Richard Nixon during the Eisenhower administration. Under discussion were the types of covert actions outlined in George Kennan's National Security directive 10/2, which allowed CIA to engage in all manner of covert actions ranging from what the Agency termed "black" propaganda and sabotage to murder.

The 5412 Committee became the "Special Group" until 1964, when the name changed to the "303 Committee." At its meetings, the Director of Central Intelligence sat alongside the Assistant to the President for National Security Affairs, the Deputy Secretary of Defense, and the Deputy Under-Secretary of State for Political Affairs. CIA had emerged as a power in its own right, free of accountability and boasting of no electoral mandate.

Cautious, CIA decided that the training of a force of Haitian exiles should take place only in the Dominican Republic. Training Haitian exiles anywhere else "would create a mechanism which was too noisy, too transparent, and too anxious to be used." With a blank check from the executive branch of the government, CIA began to explore the Haitian exile communities in the Dominican Republic for recruits.

Ambassador Timmons was assigned to "get in touch with General Gérard Constant, Chief of Staff of the Haitian Army." Constant was to be advised that in the event of Duvalier's death, his own safety would be guaranteed if he could maintain civil order. The return of Haitian civilian leaders from exile would follow; the choice of who would actually assume power would be negotiated with Constant "at the critical time."

By 1965, as a result of Duvalier's terrorism, Haiti had become a powder keg. "Unacceptable elements" had crept into the inner circles of Duvalier's government where "Communist sympathizers" were tolerated. CIA funded Haitian exiles as a means of "keeping their fingers on the exiles' pulse."

The U.S. had become fearful of unrest in Haiti and of the prospect of another Cuba dawning in the Caribbean. In October, Ambassador Timmons proposed that, under the auspices of AID, through the front of a university or private foundation, the U.S. should create an "effective National Health Service for Haiti."

In December 1965, I.I. Davidson had an idea for how the U.S. might get rid of its client Duvalier. If CIA desired to create an incident, which would form the basis for the United States sending troops in Haiti, all the Agency had to do was arrange the shooting of a couple of United States Army men at a bar on the border between Haiti and the Dominican Republic. The men would be in civilian clothes, simply taking advantage of Haitian "recreation spots." The economic situation in Haiti was ripe for just such an incident, I.I. Davidson suggested to the FBI.

As of the New Year 1966, Duvalier lived on. CIA decided to rely "upon Haitians who remain in Haiti" to construct a "stable" successor government. CIA now accepted that "Duvalier's overthrow would probably have to be an inside job." Minor incursions into Haiti by dissidents based in the north came and went. A CIA-authored National Intelligence Estimate of October 1966 reflected the view that "it might prove more difficult to get a force out than to put it in, as was the case in 1915." That CIA was instrumental in the construction of U.S. foreign policy was a given.

In April 1966, Clémard Joseph Charles traveled to Italy and France. Stopping in New York, he registered at the Waldorf Astoria Hotel where his traveling companion telephoned CIA's Jim Balog. Charles had met with James Balog of CIA's New York field office in the spring of 1963; at the Park Sheraton Hotel they had spent four hours together, with Balog under Army intelligence cover.

Clémard continued to rely on CIA to become involved in the overthrow of Duvalier, and to support him, Charles, as Duvalier's successor. The fact that CIA never discouraged Charles in this ambition is reflected in his having current contact information for CIA in New York. That he was traveling on business for Papa Doc did not inhibit Charles from immediately contacting CIA – attaining the presidency of Haiti remained his first concern.

At CIA, a man named "Freund" took the call, claiming that "Captain Balog was seriously ill." Charles then grabbed the telephone and requested Balog's home telephone number. Freund provided what he called Balog's "registered pseudo minus any military title." If CIA was not ready to utilize Charles, it apparently was not yet willing to allow him out of its sights either. CIA still did not consider it in the Agency's interest to dismiss Charles, to pretend that they did not know him, as they would do, not long after, with George de Mohrenschildt.

Freund then turned to his superior, Anthony Czajkowski, for instructions on how to handle Charles. What should he say if Charles wanted to see Balog on his way home? Czajkowski remarked that Charles was eager for contact with "our captain."

CIA assets in New York were now instructed to contact "Captain Balog" when Charles returned from Europe. The memorandum describing Charles' call to Balog states: "there is no indication what Charles wants at this time." This, of course, was for the record. CIA well knew what Charles wanted, knew that Charles was traveling for Papa Doc, as he had been doing for years, and knew what was on his mind.

A routing and records sheet adds: "Important to our NYOR Office to affect contact with Captain Balog when Clémard returns from visit to Italy and France." The document describing the Waldorf call is titled: "Closed Case."

Yet it wasn't so. In retaining contact with Charles, as CIA did, the Agency was not yet relinquishing the possibility that they could utilize Charles in the unstable Haitian situation.

Charles was traveling to Europe on behalf of Papa Doc on a very particular mission. Papa Doc had instructed him to withdraw $3,000,000 from an account at the *Union des Banques Suisses,* a bank controlled by André Labbé of the French Mafia. According to Haitian historian Michel Soukar, part of this money was earmarked for the purchase of a house in Spain and to pay debts incurred by Duvalier's extravagant daughter, Marie-Denise. The source of the money was the heroin traffic. Under the guise of exporting coffee, Duvalier had been sending heroin to the United States.

Soukar writes that the arms and drug traffic emanating from Haiti in the 1960s was facilitated by Clémard Joseph Charles. Serving as an emissary for Papa Doc, Charles had met with Bill Bonanno and Joe Notaro, prominent figures in New York crime families. To these characters, Charles had conveyed the message that Duvalier "was very unhappy with the current neglect of the casinos" in Port-au-Prince.

Bonanno and his associates flew to Haiti where Duvalier offered them sole proprietorship of the casinos and slot machine business. They were authorized to handle the "coffee trade" that moved from Haiti through Venezuela, destined for the U.S. "Coffee," as noted, stood for heroin. The crime figures were displeased only when Duvalier placed phantom associates on the casino payroll.

Two flamboyant CIA-funded incursions into Haiti were organized in the late sixties. One was led by a Cuban exile, attorney and former member of the Cuban legislature named Rolando Masferrer Rojas. A figure steeped in militancy, Masferrer had assembled in Cuba a private army, two hundred strong, called *"Los Tigres."* (In Batista's Cuba many politicians surrounded themselves with a small army of bodyguards).

Masferrer was not to be underestimated. He was very intelligent and beholden to no one. He had fought in Spain on the Loyalist side, contending that "you have to fight for your principles." Wounded in the Spanish Civil War, he had lost part of his heel and would limp ever after. Masferrer had also been a member of the Communist Party in Cuba, although later he would denounce the Communists.

No Batistiano, Masferrer had hoped that Carlos Prío Soccarás would take the government back from Batista after Batista's 1952 coup. Prío had been elected president of Cuba in 1948. He was nicknamed *"El presidente cordial"* because he supported civil liberties and a strict interpretation of the Cuban constitution. His respectable history included involvement in the coup that deposed the tyrant Gerardo Machado in 1933; Prío was also a founder of the *"Partido Revolucionario Cubano Auténtico."*

Three months remained before the 1952 election, but Batista had no intention of waiting.

"Don't turn over power," Masferrer had urged Prío. But Prío suffered a failure of nerve. "I don't want any bloodshed," Prío said, and so Batista took power virtually unopposed.

On January 1, 1959, Masferrer and his brother Kiki had sailed on their yacht from Cuba to Key West with about twenty-four men aboard. Castro later claimed that Rolando had stolen $17,000,000. In fact, Masferrer had $26,000 in his pocket. The entire group had only $45,000 between them. Three months in jail was their welcome to the United States. Masferrer would remain in his country of exile for the rest of his life.

Masferrer, a strong, stocky, physically powerful man well acquainted with weaponry and guerrilla warfare, had first begun plans to invade Haiti in 1963. He was reluctant to violate United States laws, he said, or be stopped by United States authorities. To gain the approval of government officials, he made contact with I.I. Davidson. At the time, Masferrer was operating out of an office at 345 West 45th Street in New York City.

At a 1963 meeting at the Plaza Hotel, Masferrer and a group of followers discussed the possibility of obtaining financial assistance from Davidson, as well as possible United States approval through Davidson's contacts. Davidson had already promised to see what he could do. Seventy-five Cuban exiles attended the meeting. According to Davidson, he told Masferrer he would not attempt to solicit this approval for any paramilitary effort. He promised only that he would bring the information to the attention of the FBI.

It was all but impossible for either the FBI or the Justice Department to keep pace with I.I. Davidson, as Masferrer's plans were stalled. In September 1966, the FBI instituted a Registration Act investigation of Davidson at the request of the Justice Department. Among the topics under consideration was "the extent of his activities in securing information for President Duvalier."

Which side was I.I. Davidson on? All the Justice Department could do was refuse to give I.I. Davidson a waiver allowing him not to report on the activities of three of his informants – two Cubans and one Dominican. It was a measure of I.I. Davidson's importance that the letter from the Justice Department was signed by J.

Walter Yeagley, Assistant Attorney General, Internal Security Division.

It wasn't until late 1966 that Masferrer was able to assemble a paramilitary force to invade Haiti. Masferrer was pursuing his own agenda, not CIA's, although the Agency was willing to use him for its own purposes. Masferrer hoped to utilize Haiti as a base from which to wage war on Fidel Castro. Otherwise he had no particular interest in Haiti. His ambition was to be President of Cuba.

Meanwhile I.I. Davidson's informants in the Dominican Republic kept him apprised of a proposed invasion of Haiti through the Dominican Republic in August 1966 by Haitian and Cuban exiles. For his informants, Davidson had financed trips from New York and Washington to Miami. When this invasion of Haiti was stopped in Florida, Davidson took credit, arguing that this had been the result of intelligence provided by his informant.

The informant himself, whose name was Enrique A. García, told the Bureau that Davidson was working on behalf of President Joaquín Antonio Balaguer of the Dominican Republic and for Duvalier as well. Watching, the FBI pondered whether Davidson, since he was on Duvalier's payroll, was informing Papa Doc of these paramilitary efforts against him.

Although the Bureau used Davidson, they considered him "a rather unscrupulous person." They took note of Davidson's incorrect prediction back in February that should the U.S. Government not do something to assist Duvalier in getting out of Haiti, his government would collapse within nine weeks.

In a series of interviews with Masferrer in 1973, Gordon Winslow – now retired archivist and historian for the Clerk of Court, Miami-Dade County, Florida, and webmaster of Cuban-exile.com – learned about the origins of Masferrer's proposed invasion of Haiti. A U.S. Customs agent had egged Masferrer on by remarking that "with thirty good men anyone could take Haiti."

According to CIA documents from the early 1950s, Masferrer had been both a "covert" CIA asset and an "overt" one. In a November 1, 1967 Memorandum addressed to the Director of Central Intelligence, CIA General Counsel Lawrence Houston admitted that Masferrer's association with CIA began "in the late forties." Houston claims that Masferrer's relationship with CIA was "cut off completely in the early 1950s."

This was yet another CIA obfuscation, another CIA lie about the end date of an asset's service. Records reveal that well into the fifties, Masferrer was receiving money from CIA in $5,000 increments. He invested this in his own name as he siphoned off funds CIA believed it was contributing to his operations. It might be seen as embezzling, except that CIA itself operated entirely outside the rule of law. Masferrer was one among many figures CIA attempted to use, yet found they couldn't control.

For his 1966 paramilitary incursion into Haiti, Masferrer enlisted Father Jean-Baptiste Georges, who had fled from Haiti on February 1, 1963. The plan was that Father Georges would be the temporary President of a post-Duvalier Haiti. A *Santería* priestess was Masferrer's intermediary with Father Georges. Masferrer was unaware that she was a relative of one of his own men.

Others who signed on to the Masferrer operation were León Rojas, a Masferrer cousin; and Masferrer's nephew, Julio Hormilla. American soldiers of fortune who savored the adventure included a Philadelphian named Martin Xavier Casey, whom CIA had recruited in

1961 when Casey ran into an agent at an El Paso, Texas blood bank.

"We have the green light from CIA," Masferrer told the group.

Because Masferrer was not permitted legally to enter Miami at that moment – the result of an earlier brush with the law – the expedition was organized in New York where Masferrer entered into a pact of "mutual assistance" with Haitian General Léon Cantave. Cantave was "a man of great merit," Masferrer claimed.

With Cantave in power, "the Cuban exiles would have at their disposal a base of operations only forty miles from Oriente Province in Cuba." Invading Haiti and overthrowing Duvalier was but one step toward the ultimate plan: an invasion of Cuba from Haiti, and the removal of Fidel Castro.

As this joint Cuban-Haitian operation was being assembled, equipment for the invasion was stored at a farm in the U.S. run by Cuban exile and CIA asset Manuel Artime. A CIA media asset named Andrew St. George, hovering, sold the project as a documentary to CBS for $200,000. (CBS had long been close to CIA, with William Paley, its main man, a long-time CIA asset). While CIA was filming the training in the Everglades, the money disappeared.

Martin Xavier Casey later testified that there was active CIA involvement in the Masferrer enterprise from the start. The recruits were readying themselves for action when "men in white jackets" were sent by CIA to examine them. Five-page application forms had to be filled out, describing their medical status, and they were examined from the heart to the teeth.

The next time Casey encountered the "doctor" who had examined him, the man was with the FBI – a CIA man working under FBI cover. CIA was present "to help us if they could," Casey explained.

Buzzing around were CIA informants as well as members of Castro's G-2. One commander, Napoleón Vilaboa, had once worked for CIA, then for Castro in a plot to invade Panama, only to have been recruited by CIA again.

"Get rid of this guy!" CIA ordered Masferrer, referring to Vilaboa.

As always, CIA's institutional interests came first. Masferrer had approval "from this Agency," CIA admitted. Yet they didn't trust him. Lawrence Houston wrote to Assistant Attorney General J. Walter Yeagley, that CIA had been "well-informed on the plans of Masferrer and his cohorts and disseminated this information in the normal manner." One CIA informant was Masferrer's nephew, Julio Hormilla.

Another informant was the ubiquitous I.I. Davidson, who provided CIA with the most details: leadership, sources of funds, armaments and participants. CIA played what by now had become its customary duplicitous role – affecting distance, claiming ignorance and keeping its own motives and interests secret.

Late in the year 1966, Lee Harvey Oswald's cousin, Marilyn Murret, made plans to travel to Haiti and Santo Domingo for a "vacation." Frances G. Knight, director of the Passport Office in Washington, D.C., wrote to CIA's Deputy Director for Plans requesting "any information of a security nature" which may come to your attention concerning the individual (Murret) mentioned in the attached memoranda." That Knight should have consulted the head of CIA's clandestine services about Murrett suggests, at the very least, that

Oswald's cousin was a person of interest to CIA – three years after the Kennedy assassination.

On the night of January 2, 1967, in Marathon, Florida, in the Keys, the United States Customs Service arrested seventy-five people from the Masferrer group for violation of the Neutrality Act. Customs seized two boats, arms and ammunition. Participating in the arrests was Cesario Diosdado, a Bureau of Customs official on loan to CIA. Diosdado, Lawrence Houston would write, had "become so involved in working for us that for the past few years we have been reimbursing Customs for his salary and he has actually been under our direction."

CIA had an aversion to "loose talk" and it was just such loose talk about its endorsement of Masferrer's mission into Haiti that led to the Agency's scuttling it. Confused, the Justice Department asked CIA to advise them as to whether any of the people arrested – among them seventy-three "battle clad men" – had "ever been associated with CIA." CIA denied it. In fact, many had CIA connections, beginning, of course, with Masferrer himself.

CIA monitored the trial of the Masferrer operatives at the United States District Court in Miami. Charges were dropped for only one participant, the gunrunner Mitchell Livingston WerBell III, a CIA contract employee and former Batista security adviser. WerBell ran Parabellum, Inc., a CIA front for shipping arms out of the United States.

In his own defense, Masferrer claimed that his plot to invade Haiti had been approved by the U.S. government. CIA denied any relationship with him.

For a time, Lawrence Houston was worried. His denials of CIA involvement in the Masferrer operation were motivated by "the possibility of unfavorable publicity." He invoked that old chestnut, "compromise of sources and methods," which supposedly would be jeopardized if the Agency were forced to disprove Masferrer's charges in court. Houston knew that deep in the bowels of the CIA filing systems were security files for both its "Covert" (366 859) and "Overt" (352 772) relationships with Rolando Masferrer Rojas.

Houston was not confident that his order – that JM-WAVE (Miami) "technically" steer clear of the Masferrer operation – had been obeyed. He worried that Masferrer might well "take the approach that he considered the U.S. government tacitly approved his plot since it obviously knew about it and did not take action against him." Masferrer could claim that CIA had provided him with weapons out of New York. Should CIA be compelled to testify at the trial, they could not claim non-involvement, if only because Masferrer had rounded up so many CIA assets and contacts and involved them in the operation.

Houston considered that Cuban exile and paramilitary operative Eladio del Valle might have been murdered (with an ax to the skull) because, while on a visit to Haiti, he had alerted Duvalier to the impending Masferrer invasion. Del Valle was murdered on February 22, 1967; the official cause of death was multiple blunt impacts to the head, along with a gunshot wound to the chest. The proximity in time to the death in New Orleans of del Valle's associate David Ferrie, a suspect in the assassination of President Kennedy, remains a mystery.

For the record, Houston denied that del Valle had ever "worked" for the Agency, although del Valle had been involved in sabotage missions over Cuba for CIA. Rolando Masferrer disapproved of del Valle because he ran drugs, even while several of those involved, Father

Georges, Réne Léon, and even Masferrer's lawyer, enjoyed relationships with del Valle.

During the trial, an FBI man in charge of counter-ter-
rorism sent a message: "Tell Rolando to hide." Masferrer skipped bond only to be captured. Masferrer served
a prison term from 1968 to 1972. Martin Francis Xavier
Casey, whose contacts were lower in the CIA food chain,
served ten months.

When it was over, Rolando Arcadio Masferrer Rojas
concluded that CIA had no serious intention of toppling
either Duvalier or Fidel Castro. Masferrer even wondered
aloud whether Fidel Castro had been sanctioned by CIA.

A free man, Masferrer founded a weekly Miami
newspaper called *"Libertad."* He was not a man easily
silenced. He planned to attend a Washington D.C. anti-
Communist International League meeting. He knew
that safety resided in speaking out, a lesson Robert F.
Kennedy would have done well to honor rather than remaining silent about what he knew about his brother's
death.

"I see a big flash, a big explosion," the *Santería* priestess warned Masferrer. "I see one person dead and I see
people associated with this person dead."

Rolando Masferrer Rojas was murdered on October
31, 1975. His car had been wired with twenty pounds
of TNT. The dynamite originated in Czechoslovakia.
Masferrer's nephew, Rolandito, believes he was killed
by a Castro agent, but former homicide detective who
worked on the case told Gordon Winslow that the police followed leads to a lieutenant working for terrorist
Orlando Bosch. Masferrer had been exposing the Ven-
ezuelan drug cartel in *"Libertad."* For help in getting out

of jail, Bosch had made a deal with the Venezuelans for Rolando's murder.

At the time of his death, Rolando Masferrer had been living in a house owned by his cousin, Antonio Rojas. As for his possessing millions, a friend had to pay for his funeral.

It seems that everywhere in the story of the travails of Haiti, the arms dealer and propagandist I.I. Davidson makes an appearance. In 1966, Davidson had introduced himself to Joaquin Balaguer, soon to return to the presidency of the Dominican Republic; Davidson described himself as a representative of the U.S. State Department. He could pick up obsolete weapons and replace them with modern ones "at very little extra cost," Davidson promised when later he met President Balaguer in the Dominican Republic.

Davidson boasted of his close relations with Lyndon Johnson and confided that Johnson "worries ninety-eight percent of the time about Viet-Nam and the other two percent about Latin America." Davidson also confided to Balaguer that the U.S. government has decided Duvalier must go. CIA then sent intelligence about Davidson's meetings with Balaguer over to the White House.

Despite all the trouble Lawrence Houston had gone through with the Masferrer debacle, CIA did not abandon its paramilitary efforts against Duvalier. In May 1967, CIA studied "logistic support to satisfy CIA infiltration and exfiltration requirements," to be aided by both internal and external assets. The current CIA "Contingency Plan For Haiti" read, in part, "All available information on known or potential subversives in Haiti and abroad has been collated for ready use by the Intelligence

Community." CIA's only hesitation about embarking on further paramilitary operations into Haiti was that they might be infiltrated by "unacceptable Haitians."

Nine months after the Masferrer expedition was aborted, yet another CIA-financed paramilitary invasion of Haiti was organized. It was led by a veteran of the Masferrer undertaking, Colonel René Léon, who hoped to be Chief of Staff of the post-Duvalier military. Léon handled the finances whose origins, rumor had it, led directly back to Clémard Joseph Charles. Playing a prominent role once more was I.I. Davidson, who set the terms for the payment of monies from CIA to the belligerents.

As usual, Davidson claimed to the participants in the operation that he enjoyed "the support of the U.S. Department of State and the Central Intelligence Agency." Registered agent for Duvalier though he may have been, I.I. Davidson's first loyalty, when it wasn't to Israel, was to the Agency. The financial backing for the operation, I.I. claimed, would come from "prosperous U.S. businessmen, the principal one being the son of a U.S. admiral."

"You don't ask," says Howard K. Davis, the co-pilot of the Super Constellation that flew into Haiti and bombed the Presidential palace, the centerpiece of this operation. Davis had been acquainted with I.I. at least since 1959 when he had contacted Davidson about obtaining twenty-four .50 caliber machine guns to be used in his anti-Castro activities. Davidson had requested that Davis put his request in writing. He promised that he would then contact Munitions Control for the authority to obtain the guns. Davis found this request preposterous. His instinct was proven correct when five days later Davidson contacted the FBI and told them everything.

Davis is certain that CIA provided the weapons for the 1967 paramilitary mission into Haiti. The bombing was a diversionary part of the mission, to distract the Haitians from the main action – which was the movement of an army battalion commanded by Réne Léon from Cap-Hatïen into Port-au-Prince.

Together with Martin Xavier Casey, Davis flew to Atlanta to arrange for the delivery of heavy weapons, which would come not from within the continental United States, but from outside. Approximately twenty Haitians and a coterie of CIA-connected Americans trained for the expedition for several months in the Florida Everglades, using live ammunition.

CIA also set up a camp for the Haitians in Florida near the Okefenokee swamp where they trained in wet suits and infrared goggles. It was at this camp that a man was shot in the face and died. Training resumed in the Turks and Caicos Islands where one of the Haitians had sexual relations with so many local women that he was accused of single-handedly setting off a gonorrhea epidemic. The local police demanded that the Haitians leave the islands.

Réne Léon himself hadn't been there. Impatient and refusing to train on the South Caicos, Léon was anxious to proceed directly to Cap-Hatïen where a battalion of the army waited for him. Then, victorious, they would march into Port-au-Prince.

The invaders wore camouflage labeled, "Big Game: Styled by Broadway." There was no doubt that their point of embarkation was the United States.

At last the Super Constellation set forth on its distraction mission as Colonel Léon waited at Cap-Hatïen to move stealthily into the capital. Beside Howard K. Davis sat the pilot, Jim Carlin. For explosives, they carried 53 gallon-drums of jet fuel, mixed with a non-detergent soap. One bomb had too short a fuse and exploded in the air, shaking the plane. Another dropped to the ground, unexploded.

On the plane's first pass, they encountered no resistance from Duvalier's Palace Guard. But on their second and third efforts, they were met by anti-aircraft guns planted on the roof as well as on the ground. They were now flying less than three hundred feet above ground level. The plane's massive wings were blocking their sights, so they were unable to fire their machine guns with any accuracy.

During their final pass, a bullet penetrated the fuel tank. Then a shell exploded in the cockpit, piercing the oxygen tank. The cockpit filled with smoke.

From the rear, Martin Xavier Casey was tossing out napalm. Then he grabbed the fire extinguisher and rushed to the cockpit, forgetting that he had tied a rope around his waist – so that he caromed back to the rear of the plane.

Unloading a drum filled with jet fuel, Casey set the west wing of Duvalier's palace on fire. The flight engineer was hit in the head with shrapnel. In the street below, six people were killed.

The Super Constellation now boasted more than a hundred bullet holes. Crackerjack aviators, Carlin and Davis managed to limp the plane to Cap-Hatïen. There they found military vehicles blocking the runway. The people with whom they were supposed to meet up had long since fled. Carlin and Davis headed north now to the Bahamas to buy fuel to take them and Léon back to the United States. A thunderstorm prevented their landing in the Bahamas.

The fuel gauges of the Constellation read "empty." Finally, they spotted a small airfield. Carlin landed the plane only to discover that they had arrived at an auxiliary U.S. Air Force base. Everyone on board was detained.

They were interviewed by a representative of that "friendly" intelligence service, MI6. Then they were flown back to the U.S. and charged with violating the Neutrality Act. At their trial in 1969, Léon was sentenced to three years in prison; Howard K. Davis got eighteen months. CIA issued a boilerplate disclaimer: "Forces under the leadership of Haitians based in the United States bombed Port-au-Prince and Cap-Hatïen" and "landed mercenaries" near Cap-Hatïen.

Duvalier's foreign minister demanded that the U.S. government "investigate and interdict any illegal acts of Haitians based in the United States." The Haitians claimed that the U.S. aircraft had been flown by U.S. pilots, using U.S. military equipment, which was true. Later the Haitian government put on trial as one of the invaders a former exile, whose name was changed to "Gérard Pierre." It turned out that "Gérard Pierre" was a Port-au-Prince schoolteacher, and had not been part of the invading group.

Duvalier threatened "another missile crisis based on Haitian exiles broadcasting programs from the U.S. calling for the overthrow of Duvalier."

Nicholas Katzenbach, still working for Lyndon Johnson, lied for the U.S. There was "no basis for Haitian allegations against the United States," Katzenbach declared. Yet a State Department document admits that "the B-25 used in the expedition may well have come from the United States." Then, the document claims, the government had "stopped it [the operation] cold and got convictions." This, of course, they had not done.

After they had served between 90 and 120 days, a judge suddenly turned Howard K. Davis, Martin Xavier

Casey and the other prisoners loose. The Agency had not abandoned them entirely.

Later Howard K. Davis reflected that, had they been able to return for another foray that night, Duvalier might well have left the country.

* * *

Readers might by now surely have concluded that Clémard Joseph Charles had been abandoned by CIA, that his chance to become President of Haiti had evaporated, and that CIA was done with him for good. Yet it wasn't so.

CIA continued to remain close to Clémard Joseph Charles. His case officer in 1967 was named "Francis D. Rachfield," alternate name "Matthew H. Chubb." (It has proven impossible, well into the new millennium, to determine which was the real name, and which the pseudonym).

A fragment of a Rachfield file on Charles covers the spring of 1967. On March 15, 1967, Charles requests of Rachfield, "if possible to pass a msg [message] out of channels directly to CHIEF LNPURE." Rachfield notes that Charles was "very pro-WOLADY," suggesting the continuing trust Charles placed in Dorothe Matlack, WOLADY. Rachfield also notes: "well known High Levels LNHARP." The LN attached to a cryptonym suggests an OA or "Other Government Agency," here Army intelligence, to which Matlack was attached.

The INS informs Rachfield that Charles had entered the U.S. at Miami on April 30, 1967, and was again staying at the Waldorf Astoria Hotel in New York. Rachfield then summarizes the recent history of Charles' activities, beginning with his July 1964 trip to Mexico to purchase

30 U.S. surplus T-28 trainer aircraft, and his subsequent attempt to purchase 24 U.S. surplus naval craft.

On June 12, 1967, a CIA officer named Kenneth T. Ripley writes an "Assessment of Clémard Joseph Charles," as follows:

> He has played Duvalier's game to the hilt, often entrusted w/missions abroad which were, in effect contrary to US Govt. interests: (He played a principal role in the attempt to smuggle B-26 aircraft out of the US for Duvalier's use. In that connection he went to Arizona to try purchase US Air Force Surplus planes, using US citizens of suspicious nature as his agents). [See Documents pp. 430-433.]

Only a few days earlier, on June 6th, Charles had contacted Dorothe Matlack, begging her once again to support an invasion of Haiti that would depose Duvalier. He reminds her of the "kind reception" she had afforded him in 1963 and hopes "that the assistance of the U.S. would not fail us." In an emotional appeal, Charles begs that Haiti be relieved of "the tyranny and misery in which it has been considerably thrown."

Charles claims to have secured the support "of a great majority of the populations all over the Republic, including religious people, businessmen, professionals and intellectuals." His new operation has been prepared by "a military man who has with him most of the officers in the Army." These people, Charles claims, "are ready and eager to begin operations and are only awaiting word from me."

Charles then refers to a Castro plan "to introduce communist agitators in the country." Unable to fly to the

U.S. himself, he dispatched an emissary named Louis A. Brun. Then Charles thanks Matlack "for your contribution to the relief of my country and to assure you that your cooperation will ever live in my memory."

Matlack took all this to her superiors at the 902nd Military Intelligence Group, "90 Deuce." On June 9, 1967, 90 Deuce released a seven page "information report" titled "U.S. GOVERNMENT SUPPORT FOR PLOTS TO OVERTHROW THE HAITIAN GOVERNMENT." It refers to "continuing bids by Clémard Joseph Charles for U.S. government support for his plot to overthrow the Haitian government."

Army intelligence discovered that Charles had rounded up 290 soldiers, officers and men, "ready to strike at any time and kill President François Duvalier." They had only enough ammunition "to hold out for twenty-four hours."

"We are not strong enough without foreign help to stay in power," Charles had written. Charles had outlined three negative scenarios: "counteraction by fanatical Duvalier followers; an invasion attempt by Cuban-trained Haitian exiles," and "an intervention by Balaguer to support Duvalier." Balaguer remained the President of the Dominican Republic.

90 Deuce and Matlack trusted Charles no more in 1967 than they had in 1963. They knew that Charles had "the reputation of being an opportunist, shrewd, capable, and unscrupulous." They wondered at his ability to retain Duvalier's confidence, while using that advantage to "further his own efforts against Duvalier." Still, they thought he might well be selected by the U.S. as "the lesser of a number of evils."

U.S. Army intelligence was too accurate for 90 Deuce not to know that Charles' "alleged supporters" were "believed to be insignificant," his allies in the Army "suspect." They thought that neither Castro nor Joaquin Balaguer had an appetite for overthrowing Duvalier, undercutting Charles' use of that card "to force the U.S. government in his favor." For its part, CIA was now concentrating its energies on the accelerated war in Vietnam. Neither Cuba nor Haiti promised the level of profits to CIA's client corporations, defense contractors like Halliburton, that a prolonged war in Indochina would yield.

On June 14, 1967, Clémard Joseph Charles purchased an airplane ticket to Washington, D.C. His hope was to meet with Lyndon Johnson and make his case one final time. But Papa Doc had at last grown wise to Clémard's double game. When Charles arrived at the Port-au-Prince airport to board his flight to Washington, Papa Doc's men picked him up and brought him to the Palace.

"Why are you going to the United States?" Papa Doc said.

He was going to the United States to see a doctor about having his tonsils removed, Charles said. There was, in fact, nothing wrong with his tonsils.

"There are doctors in Haiti," Papa Doc said. "Our doctors are very good." Duvalier then "strongly suggested" (as 90 Deuce would learn) that Clémard Joseph Charles undergo surgery in Haiti.

Duvalier clamped Charles into a cheap downtown Port-au-Prince hospital, hot, crowded and filthy. There they operated on his throat, leaving him unable to speak.

Joe Dryer, having moved his kenaf business out of Haiti, had returned – the good people of Haiti still residing in his heart – to organize an electronic assembly plant with such customers as Emerson Electric. He would go on to employ one hundred people and continue operations into the early 1970s.

While still hospitalized, Charles managed to get a message to Dryer.

When Dryer arrived at the hospital, he found Charles in a crowded ward, soldiers standing in the doorway of the room. Unable to utter a word, Charles lay in his bed, miserable. He communicated with Dryer by writing notes.

"Could you do me a favor when you leave?" Charles wrote. "Could you take an envelope to the States for me?"

Dryer thought fast. "I'm busy in the morning," he said. "But I'm on the noon Pan American flight. I'll come a little before that." No one was safe in Port-au-Prince now.

Dryer's gamble was that he could pick up the envelope and head directly for the airport. He timed his arrival for the moment the flight was boarding so that he could pass right through customs and board the plane. Dryer counted on the fact that telephone service in Haiti was all but non-existent.

The next day Dryer collected from Charles a thick white envelope personally addressed to "President Lyndon Johnson." Then he headed for the airport where the usual crush was underway, the chaos of departing in those days from any third world country. A few nuns were on line, and some tourists, including a young German with a backpack.

Dryer got behind the German tourist and slipped Clémard's envelope into the backpack. Dryer followed the German onto the plane. Knowing Papa Doc and his *Tontons Macoutes* well, he didn't want to be caught carrying that envelope.

Just as the tourist was about to store his gear and sit down, Dryer, with stealth and courage to spare, slipped the envelope out of the backpack and placed it in the overhead bin. He had not served with U.S. Marine intelligence for nothing. He managed to get Charles' thick envelope safely to Washington.

Dryer remembers that somehow Mrs. Matlack was involved in the delivery of Clémard Joseph Charles' letter to Lyndon Johnson. But time had run out for Charles' effort to enlist CIA and 90 Deuce in his plan to replace Duvalier as president of Haiti. He was no longer free to move about, to play his dangerous double game.

CIA recorded that in June 1967 Duvalier deprived Charles "of much of his empire." Duvalier pretended to be angry that Charles had become rich and yet refused to hand over his money to his mentor and benefactor. That Charles was becoming rich in his years of doing Papa Doc's business was no secret to the "President for life," as Duvalier had named himself. Charles was stripped of his properties and his citizenship and tossed into jail.

Unsavory characters with whom Charles had done business, like Justin Bertrand, were disappointed in Clémard for having allowed political ambition to jeopardize his position in Haiti. "Ah," Bertrand said, "Clémard had to butt in politics; if he had not, he would have kept his influential position, and today I would have been the Secretary of Public Works. I had already purchased my tuxedo."

Clémard's wife, Sophie, appealed to Amnesty International – to no avail. As for CIA, they no longer knew him.

In July of 1967, CIA's chief of station in Port-au-Prince sent the chief of the Western Hemisphere Division an "Updated Listing of the Ton Ton Macoute," including those who lacked the "formal designation" of being "card-carrying members." The list was provided to the chief of the Western Hemisphere Division by Matthew

H. Chubb, aka Francis D. Rachfield – the CIA handler of Clémard Joseph Charles.

Already outdated, it named those "Haitian civilians whom Duvalier appears to favor above other members of the militia." "Clémard Joseph Charles" appears on this list. At that very moment, Charles was rotting at Fort Dimanche, Duvalier's hellhole of a prison; Haitians had nicknamed Duvalier's gulag, "*Fort La Mort.*"

Author and long-time journalist based in Haiti, Bernard Diederich, sums Charles up as a "rascal." He had played big stakes against Duvalier and lost, and he "was a crook, no doubt about it." Diederich suggests that at Fort Dimanche Charles had to have had special quarters; he would not have been housed in one of the regular cells, which were rich with disease.

EIGHT

Second And Third Acts

We do know that his death was violent."
 — Roger Pierce, speaking for Army Intelligence about Clémard Joseph Charles, who was very much alive at the time.

George de Mohrenschildt's services to the government of Haiti went uncompensated. Remaining in Haiti at the turn of the New Year 1966, de Mohrenschildt began to enlist higher authority back home for help in persuading Papa Doc to honor the terms of their contract. That contract, for oil exploration, had been for $280,380; de Mohrenschildt had also been awarded a ten-year option on a sisal concession. Whether CIA had a hand in facilitating the "oil exploration" contract in the first place, they did nothing now to ensure that de Mohrenschildt was paid for his services, whatever his actual efforts had or had not been.

De Mohrenschildt's relationship with Clémard Joseph Charles had long since broken down completely. De Mohrenschildt himself had become a pariah. Duvalier despised him. The American Embassy officials shared Papa Doc's contempt. That de Mohrenschildt was known to have been involved in the Kennedy assassination, and connected with Lee Harvey Oswald, certainly did him no service. CIA abandoned him as it did Clémard Joseph

Charles, along with no small number of other assets whose usefulness had expired.

De Mohrenschildt wrote to Senator John Tower of Texas, to Texas Congressman Joe Richard Pool, and to Roderick MacArthur at the State Department. On February 1, 1966, de Mohrenschildt appealed to President Lyndon Johnson himself. "The Government of Haiti and my concessionaire of sisal exploitation, Mr. Clémard J. Charles, ignore me," de Mohrenschildt complained.

De Mohrenschildt reminded Lyndon Johnson of his 1963 meeting with Colonel Howard Burris, with whom, he claimed, he had "retained contact." Indeed, Burris appears at least twice in de Mohrenschildt's address book. He invoked being "a Texan." Yet again he summoned the name of "the late Herman Brown of Brown and Root of Houston." And he speculated about why he, de Mohrenschildt, had fallen so precipitously out of favor.

"Could it be that we had the misfortune of having known Harvey Lee Oswald?"

The coy transposition of Oswald's name could not have fooled Johnson. Still, de Mohrenschildt reminded the president that he had played along with the government's blaming Oswald for the murder: "We had contributed our time and efforts to help the Warren Committee [sic] and we have their thanks and acknowledgement." Won't Johnson, then, "save our work in Haiti"?

The issue was no longer oil or sisal. What de Mohrenschildt meant was that the President of the United States should prevail upon Duvalier to pay him the terms of his contract.

De Mohrenschildt remained a man who knew too much, and so could not be ignored entirely. President Johnson entrusted Robert M. Sayre, the Acting Assistant

Secretary for Inter-American Affairs, to reply for him. In his letter to de Mohrenschildt, Sayre attempted to placate the beleaguered former CIA contact.

Sayre noted that the State Department "exchanged several letters with members of Congress concerning your apparent difficulties in Haiti." He claimed that the State Department was "most anxious to be of assistance to you in solving any problems you might have in that country."

Then Sayre wheeled away from the problem. Attempting to inject obscurity where there was none, he asked whether de Mohrenschildt had "a valid written contract under which you have received compensation." He bombarded de Mohrenschildt with minutiae. Have you recovered your geological maps? Sayre asked, "so that they might be described along with the date and place they were taken from you and who took them?"

"If they concern a sisal concession," Sayre added, "you should describe the concession, its date, its signatories, its terms, the way in which the concession is not being honored and the dollar or gourde losses you have suffered because it has not been honored." De Mohrenschildt found himself facing checkmate.

For six weeks after receiving Sayre's letter, de Mohrenschildt was silent. Then, on March 15, 1966 – he remained in Haiti – he wrote again to Johnson. Thanking him for Sayre's assistance, he praised Lyndon Johnson for proving "once more that you have the utmost respect for the rights of the ordinary American citizen in distress and are anxious to help all citizens in their problems." De Mohrenschildt knew well that Johnson portrayed himself as the savior of the common man.

Still, de Mohrenschildt was offered no redress. The executive branch of the U.S. government was not about to insist to Duvalier that he pay George de Mohrenschildt any money at all, let alone the munificent amount he had once been promised.

In October 1966, having skipped out on several months rent, the de Mohrenschildts boarded a Panamanian transport ship called the *Mona I.* Sailing off into the horizon, surrounded by a sullen grey-green ocean, they left Haiti behind forever. On the ship's manifest, George is listed as a "sailor," and Jeanne as a "cook." They were stone cold broke. CIA had already informed the FBI of the de Mohrenschildts' plans.

CIA had discovered that de Mohrenschildt's original contract with the Government of Haiti had fallen through, but that the government still admitted that it owed him $122,222. He planned to spend six weeks in the States and then return to Haiti without his wife to try to arrange to be compensated for his back pay in the form of real estate.

Arriving in Dallas on November 10, 1966, homeless, the de Mohrenschildts accepted the hospitality of Sam Ballen. Ballen was the Texas oil and gas executive who had testified before the Warren Commission about having spent a few hours in the company of Lee Harvey Oswald, and having accompanied him to the offices of some business in the hope of landing him a job.

After a while, the de Mohrenschildts rented an apartment of their own at 3615 Gillespie, and George tried to obtain a government contract for geological work in Latin America. But de Mohrenschildt was not now, nor would he ever again be, rescued by the U.S. government, no matter what services he had provided in times past. The government wanted nothing more to do with him.

From Dallas, de Mohrenschildt renewed his efforts to enlist powerful politicians to help him extract payment from Duvalier for his services. Although Lyndon Johnson had done nothing for him, he sent Johnson a get-well telegram, adding "many many thanks again for the kind intervention regarding my Haitian consulting assignment." Yet another letter to Johnson proposed an "Institute of Latin American Resources," to be funded through AID.

Lyndon Johnson's staff debated how to deal with de Mohrenschildt. Any reply to his entreaties should be "de minimus," they agreed. Even W.W. Rostow, Johnson's National Security Adviser, was briefed: "A lengthy file in the Office of Special Consular Services clearly indicates that de Mohrenschildt is an unstable and unreliable individual who would not hesitate to misuse or misrepresent even the slightest expression of interest."

The record does not reflect that J. Edgar Hoover enjoyed any part of the process, but the briefing of Rostow does reflect Hoover's standard operating procedure toward inconvenient witnesses. Like Nelson Delgado, who served in the Marines with Oswald, and like Sylvia Odio, whom Oswald had visited a month before the assassination, the de Mohrenschildts were now declared mentally unbalanced, unstable, and untrustworthy.

Desperate, in August 1967 de Mohrenschildt wrote Lyndon Johnson yet again. He suggested a "health corps" to dissipate race riots and "hippie propagation." By now, de Mohrenschildt's letters had been assigned to low level Johnson staff members to acknowledge.

De Mohrenschildt hired a Washington D.C. lawyer named Charles R. Norberg. From 1946 to 1951, Bruce

Adamson discovered, Norberg had been employed by CIA. Norberg's assignment now for de Mohrenschildt was to enlist foreign service officers on his behalf.

Norberg learned from Haitian officials that de Mohrenschildt had been dealing with "one Haitian government worker who had a personal stake" in his sisal enterprise. The Haitians said they were "vaguely aware" of de Mohrenschildt's presence in Haiti, but there were no official records of his "survey works." Predictably, Norberg obtained no redress for George de Mohrenschildt.

One day at a bar, de Mohrenschildt ran into Austin, Texas police intelligence officer J. Harrison, a man with a sophisticated interest in the vagaries of the Kennedy assassination.

"You know how to become a millionaire?" de Mohrenschildt said. "You go out and buy something for a buck and sell it for two bucks. Then you sell that for four bucks, and you keep on going until you have a million dollars."

On October 28, 1967, I.I. Davidson telephoned the FBI to request a meeting with Hoover's second-in-command, Clyde Tolson. Davidson confided that he had been approached by two characters – Hugh McDonald, a CIA contract agent and former chief of detectives of the Los Angeles County Sheriff's office, and Leonard Davidov, whom McDonald claimed had assisted him in the security of the Goldwater campaign in 1964.

I.I. Davidson told the FBI that Davidov was a business acquaintance of his and president of Security Associates, a burglar alarm company. Davidov told Davidson that an "Eastern group" was putting up a lot of money to learn the truth about the assassination of President Kennedy. They were working through McDonald.

McDonald, I.I. Davidson said later, was somehow involved in Las Vegas with Howard Hughes in the sale of helicopters to law enforcement agencies. McDonald had promised a share of the police helicopter business to Davidov if he would help him.

Davidov and McDonald wanted I.I. Davidson to investigate George de Mohrenschildt, whom McDonald believed "was part of the conspiracy" to assassinate President Kennedy. They wanted to know whether de Mohrenschildt was actually involved in the Kennedy assassination, and whether Lyndon Johnson had foreknowledge of the conspiracy.

Davidson accepted the assignment and flew off to Dallas, promising to inform the FBI of whatever he learned. His purpose, Davidson added, was to protect President Johnson from being "smeared." Hoover concluded that Davidson's real motive was for himself to investigate both de Mohrenschildt – and Hugh McDonald.

McDonald's book, *Appointment in Dallas: The Final Solution to the Assassination of JFK*, published in 1975, was not taken seriously by historians. In it, McDonald invents a mythological shooter named "Saul." The FBI took a dim view of the book, but decided the wiser course was to remain silent and so not grant Hugh McDonald public attention. "Should the Bureau desire inquiries," they determined, "it is felt considerable inquiry should be made through CIA." I.I. Davidson received no acknowledgement for his efforts, as of course he preferred.

As CIA enlisted *Reader's Digest* as an outlet for authors whose political views matched its own, so CIA-sponsored books appeared regularly. *Miami Herald* journalist Al Burt, who appears in CIA documents as AMCARBON-1, collaborated with Bernard Diederich on a book titled *Papa Doc: The Truth About Haiti Today*, exposing Duvalier's terrorism. AMCARBON-1, a ten-page CIA document notes, was someone willing "to carry out certain operational support tasks for the Agency." *Papa Doc*, published in 1970, seemed to provide part of the CIA rationale for overthrowing Duvalier. It was published after the Super Constellation bombing of Duvalier's presidential palace, but *Papa Doc* does not mention Masferrer, de Mohrenschildt, or Clémard Joseph Charles.

CIA retained its interest in Charles even when he was in prison and there was no possibility of his becoming President of Haiti. In a May 20, 1968 "confidential teletype," Francis D. Rachfield writes: "Charles uses pseudonym 'Jacoby' in his confidential correspondence." This was an alias exclusively used within CIA.

The name "Jacoby" does not appear in the military intelligence records on Charles. Rachfield, readers may recall, was the CIA handler or case officer assigned to Charles in the late 1960s.

On June 20, 1968, Clémard Joseph Charles paid Duvalier a ransom of $250,000 by turning over to Papa Doc a sheaf of "signed blank checks on each of his Swiss accounts." For the moment, Clémard was a free man.

Joe Dryer visited Haiti at this time, and learned from his agronome, Analous Barthelemy – who had worked on his kenaf farm, and who was to work for him on kenaf operations in Nigeria, Ghana and the Ivory Coast – that Charles was at home, under house arrest. "It's best not to get involved in the past," Analous told Dryer. What he meant was that Dryer should stay away from politics, which meant not making contact with Clémard Joseph Charles. Dryer took Barthelemy's advice.

In 1968, CIA continued to beam anti-Duvalier broadcasts into Haiti. Retaliating, Duvalier jammed the radio station signal, and attempted to extort money from American businesses: HASCO; Reynolds; the Dauphine Plantation; Pan American Airways. A typhoid epidemic raged as the country slid even more deeply into chronic poverty.

Also in 1968, George H.W. Bush and his CIA partner Thomas J. Devine traveled together to Viet Nam. CIA's eyes were set firmly now on Southeast Asia. When the Department of Defense issued Devine only an "interim" Top Secret clearance for the trip, Devine balked and pulled rank.

Devine demanded that his CIA clearance be updated to a "Standing Top Secret clearance status," the better to facilitate further trips he planned to take in the company of Mr. Bush. At CIA's Directorate of Operations, Gale Allen obliged. Project WUBRINY, identity unknown, remained in place.

Harassed mercilessly in public for facilitating CIA's war in Viet Nam, Lyndon Johnson had retreated to his ranch outside Austin. He had renounced the opportunity to run for re-election. In June 1969, George de Mohrenschildt requested permission to pay Johnson a visit at his home.

Once again de Mohrenschildt dropped familiar names: Barbara and Howard Burris; George Brown "and the late Herman Brown" of Brown & Root, now owned by Halliburton. De Mohrenschildt even invoked Jacqueline Onassis, a "former acquaintance." The purpose of his visit was "to express my appreciation for your help to me in Haiti."

De Mohrenschildt thanked Lady Bird "for her gracious help to a Haitian refugee girl whom we had smuggled out of Haiti," and promised to provide Johnson with "some amusing insights on the Auchincloss-Bouvier families, possibly interesting for memoirs." He was a man now attempting to sell something to people not inclined to buy what he was peddling.

"Do you have any interest in seeing this man?" Johnson's executive secretary asked the former President. He used a standard office form for this inquiry, since Lyndon Johnson had secluded himself even from his own staff.

Johnson placed a large check mark beside the word: "NO."

"President Johnson regrets that his schedule will not permit him to meet with you," de Mohrenschildt was informed tersely.

In April 1970, Clémard Joseph Charles became involved in yet another plot against a now ailing Duvalier. Charles financed a coup that was timed for what Duvalier's doctors had assured the conspirators would be the day of Duvalier's death. The organizer of the coup was Colonel Kesner Blain, who had noted that the Haitian Constitution with its clause granting Duvalier the presidency "for life" lacked a legal mechanism to fill a sudden presidential vacancy.

Nervous about the certainty of this declaration regarding the day that Duvalier would die, Charles consulted his friend M. Jacques Fourcand, who was one of Duvalier's doctors. He needed not only to confirm that Duvalier's illness really was terminal, but also to gain Fourcand's cooperation.

Wary, Fourcand insisted instead that Charles report the conspiracy to Duvalier. Fourcand and Charles headed for the presidential palace to expose Blain's plot. While Fourcand went into the sick man's room, Charles sat outside in the waiting room.

Ever suspicious, Duvalier perceived at once the role Charles was playing in this new conspiracy and immediately had him arrested and thrown back into Fort Dimanche prison. A revolt by the Haitian coast guard was followed by more arrests, including that of Colonel Kesner Blain. The anti-Duvalier forces had penetrated the *Service Duvalier*, and so the ensuing investigation was conducted outside its framework.

I.I. Davidson, unfamiliar with moral scruples and playing every side, declared in March 1970 that he was proud of his "personal friendship" with François Duvalier, his daughter Marie-Denise, and her husband Max Dominique. François Duvalier lived for another year. When he died on April 21, 1971, he was succeeded by his son, Jean-Claude, "Baby Doc," who offered the suffering people of Haiti more of the same.

I.I. Davidson remained a CIA source for matters relating to Haiti. His CIA contact was Mayo Stuntz, who had acquired so negative an impression of Clémard Joseph Charles in 1963. CIA now wanted to know Davidson's assessment of Baby Doc's "ability to retain the presidency....Who are his chief advisers? Will he accept guidance from his advisers?"

When Jean-Claude Duvalier considered declaring an amnesty that would bring many exiles home, Davidson forwarded this information to the State Department, which sent it on to CIA. Davidson's source was Baby Doc's brother-in-law, Max Dominque. "How successful will the new Minister of Information, Dr. Fritz Cineas, be in selling the new image of Haiti?" the U.S. wanted to know.

Meanwhile, Charles remained in prison, where he wrote hundreds of love letters and poems to his wife,

Sophie. One day in 1975, attired in the white habit of a nun, Sophie burst into a mass at Port-au-Prince Cathedral during a service when most of the worshipers were members of the diplomatic corps. Confronting the assembled parishioners, she begged for her husband's release.

George de Mohrenschildt hoped to be paid by Baby Doc for his original contract with the Government of Haiti. On May 20, 1971, he wrote for assistance to Texas Congressman Earle Cabell, who had been Mayor of Dallas when John F. Kennedy was murdered. De Mohrenschildt suggested that Haiti's sugar quota be suspended until his claim was settled.

Then, in June, de Mohrenschildt contacted his old acquaintance, George H.W. Bush, the former Andover roommate of his step-nephew Edward Hooker. Bush was now U.S. Representative to the United Nations for President Nixon.

Icy in his dealings with others, Bush forwarded de Mohrenschildt's letter to David A. Ross in the Haitian Affairs section of the Office of Caribbean Affairs. Ross knew what was required. Your contract with Duvalier was a "private matter," Ross wrote de Mohrenschildt. "You should redress your grievance in the appropriate court of competent jurisdiction."

Among other notables from whom de Mohrenschildt sought assistance in extracting at least the $100,000 some odd dollars that had been acknowledged was owed him was Henry Kissinger. Kissinger requested that American Embassy officials in Port-au-Prince "discuss the case informally" with the "appropriate" officials "with a view toward persuading [them] to enter into settlement discussions directly with Mr. De Mohrenschildt." Nothing came of it.

Broke, and nervous, de Mohrenschildt feared that he was being shadowed by CIA – as he had been, indeed, for years. Rejected by the higher-ups whom he had spent all his life cultivating, de Mohrenschildt experienced severe psychological deterioration. He babbled about fearing Blacks and Jews, the FBI and CIA. He claimed that his house was bugged. He subjected Jeanne de Mohrenschildt to domestic violence, the same kind of assaults he had visited upon his first three wives.

According to Bruce Adamson, Jeanne "stated her husband had attacked her several times, broken some of her ribs and teeth, and boxed her ear until it bled." He also made off with their last $8,000, unbeknownst to her. Jeanne's other charges rested on his emotional disarray: suicide attempts, and being "very neglectful of his appearance." She confided that he didn't wash his hair and took maybe one shower in two weeks.

Jeanne left him. They were divorced on April 3, 1973.

During this time, de Mohrenschildt overdosed on drugs. He slashed his wrists. In April 1976, he committed himself to the psychiatric ward at Dallas' Parkland Hospital, the eerie scene of John F. Kennedy's death. An affidavit by Jeanne de Mohrenschildt accompanied his commitment. Nine shock treatments were administered.

To his hospital roommate, de Mohrenschildt talked of having been in Dallas on November 22, 1963, although in fact he had been in Haiti. He insisted that Oswald had been set up. The CIA was harassing him, de Mohrenschildt whispered. Having recounted his conversations with de Mohrenschildt, the roommate took a voice stress test to demonstrate that he was telling the truth – and passed.

Out of the hospital on September 5, 1976, de Mohrenschildt wrote again to George H.W. Bush, who had now
assumed the office of Director of Central Intelligence under President Gerald Ford. Vigilantes were pursuing him,
de Mohrenschildt said in a sloppy, handwritten letter. He
was being followed. His telephone was bugged.

As he had in Port-au-Prince at the time of the Kennedy assassination, de Mohrenschildt blamed the FBI,
although the reality was that it was CIA that had more
recently been pursuing him. Invoking his misfortune of
having known Lee Harvey Oswald, he described himself
to Bush as an "elderly man who is being punished."

"Could you do something to remove this net around
us?" de Mohrenschildt begged Bush. "This will be my last
request for help and I will not annoy you anymore."

"I do know this man DeMohrenschildt," Bush wrote
in a memo to his staff. He was "an uncle to my Andover roommate," and "knew Oswald before the assassination of President Kennedy." Bush, as Hoover had said in
1963, had been "briefed." A close friend and collaborator
of CIA's WUBRINY/1, Thomas J. Devine, Bush was well
aware that de Mohrenschildt had "got involved in some
controversial dealings in Haiti."

"My staff has been unable to find any indication of
interest in your activities on the part of Federal authorities in recent years," Bush wrote to de Mohrenschildt in a
supercilious rebuff. Bush closes by hoping that his letter
"has been of some comfort to you." Having addressed de
Mohrenschildt condescendingly by his given name, he
signs the letter "George Bush."

Bush then turned the matter over to the appropriate
CIA component. CIA Counter Intelligence now contacted the FBI. CIA requested "information on the current
activities and location of a Mr. George de Mohrenschil-

dt who has attempted to get in touch with the Director, CIA." Counter Intelligence, perhaps the most arrogant of the Agency components, having assumed the personality of its long-time chief, James Angleton, requested that the matter be handled "on a priority basis."

The FBI had had enough of CIA's requests for its collaboration in the handling of de Mohrenschildt. The Bureau refused CIA's request outright. They could not "conduct investigation under AG (Attorney General) guidelines," the FBI replied.

In the last year of his life, 1977, de Mohrenschildt was bedeviled by the Kennedy assassination. He traveled to the Netherlands with Dutch journalist Willem Oltmans, who had promised to pay him for interviews. Oltmans was no stranger to the Kennedy assassination story. In April 1967, a decade earlier, Oltmans had gone to the FBI with information he had obtained from "someone in Western Europe" that "George de Mohrenschildt was the principal organizer in the assassination of President Kennedy."

Oltmans had added that George's upright brother Dimitri was "possibly the second assassin," while suggesting at the same time that it could not have been the case. Since Professor Dimitri von Mohrenschildt, a CIA asset of long standing, was the unlikeliest of assassins, Oltmans seemed to be suggesting that neither Dimitri nor CIA could have been involved.

Oltmans had, in fact, traveled to Dallas in 1968 to do research into the assassination, requesting FBI protection when he did so. Oltmans' behavior raises the ubiquitous question hovering over these scoundrels surrounding de Mohrenschildt, and their escapades: who knows who is working for whom?

Nonetheless, in October of 1968, there was Oltmans arriving at the de Mohrenschildts' apartment in Dallas with a CBS television crew – taping for forty minutes. Oltmans taped the couple again in 1969, this time for nearly *nine hours.*

In 1977 , de Mohrenschildt, reflecting that he must not have been displeased with Oltmans, agreed to "confess all" to the Dutchman – but only in the Netherlands.

A pre-interview was set up in Dallas, where Oltmans found de Mohrenschildt a changed man – nervous and very frightened, not the sun-tanned, robust tennis player Oltmans remembered from 1969. Now de Mohrenschildt was living in an apartment owned by Bishop College, a small black school outside Dallas where he taught. As an adjunct, he was paid $1600 a month. He had come to the dead end of his adventurous life.

At the college library, de Mohrenschildt told Oltmans, "I have to tell the story as it really was." He said that he feared going to jail. "I am responsible," he said. "I feel responsible for the behavior of Lee Harvey Oswald. Because I guided him. I instructed him, to set it up." History reflects that this was not exactly the case. Oswald was framed during the summer of 1963, primarily in New Orleans and in the state of Louisiana, while George de Mohrenschildt was safely in Port-au-Prince.

Consistent with the paranoia that had led to his frantic final letter to CIA Director George H.W. Bush, de Mohrenschildt repeated to Oltmans, "they are after me." De Mohrenschildt added, "even the Jewish Mafia is after me," a return to the old anti-Semitism he had evinced decades earlier. He wanted to be taken to Europe where he might talk freely.

Oltmans had told his superiors that de Mohrenschildt said he had instructed Oswald on how to go about the assassination of President Kennedy. Dutch television then pushed him to get de Mohrenschildt to Holland so they could have a scoop.

Before they departed, Oltmans drove de Mohrenschildt from Dallas to Houston, a ticket from Houston to Holland in hand. In New York, over dinner, de Mohrenschildt confided to Oltmans that he had saved his life since, in Dallas, "Either I talk or I go, they will drive me mad, or I will kill myself." De Mohrenschildt had withdrawn several thousand dollars from the Dallas Oak Cliff Bank and Trust and carried the cash in his attaché case.

The purpose of the trip to the Netherlands was "to discuss eventual TV appearances and a book on Lee Harvey Oswald and my friendship with him," de Mohrenschildt later recounted. During these appearances, he provided snippets of his story. "I played the devil," he said, in relation to Oswald, and this was true. He admitted to having known Oswald's assassin, Jack Ruby, and a gun dealer named Lester Logue, who testified that he offered soldier of fortune Loran Hall $50,000 to take part in the Kennedy assassination. De Mohrenschildt claimed to have done an oil survey with Logue in Cuba for Batista.

Oltmans later testified that de Mohrenschildt had told him Oswald "had many friends among the Cubans," and that Oswald had followed de Mohrenschildt's "detailed instructions on how to set up an ambush of President Kennedy." (But when the House Committee's Chief Counsel Robert Tanenbaum asked Oltmans how many shooters were involved in Dealey Plaza, Oltmans hedged and couldn't find his notes, claiming the notes were in Amsterdam). De Mohrenschildt had also stated, according to Oltmans, that he was "not sure" whether Oswald himself was a shooter.

De Mohrenschildt had also suggested to Oltmans that orders for the assassination issued ultimately from oilman H.L. Hunt, for which no evidence over all these years has ever emerged. (See the "Addendum" to this book.)De Mohrenschildt claimed that CIA and the FBI were "involved in the assassination," an immediate contradiction since H.L. Hunt was at war with CIA, and never wittingly had anything to do with the Agency.

A description of the harrowing trip to Holland appears in an affidavit from Brussels, dated March 11, 1977 and signed by de Mohrenschildt. It was discovered among his papers after his death. In Brussels, de Mohrenschildt relates, Oltmans took him to a meeting with a clairvoyant, who had connected his name with Oswald. In this circus of a charade, a member of Dutch television, Karl Enklraar, was present to negotiate for de Mohrenschildt's unpublished manuscript, "I was a Patsy, I was a Patsy."

The next day, a publisher from "Stranghold Publications" wanted to give de Mohrenschildt a contract for "a sensational book on Oswald and his influence on him."

"How sensational?" De Mohrenschildt demanded, stepping back. Among de Mohrenschildt's revelations, according to Oltmans in his later testimony before the HSCA, was that he believed that "Oswald loved President Kennedy. He could never have killed President Kennedy."

Over the years of his acquaintance with Oltmans, de Mohrenschildt contradicted himself repeatedly. Once he even said, "I killed Kennedy, of course," and then gave Oltmans a photograph, writing on the back, "From the biggest crook in the Western Hemisphere, George de Mohrenschildt."

In Europe, de Mohrenschildt and Oltmans could not come to an agreement on the book. By this time, de

Mohrenschildt was in disarray. He telephoned an old friend from Antwerp, who took him in. Before long he fled, leaving behind all his belongings, from his pipe to his keys. His $4600 worth of American Express Travelers' Checks disappeared.

De Mohrenschildt had noted that Oltmans had grown skilled in forging his signature, which may or may not have been a symptom of paranoia, but Oltmans managed to cash some of de Mohrenschildt's travelers' checks in Brussels. De Mohrenschildt's final thrust was that the interviews were his and his wife's property. Neither Oltmans nor Dutch TV had been entitled to use any portion of them.

When Oltmans returned to the United States, he passed de Mohrenschildt's telephone number over to the House Select Committee on Assassinations. They in turn assigned the matter to their chief investigator, Gaeton Fonzi.

De Mohrenschildt's complaints ranged from Oltmans' "unrestrained homosexuality" to his demands for book and television appearances. Later Oltmans would acknowledge to Bob Tanenbaum, interviewing him for the House Select Committee on Assassinations: "I am a homosexual...everyone in Holland knows this...." Oltmans also admitted under questioning from Tanenbaum that since contracts had not been signed, de Mohrenschildt never actually revealed the details of what he knew about the assassination.

De Mohrenschildt's brief sojourn in Holland was the final adventurist escapade of his life. Yet, his desire to tell what he knew about Oswald and the Kennedy assassination had not abated; he was ready, finally, to tell what he knew. De Mohrenschildt arranged a meeting with *Reader's Digest* in New York on March 15, 1977 with journalist Edward Jay Epstein and editor in chief, Fulton Oursler, Jr. At the close of March 1977, de Mohrenschildt agreed, for $4,000, to be interviewed by Epstein for *Reader's Digest*; $2,000 would be paid to him in advance.

The interview would take place in Palm Beach where de Mohrenschildt was staying with Nancy Tilton at the urging of his daughter, Alexandra, who was also in residence. "Papa, come back to Palm Beach, I will save you," she had said when she learned he was going to Holland.

Never a stranger to money, Tilton resided at a palm-studded property in a mansion facing the ocean at Manalapan Beach, just south of Palm Beach. It was a property of staggering beauty, on one side fronting the Atlantic Ocean, and on the other the Intercoastal Waterway.

In 1977, Joe Dryer happened also to be living in Palm Beach. Taking advantage of his Columbia University MBA in securities analysis, he was employed by Goodbody Company, an old investment firm with a Palm Beach branch. On weekends, he pursued his kenaf business, flying to Colombia and Ecuador.

One evening at a dinner party, Dryer had been seated next to a prominent local socialite named Dr. Wynne Sharples Denton, now Balinger. They had much in common. One of Dryer's sons had dated her daughter. There was also another connection. Dryer could not resist the clarion call of his curiosity. Dryer asked Balinger about the man to whom she had been married for five years, George de Mohrenschildt.

"I don't want to remember that man," Wynne Balinger said, closing the door firmly on the subject.

On the morning of March 29th, Epstein interviewed de Mohrenschildt at the Breaker's Hotel in Palm Beach. He told Epstein that, "he had maneuvered Oswald around and put him in touch with the 'right people' in the Dallas area." It was during this meeting with Epstein that de Mohrenschildt stated for the first time that CIA's J. Walton Moore had requested that he "keep tabs on Oswald." After a while, they took a break.

At about eleven a.m. that morning, the telephone rang in Joe Dryer's office.

"I'm here in town," George de Mohrenschildt said, sounding very friendly. "I've only just arrived. Can you have lunch with me today?"

Dryer didn't like de Mohrenschildt any more now than he had in Haiti. But he had wondered over the years what had happened to him. None of Dryer's acquaintances had heard from de Mohrenschildt.

Piqued by the curiosity that was to remain lively even into his nineties, Dryer was intrigued, not least because of de Mohrenschildt's connection to the Kennedy assassination. He was certain too that among the subjects they would discuss would be the years they had shared in Haiti, the Duvalier regime, and the fate of Clémard Joseph Charles.

"George, I can't," Dryer said, "but I'll have lunch with you tomorrow."

"Tomorrow will be fine," de Mohrenschildt said. "I'm here for a few more days."

"Where do I go?" Dryer said.

"I'm staying at a friend's house – it's right on the beach," de Mohrenschildt said, giving Dryer the address of Tilton's mansion. They agreed on the time they would meet for lunch the next day.

"I have some very important news to tell you. I have things to discuss," de Mohrenschildt added, in the same cheerful voice. Dryer didn't pursue the "important news" – there was no time. He figured they would discuss it over lunch the following day.

* * *

By late March 1977, the House Select Committee, re-investigating the Kennedy assassination and already having interviewed Willem Oltmans, had some questions for George de Mohrenschildt. While de Mohrenschildt was being interviewed by Edward J. Epstein, Committee investigator Gaeton Fonzi drove up to Tilton's mansion. Learning that de Mohrenschildt was out, Fonzi left his card.

Having interviewed Alpha 66 terrorist Antonio Veciana at length, Fonzi figured that when de Mohrenschildt on his "oil exploration" mission in 1957 "went to Yugoslavia to work for the International Cooperation Administration, he was operating under the same type of set-up" as would have been arranged for Veciana in La Paz by his own CIA handler.

In Cuba, Veciana had been an accountant at a bank owned by Julio Lobo, the sugar broker. After the disaster at the Bay of Pigs in 1961, Veciana became part of an anti-Castro terrorist group called "Alpha 66," its goal to bring Castro down "by the bullet" and to employ commando style raids. CIA funded Alpha 66, along with other groups, and over time provided Veciana, through his handler "Maurice Bishop," with at least $253,000; among those, in addition to Veciana, that Bishop met in Dallas in August 1963, according to Veciana, was – Lee Harvey Oswald.

Fonzi, a natural as an investigator, had been the person to interview Veciana and extract from him the name "Maurice Bishop" – a pseudo, Fonzi would conclude, for David Atlee Phillips. Fonzi had also discovered that Bishop College, where de Mohrenschildt had been teaching and that had "once got a lot of publicity in Dallas as a result of some Red-inspired campus agitators," had "all along been funded by the CIA." Fonzi had also connected de Mohrenschildt with Brown & Root, long a redoubt of CIA assets. That was an old story.

When de Mohrenschildt returned from the Epstein interview, his daughter Alexandra handed him Fonzi's card. Authorities later concluded that shortly thereafter, de Mohrenschildt went upstairs, placed a shotgun in his mouth and ended his life. He was sixty-five years old and, officially, a suicide. Typical of de Mohrenschildt, he died at the home of one of his wealthy connections, the cousin of one of his rich ex-wives.

"I'd bet my last penny that de Mohrenschildt did not intend to take his life," Joe Dryer says. Dryer remembers that de Mohrenschildt had "wanted to talk. He knew I had connections, if he was going to launch himself on some disclosure....Murdered. No doubt about it. I knew he was murdered."

Dryer discovered that the maid had heard a car drive away. There had been no shells for the shotgun anywhere nearby. De Mohrenschildt's daughter, whom he apparently loved, was in the house – all were factors casting a verdict of suicide into doubt.

Even one of Oltmans' government interrogators, Representative Stewart McKinney (R-Conn), had been skeptical. Having "been subjected to such mental anguish," McKinney suggested, De Mohrenschildt had wished to tell his story, and had finally begun to do so. Would the mere appearance of Gaeton Fonzi, offering him yet another opportunity to talk, really have precipitated his taking his life?

Dryer, who had lost every close friend he had at Iwo Jima, except one, says you can tell from people's voices whether they are under stress. De Mohrenschildt had been calm, even cheerful. He was extending an invitation, a social lunch between himself and Dryer. It would have been just like him to use an approach such as discussing their mutual experiences in Haiti "to lead into other subjects." George was a smooth character, Dryer says. He wasn't blunt.

"While the newspapers said he was despondent and sick, overdrugged," Dryer adds, "that wasn't true at all. He was perfectly sociable. He wanted to talk and he knew we had always had some respectful conversations. He knew too that I had some connections. If he was planning to launch himself on some sort of disclosure, he was coming to the right person."

Still manning the Dallas CIA field office, J. Walton ("Jim") Moore clipped the news stories reporting de Mohrenschildt's death and sent them to the chief of CIA's Domestic Contact Division. "Nothing new, is there?" he scribbled on a cover sheet over the *Dallas Times Herald* article stating that the House Select Committee had uncovered "new, unproven evidence on Oswald's ties with CIA, FBI."

Five days after de Mohrenschildt's death, on April 4, 1977, Russ Holmes completed CIA's official report on George de Mohrenschildt. It ran to over one hundred pages. CIA "dropped their interest in de Mohrenschildt's activities by the mid-to-late 1960s," Holmes wrote. In its file, the FBI dismissed de Mohrenschildt as an "international playboy."

Jeanne de Mohrenschildt found it highly unlikely that her former husband would have committed suicide. In

May 1978, Jeanne gave an interview to writer Jim Marrs for the *Fort Worth Star-Telegram*. She claimed that, during World War II, de Mohrenschildt had served as an agent "for the German underground." She knew that there were no cartridges in the room where George was found dead.

"He would never commit suicide and he would never commit suicide in that manner," she said. "He hated guns. He was eliminated before he got to that Committee because someone did not want him to get to it."

Among George's "closest friends at the time of the assassination," Jeanne said, "were Dallas' top CIA man [J. Walton Moore] and a Fort Worth man connected with some military-oriented organization." This was Max Clark, the attorney who had headed security for a division of General Dynamics.

Jeanne Le Gon de Mohrenschildt outlived George by sixteen years. Near the end, she was living in a $450 a month cramped room in a Los Angeles house owned by her brother. The one item of value she retained from her days with de Mohrenschildt was the "backyard photograph" inscribed to George by both Marina and Lee Oswald, the photograph in which Oswald holds the "alleged assassination rifle."

The clear suggestion is that Jeanne believed the photograph to have been genuine, and not doctored, despite the anomaly of Oswald's holding two contending newspapers, *The Worker*, and its archenemy Trotskyist paper, *The Militant*. This grotesque detail, irrelevant to whether a different head was affixed to the body, points to Oswald as jokester, a cynic, a man who – like his mentor George de Mohrenschildt – believed in nothing and was for sale.

Jeanne had hoped to sell the photograph for enough money to buy herself a new convertible automobile.

However, the photograph was taken from her by a photographer named Farris Rookstool, who worked for the FBI in Dallas in a minor capacity. In October 1992, a year before Jeanne de Mohrenschildt's death, Rookstool flew out to California, met with her, and after much courting and proffering of gifts, extracted the photograph. Rookstool promised that on her behalf he would sell it to the highest bidder.

She never saw the photograph or Farris Rookstool again. Later Rookstool admitted that he was not an FBI agent at all. Jeanne de Mohrenschildt died on January 21, 1993.

In 1977, the year of George de Mohrenschildt's death, Baby Doc released Clémard Joseph Charles from prison following what Haitian commentator Max Blanchet refers to as "a vigorous campaign in the US on behalf of Mr. Charles." Such a campaign could only have been engineered by CIA; it was definitely not in the style of "90 Deuce."

Charles immediately flew to the United States where he recovered at a Boston hospital. Whatever remained of the money he had stashed in Switzerland had vanished. He tried to enlist Joseph Dryer to fly to Switzerland in quest of the missing cash, but Dryer declined.

The law came calling on I.I. Davidson in 1980 when his insurance bribery schemes with Louisiana Mafia boss Carlos Marcello were exposed by their erstwhile partner and colleague, Joseph Hauser, who had been taping their conversations. Hauser had been carrying an attaché case with the tape recorder inside, exciting I.I.'s suspicion. Careless for once, I.I. had let his concern pass. One side of him knew he was being taped, the other reflected Davidson the overreacher, the wheeler dealer who believed that his connections were too high for him to be anything other than immune to the law. Hadn't he operated outside the law for years?

It all came out: how Davidson and Hauser had conspired to obtain the Teamsters' Southeast and Southwest Health and Welfare Fund life insurance contract by bribing the fund's trustees. In Florida, together with mobster Santos Trafficante, they had conspired to garner labor union insurance contracts by offering union officials huge kickbacks. The *eminence gris* presiding over it all was Carlos Marcello. This byway in Davidson's biography reflects back on de Mohrenschildt, and the company he kept, the people with whom he was connected in Haiti and elsewhere. Among them were de Mohrenschildt's own Mafia cohorts, people like Herbert Itkin.

"If I get knocked out of the box," Davidson told federal investigators, "it's going to hurt this country. I'm involved in some sensitive stuff overseas. I am talking to people who our own people can't talk to." Davidson pointed to his Diary entry for January 4th (1980): "National Security Council," it read.

Marcello forgave I.I., whom he called "Irv," for having introduced him to the duplicitous Joe Hauser: "Don't worry about it," Marcello said. "We still friends." Always, Marcello had trusted Davidson, and once handed over $500,000 to Jimmy Hoffa in Davidson's presence, money destined for Richard Nixon's war chest.

As for Davidson, to his face he called Marcello the "Boss," but behind his back Marcello was "Uncle Snookems." Davidson had long been a man who feared no one. He knew how to keep his many clients happy with him. He was exactly what he had admitted to being: a mover and shaker, welcoming all manner of clients, from Mafia kingpins and the Teamsters and Hoffa to heads of state, from Presidents of the United States to tinhorn dictators at the helm in Latin American "republics."

For his insurance schemes with Carlos Marcello, on June 17, 1980, Davidson was indicted on twelve counts of "racketeering and mail and wire fraud," as well as "conspiracy involving an alleged scheme to obtain insurance contracts in Louisiana by bribery."

Marcello went to jail, but Davidson was found not guilty on all twelve counts. He walked out of federal court a free man, murmuring, "I'm upset, I'm upset about the others." Before long I.I. Davidson had returned to, as author John H. Davis writes, "business as usual."

In 1980, the United States granted Clémard Joseph Charles political asylum. He wrote an article in October 1981 published in the *New York Times* and in the *Des Moines Register*, among other places, explaining how he had spent ten years in prison in Haiti because he "was in opposition to cruelty and tyranny." Charles encouraged the U.S. to grant Haitians the same privilege of asylum that the Cuban boat people enjoyed. He was renewing his effort to fight the "Tonton Macoute" and "the corrupt and venal Duvaliers."

Texas journalist Pete Brewton has reported that after Charles moved to the United States, he laundered money used to bribe union officials on behalf of Mario Renda. Renda, in turn, brokered money for Adnan Khashoggi, Mohamed Fayed's once and future mentor. This money had been "skimmed from union pension fund deposits."

Clémard Joseph Charles had swum within the sea of Duvalier's corruption as well as CIA drug trafficking. Now, broke and in exile, he turned to those Duvalier minions with whom he had done business in palmier days. Charles used his old contacts, including Mohamed Fayed, to turn the money into untraceable cash by first wiring it to Swiss bank accounts.

In these years, Charles did business with the Miami lawyer who represented Lawrence Freeman, a disbarred attorney and convicted money launderer for a cocaine smuggler named Jack Devoe. Lawyer Freeman in turn was a former law partner of CIA's Paul Helliwell, who laundered money for Miami crime boss Santos Traficante.

Clémard Joseph Charles continued under the scrutiny of the 902nd Army Intelligence Group. A Defense Intelligence Agency document states, as a factual matter, that Charles died in Haiti in 1981. Charles died under "bizarre circumstances," declared army intelligence veteran Roger Pierce, replying to an inquiry about Charles filed under the Freedom of Information Act by Washington, D.C. lawyer and former U.S. Senate investigator, Bernard Fensterwald.

Pierce had told Fensterwald with a straight face, as if his words were true, that Charles was dead. He wasn't.

His information, Pierce lied, came from the U.S. army attaché in Port-au-Prince. Defense Intelligence Agency records on Charles remain classified, Pierce added, despite Charles' death. The revelation of his activities "would still raise all sorts of hell in the Caribbean." Pierce insisted that Charles had "received little or no sympathy or help from the U.S. government."

The freedom of information suit filed to uncover the story of Clémard Joseph Charles and the CIA met with a wall of resistance from the U.S. military. Major General William E. Odom testified under oath that, "no portion of the documents at issue could be segregated and released without causing harm to the national security." Only Charles' longtime relationship with CIA could account for the decision to conceal all records on a disgraced Haitian banker who had run afoul of the vicious Papa Doc.

Presiding over the freedom of information suit to release the records on Charles was United States District Judge John A. Pratt. Pratt had memorized CIA boilerplate arguments for keeping its activities secret from the public. "Disclosure of the records would reveal the identities of case officers and confidential sources as well as the circumstances of their operations," Pratt intoned, adding that "release of the material may also have an adverse effect on working relationships with foreign intelligence agencies." In lying about Charles' death, Army intelligence was making a desperate attempt to prevent anyone from reaching Charles and hearing what he had to say.

Clémard Joseph Charles was still very much alive in the 1980s. Not only was he not dead, but he had not given up his ambition to be president of Haiti. Charles declared himself chairman of a "Federation For The Liberation of Haiti." He continued to plead for United States help in the retaking of "our homeland," while promising that Haiti would not become a "second Cuba."

In 1984, from a base in the United States, Charles helped organize protests in Haiti against the rule of Baby Doc.

In 1986, following the fall of Baby Doc, a civilian-military junta called the National Council of Government (CNG) took power in Haiti. The new CIA-inflected regime welcomed the return of its exiled citizens, and in February Clémard Joseph Charles returned to Haiti.

Soon after his arrival, Charles founded the Alliance For The Renewal of Haiti, one of fifteen new political parties sponsoring candidates for the presidency.

Charles held a news conference at the Port-au-Prince Holiday Inn. If he were elected president, Charles promised, he would provide the people of Haiti with pigs to replace those wiped out by disease near the end of the Duvalier regime.

An "Electoral Council," set up to review the viability of candidates for the presidency, rejected Charles on the ground of his long association with Papa Doc. Charles was labeled an "architect of the dictatorship," which he had been, even as, simultaneously, he had been attempting to overthrow the dictator. Charles appealed the Council's decision to the Haitian Supreme Court, only to have his appeal rejected. He was declared ineligible to run for president of Haiti in the elections of 1987.

Endlessly energetic, back in the United States in 1988, Clémard Joseph Charles turned up as a principal in a tax-exempt charitable corporation called the "St. Charles Pacific Peace Organization." It was incorporated as a non-profit entity with the power to raise money for all manner of profit-making activities, so long as they were devoted to "elevating the standards of health."

The treasurer of this corporation turned out to be a long-time soldier of fortune, anti-Castro operative and Watergate burglar, Frank Sturgis. Also known as "Frank Fiorini," Sturgis was among those CIA assets whose activities had been reported to Frank O'Brien at the New York field office of the FBI by Michael J.P. Malone.

Sturgis had for years been on the periphery of CIA operations. His name appears as having been recruited for CIA's "Operation 40," a group organized by Allen Dulles in 1959 for anti-Castro operations. Called *"La Compañía de Inteligencia y Reconocimiento,* Operation 40 boasted among its participants CIA assets Colonel William Bishop and David Sánchez Morales. "Fiorini's activities were well known to CIA," Alexander I. Rorke, Jr., Sturgis' fellow soldier of fortune, told the FBI. Whatever Fiorini had done, Rorke said, "was done on instructions from CIA."

Rorke himself had recommended to CIA that it utilize Fiorini/Sturgis in its Cuban missions. For confirmation, Rorke had directed the Bureau to Commander Andy Anderson of the U.S. Navy who "had been assigned to CIA's covert office in New York." Clémard Joseph Charles' connections with CIA remained into the 1980s.

Yet another link among the characters in this intrigue is that Rolando Masferrer Rojas had been observed paying off CIA money to Rorke for his anti-Castro operations. This was only a few days before, in late September 1963, Rorke and Geoffrey Sullivan had left on the mysterious flight/mission bound for Cuba, apparently, from which they never returned.

Under a listing in the *Miami Herald* of new nonprofit corporations, sometime in the late 1980s, Gaeton Fonzi discovered the "St. Charles Pacific Peace Organization." Frank Sturgis appeared as "Treasurer." Clémard Joseph Charles' name was there as well. Fonzi reached for the telephone and called Sturgis.

Sturgis laughed. "I told you somebody would see it!" his wife called out. Sturgis refused to tell Fonzi anything about his relationship with Clémard Joseph Charles. How they came to know each other would remain yet another mystery.

In 1989, still very much alive and now sixty-six years old, Charles, the director of four Miami companies, was living in a split-level Jamaica Estates house at 178-44 Grand Central Parkway in Queens, New York. His office was his kitchen table, his equipment a telex, fax and telephone. From this home office, Charles concocted a fraudulent banking pre-Ponzi scheme that reached to heads of state and the PLO. Charles claimed to be operating as the "Bank of Haiti," although he was not authorized to do business either in New York State or in Haiti.

On July 6th, a knock at the door was followed by the appearance of FBI agents. They arrested Charles on federal bank fraud and conspiracy charges. Charles was accused of defrauding his investors, which included drug dealers as well as financial institutions, of tens of millions of dollars.

Among Charles' machinations was a worthless $12 million letter of credit used to defraud banks in India with the unwitting assistance of the National Westminster Bank. Charles also attempted to extract $25 million from another bank by proposing a $500 million deal in U.S. government bonds to be provided by his own non-existent bank.

He tried to hit on the American Express bank for $12 million using a non-existent line of credit. The Royal Bank of Canada, once utilized by Mohamed Fayed and by George de Mohrenschildt, was another of his targets. Charles attempted to steal $200 million in exchange for phony bank notes.

Charles had issued three letters of credit for $6 million (in total) to the PLO, Iraq, and Libya as security for loans made to a candidate for the presidency of the Dominican Republic. Charles' intended victims included the PLO; the Economic Ministries of Iraq and Libya; and a Dominican presidential candidate. The wild schemes stretched even to South Africa, from which Charles was accused of stealing $70 million from individuals and institutions.

Armed with search warrants, the FBI and the Internal Revenue Service seized from Charles' home numerous bank records and documents. U.S. Attorney Andrew Maloney "said the agents also seized the bank's account at the French American Bank of Manhattan, but he said he did not know how much money it held," wrote Pete Bowles in *Newsday*, on July 7, 1989 ("Haiti Exile Busted in Bank Scam").

There were fake letters of credit, promissory notes, and evidence that the address of a "mortgage company" that was part of Clémard Charles' operation was in fact an apartment belonging to one of the defendants. "It's a totally bogus bank which operated a fraudulent scheme to get money from investors, who got back paper which was worthless," Maloney explained later.

Some of the money had been earmarked to fund Charles' upcoming 1990 campaign for the presidency of Haiti. So extensive was the fraud that bail was set for $2.5 million dollars. Three other bank officials were arrested with Charles, including his forty-three-year-old son, Victor Charles, the bank's executive vice-president.

In the process of extricating himself, Charles claimed that he was no longer in touch with Mohamed Fayed.

Released on bail, Charles fled from the United States and once again returned to Haiti. Now a fugitive from justice, he presented himself yet again in 1990 as a candidate for the presidency of Haiti. This time the Electoral Council disqualified him, as a "Duvalierist banker," from running in the December 16th general election because he was "wanted in the United States."

Charles returned to the United States where he died in 1991. Two years after his death, there remained a lien and a civil judgment pending against him.

John Whitten, who had supervised the surveillance of George de Mohrenschildt in Haiti – on James Angleton's orders, operating under the pseudonym "John Scelso" – had retired from CIA. Whitten moved to Vienna where he purchased an apartment and immersed himself in the world of music. He sang with the Vienna Men's Choral Society, and published articles on music. Whitten's specialty was Johann Strauss.

In the late 1990s, CIA was pressured by the Assassination Records Review Board (ARRB) to release "John Scelso's" real name. General Counsel of the ARRB, Jeremy Gunn, flew to Vienna on August 22, 1996, accompanied by a CIA lawyer.

Now seventy-five years old, Whitten became emotional. "On the verge of tears," he begged that his real name not be released. He had committed perjury when applying for residency in Austria, he said. He had lied about having worked for CIA. Now he feared "criminal penalties."

"Extremely distraught," he feared "Islamic terrorists." There had been "several assassinations" in Vienna in recent years, including one of a city councilman. "You must know about the kidnapping and killing of our colleagues around the world," Whitten said.

Should his name be exposed as a former CIA operative, he would be obliged to leave Vienna. Where would he go? Whitten promised that no matter what happened, he "would never betray the CIA by telling anyone about his work as an intelligence officer." He closed his written appeal to the Agency, "With bitter resolve."

CIA obliged. "John Scelso" died in January 2000. Only in 2002 did the Agency make public his real Whitten surname.

George de Mohrenschildt settled into oblivion. He would be remembered in history, if at all, as having shepherded Lee Harvey Oswald around Dallas and Fort Worth prior to the assassination of President Kennedy. Clémard Joseph Charles was condemned in Haiti ever after as a person who facilitated the cruelty and madness of the Duvalier dictatorship, as Duvalier's "bagman." CIA's betrayals of both men would remain invisible, secured firmly under the radar of intelligence contradictions.

Both men were victims of CIA's habit of discarding brutally those assets for whom it no longer had any use. Their stories expose the ruthlessness of CIA's treatment of those whom it draws into the circle of its promises. The experiences of these men reveal that the Agency was more interested in its own health as an institution than in human needs, whether of the Haitian people or of its own assets.

CIA's long-term interest in George de Mohrenschildt, and the Agency's role in connecting him to Clémard Joseph Charles, replicates CIA's assignment to de Mohrenschildt in the matter of Lee Harvey Oswald. Just as de Mohrenschildt mentored a potential CIA-approved candidate for the presidency of Haiti, so de Mohrenschildt had been enlisted by CIA to focus on Oswald, future suspect in the assassination of President Kennedy. The common denominator in the fates of both Clémard Joseph Charles and Lee Harvey Oswald was CIA.

That the Duvaliers, *pere et fils* both, wreaked havoc on the people of Haiti was never a factor in the Agency's machinations to remove these virulent dictators. Despite CIA propaganda, "black" and otherwise, about "promoting democracy" in the world, CIA's agenda in Haiti, as in Vietnam, was to impose a social order amenable to its corporate sponsors and allies. Never did CIA act on behalf of the people who funded its budget.

Just as CIA's preoccupation with the 1956 Suez crisis had meant it would not aid the Hungarian revolution of that year, so CIA now viewed Vietnam as a more fertile arena than Haiti for the enterprises of its corporate allies like Halliburton (in the name of Brown & Root, its new subsidiary), and Bechtel, a somewhat lesser partner in that war. Vietnam was a richer vein to tap than either Haiti or Cuba, because the scale of operations was much vaster and the likely duration of a war there more promising.

CIA did not cease to exert its influence in Haiti after the fall of the Duvaliers. That Haiti should be ruled by anyone not under CIA control would not be tolerated. Clémard Joseph Charles had been correct in approaching military intelligence and CIA out of the conviction that without their backing, he could not secure the presidency of Haiti.

In 1986, CIA created the Haitian National Intelligence Service (NIS), whose primary function was to operate and command the trafficking of cocaine, with the collateral enrichment of those so engaged. Haiti continued to be a way station in the drug trade that moved from Colombia through Haiti to the United States in one dedicated seamless trajectory.

In Haiti's 1987 presidential election, CIA funded the opponents of Catholic priest Jean-Bertrand Aristide. If CIA had permitted the Duvaliers to remain in power, they were not so generous with Aristide, who had termed capitalism a "mortal sin." Among Aristide's "sins" was that he had criticized U.S. support of the Duvaliers.

CIA's disinformation campaign against Aristide included CIA officer Brian Latell's informing the U.S. Congress that Aristide was "unbalanced." He was a manic-depressive, who had been in a mental hospital in Canada, CIA claimed.

Aristide was elected nonetheless, but remained in power for a scant eight months. The officers of the military coup of 1991 had been on CIA's payroll for years. CIA had been ready to unleash covert action in Haiti as early as 1988, only to be thwarted, temporarily, by the Senate Select Committee on Intelligence.

Along the way, CIA placed Haitian paramilitary leader Emmanuel Toto Constant, son of a Duvalier general, on its payroll. Through his "Front for the Advancement and Progress of Haiti" (FRAPH), Constant unleashed murder and mayhem, touchstones of the Duvalier governments. Constant specialized in the murder of civilians. He acknowledged openly that he had assassinated the Minister of Justice and boasted of having been invited to Bill Clinton's inaugural balls.

In 1994, CIA gained authorization to spend $12 million on covert operations to remove the very same military leaders it had supported in its coup against Aristide. President Bill Clinton restored Aristide to office in 1995, but at a price. As Allan Nairn points out in a groundbreaking article in *The Nation* magazine, Aristide "had agreed to accept a U.S. occupation," something he had long opposed. In August 1994, Aristide endorsed a structural adjustment program drafted by the World Bank, the I.M.F. and U.S. AID." Axel Peuker, the World Bank's Haiti desk officer, told Nairn that the return of Aristide "will mean a chance to make Haiti interesting for foreign investors."

According to Nairn, Aristide was "essentially forced to agree to abandon the economic program of the popular movement, a program of redistributing wealth from the rich to the poor." It was Clinton and his National Security Adviser, Anthony Lake, who pressured Aristide to sign on to the World Bank/I.M.F. program.

Aristide's return to Port-au-Prince in a US helicopter, surrounded by US Special Forces people, meant "the beginning of the end of the popular movement in Haiti... and...the beginning of Aristide's own corruption." The popular movement that had brought down Baby Doc was over. Now Aristide, having been corrupted, his principles in tatters, began to enlist gangs to fight his opponents.

FRAPH, the paramilitary mercenaries encouraged and funded by CIA, was still doing business in Haiti.

Compared to its posturing paramilitary operations designed to fail during the Duvalier years, CIA unfurled new operations in Haiti on a scale it had not displayed before. WikiLeaks was to reveal U.S. cables from the Embassy in Port-au-Prince indicating U.S. support for a UN military force to occupy Haiti after the 2004 removal of President Jean-Bertrand Aristide. An October 1, 2008 cable from then-Ambassador to Haiti Janet Sanderson reiterated the point. "The UN Stabilization Mission [MINUSTAH] in Haiti is an indispensable tool in realizing the core USG policy interests," it reads.

The underlying theme was, yet again, keeping Haiti open to foreign, especially U.S., corporate investment. As Sanderson writes, among evils attendant upon "a premature departure of MINUSTAH" would be "a sharp drop in foreign and domestic investment, and resurgent populist and anti-market economy political forces."

Although MINUSTAH, the UN force in Haiti, had cost the U.S. and its allies two billion dollars by 2008, Sanderson wrote that the UN force was "a financial and regional security bargain for the USG." Sanderson added: "In the current context of our military commitments elsewhere, the U.S. alone could not replace this mission." One alternative pondered, the commitment of French troops, was considered not acceptable, given Haiti's history. The title of Sanderson's "confidential" cable is "Why We Need Continuing MINUSTAH Presence In Haiti."

Another WikiLeak features a February 2010 cable from Ambassador Joseph Merton. It quotes the political office director of MINUSTAH, Lizbeth Cullity, warning the U.S. Embassy that opponents of President Réne Préval might "take advantage of public dissatisfaction to organize protests, weaken the GOH [Government of Hatai], and seek...access to the control of funds."

Cullity argued that the big challenge for President Réne Préval was to manage Haiti's earthquake relief efforts "while keeping displaced and unemployed residents from resorting to violence if their needs or expectations are not met." Cullity recognized the danger: that Préval's opponents would take advantage "of public dissatisfaction to organize protests, weaken the GOH, and seek concessions (patronage and, ultimately, access to and control of funds)."

Among Préval's priorities, according to this cable from Ambassador Joseph Merton – and distributed to the White House, the National Security Council, HQ USSOUTHCOM based in Miami, and the Joint Chiefs of Staff – was to "strengthen the powers of the president." It was *La Ronde*, the Duvalier years all over again. It meant reinforcing U.S. economic and political control over the impoverished Haitian population, using the catastrophe of the earthquake as cover and pretext. This was U.S. policy in Haiti as of the new millennium with UN forces functioning as thinly disguised US agents, no different from the so-called "coalitions of the willing" used as cover for the U.S. invasions and occupations of Iraq and Afghanistan.

As I hope this narrative has revealed, the history of Haiti has been shaped by U.S. interventions, first by the military, and then, for the next sixty years, by CIA. The events involving George de Mohrenschildt and Clémard Joseph Charles during the Duvalier regimes foreshadowed the continued misery of the Haitian people. As CIA hovered then, aspiring to control the Government of Haiti, so it would in the years to come. Its notable victim was Jean-Bertrand Aristide.

Haiti stands as an example of how destructive U. S. involvements in the internal affairs of other countries have been, and how they have been characterized by a callous indifference to the needs of the people. CIA in particular has revealed that its interest overwhelmingly has been its own well being as an institution; it has nurtured above all else its power to make policy unimpeded by any branch of the U.S. government, elected or otherwise. Nowhere more lucidly than in Haiti has that reality been made manifest.

NOTES

CHAPTER ONE:
ONE: HAITI: AN ADOPTIVE TEXAN WITH SOME INTELLIGENCE CONNECTIONS

1: "He was a fey character": Fragment of a letter from Edward Browder to historian Bruce Adamson.

1: "I find out he's also hooked": Don DeLillo, *Libra* (Simon & Schuster: New York, 1981), p. 74.

2: The best source for the story of the Haitian revolution is C. L. R. James, *The Black Jacobins: Toussaint L'Ouverture and the San Domingo Revolution* (Vintage Books: New York, 1989). Second edition, Revised.

3: "They were mistaken": James, p. 374.

3: Pétion's condition was that Bolívar free the slaves in the territories he liberated: David Nicholls, *From Dessalines to Duvalier: Race, Colour and National Independence In Haiti* (Rutgers University Press: New Brunswick, New Jersey, 1996), p. 46. In July 1816, Bolívar proclaimed the end of slavery in Venezuela.

3: "the guarantee of the liberty of the blacks": James, p. 374.

4: two companies of Marines: James Ferguson, *Papa Doc, Baby Doc: Haiti And The Duvaliers* (Basil Blackwell: Oxford, UK, 1987), p. 22.

4: "action is evidently necessary": Ibid., Ferguson. p. 22.

4: "in broad daylight": Marines remove gold from the Bank of Haiti: Juan José Arévalo, *The Shark And The Sardines*, translated by June Cobb and Dr. Raul Osegueda (Lyle Stuart: New York). Originally published in 1961. p. 171.

4: Brown & Root…to build the Péligre Dam: Joseph A. Pratt & Christopher J. Castaneda, *Builders: Herman and George R. Brown* (Texas A & M University Press: College Station, Texas, 1999), pp. 134-135.

5: Duvalier gives the army a $400,000 bribe: Interview with Michel Soukar, Haitian historian, in *Haiti Observateur*, May 2, 2007.

6: "could redeem themselves only by thinking black": Robert I. Rotberg (with Christopher K. Clague), *Haiti: The Politics of Squalor* (Houghton Mifflin Company: Boston, 1971, p. 165.

7: Wieland sent an entire rifle company to Haiti answering Duvalier's request for a U.S. military mission: Bernard Diederich & Al Burt, *Papa Doc: The Truth About Haiti Today* (Avon Books: New York, 1969), p. 96.

7: an invading Castro brigade: Interview with CIA officer, John Quirk, January 20, 2010.

8: a $4,300,000 loan as the U.S. poured millions of dollars into Haiti to prop up Duvalier: Diederich and Burt, op. cit., pp. 127-128.

8: "the measure of Duvalier's extraordinary force of character....": Robert Debs Heinl and Nancy Gordon Heinl, *Written In Blood: The Story of the Haitian People 1492-1995* (University Press of America, Inc.: Lanham, Maryland, 2005), p. 584.

8: Marx, Lenin, Atatürk: Ibid., p. 584.

9: "bring President Kennedy to his knees": Bernard Diederich and Al Burt, Ibid. p. 173.

9: Murchison a Duvalier lobbyist: Letter from Raphael Quisdueya to Dear Mr. Garrison. Undated. Records of the Garrison investigation. Courtesy of Lyon Garrison.

9: HAMPCO shipped 1,609,886 pounds of meat in 1962: Bruce Adamson, *Oswald's Closest Friend: The George de Mohrenschildt Story*, Volume VI, p. 131. See also, Adamson, Volume V, pp. 110, 131.

9: "certain deficiencies": Diederich and Burt, p. 344.

10: Bobby Baker made the trouble evaporate: Diederich and Burt, p. 344.

10: Lyndon Johnson receives a kickback: Attorney General Robert F. Kennedy was looking into Bobby Baker's speeding the clearance of meat: Adamson, *Oswald's Closest Friend: The George de Mohrenschildt Story*, Volume VI, p. 131. A *New York Times* story on the subject appeared on November 13, 1963. For more press reporting on how Baker was splitting fees with Lyndon Johnson, see "Baker, U.S. Aide Split Meat Fees, Probe Told," *The Evening Star*, January 4, 1964.

10: shakedowns and harassment: Diederich and Burt, p. 166.

11: de Mohrenschildt states in August 1964 in Haiti that he was born in Sweden of Swedish parents: AGENCY: FBI. RECORD NUMBER: 124-10135. AGENCY FILE NUMBER: 100-32965-306. ORIGINATOR: CIA. FROM: ANGLETON, JAMES. TO: DIRECTOR, FBI. DATE: 04/05/65. PAGES: 29. SUBJECTS: DEMOH, POST-OSWALD PERIOD, HAITIAN CONNECTION. NARA.

12: George de Mohrenschildt was entitled to call himself a Baron by virtue of a title granted the "Morenskildes" by Queen Christine of Sweden in 1650. For biographical detail on de Mohrenschildt, see: CIA. 104-10431-10035. AGENCY FILE NUMBER: RUSS HOLMES WORK FILE. TITLE: DEMOHRENSCHILDT, GEORGE SERGIUS [DRAFT BIOGRAPH]. PAGES: 100. JFK-RH18:F1 1998.09.16.08:35:55:280128. NARA. See also the eleven volumes of Bruce Adamson's *Oswald's Closest Friend: The George de Mohrenschildt Story*. Volume One, "1,000 Points of Light: The Public Remains In The Dark." On the cover is a rare photograph of the nineteen-year-old de Mohrenschildt provided to Adamson by Dimitri von Mohrenschildt. Santa Cruz, California: 1996. See also: United States Civil Service Commission file on George de Mohrenschildt. NARA.

12: begging for food, living like "an animal": George de Mohrenschildt offered this description of his childhood to Igor Voshinin, a Russian friend in Dallas, who reported it to the FBI. The interview with Voshinin is available in the FBI file of George de Mohrenschildt, 100-32965.

13: de Mohrenschildt's father recruited by Allen Dulles: Loftus and Aarons, *The Secret War Against The Jews: How Western Espionage Betrayed the Jewish People* (St. Martin's Press: New York, 1994), p. 598, note 78.

13: George and Dimitri attempt to bring their father into the United States in 1940: See George de Mohrenschildt to Honorable Hugh R. Wilson, Department of State. FBI file of George de Mohrenschildt.

13: Dimitri von Mohrenschildt approved by CIA on April 11, 1950: Memorandum from Personnel Security Division, Office of Security, 13 August 1958, cited in Russ Holmes Work File draft biography of George de Mohrenschildt.

14: *Russian Review* was invited to collaborate with CIA radio component AmcomLib (later renamed Radio Liberty): Spencer Williams to Dimitri von Mohrenschildt, December 9, 1956. Reprinted in Bruce Adamson, *Oswald's Closest Friend*, Volume IV, p. 78.

17: De Mohrenschildt invents a brother who was executed by Hitler: FBI. To: Director. From: Los Angeles. 100-32965-215. March 11, 1964. FBI file of George de Mohrenschildt. 100-32965.

17: he claimed to have served with British intelligence: FBI interview with Henry J. Doscher. March 23, 1964. TO: Legat London. FROM: Director, FBI. FBI file of George de Mohrenschildt.

18: "always seemed to associate with very fine people": This and the other details of de Mohrenschildt's early life in the United States may be found in his FBI file.

21: See FBI report dated February 25, 1964 re FBI calling Charles Scribner's Sons: "They never published a book called *The Son of the Revolution* or anything by de Mohrenschildt." The FBI also checked the catalogues of the New York Public Library and of the Library of Congress. Special Agent James E. Freaney did this investigation.

22: De Mohrenschildt applies for a re-entry permit from Mexico: See: Department of State, Visa Division. January 20, 1943. MEMORANDUM FOR THE FILES. See also: Application For Permission To Depart From The United States: He is "in a ticklish position," de Mohrenschildt writes, "as to how I shall come back if I am reclassified and called to the U.S. Army, very peculiar situation." From the record, it's clear that he had no desire to serve with the U.S. forces in World War II. By now, of course, the Army certainly would not have had him. The verdict of the Interdepartmental Committee is dated February 12, 1943. See also: Navy Department; Office of the Chief of Naval Operations, Office of Naval Intelligence. December 15, 1943. Memorandum for Visa Division, Department of State. Subject: VON MOHRENSCHILDT, George Sergius. Lilia Pardo Larin was also considered a "Nazi suspect." When she did receive a ten day visa to visit the United States in 1942, she had to promise neither to see nor to contact George de Mohrenschildt.

25: "the noble profession of gigolo": Lilia Pardo Larin to George de Mohrenschildt. October 17, 1942. FBI file of George de Mohrenschildt.

26: "films of a pro-Nazi nature": HSCA Staff Report of the Select Committee on Assassinations. March 1979.

27: suspected of being a German propagandist. Report of Investigation. A. J. Cronin, Investigator. September 24, 1957. United States Civil Service Commission investigation into George de Mohrenschildt for the International Cooperation Administration.

27: de Mohrenschildt claims employment with the Economic Resources French Military Mission in 1941 and 1943: Report of Investigation. Name of Investigator: Joseph Aronson. Dates of Investigation, August 20, 21, and 22, 1957. Investigations Division of the United States Civil Service Commission file on George de Mohrenschildt.

28: "OSS non-citizen agent in Mexico": Bruce Adamson, *Oswald's Closest Friend: The George de Mohrenschildt Story: The Paine Dulles Felt Must Be Let Luce*, Volume VI, p. 3. Adams refers to a NAVIN-VSERV intelligence document.

28: "alleged to be a Nazi espionage agent": CIA. 104-10009-10124. AGENCY FILE NUMBER: 201-289248. FROM: HELMS, RICHARD, DD/P, CIA. TO: RANKIN, J. LEE, GEN COUNSEL, WC. TITLE: GEORGE AND JEANNE DE MOHRENSCHILDT. DATE: 06/03/1964. PAGES: 9. COMMENTS: OSW14 : V54 : 1993.06.21.17:31:03.900140. NARA.

28: he kicked Dorothy in the abdomen and hit her on the head with a hammer: See United States Department of State, Federal Bureau of Investigation document. March 9, 1964. 3 pages. Re: GEORGE DE MOHRENSCHILDT, JEANNE DE MOHRENSCHILDT. FBI file of George de Mohrenschildt.

28: "kissing and pawing other women": FBI. Interview with Mrs. Olga B. Markov. SAs John R. Wineberg and Thomas F. Lewis. March 25, 1964. FBI file of George de Mohrenschildt.

28: the children would probably be born without arms or legs: FBI. Report of Richard B. Kellogg. March 17, 1964. Miami. FBI file of George de Mohrenschildt.

29: nightmare of a marriage: De Mohrenschildt was with Dorothy Pierson from June 1943 to January 1944.

30: De Mohrenschildt financed his studies at the University of Texas, in part, with a grant from the "Russian Student Fund." This was the same organization that sponsored his brother Dimitri's *Russian Review*.

30: "ponies": de Mohrenschildt cheats on examinations: Civil Service Commission interview with Dr. Wynne Sharples, 1957.

31: "neglected his job": Civil Service Commission investigation of de Mohrenschildt by Wilbur L. Rusho. August 20, 1957. Part of OPM (CSC) file on de Mohrenschildt available in HSCA, Box 132.

32: mental illness: Phyllis Washington was termed a "borderline mental case": See FBI. "Background Information Regarding Phyllis de Mohrenschildt, Former Wife of George de Mohrenschildt." FBI file of George de Mohrenschildt.

33: "doesn't know right from wrong": Dr. Wynne Sharples spoke about de Mohrenschildt for the United States Civil Service Commission investigation. The interviewer was Philip E. Kosky, Sept. 18, 19, 20, 23, 1957.

35: "forced to spend considerable sums of money on occasion to bail de Mohrenschildt out of various oil deals": Interview with Mr. Samuel Butler. Report of J. Hale McMenamin. February 28, 1964. FBI file of George de Mohrenschildt.

36: "not a competent or aggressive business partner: FBI interview with Edward Walz. March 4, 1964. FBI file. SUBJECT: Clémard Joseph Charles. FOIPA # 224,861. C.A.#:82-2156. NARA.

36: for de Mohrenschildt's law suits against Wynne Sharples, See FBI report February 25, 1964. Special Agents Charles Silverthorn and John R. Wineberg, at Philadelphia. FBI file of George de Mohrenschildt.

37: Schlumberger as a CIA partner: See CIA records which reveal its relationship with Schlumberger: CIA. 104-10104-10178. FROM: CHIEF, CI/R&A) (ROCCA), TITLE: GARRISON AND THE KENNEDY ASSASSINATION. MEMO #4. (LIST OF PERSONS WHO HAVE HAD CONTACT WITH CIA AND ALSO HAVE BEEN INVOLVED IN GARRISON INVESTIGATION). DATE: 06/20/67. PAGES: 12. JFK37:F11 1993.07.26.10:40:48:590620. NARA.

37: The Garrison investigation provoked CIA to release information of its longstanding relationship with the Schlumberger Well Surveying Corporation of Houston: CIA. 104-10435-10025. RUSS HOLMES WORK FILE. TO: DIRECTOR, CIA. FROM: [REDACTED]. TITLE: MEMO: GARRISON'S CHARGES AGAINST CIA. 09/15/67. 6 PAGES. JFK-RHO2:F050-1 1998.11.16.12:53:17:780129. NARA.

37: "extensive CIA traces on this company": Enclosure 24 of CIA. 104-105150-10035. TITLE: MEMO NO. 2: GARRISON AND THE KENNEDY ASSASSINATION. 05/08/67. 32 PAGES. JFK64-25:F3 1999.0217.10:10:17:733120. NARA.

37: "three or four subsidiaries elsewhere": CIA. 104-10435-10009. RUSS HOLMES WORK FILE. FROM: DDO/PIC TO: CI STAFF. TITLE: OFFICIAL ROUTING SLIP WITH ATTACHED RESANITIZED COPY OF MEMO #8 OF THE GARRISON PACKAGE. DATE: 1/12/68. JFK-RHO2:F050-1. 1998.11:16:10:30:32:373129: NARA.

37: address book: we are indebted to Bruce Adamson, whose research efforts uncovered the de Mohrenschildt address book, and who has scrutinized its entries.

37: at least ten CIA assets or employees: Adamson, Volume One, p. 18A.

38: Samuel Washington supervises two hundred and fifty CIA employees: See Adamson, Volume XI, p. 4. A detailed biographical portrait of Samuel Washington appears in this volume.

39: "get even with the world": Interview with Dimitri Djordjadze, Representative, Christie. Mitchell Oil Company, Fidelity Union Life Building, Dallas. Investigation by V.A. Memmolo. September 9 and 10, 1957. United States Civil Service Commission.

39: International Cooperation Administration: Neither the Warren Commission nor the House Select Committee on Assassinations could discover any records from an "International Cooperation Administration." Obviously they had been purged.

40: CIA and ICA are interchangeable, one and the same. The following document appears in CIA's file of documents relating to the Research Institute of America: MEMORANDUM FOR THE RECORD: SUBJECT: Soviet Repatriation campaign – Mr. Max Rabb/ White House Interest. 19 March 1956. Signed by F. M. Hand. The entire file contains CIA documents: CIA. 104-10070-10296. TITLE: CONTACTS WITH RESEARCH INSTITUTE OF AMERICA/LEO CHERNE, 18 JANUARY 1952-19 AUGUST 1957. SUBJECTS: CHERNE, LEO; R.I.A. JFK14:F34 1999.02.22.15:23:03:750120. NARA.

41: Dulles knows the "name of every city, town, river": Mary Bancroft, *Autobiography of a Spy*. (New York: Morrow, 1983), p. 186.

41: Yugoslavia now buys oil and oil machinery: See "Yugoslavia Oil Program Seen," *Dallas Times-Herald*, December 4, 1957.

42: de Mohrenschildt is in Yugoslavia for eight months: See: "Dallas Oil Experts To Aid Yugoslavia," *Dallas Times-Herald*, January 17, 1957.

42: ten separate reports: The document listing de Mohrenschildt's reports to CIA is: CIA. 104-10518-10078. FROM: CI STAFF. TO: SUPPORT BRANCH DIVISION, 00. TITLE: REPORT: REPORTS RECEIVED FROM GEORGE DE MOHRENSCHILDT. DATE: 04/20/64. PAGES: 2. JFK64-52:F3 1999.03.12.13:43:01:060128. NARA.

42: de Mohrenschildt's CIA affiliation an "open secret": George Kitchel tells Bruce Adamson that de Mohrenschildt worked for CIA: Adamson, *Oswald's Closest Friend*, Volume III, p. 64.

43: this August 13th document is referenced in a document from the Director of Central Intelligence to the Deputy Director, Plans, and also indicates that de Mohrenschildt had long been of Agency interest: CIA. 104-10244-10247. FROM: DIRECTOR, CENTRAL INTELLIGENCE AGENCY. TO: DEPUTY DIRECTOR, PLANS. TITLE: LETTER: DEAR SIR: FOR YOUR INFORMATION I AM ENCLOSING COMMUNICATIONS WHICH MAY BE OF INTEREST TO YOU. DATE: 03/17/64. PAGES: 2. SUBJECTS: DEMOHRENSCHILDT. JFK64-5:F16B. 1998.06.08.12:58:57:356128: ATTACHED, REPORT. NARA.

43: CIA's "proprietary" corporations: Taylor Branch and George Crile III, "The Kennedy Vendetta: How the CIA waged a silent war against Cuba," *Harper's Magazine*, August 1975, p. 51.

44: the alias "Phillip Harbin": Robert J. Drummond, Jr., Director, United States Civil Service Commission, Bureau of Personnel Investigations, To Mr. G. Robert Blakey. AGENCY: HSCA. RECORD NUMBER: 180-10087-10309. AGENCY FILE NUMBER: 0006857. DATE: 03/02/78. PAGES: 88. SUBJECTS: DE MOHRENSCHILDT, GEORGE, EMPLOYMENT. DEMOHRENSCHILDT'S civil service file is in Box 132. NARA. A portion of de Mohrenschildt's Bureau of Personnel Investigation file containing the Department of State and Federal Bureau of Investigation reports was transferred to the Civil Service Commission's "relocation" facility in Suitland, Maryland, "to await destruction."

44: De Mohrenschildt borrowed money from friends, yet he paid them back: For example, while he was negotiating his Haiti deal he borrowed $600 from Thomas J. Attridge, the Deputy Manager of the Equitable Life Assurance Society of the United States. See Interview with Attridge by Special Agent Raymond P. Yelchak. March 3, 1964.

44: "scrimped and saved...had enough money to do as they pleased": FBI interview with Gary Taylor by Special Agents Robert E. Bashaw and James J. Ward. December 3, 1963. FBI file of George de Mohrenschildt.

44: not working "steadily": FBI interview with Ilya A. Mamantov, November 23, 1963. This interview is Warren Commission Document 205. 100-10461. Agents interviewing Mamantov were Emory E. Horton and Ural E. Horton, Jr. NARA.

45: "very interested sexually in the daughter of one of his wives: FBI. Report of T-4 (Los Angeles). Special Agent Riley L. Millard. March 16, 1964. T-4 was unique among de Mohrenschildt's acquaintances in keeping his name off the record.

45: George de Mohrenschildt wrote to Honorable George C. McGhee on October 19, 1962; McGhee replied on October 22nd. Both letters appear in the FBI file of George de Mohrenschildt.

47: de Mohrenschildt's proposal for a "Haitian Holding Company". Letter appended to CIA. 104-10518-10078. TITLE: REPORT: REPORTS RECEIVED FROM GEORGE DE MOHRENSCHILDT. DATE: 04/20/64. SUBJECTS: DEMOHRENSCHILDT. NARA. A copy of the blueprint appears in the FBI file of Clémard Joseph Charles.

47: "you and Texas": Clémard Joseph Charles to George de Mohrenschildt. De Mohrenschildt Exhibit No. 2. Warren Commission Hearings, Volume XIX.

47-48: Texas foundations: See: E. W. Kenworthy, "Triple Pass: How C.I.A. Shifts Funds," The New York Times, February 19, 1967, p. 1, 26; "House of Glass," Newsweek, March 6, 1967, p. 32; Richard Harwood, "Secret Use Of Public's Money: CIA and Foundations," Houston Chronicle, February 26, 1967, Section 1, p. 2; Vitaly Petrusenko, A Dangerous Game: CIA and the Mass Media, translated from the Russian by Nicolai Kozelsky and Vladimir Leonov. Published by Interpress. Prague, Czechoslovakia; Memo From The Desk of Earle Cabell, February 20, 1967. Note to General Philip H. Bethune. DeGolyer Library. Southern Methodist University. Papers of Earle Cabell. Box 22, Folder 16; CIA. 104-10117-10203. FROM: HALL, SARAH K. TO: CHIEF, LEOB/SRS. TITLE: MEMO: DECEMBER 1967 "RAMPARTS" ARTICLE ENTITLED 'THE CIA'S BROWN AND ROOT DIMENSIONS.' DATE: 12/20/67. PAGES: 8. SUBJECTS: "RAMPARTS"; BROWN AND ROOT. NARA.; CIA. 104-10059-10026. FROM: WITHHELD. TO: DDP. TITLE: INDICATIONS OF THE SCOPE AND POSSIBLE DAMAGE OF NEW ALLEGATIONS BY RAMPARTS MAGAZINE. DATE: 11/25/68. PAGES: 48. SUBJECTS: MEDIA REPORT; RAMPARTS MAGAZINE. JFK8f11 1993.07.08.15:45:04:500340. DDP INTERNAL MEMO WITH ANNEX A-F. IN 11/97. ARRB DECLARED ALL BUT THE PARAGRAPH ON THE IRC AS NBR. NARA. (NBR is "Not Believed Relevant").

Notes

50: de Mohrenschildt claims he will be in charge of the "Haitian Government Development Projects," including a large air field: FBI interview with Mr. and Mrs. Edward Robert Thomas. April 1, 1964. FBI file of George de Mohrenschildt.

50: de Mohrenschildt attempts to enlist Jean de Menil as an investor in his Haitian Holding Company: De Mohrenschildt Exhibit No. 5, George de Mohrenschildt to Jean de Menil, July 27, 1962. Warren Commission Hearings, Volume XIX. See also: George de Mohrenschildt to Mr. Jean de Menil, August 7, 1962. De Mohrenschildt Exhibit No. 16. Warren Commission Hearings, Volume XIX.

50: de Mohrenschildt assumes that his "American connections" facilitated his contract with Duvalier: Edward Jay Epstein, *The Assassination Chronicles: Legend,* (Carroll & Graf Publishers, Inc: New York, 1992), p. 559.

51: De Mohrenschildt invites oil men to lunch at the Petroleum Club to raise money for his efforts in Haiti: FBI interview with Morris I. Jaffe. March 4, 1964. Special Agent Carl E. Underhill. FBI file of George de Mohrenschildt.

51: De Mohrenschildt asks Paul M. Raigorodsky for $100,000: FBI interview with Paul M. Raigorodsky, March 5, 1964. Special Agent Richard L. Wiehl. Raigorodsky thought that de Mohrenschildt was "too immoral to be concerned with politics." A parallel comment was made by Henry Rogatz: "George was too much of a coward to ever be subversive." (FBI interview with Henry Rogatz, February 29, 1964. Special Agent Richard L. Wiehl).

51: De Mohrenschildt tells people he can be reached in Haiti through Clémard Joseph Charles at the *Banque Commerciale d'Haiti:* FBI file, CLÉMARD JOSEPH CHARLES. 82-2156. March 4, 1964. 100-32965-143. Interview with Edward J. Walz. Fensterwald file. AARC.

52: Orlov a handball partner of J. Walton Moore: Adamson, Volume I, p. 20.

53: Sam Ballen: See Ballen's testimony before the Warren Commission, March 24, 1964. Volume IX, pp. 46ff. See also: Interview with Samuel Ballen by V.A. Memmolo, September 9 and 10, 1957 for the United States Civil Service Commission.

54: later Moore corrected himself. J. Walton Moore admitted that he had interviewed de Mohrenschildt in 1957 only when he himself was interviewed on March 14, 1978 before the House Select Committee on Assassinations. Moore had already told something closer to the truth to the Acting Chief of the CIA's Contacts division in a memorandum dated May 1, 1964. This document turned up in de Mohrenschildt's own CIA file.

54: "debriefing" purposes: CIA. J. Walton Moore personnel file. Fitness Report. April 1, 1963-March 31, 1964. George de Mohrenschildt 201 file: Memorandum. April 3, 1977 to CHIEF, DCD. See also: May 1, 1964, To: Acting Chief, Contacts Division. FROM: Dallas resident agent. The Staff Interview of James Walton Moore, March 14, 1978 is HSCA 014893.

54: Clay Shaw, a CIA asset: See Joan Mellen, *A Farewell To Justice: Jim Garrison, JFK's Assassination and The Case That Should Have Changed History* (Potomac Books: Dulles, Virginia, 2005). PERMINDEX documents appeared in Clay Shaw's CIA file three years before the Kennedy assassination and included a March 24, 1967 "Memorandum Regarding trace results on persons connected with Centro Mondiale Commerciale (World Trade Center)," Italian subsidiary of PERMINDEX. For Shaw being "highly paid" by CIA, see: op. cit: CIA. 104-10337-10006. AGENCY FILE NUMBER: PROJFILES – CIA MATTERS. FROM: J. KENNETH MCDONALD. TO: DIRECTOR OF CENTRAL INTELLIGENCE. TITLE: CIA MATTERS-JFK RECORDS, BACKGROUND. DATE: 02/10/1992. PAGES: 82. SUBJECTS: JFK ASSASSINATION. UNIT INDEX. JFK RECORDS. JFK-M-21 : F7 : 20030804-974400 : UNIT INDEX. NARA.

55: Shaw "a highly paid CIA contract source": AGENCY: CIA. RECORD NUMBER: 104-10337-10006. RECORD SERIES: JFK. AGENCY FILE NUMBER: PROJFILES – CIA MATTERS. FROM: J. KENNETH MCDONALD. TO: DIRECTOR OF CENTRAL INTELLIGENCE. TITLE: CIA MATTERS – JFK RECORDS, BACKGROUND. DATE: 02/10/1992. PAGES: 82. JFK-M-21 : F7 : 20030804-974400 : UNIT INDEX.

55: "I would never have contacted Oswald": Edward Jay Epstein, *The Assassination Chronicles*, p. 559.

55: "keep tabs on Oswald": Ibid.

55: agencies that held files on George de Mohrenschildt: CIA. 104-10009-10124. AGENCY FILE NUMBER: 201-28948. FROM: HELMS, RICHARD, DD/P, CIA. TO: RANKIN, J. LEE, GEN COUNSEL, WC. TITLE: GEORGE AND JEANNE DE MOHRENSCHILDT. DATE: 06/03/1964. PAGES: 9. SUBJECTS: DEMOHRENSCHILDT, ICA. COMMENTS: OSW14 : V54 :1993.06.21.17:31:03:900140. NARA.

CHAPTER TWO: CLÉMARD JOSEPH CHARLES TEAMS UP WITH GEORGE DE MOHRENSCHILDT

59: Thomas J. Devine remains with Project WUBRINY, and is "a cleared and witting contact in the investment banking firm which houses and manages the proprietary corporation WUSALINE": 30 January 1968. MEMORANDUM FOR: DO/Security. SUBJECT: Thomas James Devine -201-267708 OS#42069. Signed by Gale Allen, DO/CO. NARA.

59: a teacher in rural schools: CIA. Office of Central Reference. Biographic Register. HAITI. Clémard Joseph L. Charles, President and General Manager, Commercial Bank of Haiti. 3 pages. July 1964. NARA.

60: an enterprising American businessman named Joseph F. Dryer, Jr.: The story of Dryer's adventures in Cuba and Haiti, and his relationship with Clémard Joseph Charles, derives from the author's Interview with Dryer, January 8, 2010.

60: world production of jute: "Ready Market Reported For Kenaf Fiber In Cuba": Papers of Czarnikow-Rionda. University of Florida Czarnikow-Rionda collection. See also: "Kenaf In Cuba: Up To Now We Have All Been Failures," THE SUGAR JOURNAL. November 1957, pp. 18-24. "The Sugar Journal" was published out of New Orleans.

60: Dryer's kenaf business in Cuba. Ibid. Fonzi interview with Joseph Dreyer. See also: Jack Hemingway, "A Life Worth Living: The Adventures of a Passionate Sportsman" (*Sports & Recreation*: 2004), pp. 127-128.

61: December 15, 2009, January 8, 2010, and subsequent letters and telephone conversations.

62: Malone calls Dryer "a very good man": Michael J. P. Malone to Mr. Alfonso Fanjul, Cuban Trading Company, October 17, 1957.

63: Joseph F. Dryer meets Clémard Joseph Charles in Cuba: Interview by the author with Joseph F. Dryer, Jr., January 8, 2010. HSCA. MEMORANDUM. July 7, 1978. TO: G. Robert Blakey. FROM: Gaeton Fonzi. Re: Interview with Joseph Dryer. Courtesy of Mr. Fonzi.

66: "situation in Cuba seems to be more eased": Memorandum from Michael J. P. Malone to Mr. James A. O'Hara, January 7, 1959. Czarnikow-Rionda collection, University of Florida. See also: Memorandum. To: Mr. H. G. Atkinson. From: D. Rivera. Date: February 9, 1959. Ref: "Kenaf." Czarnikow-Rionda Collection, University of Florida.

66: Czarnikow considers Dryer's offer to invest in Haiti; Dryer sends Czarnikow a memorandum: "Investment Potential of the Kenaf Industry in Haiti": James A. O'Hara to Michael J. P. Malone, February 2, 1959. Malone files. Papers of Czarnikow-Rionda, University of Florida.

67: Czarnikow turned Dryer down, and chose not to invest in his operations in Haiti (and Guatemala): Conversation with Joseph F. Dryer, Jr. November 25, 2009.

67-68: Charles and two Miami citizens found the "Haitian Industrial Mortgage Bank": FOREIGN SERVICE DISPATCH. FROM: Amembassy, PORT-AU-PRINCE. TO: THE DEPARTMENT OF STATE, WASHINGTON. September 30, 1959. REF CERP Section D, Items II-A-2 and V-A-3. "Establishment of 'Haitian Industrial Mortgage Bank.'"

68: "building assembly plants in Haiti": FOREIGN SERVICE DISPATCH. FROM: Amembassy, PORT-AU-PRINCE. TO: THE DEPARTMENT OF STATE, WASHINGTON. October 30, 1959. Signed: David R. Thomson, Second Secretary of Embassy. (This is a Department of State document).

69: showered Charles with honors: Elizabeth Abbott, *Haiti: The Duvaliers and Their Legacy* (McGraw-Hill Book Company: New York, 1988), p. 181.

69: Clémard Joseph Charles is being tracked by the 902nd Military Intelligence Group out of Fort Holabird. The documents reflecting the military surveillance of Charles, marked INSCOM/CSF, were released from the historical section and are sometimes known as the "IRR" records (Investigative Records Repository, residing at Fort Meade, which houses the records of the 902nd Military Intelligence Group.). AGENCY: INSCOM/CSF. RECORD NUMBER: 194-10014-10166. RECORD SERIES: DOD AFFILIATED PERSONNEL AND INCIDENT INVESTIGATIONS. AGENCY FILE NUMBER: AA851401WJ – PAGE 130.

69: an FBI check on Charles' activities in Miami: FROM: FBI. TITLE: MEMORANDUM. DATE: 08/17/62. PAGES: 1. SUBJECTS: CHARLES, CLÉMARD J.; SCHULWOLF, FRANK. NARA.

69: Army Intelligence attempts to assess Charles' character: AGENCY: INSCOM/CSF. RECORD NUMBER: 194-10014-10154. AGENCY FILE NUMBER: AA851401WJ – PAGES 97-98. FROM: USARMA PORT AU PRINCE. TO: DEPTAR FOR ACSI. TITLE: MESSAGE. DATE: 05/01/63. PAGES: 2. SUBJECTS: CHARLES, CLÉMARD J. NARA.

69: Charles not a good looking man and lacked charisma: Interview with journalist and long-time resident in Haiti, Bernard Diederich, July 31, 2011.

69: CIA had long been interested in intervening in Haiti. See CIA document dated June 11, 1965, and marked "SECRET EYES ONLY" which provides some of this history: MEMORANDUM FOR: ARA-Mr. Vaughn. FROM: INR/DDC – Murat W. Williams. SUBJECT: Minutes of the 303 Committee Meeting June 10, 1965. Date: June 11, 1965. 2 pages: NARA. This document was filed under "Cuba," hence its release under the JFK ACT.

ARA stands for the Bureau of Inter-American Affairs for Latin America and the Caribbean. Jack H. Vaughn, until the previous March, had been Assistant Secretary of State for Inter-American Affairs. INR/DDC, the Bureau of Intelligence and Research, was closely connected to CIA's Office of Security. Murat W. Williams was a Foreign Service officer who had been Ambassador to El Salvador until June 1964.

69: Herbert Itkin blows the whistle on a CIA plot to assassinate President François Duvalier: CIA. 104-101007-10143. FROM: HOUSTON, L.R. OGC (Office of General Counsel). TO: MFR. TITLE: HERBERT ITKIN – DRAFT MEMO. DATE: 11/20/1968. PAGES: 6. SUBJECTS: ITKIN, H. JFK38:F10 1994.04.12.12.18.58:48:850006. NARA.

72: "Paradise in Chains": Charles F. Willis, Jr. to Allen Dulles, October 12, 1960. Dulles papers. Princeton University.

72-73: Schlesinger proposes a "black operation": Memorandum From The President's Assistant (Schlesinger) to President Kennedy. February 11, 1961. Foreign Relations of the United States, 1961-1963. Volume X, Cuba, January 1961-September 1962. Document 43.

73: "no one on the scene now": Memorandum Prepared in the Department of State. March 23, 1961. "Memorandum on United States-Haitian Relations." Foreign Relations of the United States, Volume XII, American Republics. Document 365.

73: "whatever is done will be attributed to the United States": Paper Prepared in the Central Intelligence Agency. Foreign Relations of the United States, 1961-1963, Volume XII, American Republics. Document 381.

73-74: For the debates within the U.S. government regarding what to do about Haiti, See: Special National Intelligence Estimate, "Short-Term Prospects in Haiti," dated June 7, 1961, prepared by the Central Intelligence Agency, and the intelligence components of the Departments of State, the Army, the Navy, and the Air Force, and the Joint Chiefs of Staff, and submitted to the U.S. Intelligence Board. Foreign Relations of the United States, Volume XII, American Republics. Document 369.

73: "an active covert role": Letter from the Assistant Secretary of State for Inter-American Affairs (Martin) to the Ambassador to Haiti (Thurston). August 11, 1962. Foreign Relations of the United States, Volume XII, American Republics. Document 373.

74: "Another coup really doesn't do any good": Quoted in Tim Weiner, *Legacy of Ashes: The History of the CIA* (Doubleday: New York, 2007), p. 190.

74: "This is too long": Summary Record of the 509th National Security Council Meeting. March 13, 1963. Subject: Latin American Policy. Foreign Relations of the United States, Volume XII, American Republics. Document 377.

74: Kennedy suspended shipments of war materiel: Memorandum Prepared in the Department of State. January 21, 1963. "Haiti Situation and United States Policy." Foreign Relations of the United States, Volume XII, American Republics. Document 374.

74: "to meet a United States military requirement": Memorandum From the Executive Secretary of the Department of State (Brubeck) to the President's Special Assistant for National Security Affairs (Bundy). August 8, 1962. Foreign Relations of the United States, Volume XII, American Republics, Document 373.

75: "promising Haitian exiles": Memorandum From The Executive Secretary of the Department of State (Brubeck) to the President's Special Assistant for National Security Affairs (Bundy). June 1, 1962. Foreign Relations of the United States, Volume XII, American Republics. Document 371. See also: Document 373. This document was concurred in formally by the Central Intelligence Agency.

75: a "paramilitary operation involving an invasion of Haiti": Church Committee Boxed files. 157-10011-10024. Testimony of DCI William Colby, 21 May 1975. NARA.

75: "a heavy shipment of large arms from a U.S. government agency": CIA Sept. 17, 1962. Received from Charles McCarthy, I & NS (Immigration and Naturalization Service). 10:15 A.M. CIA cable. NARA.

75: more than eight such invasions and attempted coups: Mark Danner, *Stripping Bare The Body: Politics, Violence, War* (Nation Books: New York, 2009), p. 6.

75: Clémard Joseph Charles values his personal investments at $500,000: FROM: Amembassy, PORT-AU-PRINCE. SUBJECT: Conversation with Clémard Joseph Charles of the Commercial Bank of Haiti on April 18 1963. REF Embassy A-406. April 11, 1963.

75: "favorable relations with well-placed Duvalier regime figures": Clémard Joseph Charles visited the U.S. Embassy in Port-au-Prince on February 16, 1963: OFFICIAL USE ONLY. TO: DEPARTMENT OF STATE. FROM: Amembassy, PORT-AU-PRINCE. SUBJECT: Banking. Balance Sheet of the *Banque Commerciale d'Haiti*. DATE: February 16, 1963. For the *Chargé d'affairs*, Robert B. Hill, First Secretary of Embassy.

76: granting a Canadian the right to handle all public transportation of merchandise: Diederich and Burt, *Papa Doc*, pp. 342-344.

76: SHADA and Duvalier transferring SHADA to the bank of Clémard Joseph Charles: Raphael Quisqueya to Dear Mr. Garrison. Courtesy of Lyon Garrison.

77: Robert Debs Heinl and Nancy Gordon Heinl repeatedly refer to Charles as a Duvalier bagman. See, for example, *Written In Blood*, p. 541 and p. 684.

77: perhaps CIA wants to talk to him about his business enterprises: Notes of Bernard Fensterwald labeled "Charles." Courtesy of James H. Lesar.

78: Charles wrote a nine-page document: Available in the Bernard Fensterwald file on Charles. Available from AARC, Washington, D.C. Courtesy of James H. Lesar, President.

78: De Mohrenschildt writes to Colonel Roy J. Batterton, Jr: George de Mohrenschildt to Colonel Roy J. Batterton, Jr. April 5, 1963. AGENCY: INSCOM/CSF RECORD NUMBER: 194-10014-10153. RECORDS SERIES: DOD AFFILIATED PERSONNEL AND INCIDENT INVESTIGATIONS. AGENCY FILE NUMBER: AA851401WJ – PAGE 96. NARA. Note: INSCOM stands for U.S. Army Intelligence and Security Command. OACSI stands for Office of the Assistant Chief of Staff for Intelligence, which was Dorothe Matlack. INSCOM's chronology of the comings and goings of Clémard Joseph Charles and George de Mohrenschildt is four pages long, single-spaced and marked "Secret." Bruce Adamson uncovered the thank you note to Colonel Roy J. Batterton, Jr.

78: George de Mohrenschildt writes to Honorable Lyndon Johnson, April 17, '63. LBJ Library, Austin, Texas.

79: the reply from Lyndon Johnson's office is dated April 18th: Walter Jenkins to Mr. Mohrenschildt. April 18, 1963. LBJ library, Austin, Texas. It was Bruce Adamson who originally discovered this correspondence.

79: de Mohrenschildt deposits a check for $1,200 in his savings account: Adamson, *Oswald's Closest Friend: The George de Mohrenschildt Story*, Volume V, p. 66.

80: Howard Burris: I am indebted for this information to Bruce Adamson. Adamson examines the unlikelihood of Lyndon Johnson's having de Mohrenschildt's April 17th letter answered the very next day.

80: in New York, Clémard Joseph Charles meets a "former journalist": CIA Office of Central Reference Biographic Register, Central Intelligence Agency, July 1964. Report on Clémard Joseph L. Charles, President and General Manager, Commercial Bank of Haiti. NARA.

81: In New York, Joe Dryer meets with Clémard Joseph Charles. This account of their meeting in New York derives from Interviews with Joseph F. Dryer, Jr.

82: "a firm dealing in the import and export of fibers": FBI. NY 100-10310. Report by SA William W. Hamilton. NARA. (Dryer did not remember having initiated this check on de Mohrenschildt).

82: Dryer reports to Army Intelligence about de Mohrenschildt, Lyndon Johnson and Clémard Joseph Charles: AGENCY: INSCOM/CSF. RECORD NUMBER: 194-10014-10165. AGENCY FILE NUMBER: AA851401WJ – PAGES 128-129. TITLE: LETTER. PAGES: 2. SUBJECTS: CHARLES, CLÉMARD J. NARA.

83: Stone and Devine meet at the Knickerbocker Club: CIA. 104-10436-10014. TITLE: CONTACT REPORT. A MEETING WAS HELD IN THE LIBRARY OF THE KNICKERBOCKER. DATE: 04/25/63. PAGES: 8. SUBJECTS: DEMOHRENSCHILDT. JFK-RHO7:F124-2 1998.11.20.12:29:11:013128. NARA.

83: Gale Allen recommends Devine: this document is dated 30 January 1968. From: Gale Allen, DO/CO.

83: Other commercial enterprises under CIA aegis using the WU digraph included: WUPUNDIT, WURAISIN and WUSENDER. Apparently several publishing ventures were grouped under the WU digraph.

84: Richard E. Snyder was a CIA employee: CIA. 104-10181-10263. FROM: SNYDER, RICHARD E. TO: BRADLEY, NORMAN. TITLE: LETTER: DEAR BRICK. DATE: 03119/57. PAGES: 3. SUBJECTS: SNYDER. JFK64-17:F13 1998.07.31.05:44:41:310129. 2 PAGE LETTER AND ENVELOPE. NARA. See also: MEMORANDUM TO DEPUTY PERSONNEL OFFICER. SUBJECT: SNYDER, RICHARD. 3 PAGES including OFFICE MEMORANDUM, UNITED STATES GOVERNMENT.18 Feb 57. See also: Final Report of House Select Committee on Assassinations, pp. 214-215. This report exposes that Snyder lied under oath to the Committee.

85: Dean Lippincott opposed student groups inviting liberal speakers like Howard Fast and Alger Hiss.

85: The author cannot confirm or deny whether CIA was successful in recruiting Brzezinski.

86: George Bush wrote to Thomas J. Devine as "T": See: George H.W. Bush to Thomas J. Devine, Feb. 6th, 1965 in George Bush, *All The Best, George Bush: My Life In Letters And Other Writings* (Scribner: New York, 1999), p. 94.

87: "for use of subject in Project WUBRINY operations": 30 January 1968. MEMORANDUM FOR: DO/Security. SUBJECT: Thomas James Devine -201-267708. OS #42069.

87: WUSALINE is housed by Devine: CONTACT REPORT. IX-95. 26 April 1963. WUBRINY – Haitian Operations. CIA. 104-10070-10076. FROM: CHIEF/DO/COEO. TO: DO/COBO. TITLE: CONTACT REPORT WUBRINY HAITIAN OPERATIONS. DATE: 04/26/63. PAGES: 3. SUBJECTS: HAITIAN OPS DEMOHRENSCHILDT. JFK14:F41 1992.07.31.11.47:55:210047. NARA.

88: "meshing with and protecting....": Kirkpatrick Sale, "Spies With and Without Daggers," in *Uncloaking the CIA*, ed. Howard Frazier. (The Free Press: New York, 1978), p. 152.

89: Bush's involvement in WUBRINY/LPDICTUM: CIA. FROM: CHIEF, COVER & COMMERCIAL STAFF. TO: DEPUTY DIRECTOR OF OPERATIONS. 29 November 1975. The occasion for the creation of this document was CIA's own investigation of George H.W. Bush's history with them at the time of his 1975 confirmation hearings as Director of Central Intelligence.

89: "WUBRINY/LPDICTUM involved in proprietary commercial operations in Europe": 27 November 1975. MEMORANDUM FOR: Deputy Director of Operations. SUBJECT: Messrs. George Bush and Thomas J. Devine. Signed [03] Chief, Cover & Commercial

Notes

Staff. This memo went to the Directorate of Operations/Security in reference to Mr. Devine. The "Postponement Code" [03] designates a CIA employee.

89: a memorandum from J. Edgar Hoover, in which Hoover outs "Mr. George Bush of the Central Intelligence Agency" is dated November 29, 1963. TO: Director, Bureau of Intelligence and Research, Department of State. FROM: John Edgar Hoover, Director. Subject: ASSASSINATION OF PRESIDENT JOHN F. KENNEDY, NOVEMBER 22, 1963. 2 PAGES. 62-109060-1396. NARA.

90: the photographic analyst named George William Bush swore under oath before the United States District Court for the District of Columbia on September 21, 1988 that he had never been debriefed by either CIA or FBI: "I am not the Mr. George Bush of the Central Intelligence Agency referred to in the Memorandum," he testified.

90: Bill Devine refuses to confirm or deny: See Joseph McBride's article in *The Nation*, August 13/20, 1988. See also: McBride, "The Man Who Wasn't There: 'George Bush,' CIA operative," *The Nation* magazine, July 16-23, 1988. Another of George H.W. Bush's unexplained actions occurred on the day of the Kennedy assassination when he telephoned the brother of his friend George Kitchel, an FBI agent named Graham "Kitchell," to report on a possible suspect, James Parrott. It was as if Bush were establishing his location outside of Dallas; Parrott had nothing whatsoever to do with the assassination: See: FBI. TO: SAC, HOUSTON. FROM: SA GRAHAM W. KITCHELL. 11-22-63. NARA.

90: cover jobs for CIA employees: Joseph J. Trento, *Prelude to Terror: The Rogue CIA and The Legacy of America's Private Intelligence Network* (Carroll & Graf: New York, 2005), pp. 13-14.

90: Neil Mallon is well known to Allen Dulles: Anthony Kimery, "George Bush and the CIA: In the Company of Friends," *CovertAction Quarterly*, Number 41, Summer 1992. Kimery cites a March 25, 1953 letter from Prescott Bush to President Eisenhower's National Security adviser C. D. Jackson, dated March 26, 1953.

91: George H.W. Bush's association with CIA through Zapata Off-Shore: See Kimery, Ibid., p. 62. Bush created a company called "PERMARGO" of which Zapata would own 50%, circumventing Mexican law requiring all drilling contracts to be held by Mexican nationals. His partner, Jorge Díaz Serrano, would be convicted of defrauding the Mexican government of $58 million dollars. Involved as well was H. Neil Mallon, who had recommended that Bush become involved in the scheme. See: Jonathan Kwitney, "The Mexican Connection of George Bush," *Barron's National Business and Financial Weekly*, September 19, 1988.

91: "a part-time purchasing front for the CIA": John Loftus, *The Secret War Against The Jews*, p. 368.

91: only a "general knowledge" of how CIA operated: George Bush, *Looking Forward: An Autobiography* (Bantam Books: New York, 1988), p. 165.

91: Clémard Joseph Charles and George de Mohrenschildt visit Devine at his office: The meeting between Charles, de Mohrenschildt and Devine at Devine's office is described in CIA. 104-10070-10076. FROM: CHIEF/DO/COEO. TO: DO/COEO. TITLE: CONTACT REPORT WUBRINY HAITIAN OPERATIONS. DATE: 04/26/63. PAGES: 3. SUBJECTS: HAITIAN OPS, DEMOHRENSCHILDT. JFK14:F 41. 1993.07.31.11:47:55:210047. NARA. Charles has been "the subject of earlier Contact Report," the document reads.

92: "sisal plantation...they never went near": Gaeton Fonzi, *The Last Investigation* (Thunder's Mouth Press: New York, 1994), p. 313.

93: "not appropriate for a banker to ask for money": Memo to C. Frank Stone. From: WUBRINY – Haitian Oper. April 26, 1963. Handwritten. This document includes a history of what the Agency had on its asset de Mohrenschildt. It leaves no doubt that in April 1963 de Mohrenschildt was of Agency interest.

93: assassins fire upon the limousine carrying Duvalier's children: Telegram From The Embassy in Haiti to the Department of State. May 2, 1963. Foreign Relations of the United States, Vol. XII, American Republics. Document 378.

94: Matlack's clearance: See: MATLACK, Mrs. Dorothe – Dept of Army, G-2 (Operations Br). 3 March 1953. MEMORANDUM FOR: Chief, Physical Security Division/OS SUBJECT: Renewals of CIA Building Passes. 15 December 1960. Available on www.maryferrell.org.

94: "a real black intelligence arm of the Pentagon": Dick Russell interview with L. Fletcher Prouty in *The Man Who Knew Too Much* (Carroll & Graf: New York, 1992), p. 319.

95: Clémard Joseph Charles' bank is rated a poor third: AGENCY: INSCOM/CSF. RECORD NUMBER: 194-10014-10154. RECORDS SERIES: DOD AFFILIATED PERSONNEL AND INCIDENT INVESTIGATIONS. AGENCY FILE NUMBER: AA851401WJ – PAGES 97-98. FROM: USARMA PORT AU PRINCE. TO: DEPTAR FOR ACSI. TITLE: MESSAGE. DATE: 05/01/63. SUBJECTS: CHARLES, CLÉMARD J. NARA.

95: Kail in Cuba reported on the Cuban Army: MEMORANDUM – July 24, 1978. TO: G. Robert Blakey. FROM: Gaeton Fonzi. RE: COLONEL SAMUEL G. KAIL, U.S. Army (Ret.). Courtesy of Gaeton Fonzi. Kail managed to remain in Cuba from June 3, 1958 to January 4, 1961.

95: Antonio Veciana and Col. Sam Kail: See Antonio Veciana, Testimony before the House Select Committee on Assassinations, Volume X, pp. 37-56. "Anti-Castro Activities and Organizations." Appendix to Hearings Before The Select Committee on Assassinations of the U.S. House of Representatives. Ninety-Fifth Congress. Second Session. See also: Memo. January 10, 1978. To: Bob Blakey. From: Gaeton Fonzi. Re: Conversation with Senator Schweiker re David Phillips and Military Intelligence. Courtesy of Gaeton Fonzi.

95: Lansdale promotion – see page 334.

96: applying for access to CIA headquarters: SECURITY FILE ON SAMUEL GOODHUE KAIL. 1993.07.24.09:42:23:590310. JFK Box # 43.

96: Alva Revista Fitch and Roland Haddaway Del Mar: See 1972-73, "Who's Who In America."

96: Dryer writes to General Fitch about Clémard Joseph Charles: Letter of Introduction from Joseph Dryer to "Jackie Cooksey": Gen Fitch (Mrs. Cooksey), "Dear Jackie." AGENCY: INSCOM/CSF. RECORD NUMBER: 194-10014-10162. RECORD SERIES: DOD AFFILIATED PERSONNEL AND INCIDENT INVESTIGATIONS. AGENCY FILE NUMBER: AA851401WJ – PAGES 124-125. FROM: DRYER, JOSEPH F. JR. TO: COOKSEY, JACKIE. 2 PAGES. SUBJECTS: CHARLES, CLÉMARD J. NARA.

97: for Colonel Kail's visit to Joseph Dryer, see: AGENCY: INSCOM/CSF. RECORD NUMBER 194-10014-10158. RECORDS SERIES: DOD AFFILIATED PERSONNEL AND INCIDENT INVESTIGATIONS. AGENCY FILE NUMBER: 11851401WJ – PAGE 106. FROM: KAIL, SAMUEL G. TITLE: MEMORANDUM OF VISIT. PAGES: 1. SUBJECTS: CHARLES, CLÉMARD J. NARA. See also: AGENCY: INSCOM/CSF. RECORD NUMBER: 194-10014-10165. RECORDS SERIES: DOD AFFILIATED PERSONNEL AND INCIDENT INVESTIGATIONS. AGENCY FILE NUMBER: AA851401WJ – PAGES 128-129. TITLE: LETTER. UNDATED. 2 PAGES. NARA.

98: Dryer praises the "honesty" and "ability" of Clémard Joseph Charles: INSCOM. CHRONOLOGY OF DATA CONCERNING MR. CLÉMARD JOSEPH CHARLES (HAITIAN). 9 May 1963. AA851401WJ. PAGES 101-104.

99: useful to CIA in Operation Mongoose: Fonzi, *The Last Investigation*, p. 312.

100: Duvalier would "kill my family": AGENCY: INSCOM/CSF. RECORD NUMBER: 194-10014-10159. RECORDS SERIES; DOD AFFILIATED PERSONNEL AND INCIDENT INVESTIGATIONS. AGENCY FILE NUMBER; AA851401WJ. PAGES 107-108. NARA.

100: Charles expresses his wish to present President Kennedy with his plan to save Haiti "from Duvalier and Communism": AGENCY: INSCOM/CSF. RECORD NUMBER: 194-10014-10159. AGENCY FILE NUMBER: AA851401WJ – PAGES 107-108. TITLE: MESSAGE. DATE: 05/23/63. SUBJECTS: CHARLES, CLÉMARD J., HAITIAN POLITICIANS. NARA.

101: "as soon as the Duvalier crisis is resolved": CIA. 10 MAY 1963. MEMORANDUM FOR THE RECORD. SUBJECT: CLÉMARD JOSEPH CHARLES.

101: "without his Texan friend and business partner": CIA. 104-10164-10444. TITLE: JOSEPH CHARLES, CLÉMARD. 1 PAGE. NARA.

105: "CIA should have Charles": AGENCY: INSCOM/CSF. RECORD NUMBER: 194-10014-10163. RECORDS SERIES: DOD AFFILIATED PERSONNEL AND INCIDENT INVESTIGATIONS. AGENCY FILE NUMBER: AA851401WJ – PAGE 126. FROM: ANN. TO: MRS. MATLACK. PAGES: 1. SUBJECTS: CHARLES, CLÉMARD J.; MR. BALOG. NARA.

105: for details of the planning of the May 7th luncheon at the Willard Hotel: See: INSCOM/CSF. CHRONOLOGY OF DATA CONCERNING MR. CLÉMARD JOSEPH CHARLES (HAITIAN). 9 May 1963. pp. 101-104. NARA.

THREE: HAS CIA ABANDONED CLÉMARD? GEORGE DE MOHRENSCHILDT IN HAITI

107: "Come on down to Haiti": Bruce Campbell Adamson's telephone conversation with Thomas Josten, quoted in *Oswald's Closest Friend: The George de Mohrenschildt Story*, Volume VIII, p. 85.

108: "ambitions": The ambition of Clémard Joseph Charles was to be the President of Haiti: "Chronology of Data Concerning Mr. Clémard Joseph Charles (Haitian)." 9 May 1963. INSCOM/CSF.

108: the suggestion that Charles see Wise of AID was made by Lyndon Johnson: CIA. Secret document. May 22, 1963, available at http://www.maryferrell.org/mffweb/archive/viewer/showDoc.do?absPageId=545500&ima...

109: letter from William Stix Wasserman: See Bruce Adamson, *Oswald's Closest Friend: The George de Mohrenschildt Story*, Volume XI, pp. 34-35ff.

109: "men with Charles' ability": William S. Wasserman to The Honorable Hubert H. Humphrey. May 6, 1963. AGENCY: INSCOM/CSF. RECORD NUMBER: 194-10014-10157. RECORDS SERIES: DOD AFFILIATED PERSONNEL AND INCIDENT INVESTIGATIONS. AGENCY FILE NUMBER: AA851401WJ – Page 105.

109: "I knew the Texan wasn't there to sell hemp": HSCA document No. 015042. Staff interview with Dorothe Matlack. September 4, 1978. NARA.

112: "no record of a current operational interest in subject": CIA. 10164-10443. TITLE: TRACE REQUEST JOSEPH CHARLES, CLÉMARD. 05/08/63. NARA.

113: Stone's requests for traces on de Mohrenschildt: A file was found in the Western Hemisphere/Mexico office: IX No. 130. 9 May 1963. MEMORANDUM FOR: DO/

COEO. ATTENTION: MR. C. FRANK STONE. SUBJECT: Trace reply – George de MOHRENSCHILDT. REFERENCE: Telephone request of 26 April 1963 requesting traces on subject above. Signed: Anna Panor DO/HQT. NARA.

113: "We're going to bring down Papa Doc": CIA. CONTACT REPORT. 9 May 1963. FROM: CHIEF, DO/COEO. NARA.

114: Despite all the hesitation, Army intelligence was still interested in Charles and de Mohrenschildt on May 10th: AGENCY: INSCOM/CSF. RECORD NUMBER: 194-10014-10155. PAGES: 99-100. FROM: SELECMAN, T. H. TO: USARMA PORT AU PRINCE HAITI. TITLE: JOINT MESSAGEFORM. DATE: 05/10/63. PAGES: 2. SUBJECTS: CHARLES, CLÉMARD J.

114: "whatever data is available to you": Ibid. INSCOM/CSF, pp. 99-100.

115: Stone and Devine meet at the Sheraton East Hotel in New York on May 15, 1963: CIA. CONTACT REPORT. 15 May 1963. WUBRINY – George deMOHRENSCHILDT-Haiti. IX-171. FROM: C. FRANK STONE, III, CHIEF/DO/COEO. NARA.

115: "derogatory information regarding the U.S.A....": CONTACT REPORT IX-171. 15 May 1963. WUBRINY – George de MOHRENSCHILDT – Haiti. Signed: C. FRANK STONE, III, Chief, DO/COEO. NARA.

116: "next President of Haiti": CIA. 104-10528-10109. ORIGINATOR: CIA. FROM: MEXICO CITY. TO: DIRECTOR. TITLE: CABLE: CLAIM OF THE MINISTER OF TOURISM IN HAITI THAT HE WILL BE THE NEXT PRESIDENT OF HAITI. DATE: 11/04/63. SUBJECTS: RETTIE. 1 PAGE. JFK64-47:F10 1999.07.07.09:53:104:856128. NARA.

116: "some Texas financial backing": CIA. 21 May 1963. IX-193. CONTACT REPORT. WUBRINY – George de MOHRENSCHILDT. FROM: C. Frank Stone, III, chief, DO/COEO. NARA.

116: "sterile line": CIA. 104-10166-10143. FROM: WITHHELD. TITLE: WITHHELD. DATE: 05/21/63. 2 PAGES. CONTACT REPORT. WUBRINY – George de MOHRENSCHILDT. IX-193. FROM: FRANK STONE, III, CHIEF/DO/COEO. JFK64-5: F16B 1998.01.21.16:05:31:890107. NARA.

116: "involvement in any program to unseat Duvalier": National Security Action Memorandum No. 246. To the Secretaries of State, Defense and the Director of Central Intelligence. Foreign Relations of the United States, Volume XII, American Republics, Document 384.

117: "the danger of communist activity": Memorandum of Conversation, June 1, 1963. Foreign Relations of the United States, Volume XII, American Republics, Document 386.

117: "not more than a battalion of United States forces": Memorandum of Conversation. June 18, 1963. Foreign Relations of the United States, Volume XII, American Republics, Document 389.

118: de Mohrenschildt's oil survey contract is bogus: "CONFIDENTIAL." Signed by V. E. Blacque, Commercial Officer. For the Ambassador, pp. 2-3. Courtesy of Jim H. Lesar from the Fensterwald file on Clémard Joseph Charles.

118: de Mohrenschildt uses existing surveys: Raphael Quisqueya to Dear Mr. Garrison. Files of Jim Garrison. Courtesy of Lyon Garrison.

119: General Léon Cantave: Telegram From The Department of State to the Embassy in Haiti. May 14, 1963. Foreign Relations of the United States, Volume XII, American Republics, Document 380.

Notes

119: "CIA has a commitment to the failure of this effort": Memorandum From The Executive Secretary of the Department of State (Read) to the President's Special Assistant For National Security Affairs (Bundy). August 14, 1963. Foreign Relations of the United States. Volume XII, American Republics, Document 390.

120: "CIA could not resist the temptation": Robert Emmett Johnson, "I Stuck Pins In A Voodoo Dictator," *TRUE* magazine. April 1968.

120: "the big man in the White House": This incident was recounted to Gaeton Fonzi by Joseph F. Dryer, Jr., who heard the story from a CIA informant in Haiti, Jacqueline Lancelot: Memorandum – July 7, 1978. TO: G. Robert Blakey. FROM: Gaeton Fonzi. RE: Interview with JOSEPH DRYER. Courtesy of Mr. Fonzi.

121: Gary Taylor tells FBI that no one has more influence over Oswald than George de Mohrenschildt. FBI. Report of SAs Robert E. Bashaw and James J. Ward. December 3, 1963. FBI file of George de Mohrenschildt.

121: "Don't we know someone by that name?" CIA. MEMORANDUM FOR: Mr. J. Lee Rankin, General Counsel, President's Commission on the Assassination of President Kennedy. SUBJECT: Statement reportedly made by George and Jeanne DE MOHRENSCHILDT concerning Lee Harvey OSWALD and the Assassination of President Kennedy. July 8, 1964. Signed: Richard Helms, Deputy Director For Plans. NARA.

121: De Mohrenschildt's letter to Thomas J. Attridge is available in his FBI file.

124: "a Mr. Parker of the FBI": Oltmans testimony before Robert Tanenbaum, deputy counsel of the HSCA, taken under oath: HSCA 180-10105-10250. AGENCY FILE NUMBER: 014316. FROM: OLTMANS, WILLEM. TITLE: TESTIMONY OF WILLEM OLTMANS. 04/01/77. PAGES: 143. NARA.

124: "Boy! I can assure you it is a pleasure not to be in Texas": George de Mohrenschildt to Everett D. Glover, January 15, 1964. FBI file of George de Mohrenschildt, 105-862.

124: Dabney A. Austin sues de Mohrenschildt for selling him an invalid oil lease: Oswald arrives while Austin is paying de Mohrenschildt $500: FBI. Report of SA Earle Haley and Robley D. Madland. March 3, 1964. FBI file of George de Mohrenschildt. See also: Report of SA W. James Wood. March 14, 1964.

125: "Murchison/Davidson interest in Haiti": Telegram From The Embassy in Haiti to the Department of State. December 18, 1963. Volume XXXII, Dominican Republic; Cuba; Haiti; Guyana. Document 325.

126: "ground up to make sausages…": G. R. Schreiber, *The Bobby Baker Affair* (Henry Regnery Company: Chicago, 1964), p. 129. Schreiber mistakenly calls Isadore Irving Davidson "Irvin," but there is no mistaking that he is writing about I.I. Davidson.

126: I.I. Davidson, a "five percenter": FBI. 124-10078-10257. Agency file number: 62-109060-5837. FROM: BISHOP, E. E. TO: DELOACH. DATE: 11/01/67. PAGES: 3. SUBJECTS: JFK, ASSISTANCE, INTV, DAVIDSON, I. IRVING. NARA.

127: Davidson is a lobbyist for CIA: John H. Davis, *Mafia Kingfish: Carlos Marcello And The Assassination of John F. Kennedy* (McGraw-Hill Publishing Company: New York, 1989), p. 154.

127: Davidson worked for the International Cooperation Administration: Adamson, *Oswald's Closest Friend*, Volume XI, p. 67.

127: Davidson was "well known to CIA": FBI. 124-10302-10106. AGENCY FILE NUMBER: 2-1423-133. FROM: DIRECTOR, FBI. DATE: 07/30/69. PAGES: 52.

SUBJECTS: IID. CORRELATION SUMMARY, SEE REFERENCES, AKA. POLIT. CONSPIR, REVOLUTIONARY, CRIMINAL ACT, SUR, TESUR. NARA.

127: Davidson reports on the Cuban Revolution to the FBI: FBI. RECORD NUMBER: 124-10294-10058. RECORDS SERIES: HQ. AGENCY FILE NUMBER: 2-1423-4TH NR 39, 5TH NR 39, 6TH NR 39. FROM: DAVIDSON, I. IRVING. TO: ASSISTANT DIRECTOR, FBI. DATE: 06/11/59. PAGES: 6. SUBJECTS: IID, COMMUNIST INFLUENCE, CUBA, ACA. NARA.

128: "they are really going to give it to him": AGENCY: FBI. RECORD NUMBER: 124-10294-10034. RECORDS SERIES: HQ. AGENCY FILE NUMBER: 2-1423-31. FROM: SAC, WMFO. TO: DIRECTOR, FBI. DATE: 04/08/59. PAGES: 4. SUBJECTS: IID, ASSOC, ANTI-CASTRO MOVEMENT, DC, CASTRO VISIT, INSTR, RCK. NARA.

128: CIA divers blow up the ship loaded with weaponry: Interview with Alberto Fernandez, October 31, 2009.

128-129: Davidson assisted crime boss Carlos Marcello: Davis, p. 308.

129: CIA purchases arms from I.I. Davidson: See: CIA. 104-10216-1-100. FROM: CHIEF, FORMAT SECTION. TITLE: MEMORANDUM FOR THE RECORD: SUBJECT: 1. IRVING DAVIDSON. DATE: 07/31/1974. PAGES: 2. SUBJECTS: DAVIDSON. JFK64-51: F16 : 1998.04.28.20:23:53:500115. NARA.

129-130: how I.I. Davidson came to be hired by Papa Doc: See: Laurence Stern, "Senate Probe Brought New Client to Lobbyist," *Washington Post*, January 4, 1964.

130: Ramsay Clark did not like J. Walter Yeagley any better than I.I. Davidson did: Ramsay Clark interview with Joan Mellen, February 21, 2000.

132: George de Mohrenschildt runs a salon in Port-au-Prince...ship of fools: For a chronology of de Mohrenschildt's active social life, See: CIA. 104-10166-10266. FROM: WITHHELD. TO: CHIEF, KUDESK. TITLE: INFORMATION CONCERNING GEORGE DE MOHRENSCHILDT'S CONTACTS WITH THE POLISH COMMERCIAL DELEGATION IN PORT-AU-PRINCE. DATE: 01/29/1965. PAGES: TWO. JFK64-5 : F17 : 1998.01.27.18:31:23:716102. NARA.

132: CIA enlists "Conrad V. Rubricius" to spy on de Mohrenschildt, and attend his dinner parties: CIA. 104-10166-10139. AGENCY ORIGINATOR: CIA. FROM: CHIEF OF STATION, PORT-AU-PRINCE. TO: CHIEF, WHD. TITLE: THE DEMOHRENSCHILDTS AND RUBRICIUS ARE MEMBERS OF THE PÉTIONVILLE CLUB AND OFTEN PLAY TENNIS TOGETHER. DATE: 06/16/1964. PAGES: 2. JFK64-5:F18 1998.01.21.15:50:34:810107. NARA.

134: "beautiful mulatto": MEMORANDUM – July 7, 1978. TO: G. Robert Blakey. FROM: Gaeton Fonzi. RE: Interview with JOSEPH DRYER.

134: "octoroon": Interview with Susan Rich, August 16, 2011.

138: Aubelin Jolicoeur: Christopher Lehmann-Haupt, "Aubelin Jolicoeur, Haitian Muse, Dies at 80," *The New York Times,* March 6, 2005. Conversation with Joseph F. Dryer, Jr., August 23, 2011.

138: the telephone rings at the Hotel Oloffson: Interview with Edward Ridgeway Harris, January 10, 2010. Harris worked with Joseph F. Dryer, Jr. in his Haiti kenaf operation. The Hotel Oloffson is a character in Graham Greene's novel about Haiti, *The Comedians.*

139: $250,000 has been deposited in de Mohrenschildt's bank account: HSCA testimony of Joseph Dryer.

144: 450,000 people in a nation of ten million: *The New York Times,* October 19, 2011.

FOUR: PHILIPPE THYRAUD DE VOSJOLI: EVERYONE IS CONNECTED

145: "He's writing a book": Interview with Joseph F. Dryer, Jr.

146: French Communist Party: De Vosjoli learned that the Soviet Union had assigned the French Communist Party the role of liaison with Latin American Communist parties: P.L. Thyraud de Vosjoli, *Lamia* [CODE NAME 'LAMIA'] (Little, Brown and Company: Boston, 1970), pp. 231-232.

146: "the colored population": de Vosjoli, Ibid., p. 223.

146: de Vosjoli investigates the activities of French Communists in the 1959 Cuban invasion of Haiti: Ibid., p. 285.

146: a "way with his eyes": So Philippe de Vosjoli describes himself in the novel *Topaz*, ghost written for him by Leon Uris, *Topaz: A Novel* (McGraw-Hill Book Company: New York, 1967), p. 26.

147: de Vosjoli arranges to provide CIA with intelligence about Indochina in exchange for war supplies: de Vosjoli, *Lamia*, p. 221.

147: Walter Bedell Smith asks de Vosjoli to confer a posthumous Legion of Honor on Joe Kennedy, Jr.: de Vosjoli, Ibid., p. 223.

148: Fulgencio Batista tries to bribe a U.S. Senator, and de Vosjoli reports this information to James Angleton: FBI. RECORD NUMBER: 124-90138-10047. AGENCY FILE NUMBER: CR 62-70441-157. FROM: PAPICH. TO: FROHBOSE. DATE: 07/20/59. SUBJECTS: CIA LIAISON MATERIAL. NARA.

149: even his "worst enemies": *Lamia*, p. 76.

149: "could have become chief": Ibid., p. 250.

149: "beyond reproach," Ibid., p. 300.

149: Soustelle advocates overthrowing de Gaulle: James D. LeSueur, *Uncivil War: Intellectuals and Identity Politics During the Decolonization of Algeria* (The University of Pennsylvania Press: Philadelphia, 2001), p. 4.

149: "most notorious fascist organizations in French history: James D. LeSueur, p. 56. In New Orleans, one of detective Guy Banister's operatives, a future lawyer named Tommy Baumler, remarked that "those who killed John F. Kennedy were those who wanted to kill de Gaulle."

149: Bissell and Helms eat lunch with Jacques Soustelle, courtesy of Philippe de Vosjoli: Andrew Tully, *CIA: The Inside Story* (William Morrow: New York, 1969), pp. 45-53.

158: *Le Monde* writes that "some American agents more or less encouraged Maurice Challe": Tully, p. 49.

150: Soustelle and *Time* magazine: "World: Scapegoat Wanted," *Time*, May 12, 1961.

150: Pierre Salinger calls Allen Dulles and is briefed by Richard Helms: Tully, op. cit., pp. 49-50. Tully in his acknowledgements thanks both Pierre Salinger and "former CIA Director Allen W. Dulles." Later Dulles regretted ever having talked to Tully. See Dulles papers, Princeton University.

151: Nagy a long-time CIA asset: See: CIA. 104-10213-10146. Title: Correspondence with FBI on CIA/FBI Liaison Agreement in 1948. 18 pages. See also: Memorandum. 13 September 1948. For: Admiral Sidney W. Souers, Executive Secretary, NSC. VIA. Admiral R. H. Hillenkoetter, Director of Central Intelligence. From: Frank G. Wisner, Assistant

Director, CIA. Subject: Cooperation with FBI. NARA. See note for p. 22, line 4: Nagy personally recruited to PERMINDEX New Orleans CIA contract employee Clay Shaw.

151: Nagy a munificent contributor to Jacques Soustelle. See: Paris Flammonde, *The Kennedy Conspiracy: An Uncommissioned Report On The Jim Garrison Investigation* (Meredith Press: New York, 1969), p. 216ff.

151: CIA operatives who let their own politics show: Tully, p. 55.

151: CIA definitely supported Soustelle's putsch: Bissell and Helms meet with Jacques Soustelle: See also: Douglas Valentine, *The Strength of the Wolf: The Secret History of America's War On Drugs* (Verso: New York, 2004), p. 270.

151: "at the expense of democracy itself": quoted in Hugh Wilford, *The Mighty Wurlitzer: How The CIA Played America* (Harvard University Press: Cambridge, Massachusetts, 2008), p. 75. Paul Sakwa made this statement in "Chief/Covert Action/Vietnam," 2 August/11 December 1976, 63.5. Victor Reuther Papers, Archives of Labor and Urban Affairs. Wayne State University, Detroit, Michigan.

151: Allen Dulles enlists de Vosjoli to go to Cuba: *Lamia*, p. 289.

152: McCone thanks de Vosjoli "in private": *Lamia*, p. 297.

153: Senator Keating has been "reliably informed" of the arrival in Cuba of Soviet Combat troops: See Arthur J. Olsen, "Boats Off Cuba Fire At U.S. Navy Plane; Havana Caution," *The New York Times*, September 1, 1962, pp. 1-2. See also: "I am reliably informed...those CIA bastards": Richard Reeves, *President Kennedy: Profile Of Power* (Simon & Schuster: New York, 1993), p. 345. Reeves is quoting from Kennedy's interview with journalist Sander Vanocur.

161: "de Vosjoli was recruited and worked for us": See Tom Mangold's discussion of Philippe de Vosjoli and his relationship with CIA in *Cold Warrior: James Jesus Angleton: The CIA's Master Spy Hunter* (Simon & Schuster: New York, 1991), pp. 120-135. See also: "A Head That Holds Some Sinister Secrets," *LIFE*, Vol. 64, Number 17, pp. 30-39, which includes a memoir by de Vosjoli, "So Much Has Been Swept Under The Rug," and an afterword by *The Sunday Times* (London) reporter, John Barry, "Broad Impact of 'Martel' Everywhere But France." "Martel" was the pseudonym de Vosjoli gave to Golitsyn. CIA called him "John Stone" or AELADLE-1

155: Donald Deneselya works as Golitsyn's administrative assistant: Interview with Donald Deneselya, December 20, 2009.

154: Angleton helped to arrange de Vosjoli's permanent residence: See website of Edward Jay Epstein, Diary, April 26, 1980: http://www.edwardjayepstein.com/diary/devosjoli.htm

156: De Gaulle calls de Vosjoli a "defector to the CIA": "A Head That Holds Some Sinister Secrets," *LIFE* magazine feature, "The French Spy Scandal," April 26, 1968, Volume 64, No. 17, p. 31.

157: "I was in hiding from paid killers": *Lamia*, p. 225.

158: Juanita de Córdoba: *Topaz*, p. 96.

158: "a woman of prominence": *Topaz*, p. 95.

159: "grip on the throat of the country": "Topaz," p. 326.

159: Uris was paid merely to sign the contract: Interview with Joseph F. Dryer, Jr. January 8, 2010.

159-160: only a three-page summary of de Vosjoli's interview with HSCA has been made public: HSCA. 180-10080-10025. AGENCY FILE NUMBER: 008534. FROM: DE VOSJOLI, PHILLIPE THYROUD [SIC]. 05.09/78. PAGES: 3. SUBJECTS: SERVICE DE

DOCUMENTATION EXTÉRIERE ET DE CONTRE-ESPIONAGE. BOX 156. NARA. The interviewer was James P. Kelly.

FIVE: A SHEIKH FROM KUWAIT

162: Jack Cogswell: See the following records: OUTSIDE CONTACT REPORT. Gaeton Fonzi. Jack Cogswell. 3/23/2978; MEMO 4/21/76. TO: Dave Marston. FROM: Gaeton Fonzi. Courtesy of Mr. Fonzi; CIA. 104-10181-10408. From: Bryan R. Waidley. SUBJECTS: Meetings with James K. Cogswell aka Jack Cogswell. DATE: 5/31/66. PAGES: 3. JFK64-17:F17 1998.08.04.08:29:20:466128. NARA; CIA. RECORD NUMBER: 104-10192-10448. FROM: CHIEF, NEW YORK OFFICE. TO: ACTING CHIEF, CONTACT DIVISION. TITLE: MR. JAMES COGSWELL/MRP REPRESENTATIVE TO NEW YORK. DATE: 04/10/62. PAGES: 2. JFK64-27:F20A 1998.09.02.09:56:09:653129. NARA; CIA. RECORD NUMBER: 104-10271-10021. FROM: JMWAVE. TO: DIRECTOR. TITLE: CABLE: MRP EXILE LEADER JOAQUIN GODOY Y SOLIS HAS FRIEND [SIC] IN NYC NAMED JACK COGSWELL. DATE: 11/22/61. PAGES: 1. JFK64-27:F20A 1998.09.02.09:44:57:513129. NARA.

162: Cogswell reported to David Atlee Phillips in Havana: Phillips HSCA testimony, p. 42.

164: "I did some favors": Aldereguia Once Worked With FBI," *Miami News*, March 27, 1978. See http://www.latinamericanstudies.org

167: "may possibly be a contact of that agency": FBI. Special Agent Charles M. Beall, Jr. contact L. B. Hogle at CIA's Office of Security. March 19, 1964. FBI file of George de Mohrenschildt.

168: "wealthy people for friends": FBI interview with Mr. and Mrs. Edward Robert Thomas. April 1, 1964. FBI file of George de Mohrenschildt.

168: Clémard Joseph Charles traveled to Mexico City "to purchase cheap sisal cordage machinery": INCOMING TELEGRAM. Department of State. February 24, 1964.

171: Hoover wrote to the Director of Central Intelligence about de Mohrenschildt's identification of CIA's J. Walton Moore as an FBI agent.

172: for preparations for the de Mohrenschildt's trip to Washington, D.C. to testify before the Warren Commission, see: Incoming Telegram, Department of State. From: AMEMBASSYPORTAUPRINCE. To: SECSTATEWASHDC. April 16, 1964. 013603. Signed Timmons. See also: Outgoing Telegram, Department of State, April 18, 1964. 11766.

172-173: CIA circulates the reports Counter Intelligence received from George de Mohrenschildt: CIA. 104-10518-10078. FROM: CI STAFF TO: SUPPORT BRANCH CONTACT DIVISION, 00. TITLE: REPORT: REPORTS RECEIVED FROM GEORGE DE MOHRENSCHILDT. DATE: 04/20/64. SUBJECTS: DEMOHRENSCHILDT. JFK64-52:F3 1999.03.12.13:43l01:060128. NARA.

173: George de Mohrenschildt is met at National Airport by Dorothe Matlack: Fletcher Prouty to Jim Garrison, March 6, 1990. Available at http://www.prouty.org.

174: He was dealing with Duvalier on a man-to-man basis: U.S. Department of State Report of John R. Wineberg. April 14, 1964. Available in George de Mohrenschildt's FBI file.

175: at the State Department: Document describing de Mohrenschildt's visit when he was in Washington, D.C. testifying before the Warren Commission. 3 pages. 100-32965; 100-38965-5-? Header illegible. Part of de Mohrenschildt's FBI file.

176: he has found oil "near the Santo Domingo border": FBI. Report of SA W. L. Daleymple. March 26, 1964. FBI file of George de Mohrenschildt.

176: Justin Bertrand gives Clémard Joseph Charles "two or three hundred thousand dollars" for safekeeping: Patrick Lemoine, *Fort-Dimanche, Dungeon of Death* (Trafford Publishing: fordi9: Uniondale, New York, 2011), p. 123. "Operator": Conversation with Bernard Diederich, July 30, 2011.

177: "no information establishing a link between the de Mohrenschildts and Lee Harvey Oswald or his family": TO: Director, Federal Bureau of Investigation. Attention: Mr. S. J. Papich. FROM: Deputy Director for Plans. Subject: George and Jeanne de MOHRENSCHILDT. July 9, 1964. 100-32965-298. Available in FBI file of George de Mohrenschildt.

177: "At CIA headquarters....": CIA. 104-10009-10124. AGENCY FILE NUMBER: 201-28948. FROM: HELMS, RICHARD, DD/P, CIA. TO: RANKIN, J. LEE, GEN COUNSEL, WC. TITLE: GEORGE AND JEANNE DE MOHRENSCHILDT. DATE: 06/03/1964. PAGES: 9. SUBJECTS: DEMOHRENSCHILDT, ICA. COMMENTS: OSW14 : V54 :1993.06.21.17:31:03:900140. NARA.

177: the federal government destroys de Mohrenschildt's federal employment file. This fact was reported in the *Dallas Morning News* of April 2, 1977, and is cited by Adamson, *Oswald's Closest Friend: The George de Mohrenschildt Story: Zapruder, Bush & The CIA's Dallas Council On World Affairs*, Volume X, p. 21. In 1976, Senator Otis Pike, chairman of the House Intelligence Committee, would note that more than two hundred Top-Secret and Secret documents that CIA had turned over to the House Intelligence Committee had vanished from the face of the earth. See also: "'Top-Secret' CIA papers Missing," *San Francisco Chronicle*, March 5, 1976.

177: from the moment of his return from testifying before the Warren Commission, CIA watched de Mohrenschildt: CIA. TO: Director, Federal Bureau of Investigation. 5 April 1965. SUBJECT: Activities of George and Jeanne de MOHRENSCHILDT in Haiti. NARA. This is but one of many documents on the subject.

178: "They were safe and secure and loved Haiti": FBI interview with Morris I. Jaffe, March 4, 1964. FBI file of George de Mohrenschildt.

178: the annual per capita income was $75.00....Press release of the International Commission of Jurists, 2 Quai du Cheval-Blanc, Geneva, Switzerland, August 5, 1963. "The Socio-Political Situation in Haiti." Courtesy of Max Blanchet.

183: for de Mohrenschildt's June 20, 1964 dinner party: See: Dispatch. To: Chief, WHD. From: Chief of Station, Port-au-Prince. 23 July 1964. Dispatch symbol and number: HTPA 1359. NARA.

183: the Polish commercial attaché: For a history of George de Mohrenschildt's contacts with Galicki, see: Ibid., CIA. 104-10166-10266. FROM: WITHHELD. TO: CHIEF, KUDESK. TITLE: INFORMATION CONCERNING GEORGE DE MOHRENSCHILDT'S CONTACTS WITH THE POLISH COMMERCIAL DELEGATION IN PORT-AU-PRINCE. DATE: 01/29/1965. PAGES: TWO. JFK64-5 : F17 : 1998.01.27.18:31:23:716102. NARA.

183: "coal black": CIA used "Conrad V. Rubricius" for surveillance in Haiti of de Mohrenschildt and Clémard Joseph Charles: CIA dispatch: TO: CHIEF, WHD. FROM: Chief of Station, Port-au-Prince. Subject: George and Jeanne de Mohrenschildt. July 23, 1964. Dispatchnumber: HTPA 1359. NARA.

183: Colonel Danache told the Pan American Airways manager that he was accompanying Charles to inspect airplanes: CIA. 201 card file: CHARLES, Clémard, Joseph. See also:

Notes

HSCA MEMORANDUM. TO: GARY CORNWELL. FROM: SURRELL BRADY, Staff Counsel. RE: DE MOHRENSCHILDT SCENARIO. 11 July 1978. NARA.

185: "for pleasure": CIA. 104-10244-10259. TITLE: ONE-DEC 21 – ARRIVED PORT TWELFTH 0220Z LUGGAGE NOT INSPECTED. UNDATED. SUBJECTS: DEMOHRENSCHILDT. PAGES: 2. JFK64-5:F16B 1998.06.08.14:05:19:233128: NARA.

185: nor did he hail from Kuwait: See "Fayed's Forgotten Years: The Con Man, The Dictator and the CIA files," *The Daily Telegraph* magazine (London), 20 June 1998. See also: Maureen Orth, "Holy War At Harrods," *Vanity Fair*, September 1995.

185-186: Adnan Khashoggi: See: Michael Slackman, "An Arms Dealer Returns, Now Selling an Image," *The New York Times*, November 14, 2009, p. A7.

186: Fayed makes "side deals" when he is working for Khashoggi: Interview with Khashoggi by Maureen Orth, in "Holy War At Harrods."

186: "cover firm for the Egyptian Intelligence Service": CIA. 104-10166-10146. TO: INFORMATION REPORT. TITLE: THE UAR GOVERNMENT WAS EMPLOYING AL-NASIR TRADING COMPANY FOR ITS 'ILLEGAL' TRANSACTIONS, SUCH AS TRADE WITH FRANCE. DATE: 09/123/1960. 2 PAGES. JFK64-5 :F16B : 1998.01.21.16:17:24:780107. NARA.

187: Bozo Dabinovic: See: "Fayed's Forgotten Years: The Con Man, The Dictator & The CIA Files," *Daily Telegraph* magazine, 20 June 1998. Available online at http://www.guardianlies.com/Section%206/page35.html.

188: business, "the long-term cost to our economy": Memorandum From The Director of the Office of Caribbean Affairs (Crockett) to the Assistant Secretary of State for Inter-American Affairs (Mann). November 23, 1964. Foreign Relations of the United States, Volume XXXII, Dominican Republic; Cuba; Haiti, Guyana. Document 335.

188: another invasion of Haiti on July 8, 1964: Memorandum from Robert M. Sayre of the National Security Council Staff to the President's Special Assistant for National Security Affairs (Bundy). July 9, 1964. Volume XXXII, Dominican Republic; Cuba; Haiti; Guyana. Document 331.

190: upstairs to the bedroom: CIA surveillance of Galicki and his visitors: CIA. 104-10166-10296. FROM: COS, PORT AU PRINCE. TO: CHIEF, WHD. TITLE: ACTIVITIES OF WLODZIMIERZ GALICKI. DATE: 08/25/1964. 3 PAGES. SUBJECTS: DEMOHRENSCHILDT. JFK64-5 : F17 : 1998.01.27.20:46:950102. NARA.

190: August 9th boating trip as reported to CIA by Rubricius; arrival of Stawinski: CIA. 104-10166-10297. FROM: WITHHELD. TO: CHIEF, WHD. TITLE: GEORGE AND JEANNE DE MOHRENSCHILDT. 08/20/1964. 3 PAGES: JFK64-5 : F17 : 1998.01.27.20:49:01:280102.NARA.

191: "I'll get a gun": FBI. March 16, 1964. Special Agent Riley L. Millard. FBI file of George de Mohrenschildt.

192: could never work for more than two hours a day without getting headaches: FBI interview with Mrs. Igor Voshinin. March 6, 1964. Special Agent Richard L. Wiehl. FBI file of George de Mohrenschildt.

193: George McMillan employed in the U.S. Embassy in Moscow: Mark Lane, *Plausible Denial: Was The CIA Involved in the Assassination of JFK?* (Thunder's Mouth Press: New York, 1991), p. 69.

193: George and Jeanne de Mohrenschildt leave for New York to appear on television: CIA. 104-10166-10295. FROM: PORT AU PRINCE. TO: DIRECTOR. TITLE: GEORGE AND JEANNE DEMOHRENSCHILDT STATE THEY DEPARTING. DATE:

09/15/1964. 1 PAGE. JFK64-5 : F17 : 1998.01.27.20:43:10:623102. NARA. CIA writes: "reason for trip is to appear on TV program," as CIA monitors de Mohrenschildt's travels.

193-194: Paul Johnson reports on a dinner with the de Mohrenschildts: Dispatch. 18 Sep 1964. HTPA-1406. To: Chief, WHD. Info: Chief, KUDESK. From: Chief of Station, Port-au-Prince. Subject: George de Mohrenschildt – Subject of Memorandum of Conversation prepared by a Non-Official American in Haiti. Johnson's memorandum to CIA was dated September 12, 1964.

194: "light social contact with de Mohrenschildt": CIA. 104-10166-10275. FROM: DIRECTOR. TO: WITHHELD. TITLE: CABLE: HQ UNDERSTANDS THAT YOU HAVE BEEN FORBIDDEN TO MAINTAIN LIGHT SOCIAL CONTACT WITH IDEN. DATE: 12/10/64. JFK64-5 : F17 : 1998.01.27.19:02:36:840102. NARA.

194: EVMINOR-1 attempted to chronicle de Mohrenschildt's many meetings with Galicki: CIA. 104-10166-10266. FROM: WITHHELD [Joseph G. Benson]. TO: CHIEF, KUDESK. TITLE: INFORMATION CONCERNING GEORGE MOHRENSCHILDT'S CONTACTS WITH THE POLISH COMMERCIAL DELEGATION IN PORT-AU-PRINCE. DATE: 01/29/1965. PAGES: 2. SUBJECTS: DEMOHRENSCHELDT [sic]. JFK64-5 : F17 : 1998.01.27.18:31:23:716102. NARA.

196-197: Charles Valentine attempts to get his money back: "So small, it's ridiculous": Bernard Diederich and Al Burt, *Papa Doc: The Truth About Haiti Today*, p. 343.

SIX: GEORGE DE MOHRENSCHILDT UNDER CIA SURVEILLANCE

199: "CIA agents were stirring up the trouble": Report from Lang to McCombs, October 10, 1964. Title: "Information Only." Available in the Holland McCombs Papers. University of Tennessee At Martin.

199: Will Lang investigates Klepak and Schine. Ibid. Report From Lang to McCombs, October 10, 1964.

201: Charles tries to purchase some ships from the U.S. Navy: Tad Szulc, "Haiti Said To Seek Navy Ships In U.S.," *The New York Times*, July 17, 1964, p. 4.

201: Edward Browder's history: See: HSCA. 180-10077-10040. RECORD SERIES: NUMBERED FILES. AGENCY FILE NUMBER: 005081. FROM: BROWDER, EDWARD, FEDERAL PENITENTIARY. 01/12/78. PAGES: 13. BOX 105. NARA; Edward Browder to Information & Privacy Coordinator, Central Intelligence Agency, April 19, 1976. Document ID number: 1993.08.05.16:18:12:680006. Recseries: JFK. Agfileno: 201-289248. JFK Box #: JFK9. Vol/Folder F24. NARA.

At the time of the House Select Committee on Assassinations hearings, Browder was imprisoned at the U.S. Penitentiary on McNeil Island, Washington State, for securities fraud.

202: Frank Wisner himself dictated the reply that C.D. Jackson, the Agency asset at TIME/LIFE, was instructed to make: CIA. 104-10164-10407. TO: OCI. TO: ASHCRAFT FROM LEA BY CONNELL. THIS IS SENSITIVE. Edward Browder of E. Browder & Associates, Engineering Consultants. To: Dear Mr. Luce. NARA.

202: "He is also a facile liar and apparently enjoys inflating his reputation as a soldier of fortune": CIA. 104-10164-10073. FROM: F.F. HOLCOMB. TO: MEMO FOR DCI. TITLE: COPY OF LETTER FROM EDWARD BROWDER TO DIRECTOR, CIA. DATE: 12/20/54. PAGES: 1. JFK64-3:F22 1998.01.06.15:37:57:450109. NARA.

202: Browder claimed he had worked for Trujillo for years, with CIA support: See: HSCA. FROM: BROWDER, EDWARD, FEDERAL PENITENTIARY. DATE: 01/12/78. 180-10077-10040. NUMBERED FILES. AGENCY FILENUMBER: 005081. NARA.

Browder served eight years and four months on McNeill Island Federal Penitentiary in Steilacooom, Washington.

204: Owens' missing airplane turns up in the Bahamas having been flown there by Edward Browder: FBI. 124-10206-10455. AGENCY FILE NUMBER: CR 26-343710-1. FROM: SAC, DL. TO: DIRECTOR, FBI. DATE: 12/04/64. PAGES: 18. SUBJECTS: EB, BKG, ASSOC, AIRPLANE, CESSNA SKYKNIGHT TWIN 320, TRA, DESCR, ARMS, AMMO, HAITIAN GOVERNMENT. NARA.

204: Browder charged gasoline: FBI file of Edward Browder: RE: SIDNEY STANLEY SCHINE ET AL. p. 7.

205: Browder cashes a check signed by Clémard Joseph Charles: HSCA. January 12, 1978. Interview with Edward Browder.

205: "the White House will overrule the State Department": Memorandum From Robert M. Sayre of the National Security Council Staff to the President's Special Assistant for National Security Affairs (Bundy). July 10, 1964. Volume XXXII, Dominican Republic; Cuba; Haiti; Guyana. Document 332.

206: "unwilling to let a key witness testify": Memorandum From Robert M. Sayre of the National Security Council Staff to the President's Special Assistant for National Security Affairs (Bundy). December 30, 1964. Volume XXXII, Document 337.

206: "at least one segment of the American intelligence agencies or the military": TO: GARY CORNWELL. FROM: SURRELL BRADY. RE: DE MOHRENSCHILDT SCENARIO. 11 July 1978. Courtesy of Gaeton Fonzi.

207: Jeanne de Mohrenschildt slaps the receptionist in the face: Report from Ambassador Timmons to Kennedy M. Crockett, Director of the Office of Caribbean Affairs. December 8, 1964.

207: "muscled in on" the Embassy Commissary: Memorandum For The Record. Kennedy M. Crockett, Director, Office of Caribbean Affairs, December 8, 1964. Re: MR. AND MRS. GEORGE DE MOHRENSCHILDT. FBI file 100-32965 of George de Mohrenschildt. Two pages.

208: "speculation about Haiti's oil reserves": especially after the 2010 devastating earthquake, the Internet has been teeming with speculation about the untapped oil in Haiti: See, for example, Kristy Kershaw, "Haiti's Earthquake May Have Revealed Oil Resources," January 27, 2010, available at http://www.heatingoil.com/blog/haiti%E2%80%99s-earthquake-may-have-revealed-oil-res...; Ezili Danto, "Oil in Haiti – Economic Reasons for the UN/US occupation, October 13, 2009, available at: http://open.salon.com/blog/ezil_danto2009/10/13/oil_in_haiti_-_economic_reasons_for_; "Haiti: War Crimes and Oil," January 22, 2009, available at http://rainbowwarrior2005.wordpress.com/2009/01/22/haiti-war-crimes-and-oil/ ' Victor Thorn, "Big Oil Behind Haiti Quake?" February 23, 2010, available at http://www.americanfreepress.net/html/haiti_oil_210.html; Marguerite Laurent, "Oil In Haiti: Reasons for the US Occupation, Part II," February 27, 2010, available at http://www.globalresearch.ca/index.php?context=va&aid=17293; Peter Schlosser, "Are We in Haiti because of Oil?" January 21, 2010, available at http://www.prisonplanet.com/are-we-in-haiti-because-of-oil.html.

209: Alexandra de Mohrenschildt does not trust Mohamed Fayed: CIA. 104-10244-10259. TITLE: ONE-DEC 21 – FACT-ARRIVED PORT TWELFTH 0330Z LUGGAGE NOT INSPECTED. 2 PAGES. JFK64-5:F16B 1998.06.08.14:05:19233128. WORDS CROSSED OUT THROUGHOUT DOCUMENT, ALSO SOME SENTENCES ARE IN BRACKETS. NARA.

210: CIA tracks Fayed to the Waldorf Astoria Hotel: CIA. 104-10166-10232. FROM: STEPHEN C. MILLETT, JR. CHIEF/CI/S. TO: WITHHELD. TITLE: FA'ID IS CURRENTLY NEGOTIATING AN ARMS DEAL WITH PRESIDENT DUVALIER OF HAITI. DATE: 12/01/1964. PAGES: 1. SUBJECTS: DEMOHRENSCHILDT. JFK64-5 : F17 : 1998.01.27.15:48:47:263107. NARA.

210: Everyone in CIA wants to know about Fayed's deals: CIA. 104-10166-10278. FROM: DEPUTY DIRECTOR FOR PLANS. TO: DIRECTOR, FBI. TITLE: MOHAMMAD ABDEL FAYED. DATE: 12/02/1964. PAGES: 2. JFK64-5 : F17 : 1998.01.27.19:14:12:530102. NARA.

211: local shipping agents complain to Duvalier: INCOMING TELEGRAM: Department of State. November 12, 1964. FROM: PORT-AU-PRINCE. ACTION: SECSTATE 873. DATE: NOVEMBER 12, 11 AM. SIGNED: TIMMONS.

213: See Keith Allen, "'Unlawful Killing' – the film the British won't get to see," The Guardian, May 7, 2011. Available Online.

213: Clémard Joseph Charles assumes the concession for the rights to develop the wharf and will "assign to new company his concessionary rights": INCOMING TELEGRAM. Department of State. August 31, 1965.

214: FBI fact sheet on de Mohrenschildt: CIA. 104-10244-10247. ORIGINATOR: FBI. FROM: DIRECTOR, CENTRAL INTELLIGENCE AGENCY. TO: DEPUTY DIRECTOR, PLANS. TITLE: LETTER: DEAR SIR: FOR YOUR INFORMATION I AM ENCLOSING COMMUNICATIONS WHICH MAY BE OF INTEREST TO YOU. DATE: 03/17/64. PAGES: 2. SUBJECTS: DEMOHRENSCHILDT. JFK64-5:F16B 1998.06.08.12:58:57:356128: ATTACHED, REPORT. NARA.

214: a 1948 Wisner-Hoover memo: CIA. 104-10213-10146. AGENCY: CIA. ORIGINATOR: FBI. TITLE: CORRESPONDENCE WITH FBI ON CIA/FBI LIAISON AGREEMENT IN 1948. PAGES: 18. JFK64-48: F26 1998.10.22.14:10:26:590108. NARA.

215-216: Angleton monitors de Mohrenschildt's mail: See, for example: CIA. 104-10164-10115. FROM: WITHHELD. TO: DIRECTOR. TITLE: DEMOHRENSCHILDT MAIL INTERCEPTED. DATE: 11/10/64. PAGES: 1. JFK64-3:F29 1998.01.20.09:13:21:123082. NARA. See also: CIA. 104-10414-10133. FROM: JOHN H. WALLER, IG. TO: DIR OF CIA. TITLE: MR. DE MOHRENSCHILDT'S LETTER TO YOU DATED 5 SEPTEMBER 1976. 09/23/76. 6 PAGES. See also: CIA. 104-10164-10115. FROM: WITHHELD. TO: DIRECTOR. TITLE: DEMOHRENSCHILDT MAIL INTERCEPTED. 11/10/64. 1 PAGE. NARA.

215: It was Whitten who sent the names of people who corresponded with de Mohrenschildt to the FBI for file checks: MEMORANDUM TO: Jane Roman for the Chief of Counter Intelligence/Liaison. CIA. 104-10166-10235. NO DATE, but apparently April 1965. JFK64-5:F17 1998.01.27.15:56:44:420107. John Whitten acted for James Angleton in the monitoring of George de Mohrenschildt's mail: Ibid., CIA. 104-10166-10235.

215: the FBI demands a separate file check sheet for each name: MEMORANDUM FOR: Chief, CI/Liaison. Attention: Mrs. Jane Roman. SUBJECT: Request for FBI File Check on Associates George and Jeanne de MOHRENSCHILDT. Signed: JOHN M. WHITTEN. C/ WH/2. CIA. 104-10166-10235. FROM: WITHHELD. TO: CHIEF, CI/LIAISON. JFK64-5 : F17 : 1998.01.27.15:56:44:420107. NARA.

216: Angleton sends the FBI a twenty-nine page Memorandum: FBI. RECORD NUMBER: 124-10135-10123. AGENCY FILE NUMBER: 100-32965-306. FROM: ANGLETON, JAMES. TO: DIRECTOR, FBI. DATE: 04/05/65. PAGES: 29. SUBJECTS: DEMOH, POST-OSWALD PERIOD, HAITIAN CONNECTION. NARA.

Notes

216: "De Mohrenschildt connected Lee Harvey Oswald and accordingly of extreme interest": CIA. 104-10166-10240. FROM: DIRECTOR. TO: WITHHELD. TITLE: REQ STATION TRACES TUSTYN STRUMITTO AND (MADAME) (FNU) DE FEPOVATY, BOTH SUBJECTS HAVE RECENTLY BEEN IN CORRESPONDENCE WITH GEORGE DE MOHRENSCHILDT. DATE: 04/16/65. 1 PAGE. JFK64-5:F17 1998.01.27.16:15:39:373107. NARA.

217: Brandel "either in British or Dutch intelligence": CIA. 104-10166-10257. FROM: WITHHELD. TO: CHIEF/WH/4. TITLE: RESIDENT OF ROME, ITALY IN CORRESPONDENCE WITH GEORGE DE MOHRENSCHILDT (201-725439). DATE: 01/01/1900 [sic]. JFK64-5:F17 1998.01.27.17:24:05:436107. NARA.

217: Fedor Alekseyevich Garanin a de Mohrenschildt acquaintance: CIA. 104-10431-10038. AGENCY FILE NUMBER: RUSS HOLMES WORK FILE. TITLE: FEDOR ALEKSEYEVICH GARANIN, SUSPECT KGB, BIO. DATE: 06/24/64. PAGES: 3. SUBJECTS: GARANIN. JFK-RH18:F1. 1998.09.16.08:48:17:686128. NARA. Also available on www.maryferrell.org. See also: To: Mr. Rocca. From: Paul Hartman. Title: De Mohrenschildt's Contacts with Soviet Officials. 29 September 1964. No riff available. NARA.

217: Garanin "a member of the Soviet State Security service probably since the mid-1940's": CIA. 104-10009-10124. AGENCY FILE NUMBER: 201-289248. FROM: HELMS, RICHARD, DD/P. CIA. TO: RANKIN, J. LEE, GEN COUNSEL, WC. TITLE: GEORGE AND JEANNE DE MOHRENSCHILDT. DATE: 06/03/1964. PAGES: 9. COMMENTS: OSW14 : V54 : 1993.06.21.17:31:03:900140. NARA.

218: "one-time and casual": From: Paul Hartman. To: Mr. Rocca. Routing and Record Sheet. 29 Sep 64. XAAZ-22067. "De Mohrenschildt's Contacts With Soviet Officials." NARA.

218: "No checking with ODENVY": JMWAVE message from Desmond Fitzgerald and John M. Whitten, C/WH/2. October 28, 1964.

218: Sam Ballen's letter describing Marina's being jealous of Jeanne de Mohrenschildt is available in FBI, 124-10135-10123. James Angleton's twenty-nine page memorandum to the FBI is dated April 5, 1965.

219: "reported as French intel": CIA. 104-10166-10258. FROM: DIRECTOR. TO: WITHHELD. TITLE: REQUEST STATION ALSO ATTEMPT OPEN MAIL FROM F. SCHUMACHER AND CO., NYC, WHICH PROBABLY FROM PIERRE FREYSS, REPORTED FRENCH INTEL. DATE: 02/05/1965. SUBJECTS: ANIKEEFF. JFK64-5 : F17 : 1998.01.2717.28:16:936107. NARA.

219: "Has there been any progress in our matters?": FBI. RECORD NUMBER: 124-10135-10123. AGENCY FILE NUMBER: 100-32965-306. ORGINATOR: CIA. FROM: ANGLETON, JAMES. TO: DIRECTOR, FBI. DATE: 04/05/65. PAGES: 29. SUBJECTS: DEMOH, POST-OSWALD PERIOD, HAITIAN CONNECTION. NARA.

220: "Polish citizen": CIA. TO: CHIEF, WH/POLAND. TITLE: MEMORANDUM FOR: POLISH CITZEN IN CORRESPONDENCE WITH GEORGE DE MOHRENSCHILDT IN HAITI. DATE: 02/14/1965. PAGES: 1. JFK64-5 : F17 : 1998.06.09.08:45:44:500128. NARA.

220: a letter comes for de Mohrenschildt from a post office box in Switzerland: CIA. 104-10166-10259. FROM: WITHHELD [John Whitten]. TITLE: LETTER FROM GENEVA, SWITZERLAND TO GEORGE DE MOHRENSCHILDT. DATE: 02/04/1965. PAGES: 1. SUBJECTS: DE MOHRENSCHILDT. JFK64-5 : F17 : 1998.01.27.17:57:09:590102. NARA.

220: de Mohrenschildt has "connections with two foreign intelligence services": CIA. 104-10244-10292. FROM: JOHN WHITTEN, C/WH/2. TO: CHIEF/WH/POLAND. TITLE: MEMORANDUM FOR: POLISH CITIZEN IN CORRESPONDENCE WITH GEORGE DE MOHRENSCHILDT IN HAITI. DATE: 02/04/1965. JFK64-5 : F17 : 1998.06.09.08:44:500128. NARA.

220: "of extreme interest to the Federal Bureau of Investigation": CIA. 104-10166-10259. FROM: WITTHELD. [John Whitten]. TITLE: LETTER FROM GENEVA, SWITZERLAND TO GEORGE DE MOHRENSCHILDT. DATE: 02/04/1965. 1 PAGE. JFK64-5: F17 : 1998.01.27.17:57:09:590102. NARA.

220: "former Kubarker": CIA. 104-10166-10265. FROM: WITHHELD. TO: DIRECTOR. TITLE: REQUEST STATION ATTEMPT EFFECT ENTRY ALL LETTERS. DATE: 02/01/1965. JFK64-5 : F17 : 1998.01.27.18:27:14:483102. NARA.

221: "attempt effect entry": Ibid., CIA. 104-10166-10265.

221: "so that KUBARK may continue to discharge its responsibilities to ODYOKE": CIA. 104-10166-10275. FROM: DIRECTOR. TO: WITHHELD. TITLE: CABLE: HQ UNDERSTANDS THAT YOU HAVE BEEN FORBIDDEN TO MAINTAIN LIGHT SOCIAL CONTACT WITH IDEN. DATE: 12/10/1964. 1 PAGE. JFK64-5 : F7 : 1998.01.27.19:02:36:840102. NARA.

221: "not mention proposed operational use of EVMINCE": CIA. 104-10166-10272. FROM: WITHHELD. TO: DIRECTOR. TITLE: AMBASSADOR DID NOT SEE PARA 2 REF. SUBJECTS: KUBARK; EVMINCE; MOHRENSCHILDT, G. JFK64-5 : F17 : 1998.01.27.18:52:07:420102. NARA.

221: "if the Agency developed or received any information": FBI. To: Mr. D. J. Brennan, Jr. From: Mr. S. J. Papich. Subject: George de Mohrenschildt; Internal Security. March 16, 1965. The Bureau's reply is dated March 18th. FBI file of George de Mohrenschildt.

221: Jean K. Saurel: CIA. 104-10166-10262. FROM: DEPUTY DIRECTOR FOR PLANS. TO: DIRECTOR, FBI. TITLE: SAUREL, JEAN K. DATE: 02/02/1965. PAGES: 2. JFK64-5 : F17 : 1998.01.27.18:16:57:840102. NARA.

222: Paul Hartman informs Hoover of what he knows about Jean K. Saurel: CIA. 104-10166-10262. FROM: DEPUTY DIRECTOR FOR PLANS. TO: DIRECTOR, FBI. TITLE: SAUREL, JEAN K. DATE: 02/02/1965. 2 PAGES. JFK64-5 : F17 : 1998.01.27.18:16:57:840102. NARA.

223: correspondence between J. Edgar Hoover and J. Lee Rankin with respect to making public personal information about the Paines and the de Mohrenschildts: See J. Edgar Hoover to Honorable J. Lee Rankin, October 23, 1964 and J. Lee Rankin to Hoover, November 18, 1964. FBI file of George de Mohrenschildt.

224: de Mohrenschildt discovers bauxite, "not told anyone else of his discovery": CIA. 104-10166-10256. FROM: RID TO: C/WH/2. DATE: 02/08/65. PAGES: 3. JFK64-5 : FA7 : 1998. 01.27.17:21:07:780107. NARA.

224: EVMINCE/1 does not want the news of de Mohrenschildt's discovery of bauxite to be revealed; the Chief of the Western Hemisphere Division wants to know how George de Mohrenschildt is doing in business: CIA. 104-10166-10247. TITLE: POSSIBLE ECONOMIC STANDING OF GEORGE DE MOHRENSCHILDT. JFK64-5:F17: 1998.01.27.16:45:09:543107. NARA. To keep EVMINCE/1 "perfectly clean," CIA did not disseminate the information. CIA remained interested in de Mohrenschildt's finances.

224-225: EVMINCE-1 rummages through Galicki's garbage and discovers that de Mohrenschildt has sold sisal to Galicki: CIA. 104-10166-10256. FROM: RID. TO: C/WH/2. TITLE: SALE OF SISAL BY GEORGE DE MOHRENSCHILDT. DATE:

02/08/1965. PAGES: 3. SUBJECTS: DE MOHRENSCHILDTS. JFK64-5 : F17 : 1998.01.27.17:21:07: 780107. NARA.

SEVEN: THE PARAMILITARY GAME

227: "we have the green light": Interview with the nephew of Rolando Masferrer Rojas, "Rolandito" Masferrer.

227: "There will be no Cuba": Graham Greene, *The Comedians* (The Viking Press: New York, 1966), p. 249.

227: a cornucopia of invasions sponsored by the CIA. See: Intelligence Memorandum. May 13, 1965. Foreign Relations of the United States. Volume XXXII, Dominican Republic, etc. Document 342.

228: The "303 Committee": See "The U.S. Government and the Vietnam War, Executive and Legislative Roles and Relationships, Part I, 1945-1961. "Prepared for the Committee on Foreign Relations, U.S. Senate, by the Congressional Research Service, printed by the U.S. Government Printing Office, Washington, D.C., 1984, pp. 308-310.

228: the Joint Chiefs send their own list of "four potentially useful Haitian officers": Memorandum From The Deputy Director for Coordination of the Bureau of Intelligence and Research (Williams) to the Assistant Secretary of State for Inter-American Affairs (Vaughn). Foreign Relations of the United States, Volume XXXII, Document 345.

228: Clémard Joseph Charles was not on anyone's list: Memorandum Prepared for the 303 Committee. June 15, 1965. Volume XXXII, Document 345.

228: "Haiti-The Threat and Possible Pre-emptive Measures": June 11, 1965. MEMORANDUM FOR: ARA – Mr. Vaughn. FROM: INR/DDC – Murat W. Williams. SUBJECT: Minutes of the 303 Committee Meeting June 10, 1965. NARA.

229: "Communist sympathizers are tolerated": Memorandum Prepared for the 303 Committee, June 15, 1965, Document 345.

229: "a matter of keeping their fingers on the exiles' pulse": Diederich & Burt, p. 232.

229: "effective National Health Service": Telegram From The Embassy in Haiti to the Department of State. October 21, 1965. Foreign Relations of the United States, Volume XXXII, Document 349.

230: "recreation spots": FBI. 124-10301-10027. RECORDS SERIES: HQ. AGENCY FILE NUMBER: 2-1423-2ND NY 111. FROM: WANNALL, W. R. TO: SULLIVAN, W. C. DATE: 12/14/65. PAGES: 2. SUBJECTS: IID, BKG, EMP, ASSOC, HAITI, OPINION, REVOLUTIONARY ACT. NARA.

230: "Haitians who remain in Haiti": Information Memorandum From The Assistant Secretary of State for Inter-American Affairs (Vaughn) to the Under-Secretary of State for Economic Affairs (Mann). January 5, 1966. Foreign Relations of the United States, Volume XXXII, Document 351.

230: "Duvalier's overthrow would have to be an inside job": National Intelligence Estimate. October 27, 1966. Foreign Relations of the United States, Volume XXXII, Document 358.

230: CIA incursions into Haiti: See Intelligence Memorandum. May 13, 1955. Foreign Relations of the United States, Volume XXXII, Document 342.

230: "it might prove more difficult to get a force out than to put it in": Ibid., National Intelligence Estimate. October 27, 1966.

230: Charles heads for Italy and France.... "our captain": CIA. 104-10166-10174. FROM: NYOR. TO: WITHHELD. TITLE: CLOSED CASE 40,556 CLÉMARD

CHARLES OF HAITI AND RR SHEET. DATE: 04/071966. PAGES: 2. JFK64-5 F19:1998.01.24.09.11:44:326108. NARA.

232: Clémard Joseph Charles serves as an intermediary for Duvalier in his receiving money from the French Mafia: "François Duvalier s'était enrichi grâce au traffic de la drogue, révèle Michel Soukar," April 25, 2007. Available on the Internet. The "café" (heroin) made its way from Haiti to Venezuela before it arrived in the United States.

232: Charles, Duvalier and Bill Bonanno in Haiti: See: Bill Bonanno, *Bound By Honor: A Mafioso's Story* (St. Martin's Press: New York, 1999), pp. 179-182.

234: meeting of Masferrer and his followers at the Plaza Hotel: FBI. 124-10301-10058. RECORDS SERIES: HQ. AGENCY FILE NUMBER: 2-1423-3RD NR 90. FROM: SAC, WMFO. TO: DIRECTOR, FBI. DATE: 08/09/63. PAGES: 4. SUBJECTS: IID, BKG, ASSOC, INVASION, HAITI. NARA.

234: "the extent of his activities in securing information for President Duvalier: FBI. RECORD NUMBER: 124-10301-10013. RECORDS SERIES: HQ. AGENCY FILE NUMBER: 2-1423-121. FROM: YEAGLEY, J. WALTER. TO: DAVIDSON, I. IRVING. DATE: 10/07/66. PAGES: 4. SUBJECTS: IID, ASSOC, ROJAS, ARSENIO, MIRABEL, HUGO, GARCÍA, ENRIQUE, HAITI, EXILES US. NARA.

235: Masferrer wanted to be President of Cuba: email from Gordon Winslow, November 29, 2009, based on Mr. Winslow's interviews with Masferrer.

235: "a rather unscrupulous person": FBI. 124-10301-10023. RECORDS SERIES: HQ. AGENCY FILE NUMBER: 2-1423-113. FROM: WANNALL, W. R. TO: SULLIVAN, W. C. DATE: 04/18/66. PAGES: 2. SUBJECTS: IID, ASSOC, POLIT, HAITI, GOVERNMENT COLLAPSE. NARA.

236: Masferrer siphoned off money: Interview with Anselmo Aliegro, November 12, 1999.

236: *Santería* priestess: Ibid. email from Winslow, November 29, 2009.

237: Masferrer calls Cantave "a man of great merit": CIA. Country: Cuba, Haiti, Dominican Republic. Report No. TDCSDB-3/656,079. 16 August 1963. Subject: Plans of Rolando Arcadio Masferrer Rojas To Assist General Léon Cantave In Haiti and Then Overthrow Fidel Castro Ruz. Masferrer hoped to recruit as many members of the 2506 Brigade (Bay of Pigs veterans) as he could. This report was disseminated to several agencies, including CINCLANT; CINSCO; COMNAVKEYWEST; MIAMI REPS OF STATE; the U.S. Coast Guard; Border Patrol; INS; FBI and Customs.

237: men in white jackets: Interview with the late Martin Xavier Casey, November 1999.

238: "disseminated this information in the normal manner": 16 December 1966. Lawrence R. Houston, General Counsel, to The Honorable J. Walter Yeagley. NARA.

238-239: In the midst of these paramilitary operations against Haiti, Oswald's CIA-employed cousin Marilyn Murret plans a vacation to Haiti, and Frances Knight asks the DD/P for guidance: DEPARTMENT OF STATE. FROM: KNIGHT, FRANCIS G. TO: DEPUTY DIRECTOR, PLANS. TITLE: LETTER TO DD/PLANS RE REQUEST FOR INFO ON MARILYN DOROTHEA MURRET. DATE: 01/67/67. PAGES: 4: SUBJECTS: HAITI, MURRET, MARILYN, PASSPORT OFFICE. JFK16:F56 1993.07.16.09:41:56:090470: FBI LIAISON REPORT. ATT. NARA.

239: "loose talk about agency endorsement of Masferrer's mission led to the Agency scuttling it": MEMORANDUM FOR: Director of Security. FROM: Curtis R. Rivers. SUBJECT: Dade County Request for Agency Assistance Regarding the Death of Johnny Rosselli. 18 October 1976. 6 pages. NARA.

239: "ever been associated with CIA": 1 February 1967. MEMORANDUM FOR: Deputy Director for Plans. Director, Domestic Contact Service, Director of Security. SUBJECT: Masferrer Prosecution, Miami, Florida. OGC 67-0181. Signed by Lawrence R. Houston, General Counsel. cc: Chief, WH Division. NARA.

239: CIA monitored the trial of the Masferrer group: CIA. OGC. 67-1772. MEMORANDUM FOR: CHIEF, WH DIVISION. FROM: JOHN K. GREANEY, ASSISTANT GENERAL COUNSEL. SUBJECT: Masferrer Trial, Miami, Florida. This document is one of several revealing CIA's interest in Masferrer's attempted invasion of Haiti. CIA alarm at being exposed is reflected as well in a letter from Lawrence R. Houston to Assistant Attorney General J. Walter Yeagley of the Internal Security Division of the Justice Department dated 20 October 1967. (OGC 67-1993). 4 pages. NARA.

239: Parabellum, a front for shipping arms out of the United States: Conversation with Rolando P. Masferrer, Jr., who was a vice president for Parabellum.

240: Security files existed for Rolando Masferrer Rojas: MEMORANDUM FOR: Director of Security. FROM: Curtis R. Rivers. SUBJECT: Dade County Request for Agency Assistance Regarding the Death of Johnny Rosselli. NARA. Masferrer both a "covert" and an "overt" CIA asset: MEMORANDUM FOR: Director of Central Intelligence. 1 November 1967. OGC 67-2059. From: Lawrence R. Houston. NARA.

240: weapons out of New York: Interview with Rolando P. (Rolandito) Masferrer, Jr., nephew of Rolando Masferrer Rojas, November 14, 1999.

240: Masferrer disapproved of del Valle because he ran drugs: Ibid. interview with Rolando P. Masferrer, Jr.

241: whether CIA had sanctioned Fidel Castro: Interview with Rolando P. Masferrer, Jr.

242: I.I. Davidson introduces himself as a representative of the U.S. State Department: CIA. 104-10216-10066. FROM: WITHHELD. TO: DIRECTOR. TITLE: ACCORDING TO SUBJECT, DURING AFTERNOON OF 3 DEC, ONE I. IRVING DAVIDSON, VISITED BALAGUER AT PALACE. DATE: 12/08/1966. SUBJECTS: WITHHELD, DAVIDSON, IRVING JJF64-51: F14 :1998.04.25.16:04:58:983102. NARA.

242: CIA tracks Davidson's movements in 1966: CIA. 104-10216-10065. FROM: DIRECTOR. TO: WITHHELD. TITLE: SUBSTANCE REF INFO BEING PASSED ON HIGHLY RESTRICTED BASIS, PROTECTING SOURCE. 12/06/1966. PAGES: 1. SUBJECTS: TRACES, WITHHELD. JFK64-51: F14 : 1998.04.25.16:02:27:340102. NARA.

242: CIA sent intelligence on I.I. Davidson's meetings with Balaguer to the White House: CIA. 104-10234-10259. FROM: ESTERLINE, JACOB, AC/WESTERN HEMISPH. TO: DIRECTOR OF CENTRAL INTELLIGENCE. TITLE: MEMO: IRVING DAVIDSON. DATE: 12/08/66. PAGES: 3. SUBJECTS: DAVIDSON, IRVING. JFK64-51:F14: 1998.09.19.09:28:46:500109. NARA.

242: I.I. Davidson finances trips for his informants regarding an invasion of Haiti from the Dominican Republic: FBI. RECORD NUMBER: 124-10301-10016. RECORDS SERIES: HQ. AGENCY FILE NUMBER: 2-1423-118. FROM: YEAGLEY, J. WALTER. TO: DIRECTOR, FBI. DATE: 09/14/66. PAGES: 2. SUBJECTS: IID, ASSOC, HAITI, INVASION, TRA, B/F INT. NARA.

242: Davidson working simultaneously for Duvalier and Balaguer: FBI. 124-10301-10018. RECORDS SERIES: HQ. AGENCY FILE NUMBER: 2-1423-1ST NR 116. FROM: SAC, NY. TO: DIRECTOR, FBI. DATE: 08/08/66. PAGES: 2. SUBJECTS: IID, ASSOC, DOMR, HAITI, INVASION, B/F INT, WEAPONS. NARA.

243: "unacceptable Haitians": "Politico-Military Contingency Plan For Haiti," May 16, 1967. "Foreign Relations of the United States," Volume XXXII, Document 361.

243: yet another paramilitary mission into Haiti was undertaken, this one with Colonel Réne Léon in charge: Interview with Howard K. Davis, January 14, 2009. The description of the operation comes from interviews with Howard K. Davis and the late Martin Xavier Casey.

243: I.I. Davidson facilitates the 1968 invasion of Haiti, with, he claims, the cooperation of the Department of State and the Central Intelligence Agency: CIA. 104-10216-10063. FROM: DD/FOR PLANS. TO: DIRECTOR, FBI. TITLE: SUBJECT: ALLEGED PLOT TO INVADE HAITI. DATE: 12/18/67. PAGES: 5. SUBJECTS: HAITI; 201-041581. JFK64-51:F14 1998.04.25.15:58:17:030102. NARA.

244: "Big Game: Styled by Broadway": See R. D. Heinl, Jr. and N. G. Heinl, *Written in Blood – The Story of the Haitian People 1492-1971* (Houghton Mifflin: Boston, 1978), pp. 657-658.

246: "Gérard Pierre," a schoolteacher, is put on trial for participating in the May 20, 1968 invasion: CIA. 104-10069-10291. FROM: WILMA R. VAN SCOY. TO: MFR (MEMORANDUM FOR THE RECORD). DATE: 07/05/1968. PAGES: 1. SUBJECT: Conversation with EVMEND-1; CHARLES, C.J. NARA. Although this document discusses a variety of subjects, CIA lists under SUBJECTS only CHARLES, C.J. See also for "Gérard Pierre": CIA radio broadcasts jammed: MEMORANDUM FOR THE RECORD. 5 July 1968. SUBJECT: CONVERSATION WITH EVMEND-1. Signed by Wilma R. Van Scoy.

246: "no basis for Haitian allegations": See Action Memorandum From The President's Special Assistant (Rostow) to President Johnson. May 21, 1968. "Foreign Relations of the United States," Volume XXXII, Document 366.

246: "may well have come from the United States." Editorial Note. Undated. "Foreign Relations of the United States," Volume XXXII. Document 368.

246: "stopped it cold and got convictions": Memorandum of Meeting. May 27, 1968. "Foreign Relations of the United States," Volume XXXII. Document 369.

247: one was "Francis D. Rachfield": Few records have survived naming Chubb-Rachfield as the CIA handler of Clémard Joseph Charles. One is CIA. 104-10177-10185. FROM: JMWAVE. TO: DIRECTOR. TITLE: PLAN WAVE CO FRANCIS D. RACHFIELD TDY HQS 19 JUL ENROUTE REF A DEBRIEFING. DATE: 07/15/1965. PAGES: 1. SUBJECTS: AMSHAM-1; HAITI. JFK64-13:F28 : 1998.03.03.17:51:10:890102. This document requests that Rachfield "discuss Haitian exile activities with Haiti desk officers in Washington, D.C." See also: CIA. 104-10077-10284. FROM: DIRECTOR. TO: JMWAVE. TITLE: CABLE: REQUEST FRANCIS D. RACHFIELD PROVIDE HEADQUARTERS WITH CABLE. DATE: 12/05/63. PAGES: 1. SUBJECTS: RACHFIELD, FRANCIS D. JFK17:F18 1995.09.12.16:56:02S:500028: The request from Headquarters is that Francis D. Rachfield provide headquarters with a "current local home address and duty telephone number." The best document regarding Rachfield and Clémard Joseph Charles is the four pages of a researcher's notes, available from HSCA (see below). Only in 2003 did CIA reveal names like "Chubb's," which was either the true name or the pseudonym. The issue was complicated by the fact that Other Government Agencies (OGA's) namely Army intelligence, had an interest in Charles.

247: "if possible to pass a msg." Rachfield/Chubb as the case officer of Clémard Joseph Charles: HSCA. RECORD NUMBER:180-10142-10009. RECORD SERIES: CIA SEGREGATED COLLECTION. AGENCY FILE NUMBER: 22-12-01. ORGINATOR: HSCA. FROM: CIA. DATE: 08/24/78. PAGES: 84. BOX 10. NARA.

247: Howard K. Davis' instinct is proven correct when I.I. Davidson reports his request for machine guns to the FBI: FBI. RECORD NUMBER: 124-10294-10046. RECORDS SERIES: HQ. AGENCY FILE NUMBER: 2-1423-4TH NR 36. FROM: DIRECTOR, FBI. TO: SAC, MM. DATE: 05/26/59. PAGES: 1. SUBJECTS: IID, DAVIS, HOWARD, TELCAL, MACHINE GUNS. NARA.

248: "He has played Duvalier's game": HSCA. RECORD NUMBER: 180-10142-10009. RECORD SERIES: CIA SEGREGATED COLLECTION. AGENCY FILE NUMBER: 22-12-01. ORIGINATOR: HSCA. FROM: CIA. DATE: 08/24/78. PAGES: 84. BOX 10. NARA.

248: "the assistance of the U.S. would not fail us": AGENCY: INSCOM/CSF. RECORD NUMBER: 194-10014-10138. RECORDS SERIES: DOD AFFILIATED PERSONNEL AND INCIDENT INVESTIGATIONS. AGENCY FILE NUMBER: AA851401WJ – PAGES 68-69. TO: MATLACK, D.K. LETTER. 06/06/67. SUBJECTS: CHARLES, CLÉMARD J; BANQUE COMMERCIALE D'HAITI (SOCIÉTÉ ANONYME DE BANQUE). NARA.

249: Louis A. Brun wrote to Dorothe Matlack, asking for a meeting to deliver a message from Clémard Joseph Charles "personally": AGENCY: INSCOM/CSF. RECORD NUMBER: 194-10014-10137. AGENCY FILE NUMBER: AA851401WJ – PAGE 67. FROM: BRUN, LOUIS A. TO: MATLACK, D. K. TITLE; LETTER. DATE: 06/12/67. SUBJECTS: CHARLES, CLÉMARD J.; B & B INTERNATIONAL CORP. NARA.

249: "90 DEUCE" produces a seven page "information report" on "U.S.GOVERNMENT SUPPPORT FOR PLOT TO OVERTHROW THE HAITIAN GOVERNMENT: AGENCY: INSCOM/CSF. RECORD NUMBER: 194-10014-10136. RECORDS SERIES: DOD AFFILIATED PERSONNEL AND INCIDENT INVESTIGATIONS. AGENCY FILE NUMBER: AA851401WJ. PAGES 60-66. NARA.

249: Opportunist: It was Joseph F. Dryer, Jr. who told military intelligence that Clémard Joseph Charles was an "opportunist": Gaeton Fonzi, MEMORANDUM – July 7, 1978. RE: Interview with JOSEPH DRYER.

250: "there are doctors in Haiti": Interview with Joseph F. Dryer, Jr., December 15, 2009. Palm Beach, Florida.

250: Duvalier "strongly suggested" that Clémard Joseph Charles have his surgery in Haiti: AGENCY: INSCOM/CSF. RECORD NUMBER: 194-10014-10136. AGENCY FILE NUMBER: AA851401WJ – PAGES 60-66. TITLE: INFORMATION REPORT. DATE: 06/15/67. PAGES: 7. SUBJECTS: CHARLES, CLÉMARD J. US GOVERNMENT SUPPORT FOR PLOT TO OVERTHROW THE HAITIAN GOVERNMENT. NARA.

252: CIA notes that Duvalier by June 1967 had deprived Charles "of much of his empire": Intelligence Information cable, June 28, 1967. Foreign Relations of the United States, Volume XXXII, Document 363.

252: Charles refused to turn money over to Duvalier: See: Elizabeth Abbott, *Haiti: The Duvaliers and Their Legacy* (McGraw-Hill Book Company: New York, 1988), p. 181 and Robert Rotberg, *Haiti: The Politics of Squalor* (Houghton Mifflin Company: Boston, 1971), p. 251.

252: "Ah, Clémard had to butt in politics": Quoted in Patrick Lemoine, *Fort-Dimanche, Dungeon of Death*, p. 123.

252: "Updated Listing of the Ton Ton Macoute": CIA. 104-10069-10063. TO: CHIEF, W.H. DIVISION. FROM: MATTHEW H. CHUBB. DATE: 11/16/67. PAGES: 9. JFK14 :F31.1993.07.14.16:26:13:310480. NARA.

253: Charles a "rascal": Interview with Bernard Diederich, July 31, 2011.

EIGHT: SECOND AND THIRD ACTS

255: "we do know that his death was violent: MEMORANDUM. FROM: Bernard Fensterwald, Jr. TO: Gary Shaw, Mary Ferrell. RE: Clémard Joseph Charles. June 30, 1983. 2 pages. Courtesy of Peggy A. Adler and James H. Lesar.

256: de Mohrenschildt writes a complaining letter to Lyndon Johnson, February 1, 1966. George de Mohrenschildt to Dear Mr. President, February 1, 1966, LBJ library, Austin Texas.

257: "apparent difficulties in Haiti": Robert M. Sayre to George de Mohrenschildt. Undated. LBJ library.

257: "valid written contract": Ibid., Robert M. Sayre to George de Mohrenschildt.

258: CIA had informed the FBI that the de Mohrenschildts were leaving Haiti. Memo from CIA Director to Director, FBI. March 15, 1966. FBI file of George de Mohrenschildt.

258: GOH owed de Mohrenschildt $122,222, etc.: FBI. SAC, Dallas to Director, FBI. October 27, 1966. FBI file of George de Mohrenschildt.

258: de Mohrenschildt tries to obtain a government contract for geological work somewhere in Latin America: FBI. Interview with Colonel Lawrence Orlov. March 1, 1967. FBI file of George de Mohrenschildt. 100-32965-316.

259: "many many thanks again": George de Mohrenschildt to the President. December 4, 1966. LBJ library.

259: "Institute of Latin American Resources": George de Mohrenschildt to Mr. Lyndon B. Johnson, December 27, 1966. LBJ library. The reply to de Mohrenschildt was signed by Milton Barall, a Deputy Assistant Administrator, who wrote to de Mohrenschildt on January 13, 1967 that they had no interest "in supporting the creation of such an institute in Texas." LBJ library.

259: "A lengthy file in the Office of Special Consular Services...": Benjamin H. Read, Executive Secretary, MEMORANDUM FOR MR. WALT W. ROSTOW, THE WHITE HOUSE. Subject: Letter from Mr. George de Mohrenschildt to the President. January 14, 1967. LBJ library.

259: low level Johnson staff: de Mohrenschildt's letter to Johnson was answered by Whitney Shoemaker, Assistant to the President. Whitney Shoemaker to Mr. de Mohrenschildt, September 6, 1967. LBJ library.

259: Charles R. Norberg had been employed by CIA: Adamson, Volume I, p. 127.

261: I.I. Davidson is asked to inquire into de Mohrenschildt's background: Adamson, Volume XI, p. 69.

261: "inquiry should be made through CIA": FBI. TO: DIRECTOR, FBI. FROM: SAC, DALLAS. SUBJECT: ASSASSINATION OF PRESIDENT JOHN FITZGERALD KENNEDY. March 7, 1983. 62-109060-7504. This letter is included in George de Mohrenschildt's FBI file.

262: "carry out certain operational support tasks for the Agency": CIA. 104-10072-10289. Title: Special Activities Report on a JMWAVE relationship. Date: 03/19/64. 10 pages. JFK15:F38 1993.08.06:14:34:43:310028. NARA.

262: "Charles uses pseudonym 'Jacoby'": HSCA. 180-10142-10009. RECORD SERIES: CIA SEGREGATED COLLECTION. AGENCY FILE NUMBER: 2-12-01. FROM: CIA. DATE: 08/24/78. PAGES: 84. DOCUMENT TYPE: NOTES. SUBJECT(S): CIA, FILES. BOX 10. NARA.

262: Clémard Joseph Charles is released after paying a ransom of $250,000: CIA. 104-10069-10291. FROM: WILMA R. VAN SCOY. TO: MFR. TITLE: WITHHELD. MEMORANDUM FOR THE RECORD. 07/05/1968. PAGES: 1. SUBJECTS: CHARLES, C. J. Signed by Wilma R. Van Scoy. NARA. This is a conversation with EVMEND-1.

262: Clémard Joseph Charles hands over a sheaf of "signed blank checks on each of his Swiss accounts:" Robert Debs Heinl and Nancy Gordon Heinl, *Written In Blood*, p. 592.

263: "a standing TS clearance": MEMORANDUM FOR: DO/Security. 30 January 1968. SUBJECT: Thomas James Devine – 201-267709 OS# 42069. FROM: Gale Allen. DO/CO. DO refers to the Directorate of Operations. CO could be "Case Officer." EO stands for External Operations.

264: "President Johnson regrets that his schedule will not permit him to meet with you": W. Thomas Johnson to Mr. Mohrenschildt, June 17, 1969. LBJ library.

264: Charles consults Duvalier's doctor: Prosper Avril, *From Glory To Disgrace: The Haitian Army, 1804-1994* (Universal Publishers: Boca Raton, Florida, 1999), pp. 176. 180. Avril, a former President of Haiti and commander of its armed forces, was trained at the U.S. Naval Intelligence School at Anacosta, Virginia.

265: Duvalier has Clémard Joseph Charles arrested again: Prosper Avril,*From Glory To Disgrace: The Haitian Army, 1804-1994*, p. 176., p. 193. For others arrested with Charles. See: CIA. Field Information Report. Country: Haiti. Mid-July 1970. SUBJECT: Current status of the "Service Duvalier (SD)." 2 pages. NARA.

265: CIA continued to use I.I. Davidson as a source on Haiti into the 1970's: CIA. 104-10216-10102. FROM: DIRECTOR, DOMESTIC CONTACT SERVICE. TO: CHIEF, WASHINGTON FIELD OFFICE. TITLE: MEMORANDUM; SUBJECT – INFORMAL DCS REQUIREMENTS FOR IRVING DAVIDSON. DATE: 05/10/71. PAGES: 2. SUBJECTS: DAVIDSON, IRVING. JFK64-51:F16 1998.04.28.20:35:22:653115. NARA.

265: Davidson reports to the State Department on Baby Doc: CIA. 104-10234-10269. ORGINATOR: DOS (DEPARTMENT OF STATE). TITLE: DEPT OF STATE TELEGRAM: CABINET WAS CONVOKED BY PRESIDENT JEAN-CLAUDE DUVALIER. DATE: 04/26/71. PAGES: 1. SUBJECTS: DAVIDSON, IRVING; DUVALIER, JEAN. JFK64-51:F16 1998.09.19.10:42:48:356109. NARA.

265: "personal friendship with Duvalier....": CIA. 104-10216-10056. FROM: WITHHELD. TO: DIRECTOR. TITLE: DURING PLANE TRIP BETWEEN WASHINGTON AND MIAMI GPDROLL SAT NEXT TO MR. IRVING DAVIDSON. DATE: 03/16/70. PAGES: 1. SUBJECTS: DAVIDSON, IRVING; GPDROLL. JFK64-51:F15 1998.04.25.14:15:42:106102. NARA.

266: a "private matter": David A. Ross to The Honorable George Bush, June 24, 1971. Quoted in Adamson.

267: de Mohrenschildt commits himself to Parkland Hospital": "De Mohrenschildt Found Fatally Shot In Florida," *Dallas Morning News*, 30 March 1977.

267: de Mohrenschildt tells his roommate that Oswald was set up: Adamson, Volume V, p. 122.

267: de Mohrenschildt's Parkland Hospital roommate passes a stress test: Adamson, Volume V, pp. 76, 127.

268: "I do know this man DeMohrenschildt": CIA. 104-10414-10142. RUSS HOLMES WORK FILE. FROM: DIR CIA. TITLE: I DO KNOW THIS MAN DEMOHRENSCHILDT, QUOTED FROM A RUSSIAN SPEAKER. DATE: 00/00/ PAGES: 1. SUBJECTS: OSWALD, LEE H., ANDOVER, ROOMMATE. JFK-RHO7:F124-2 1998.11.14.10:09:20:733108. NARA. De Mohrenschildt's letter to

Bush, "Dear George, dated Dallas, Sept. 5 (1976) is also part of the RUSS HOLMES WORK FILE.

268: "some controversial dealings in Haiti": RUSS HOLMES WORK FILE. FROM: DIR CIA. TITLE: I DO KNOW THIS MAN DEMOHRENSCHILDT, QUOTED FROM A RUSSIAN SPEAKER. NARA.

268: "my staff has been unable to find any indication of interest in your activities": CIA. 104-10414-10134. 9/28/1976. TITLE: LETTER FROM DCI TO GEORGE DE MOHRENSCHILDT. FROM: DCI BUSH, GEORGE. TO: DE Mohrenschildt. 28 September 1976. 1 page. NARA.

268: CIA/CI asks the FBI for information "on the current activities and location of a Mr. George de Mohrenschildt": CIA. September 17, 1976. From: CIA/CI Staff. To: Federal Bureau of Investigation. FBI file of George de Mohrenschildt.

269: Willem Oltmans brings the FBI the rumor that "George de Mohrenschildt was the principal organizer of the assassination of President Kennedy": FBI report 4/3/67. See also. 4/5/67. W.C. Sullivan, W.A. Branigan. FBI file of George de Mohrenschildt.

274: Nancy Tilton...Dorothy Pierson: See: Bruce Adamson, *Oswald's Closest Friend*, Volume One. Nancy Tilton told Adamson that her husband, Franklin Clark, was a first cousin to Mrs. Nelson Rockefeller.

274: "I don't want to remember that man": Interview with Joseph F. Dryer, Jr., December 15, 2009.

275: maneuvered Oswald around: FBI Attn: Intelligence Division. Deputy Assistant Director William O. Cregar. March 31, 1977. 3 pages. FBI file of George de Mohrenschildt.

275: "Can you have lunch with me today?" Interview with Joseph F. Dryer, Jr. Palm Beach, December 15, 2009.

276: "the same type of set-up that was arranged later for Veciana by Bishop": Memo. 5/27/76 TO: Dave Marston. FROM: Gaeton Fonzi. Courtesy of Mr. Fonzi.

276-277: Bishop College, a CIA-funded institution: MEMO. 5/27/76. To: David Marston. From: Gaeton Fonzi. Courtesy of Mr. Fonzi.

278: "dropped their interest in de Mohrenschildt's activities": MEMORANDUM FOR THE RECORD. 4 April 1977.

278: "Nothing new, is there?": CIA. 104-10244-10139. FROM: CHIEF, DALLAS FIELD OFFICE. TITLE: ROUTING AND RECORD SHEET: NEWSPAPER CLIPPINGS. DATE: 03/30/77. 3 PAGES. SUBJECTS: DEMOHRENSCHILDT. JFK64-5:F15 1998.06.03.08:10:42:716128. NARA.

279: Jeanne de Mohrenschildt gives an interview: Jim Marrs, "Widow Disputes Suicide," *Fort Worth Star-Telegram*, May 11, 1978, Section B, p. 1.

279: for the last days of Jeanne le Gon de Mohrenschildt: See: Arthur Pineda and Krissa Legon Kearton to Ann [sic] Buttimer, Chief Investigator, Assassination Records Review Board. Re: De Mohrenschildt photo and records. July 27, 1995. See also: Arthur Pineda to Anne Buttimer, July 17, 1995; Declaration of Krissa LeGON KEARTON, August 22, 1995. Declaration of Arthur Pineda, August 22, 1995. NARA.

280: "a vigorous campaign in the U.S. on behalf of Mr. Charles": email from Max Blanchet, July 20, 2011.

281: Davidson, Hauser scams: Davis, p. 427.

281: I.I. Davidson faces federal investigators: Davis, p. 461.

281: $500,000 to Jimmy Hoffa: Davis, p. 360.

Notes

282: Marcello forgives Davidson: Davis, p. 467.

282: Davidson is found not guilty: Davis, p. 493.

282: "business as usual": Davis, p. 506.

282: "opposition to cruelty and tyranny": Clémard Joseph Charles, "Aiding Fleeing Haitians," *The New York Times*, December 29, 1981 and "Asylum For Haitians," *Des Moines Register*, October 1, 1981, p. 17A.

282: Clémard Joseph Charles and Mario Renda: Pete Brewton, *The Mafia, CIA & George Bush* (Shapolsky Publishers, Inc.: New York, 1992), pp. 192-196, 299.

283: Charles associates with a Miami lawyer who represented Lawrence Freeman: DJ Blaze-Jeff Williamson, "CIA Savings & Loan Scams," website: http://www.freewebs.com/ renegade movement; http://www.freewebs.com/ciascams

284: "no portion of the documents at issue": United States District Court For The District of Columbia. J. Gary Shaw and Mark Allen, Plaintiffs v. Department of Defense, et. al. Defendants. Civil Action No. 82-2411. Filed, October 12, 1983. Signed. John H. Pratt, United States District Judge. Courtesy of James H. Lesar.

284-285: Clémard Joseph Charles returns to Haiti in 1986 along with other Haitian exiles: Avril, p. 192.

285: provide the people of Haiti with pigs: Don Melvin, "Hopes For Haiti Democratic Election Has Voters Looking For A New Beginning," *South Florida Sun-Sentinel,* October 28, 1987.

285: "St. Charles Pacific Peace Organization": See: Gaeton Fonzi, *The Last Investigation,* (Thunder's Mouth Press: New York, 1994), p. 313. Fonzi credits researcher Peggy Adler with having made this discovery.

285: Rorke recounts that Sturgis' activities were known to CIA: FBI. DATE: June 28, 1962. To: Director, Central Intelligence Agency, Attention: Deputy Director, Plans. From: John Edgar Hoover, Director. Subject: FRANK ANTHONY STURGIS, also known as Frank Fiorini. NEUTRALITY MATTERS. 4 pages. NARA.

286: Sturgis refused to tell Fonzi anything about his relationship with Clémard Joseph Charles: Interview with Gaeton Fonzi, January 26, 2009.

287: Clémard Joseph Charles is arrested in Queens, New York: Pete Bowles, "Haiti Exile Busted In Bank Scam," *Newsday,* July 7, 1989.

288: "wanted in the United States": See: "Ex-Militia Chief To Fight Decision Barring Him From Haiti Election," *The New York Times,* November 7, 1990. See also: "Former Tonton Macoute Leader Barred From Haitian Election" (Associated Press), *Chicago Tribune,* November 7, 1990. See also Don Bohning, "Court Won't Reinstate Two Major Candidates," *Miami Herald,* January 16, 1988.

289: John Whitten begs the ARRB and CIA not to release his real name: CIA. 104-10332-10014. AGENCY FILE NUMBER: PROJFILES-DECLASS STDS. FROM: WITHHELD. TO: NONE. TITLE: ARRB-CIA ISSUES: JOHN SCELSO. DATE: 09/27/1996. PAGES: 56. JFK-M-17 : F17 : 2000.02.15.08:46:36:437054. NARA.

291: For sources on CIA in Haiti after the Duvalier years, see: William Blum, *Killing Hope: U.S. Military and C.I.A. Interventions Since World War II* (Common Courage Press: Monroe, Maine, 2004), Chapter 55, "Haiti, 1986-1994: Human Rights, Washington Style," pp. 370-382; Tim Weiner, "Key Haiti Leaders Said To Have Been in the C.I.A.'s Pay," *The New York Times,* November 1, 1993; Dennis Bernstein and Howard Levine, "The CIA's Haitian Connection," *San Francisco Bay Guardian,* November 3, 1993.

292: Aristide agreed "to accept a U.S. occupation": See: Allan Nairn, "Haiti Under The Gun," *The Nation*, January 8/15, 1996.

292: "make Haiti interesting for foreign investors": Quoted in Letter to *The Montclarion*, October 1994, by Grover Furr.

293: "the beginning of the end of the popular movement": See Allan Nairn interview on *Democracy Now!* February 26, 2004. "Haiti: Different Coup, Same Paramilitary Leaders."

293: "The UN Stabilization Mission....": WIKILEAKS_ _SANDERSON _ _WHY _WE _NEED _CONTINUING _MINUSTAH _PRESENCE _IN _HAITI.doc: Reference ID: 08PORTAUPRINCE1381. Created: 2008-10-01 15:03 Released: 2011-01-28 21:09 Classification: CONFIDENTIAL. Origin: Embassy Port Au Prince.

294: "take advantage of public dissatisfaction": WIKILEAKS _ _HAITI _ _MINUSTAH'S _ POLITICAL_ ASSESSMENT -_STABLE _BUT _WITH_RISKS _AHEAD.webarchive. Reference ID: 10PORTAUPRINCE196 Created: 2010-02-24 19:54. Released: 2011-06-17 03.00 Classification: UNCLASSIFIED//FOR OFFICIAL USE ONLY. Origin: Embassy Port Au Prince.

A late note:

95: Transcript of ARRB Interview with L. Fletcher Prouty. Interview conducted September 24, 1996. ARRB Staff present: Wray, Barger, Zimmerman, Gunn.

Wray: During this period of time, was one of your associates General Lansdale?

Prouty: He sat in the same office - well, I mean, in the same group of offices; we were never in the same office - but I had known Lansdale back...1952, in my Pacific duties, [I] flew him quite often, and the people that worked with him. [I] met him in Manila...I knew who Lansdale was, for sure. He was a neighbor of mine in Alexandria until he died. So we worked - he was a CIA man under Air Force cover; so he was working for a while under the Director of Plans in the Air Force, and then from Director of Plans in Air Force, he went down and did the same [in] General Erskine's office, or OSO in defense. I was in OSO, we were both there. And because his cover was as a general for Air Force and I was a colonel, it appeared to people [that] I was working for him. That was good; that's what it was supposed to be. But I was working for Erskine.

Wray: When you say that he was a CIA man under Air Force cover, [you mean] he was not really a career Air Force person?

Prouty: Oh, no. He was [an] intelligence man.

Wray: And so his wearing the uniform or assuming the rank of an Air Force...I think, major general - that was purely cover for his CIA activities?

Prouty:...General LeMay called me up at my office one morning, and he had a paper in his hand, and he said, "I've got a bunch of names here of colonels that are being promoted to brigadier general, there's one on the list that I don't know anything about the son of a gun [sic]. Do you know him?" He said, "People tell me you know him." It was Lansdale. I said, "Yeah. I wrote the thing that Dulles signed that said, 'get him promoted' and since the Agency was gonna pay for the promotion...so, LeMay signed it, and Lansdale became a brigadier general...I just never knew when he made major general; then all of a sudden one day, he told me. He had an office upstairs, and I was down in JCS. And he told me the promotion had come through, and he was a major general, [the] same way. As long as Dulles would sign it - Dulles could have what he wanted...."

ADDENDUM

H.L. HUNT & SONS and CIA

Rothermel Is CIA.

— Martin Waldron
New York Times reporter

PART ONE – MR. ROTHERMEL, I PRESUME?

When it came to party politics, Haroldson Lafayette (H.L.) Hunt, was of one mind with Robert J. Kleberg, Jr., and Herman and George Brown. None was a Democrat, none a Republican. Hunt called himself "a registered Democrat who often votes Republican." Was he, then, a "middle-of-the-roader?" Was he "a conservative?"

He was "a constructive," Hunt said. Then he defined the term: A constructive is simply someone who supports "the best that can be done in public affairs and elsewhere." Hunt's ideal "supreme American patriot of our time" was Douglas MacArthur.

Harmony prevailed in the relationship between Herman and George Brown and CIA. Mutual cooperation served the needs of both. To place CIA's motives and operations into perspective, it may be useful to examine what happened when a major Texas enterprise, Hunt Oil, along with its global affiliates, refused to cooperate with CIA.

CIA did not ignore the Hunts. The Agency came calling with its customary overtures, expecting to be welcomed. But H.L. Hunt and his sons wanted no part of a symbiotic relationship with CIA. Globally operational, richer than the Browns and Steve Bechtel, the Hunts decided that CIA penetration into their enterprises might not sit well with some of the foreign leaders with whom they were doing business, Muammar Qaddafi among them.

H.L. Hunt belonged to the same generation as Herman and George Brown, and Robert J. Kleberg, Jr., but unlike them he was not a native-born Texan. Hunt was born in Fayette County, Illinois on February 17, 1889, son of a Confederate Army veteran. By 1912, precociously entrepreneurial, he was running a cotton plantation in Arkansas, an occupation disdained by Robert J. Kleberg, Jr. Unlike Texans like Gus Wortham and D.H. Byrd, who followed Kleberg's lead and raised Santa Gertrudis cattle, Hunt's son Nelson Bunker Hunt raised instead the Charolais so prized by Alberto Fernandez in Cuba.

H.L. Hunt garnered his first oil well in an Arkansas poker game. He was thirty-one years old when he arrived in Texas in 1920. Famously, he wrested an older roustabout named Daddy Joiner of his fortune. Established in Dallas, the Hunts went their own way. In 1946, a year before the Agency was founded, Hunt was already the richest of the east Texas independent oil men with a gross income of one million dollars a week.

Over the years, some Hunt employees left and beat a path to CIA's door. One was Mack Rankin, who worked for Hunt from 1955 to 1967, and then became vice-chairman of Freeport-McMoran Copper & Gold, formerly Freeport Sulphur, a CIA cover company in Cuba. There, like King Ranch's *Becerra*, it was upended by Castro's agrarian reform policy.

H.L. Hunt was more comfortable pursuing enterprises closer to home. A rare joint venture found him in Iran in 1953 signing an oil agreement with the legally-elected president, Mohammed Mossadegh. That deal blew up when CIA overthrew Mossadegh. The Hunts persistently refused to launder CIA money. Unlike Bechtel, they persisted in declining to provide cover for CIA assets.

Meanwhile H.L. Hunt settled into his Dallas niche. He published right-wing pamphlets and newsletters and sponsored radio programs like "Facts Forum" and "Life Line." Supporters of Facts Forum included the Republic National Bank and Dresser Industries. Like another Texas mogul, Hugh Roy Cullen, "possibly the wealthiest individual in Texas in the decade following World War II," and who was the largest individual contributor to Senator Joseph McCarthy's Senate re-election campaign, Hunt appreciated McCarthy. Yet if Hunt went for Barry Goldwater in 1964, so did Robert J. Kleberg, Jr.

From Lyndon Johnson, whom Hunt had supported for President in 1960, Hunt expected support for the continuation of the oil depletion allowance, a view he shared with every oil-rich Texan. In quest of the Democratic Party nomination for the Presidency in 1960, Lyndon Johnson requested that Hunt publish a pamphlet attacking his opponent, John F. Kennedy, as a Catholic who would be subservient to the Pope.

Kennedy would destroy religious freedom if he was elected, Johnson suggested. Hunt acquiesced. Later, in response to a Senate investigation, Hunt apologized for breaking federal election laws: "I was simply trying to help Lyndon," he pleaded. H.L. Hunt and Lyndon Johnson understood each other. "Future historians will praise us," Hunt wrote to Johnson in an undated letter residing in the H.L. Hunt file at the LBJ library in Austin, "for protecting the divine rights of the American corporations."

What set H.L. Hunt apart from all these Texans was his increasingly visceral dislike of both Dulles brothers. Hunt not only wanted nothing to do with CIA, but he was not shy about making his antipathy to Allen Dulles, in particular, public. Hunt sensed that there was something not straightforward about Allen Dulles.

Over a period of years, Hunt bombarded several presidents with warnings about the disloyalty to the Republic of Allen and Foster Dulles. It was a disloyalty Arthur Goldberg had suggested to President Roosevelt in the late 1930's when he called Allen Dulles a "traitor" for his dealings with high Nazi figures and corporations.

Hunt wrote to President Eisenhower, suggesting that he get rid of both Allen and Foster Dulles. Allen, Hunt complained, was "soft on Communism." Dulles was not, of course, a Communist, but a person who believed in nothing but his own Agency. Yet Hunt perceived that Dulles' loyalty was not to the United States, but to something else. That was the shadow government over which he presided. Opposing "Communism" was merely the pretext in those years for CIA's enhancing its own power and making policy as it saw fit, increasingly in the service of its defense contractor allies. Confused, yet shrewder than most, Hunt smelled a rat.

"Mr. Dulles knew and should have informed the Board [the Loyalty and Security Board]," Hunt wrote, "that Hiss had always been a suspect. Mr. Dulles is reported to have refused to consider information tendered him that Alger Hiss was a Communist or a sympathizer," Hunt wrote. It was the same charge others made when Dulles openly ignored warnings that the landing at the Bay of Pigs was certain to fail. Hunt's confusion was matched by Cuban rancher Gustavo de los Reyes, who was astonished when Dulles admitted to him that he had no intention of opposing Fidel Castro.

In his campaign against Allen Dulles, Hunt appealed to Lyndon Johnson. "Ike knows nothing," Hunt complained to Senator Johnson, "and he has been dominated by Dulles." Later, on April 28, 1961, Hunt wrote to the Vice-President, attacking the Dulles brothers who "did not work very well." Less than two weeks later, on May 8th, Hunt sent a letter to President Kennedy, warning that he was "unfortunate to have inherited from four previous administrations many of doubtful loyalty."

When John F. Kennedy declared war on the Central Intelligence Agency and began to transfer some of its powers over to a Defense Intelligence Agency, Hunt was elated. "It seems nothing which the Dulles' ever did turned out good," Hunt wrote to President Kennedy on August 22, 1961. In a February 1965 letter to President Johnson, Hunt blamed Dulles for the Bay of Pigs defeat, as did many.

II

H.L. Hunt was too rich, too powerful, and too influential for CIA to ignore his opposition. In the late 1950's, CIA placed an agent deep inside Hunt Oil. Knowing of Hunt's long-time admiration for the FBI, the Agency chose a former FBI agent, who was, simultaneously, one of their own. His name was Paul Rothermel and Hunt, naively, hired him as his Chief of Security.

The FBI had long provided CIA people with cover. Their "rivalry" was largely a myth. It was one to which Hunt fell victim. When John F. Kennedy was elected president, H.L. Hunt sent him a list of reputable FBI-trained figures to whom he might turn, reliable intelligence people who had been both with the FBI and "engaged in counterespionage." Paul Rothermel's name appeared on that list. Only the release in 1998 of the CIA/FBI cooperation agreement of 1948 would provide conclusive documentary evidence of the symbiotic relationship between the two agencies. (See pp. 389-403 of the Documents section)

Paul Rothermel was a tall, heavy-set, gimlet-eyed man with square Germanic features. He was born in Burton, Texas, on March 24, 1926, making him a month younger than Hunt's son, Nelson Bunker Hunt. Rothermel earned undergraduate and law degrees from the University of Texas. Without ever practicing law, he joined the FBI and the Special Texas Rangers.

Rothermel was clever, shrewd and calculating. He could seem avuncular, someone in whom you might confide. He did not resemble the icy operative that he was. Rothermel's hair even turned a grandfatherly snow white.

Rothermel's duties at Hunt Oil – he worked for old man Hunt, not his sons – included investigating prospective employees, ensuring corporate security, and providing "political intelligence." He was to keep Hunt informed of what he needed to know. Rothermel had bragged about his contacts with the White House, CIA and the Dallas police. Hunt was impressed.

Disloyal from the start, Rothermel reported everything that happened at Hunt Oil to both the FBI and CIA. He saw no problem with a new employee named John Brown, despite Brown's demonstrable ties to organized crime. The well-being of Hunt's company was never on Rothermel's agenda.

Rothermel's real assignment, to watch over H.L. Hunt for CIA, was not unprecedented in Agency strategy. A "former" CIA employee, Robert Maheu, played the same role for CIA with Howard Hughes that Rothermel did with Hunt. Maheu reported directly to Colonel Sheffield Edwards, then CIA's Director of Security. Maheu, also hired as a "security chief," went on to rob Hughes blind, buying real estate on Hughes' behalf while providing finder's fees to friends, like his lawyer Edward P. Morgan and Mafia operative Johnny Rosselli.

"What Maheu was doing with his time and with the Hughes fortune" was concealed from his employer, exactly as Rothermel's pursuits were unknown to H.L. Hunt. Finally, Hughes had to hire a security company called INTERTEL to rid himself of Maheu. There was one major difference between the Hughes and the Hunt situations. Unlike Rothermel, Maheu worked for a man who had long been more than willing to make his operations available to CIA as cover.

Beginning in 1963, Paul Rothermel became so preoccupied with investigating the Kennedy assassination that you would have thought he had been hired for this purpose alone. Even before the assassination took place, Rothermel spent full-time on the murder of President Kennedy. Eighteen days before the event, on November 4, 1963, Rothermel distributed within Hunt Oil an inter-office memorandum titled "POLITICS" that all but reveals his foreknowledge of the assassination, or, at least, an act of violence about to be perpetrated on the President.

There have been "unconfirmed reports of possible violence during the [presidential] parade," Rothermel writes. "If an incident were to occur the story of who perpetrated it would never come out." Rothermel claimed that he had a report "from a left-wing group" that "an incident would occur...with the knowledge of the President." The "left-wingers would start the incident in hopes

341

of dragging in any of the right side groups nearby." Then the left would "withdraw."

That a "leftist" would be involved in the murder of President Kennedy in Rothermel's planted scenario predicts Lee Harvey Oswald's being labeled a "Marxist," something he was not. That Rothermel should fabricate such a document suggests that weeks before the assassination he had already set in motion what would be his strategy for the coming decade: blaming one or another of the Hunts for planning and financing the murder of the president.

Later Rothermel would change his story. He would claim that the sources for the information contained in his November 4th memo were the FBI and groups created by right-wing General Edwin Walker at North Texas State University at Denton. Walker was the General fired by John F. Kennedy and at whom, in April 1963, Oswald took what George de Mohrenschildt, Oswald's CIA asset Texas handler, called a "pot shot." In his November 4th memo, Rothermel added that the "above information comes from a reliable informant, and while it is in the hands of law enforcement agencies, there is no publicity about it."

With the hindsight of history, it's obvious that Rothermel's motive was to strike fear into H.L. Hunt that his right-wing opinions would render him a suspect should any harm come to President Kennedy during his visit to Dallas. Rothermel advised Hunt to write some letters-to-the-editor, an activity in which Hunt indulged frequently, "pre-exposing this."

Years later, Rothermel told the FBI that his motive had been to dissuade Hunt from becoming involved in anti-Kennedy activities during the presidential visit to Dallas. Yet Hunt had no plans for public efforts against

President Kennedy, nor had he ever engaged in "anti-Kennedy activities." Hunt had written a letter dated July 11, 1963 to various political figures in the Democratic Party, including Senator Harry Byrd of Virginia. The letter strategizes about how John F. Kennedy might be defeated in the 1964 general election.

Hunt indulges in no extremist talk. He urges that a coalition be formed uniting "constructive Democratic leaders" with the Republican party machinery in each Southern state. Hunt signs his letter, "Constructively, H.L. Hunt." Hunt's approach was obviously electoral; there is not a hint or a suggestion of violence, murder or assassination, as the FBI saw at once when author Herbert Parmet naively brought the letter to the Bureau's attention in 1977. (A member of the Armed Services' CIA subcommittee, Senator Harry Flood Byrd, unlike Hunt, favored a powerful CIA, one immune to oversight. When in a telephone call Dulles read Byrd an editorial description of CIA as a "free-wheeling outfit," Byrd replied, "If you're not a free-wheeling outfit, why aren't you?")

When, in 1975 the FBI asked Rothermel directly where he obtained the information in his inflammatory November 4th memo, Rothermel blithely changed his story. Now his source was not radical groups at North Texas State University, let alone the FBI. "Members of the Dallas Police Department's Intelligence Division," he claimed, had provided him with his prescient prediction of violence befalling President Kennedy.

Rothermel was joined in his effort to cast blame on the Hunts for the assassination by other CIA assets. On November 27, 1963, a Brown & Root engineer named John Richard Salisbury told the Houston Secret Service that H.L. Hunt had said that "if Kennedy comes to Texas, he will get shot or killed." Salisbury named as his source a Hunt employee named Robert L. Norris, who had "perhaps gone to New Orleans to engage Oswald at the behest of H.L. Hunt or possibly one of Hunt's close associates." This lead soon evaporated. It was an opening salvo.

Pretending to safeguard the interests of Hunt, and using his self-imposed assignment to justify his spending an inordinate amount of his time on the Kennedy assassination, Rothermel became an important component in CIA's attempt to lay responsibility for the murder of the President at H.L. Hunt's door. Rothermel soon seized on the fact that Nelson Bunker Hunt had contributed two or three hundred dollars of the $1400 required for the ominous black-bordered "Welcome Mr. President...to Dallas" advertisement that appeared in the *Dallas Morning News* on November 22nd.

In addition to threatening President Kennedy, the advertisement also attacked CIA: "Why has the Foreign Policy of the United States degenerated to the point that the C.I.A. is arranging coups and having staunch Anti-Communist Allies of the U.S. bloodily exterminated?" To many, observing as early as 1963 how CIA departed from the stated foreign policy of the country – and its values – , the Agency seemed to be an anomaly.

Investigating the assassination for the President's Commission, the FBI requested an interview with Nelson Bunker Hunt on the strength of his financial contribution to the advertisement. Stirring the pot, Rothermel took the view that the Warren Commission was likely to charge Bunker with complicity in the murder. Rothermel advised Bunker to "consider not talking with them." No fool, having nothing to hide, Bunker ignored him.

Undeterred, Rothermel advised Bunker to meet with only one FBI agent, since if the customary two interviewed him, one could lie and then the other would back him up. Bunker ignored this advice as well. He spoke to two agents, and brought his own lawyer along.

On the far side of liberal, Bunker's politics were grist for Rothermel's mill. Bunker was also gullible, as evidenced by a scam to which he fell victim in 1964. It was perpetrated by a Princeton, New Jersey con artist who called himself "Dean Richard Pitzel." Creating a bogus organization called the "Institute of Government," ostensibly based at Princeton University, and hoping Bunker would confuse it with the Institute for Advanced Study, Pitzel lured Bunker into contributing $5,000 to sponsor a book called "White Man's Politics."

"Pitzel" listed the "Institute's" address at "199 Nashua Street," a play on Princeton's "Nassau Street," the main drag. Pitzel escaped with the cash. When Bunker investigated, he learned that no one at Princeton University had ever heard of "Richard Pitzel." A dentist did business at 199 Nassau Street.

III

On the afternoon of the Kennedy assassination, on the pretext that H.L. Hunt's Life Line radio program had been anti-Kennedy, and with Rothermel's encouragement, the FBI shuttled Hunt out of Dallas. They insisted that he hide out at the Mayflower Hotel in Washington, D.C., to the old man's intense displeasure. By Christmas, Hunt was back in Dallas.

Having struck out for the moment in implicating Bunker, Rothermel then turned to involving Hunt's third son, Lamar, as a possible assassination sponsor. Born in 1932, Lamar was the least political of the Hunt sons. A small man, soft-spoken and dignified, Lamar was compared by *Business Week* to the popular television character, "Mr. Peepers," because he too wore heavy-framed eyeglasses. The article described Lamar as a man "with a yen to be a jock" because he loved sports. Lamar Hunt had already invested in a batting cage business; a miniature golf course; and three Major League soccer teams. Lamar was also a ten percent investor in the NBA's Chicago Bulls.

No matter that he had been only a fourth string receiver at Southern Methodist University, Lamar's real passion was football. In 1960, he had sought an NFL franchise for Dallas. Lamar Hunt went on to found the American Football League; his "Texans" in 1963 became the Kansas City Chiefs. It was Lamar Hunt who christened the NFL championship game based on his children's "super ball."

Rich man's son though he may have been, Lamar Hunt favored old clothes and flew coach. When a reporter asked his father what he thought about Lamar's losing a million dollars in each of the first three years he owned his football franchise, H.L. Hunt had to chuckle.

"That's too bad," H.L. Hunt said, famously. "At that rate, Lamar will be broke in two hundred years." To another reporter, Hunt raised the figure to "two hundred and fifty years."

It was during the tumultuous football year 1963 that Lamar Hunt became ensnared in the net of Kennedy assassination politics. Rothermel discovered that Jack Ruby, Lee Harvey Oswald's assassin, and a strip club proprietor, had Lamar Hunt's telephone number in his address book. Lamar Hunt knew Jack Ruby!

As it happened, on the day before the assassination, Ruby drove a girl named Connie Trammel to Lamar's office at the Mercantile National Bank. Connie had a job interview to work at a club for teenagers that was among Lamar's minor enterprises. He had never met Lamar Hunt, Ruby told Connie Trammel, although he would like to do so. At that, Ruby asked her for Lamar's telephone number. So Connie Trammel had explained to the FBI: she gave Ruby Lamar's telephone number and he recorded it in his address book. Lamar did not hire Connie Trammel and her acquaintance with Lamar Hunt ended there.

On December 17, 1963, Lamar Hunt told the FBI that he had "never been acquainted with Jack Ruby." He couldn't think "of any reason why his name would appear in Jack Ruby's personal property." People liked Lamar Hunt, who would always return your phone call. It wasn't easy for Paul Rothermel to discredit him, but he tried.

In the ensuing years, Rothermel cultivated researchers into the Kennedy assassination assiduously. Among them was Harold Weisberg, an indefatigable pursuer of FBI and CIA records through freedom of information suits handled by his lawyer, James Lesar. Well-known to federal judges in the Washington, D.C. courts, Weisberg became a source for Paul Rothermel over the period of a decade. At one point, Rothermel paid Weisberg's airfare from New Orleans to Dallas, and for Weisberg's hotel accommodations.

As late as January 1970, Rothermel was requesting that Weisberg help him prove that Lamar Hunt knew Jack Ruby. Ruby must have arranged for Connie Trammel to see Lamar Hunt, Rothermel insisted. Yet it was not so.

Over these years, Rothermel persisted in attempting to frighten old man Hunt with the consequences of his "complicity" in the Kennedy assassination. In a memorandum to Hunt dated soon after the assassination, February 6, 1964, Rothermel wrote that "Lyndon B. Johnson is mortally afraid of being assassinated and does not trust the Secret Service to protect him. He has ordered the FBI to be present everywhere he goes with no less than two men."

If the President was vulnerable, so surely was H.L. Hunt, who had been his supporter. Rothermel added the tidbit that "Johnson has confidentially placed a direct telephone line from his office to J. Edgar Hoover's desk."

Time passed and no credible evidence linking any of the Hunts to the Kennedy assassination emerged. Meanwhile, in his efforts to ingratiate himself with researchers who might help him to implicate the Hunts, Rothermel revealed himself to possess information about the Kennedy assassination available neither to the general public nor to the Warren Commission.

After the Bay of Pigs, Rothermel claimed, CIA and the State Department together sponsored a second invasion of Cuba. It would be led by the Manolo Ray group. Ruby and Oswald were acquainted, Rothermel said, a fact the Warren Commission vehemently denied, but which was true. Often Rothermel referred to Ruby by his original name, "Rubenstein," emphasizing his Jewishness. As Hunt's right hand man, Rothermel expressed anti-Semitic views that fueled the charge that Hunt too was anti-Semitic.

In 1967, Rothermel knew in advance that *Life* magazine was preparing a story linking Orleans Parish district attorney Jim Garrison to the mob. *Life* would charge that Garrison had accepted a $5,000 gambling credit in Las Vegas, a charge that did not appear in the final printed version of the article. Rothermel also knew, somehow, that Bobby Kennedy opposed Garrison's investigation, which was true.

IV

CIA's animus toward Bunker Hunt dated from the late 1950's when Bunker pursued an oil venture in Libya. Just as in the 1950's Robert J. Kleberg, Jr. went global, investing in satellite King Ranches, so Bunker too looked abroad to expand his business. In 1957, he secured a concession in the Sarir Field, the richest oil field in Africa and the tenth largest in the world. Things were quiet in Libya until November 1961 when low sulphur oil was discovered at the Sarir Field.

A CIA document, dated December 1965, reveals a CIA plan that Bunker be persuaded to use his Middle East oil operation for CIA cover. CIA claims it has "had good cooperation on our routine requests but have no way of judging possible reaction to operational requests. Our estimate is that we see no reason we should not make a cautious approach." In Libya, CIA reasoned, the perfect position for CIA's embedded asset would be "director of oil operations" in Bunker's business.

Three times in 1966, as far as the available record reveals, CIA requested of Nelson Bunker Hunt that they be permitted to place agents in his Libyan operations. Three times Bunker declined. "My concession agreement with the Libyans prohibits me from representing a foreign government," Bunker explained. Whether or not his father's experience with CIA's overthrow of Mossadegh had any influence on his decision, he did not volunteer.

Bunker was "so rich he didn't need them," says one of Bunker's lawyers, Philip Hirschkop, a long-time civil libertarian and ACLU board member. Like his father, Bunker continued in his distrust of CIA. By the mid and late-sixties, Bunker had leased millions of acres, not only in Africa, but in Australia and Asia. It would have been useful to CIA to place operatives in Hunt's foreign enterprises. Bunker continued to turn them down.

CIA, of course, had other corporate options to provide cover for its operatives. In Libya, between 1963 and 1970, CIA's long-time ally, the Bechtel Corporation, was happy to oblige. Through C. Stribling Snodgrass, a Bechtel employee whose particular assignment was to liaise with CIA, Bechtel provided cover employment to two CIA employees in its Libyan employee relations department. Unlike Bunker, Steve Bechtel awarded CIA the right to embed itself in his Libyan operations.

CIA infiltrated Bunker's Libyan business anyway. Then CIA presented Bunker with the consequences of his having denied them his cooperation. When Qaddafi began confiscations of foreign properties in the summer of 1973, other companies were compensated for their losses, but not Bunker. By his own assessment, Nelson Bunker Hunt lost fifty billion dollars.

Bunker did not remain silent. He told Martin Waldron at the *New York Times* that his refusal to help CIA in Libya led to Qaddafi's confiscating his oil field. Scrutinizing the dynamic between CIA and the Hunts, Waldron noted the friendship between Rothermel and CIA informant *Dallas Morning News* reporter Hugh Aynesworth.

Waldron concluded that "Rothermel is CIA." CIA releases at the National Archives reveal that Rothermel sent every document he received, including personal letters from the researchers whom he cultivated, right to CIA.

V

The 1966-1969 Garrison investigation into the Kennedy assassination provided Rothermel with fresh opportunities to frighten the Hunts. "All members of the Hunt family," Rothermel announced, should "be alert to the possibility that Garrison may attempt to embarrass or even arrest them if they are in his jurisdiction."

Garrison will arrest and subpoena you, Rothermel warned H.L. Hunt. "I have information that Garrison is referring to either you or Bunker as the wealthy oil man in his probe." At one point, Rothermel, preposterously, included himself among Garrison's targets, claiming that Garrison was "trying to implicate Mr. Hunt and myself in the Kennedy assassination." H.L. Hunt immediately canceled a trip to New Orleans he had planned to visit his friend Senator Russell Long.

Garrison had indeed wondered whether H.L. Hunt had been involved in the assassination. He assigned to Hunt the code name "Harry Blue." In a six-page memo of November 3, 1967, titled "RE: H.L. Hunt," Garrison compiled a series of published sources outlining Hunt's right-wing political views. But at no point, then or later, did Garrison suggest that H.L. Hunt or any of his sons had anything to do with the assassination.

Having visited New Orleans, Harold Weisberg delivered to Rothermel a "chart of suspects" that had circulated within the Garrison investigation. Lines radiated from H.L. Hunt's name down to "Ruby" and 'Oswald." The cryptic words, "screen[ed] by Rothermel" appear. Rothermel immediately sent copies of the chart to J. Gordon Shanklin, the Special Agent in Charge of the FBI's Dallas field office, and to Congressman Earle Cabell. The Houston CIA field office also received a copy.

This chart had been drawn up by a once and future CIA employee named William C. Wood. Wood had been a "contract instructor" with CIA until he was fired for alcoholism. In February 1967, Wood reapplied for employment with the Agency. CIA seemed to have rejected him based on a March 3rd FBI report that Wood had been drinking again. Then Wood appeared at Jim Garrison's door. Garrison had an assistant telephone CIA headquarters to inquire whether the Agency had ever heard of Wood. Contrary to Agency protocols, they admitted that they had. Wood had been a CIA recruiter in New Orleans in 1963.

When Garrison took on Wood, renaming him "Bill Boxley," he had no idea that Wood was acquainted with Paul Rothermel, who had already been Wood's companion at lunch at the Dallas Petroleum Club. It wasn't long before Wood, contrary to fact, announced that H.L. Hunt was "Garrison's chief suspect." This he never was. Wood's "evidence" included that Hunt had once transposed the name of Kennedy's accused assassin as "Harvey Lee Oswald," as de Mohrenschildt would.

Rothermel now had an ally embedded in Garrison's office. "We have extended our cooperation to Garrison in his probe, hoping to help guide his investigation," Rothermel wrote to CIA's Houston field office at the turn of the New Year 1968. In a communication of January 26, 1968, Rothermel characterized Jim Garrison as "a most vindictive left-winger...he is bisexual and a clever blackmailer." It seems a curious stance for a man whose job was to provide security for Hunt Oil.

Rothermel was soon weaving a new web of falsehoods centered around Jim Garrison. "Garrison is convinced that the assassination was carried out by General

Edwin Walker with the financial support and backing of Herman and George Brown of Houston and H.L. Hunt of Dallas," he wrote. Garrison is supported, Rothermel added, "by the Stern family of New Orleans," who had also backed "an attack on H.L. Hunt."

In fact, the Sterns, despising Garrison, backed his suspect Clay Shaw. It was true that in 1965 the Sterns were enthusiastic about Garrison's running for Mayor of New Orleans, but he had never so campaigned. Yet another Rothermel-perpetuated falsehood, dated April 3, 1968, was that there was growing pressure in New Orleans for a "lunacy hearing" at which the subject would be Garrison. Then Rothermel added that "the C.I.A. seems concerned enough to be behind the movement." Rothermel could only have known such a thing from the inside.

The next day, April 4th, Wood appeared at Rothermel's door. He had come on orders from Jim Garrison, "hat in hand to explain that Garrison was in no way concerned with Mr. H.L. Hunt."

Undeterred by this setback to his plan to implicate his boss in the Kennedy assassination, Rothermel claimed that he was not certain whether Oswald "was or was not a CIA agent or an FBI informant." He quoted a soldier-of-fortune of dubious veracity named Gerald Patrick Hemming as reporting that there had been an "intelligence meeting" about the assassination attended by H.L. Hunt.

One day a package wrapped in brown paper was delivered to Garrison's office in New Orleans. Inside were three black binders of a manuscript entitled "The Plot," a title Garrison swiftly changed to "Farewell America." It described the conspiracy to assassinate President Kennedy as having been spearheaded by Texas oil men led by H.L. Hunt. This "book" appears to have been created for the sole purpose of deflecting Garrison from blaming CIA for the crime, as he had been doing.

"Contrary to the FBI," the pseudonymous author, "James Hepburn," writes, "the upper spheres of the CIA were certainly not informed of the preparations for the assassination." Hepburn allows that "rogue operatives might well have played a role in the crime," but not CIA as an institution.

Chapter Ten of *Farewell America* is titled "Oilmen." Yet only one oil man is singled out for culpability – H.L. Hunt. "Oilmen" opens with a quotation from Hunt in which he all but implicates himself: "The myth of the indispensable man must be broken if our country is to survive." The implication is that the President himself was not "indispensable."

Hepburn describes Texas as a "paradise of murder." Kennedy, a "socialist," had "assaulted the tax privileges of the Texas oil men," granting them, by Hepburn's reasoning, sufficient motive for murder. In fact, Kennedy had not, at least not yet, challenged the oil depletion allowance, but, absent source notes, *Farewell America* makes any number of unsupported and false assertions.

H.L. Hunt is characterized as possessing "his own intelligence network," although Rothermel is not mentioned by name. Hunt is termed the "big man in Texas, the richest and the stingiest, the most powerful and the most solitary of the oilmen." Then Hepburn attempts to place the murder of the President squarely at H.L. Hunt's door:

"At 12:23 on November 22, from his office on the 7th floor of the Mercantile Building, Haroldson Lafayette Hunt watched John Kennedy ride toward Dealey Plaza where fate awaited him at 12:30. A few minutes later, escorted by six men in two cars, Hunt left the center of Dallas without even stopping by his house…."

Hunt then rushes to a "secret hideaway" across the Mexican border, rather than to Washington, D.C., where he did go.

In the hope of obtaining the source notes, or "background material" for *Farewell America*, believing naively that such documentation actually existed, Garrison sent a young volunteer to France to meet with "Hepburn." At one point, as a Garrison investigation document reveals, he was taken to a Latin Quarter dive called "Club Kama," where he was introduced to a man introduced to him only as "Philippe."

Philippe had been, the young emissary was told, head of French intelligence in the United States, "a representative of the French *Deuxième Bureau*," which could only mean that "Philippe" either actually was or was impersonating Philippe de Vosjoli. De Vosjoli had resigned from the French services and defected to the United States five years earlier, in October 1963. (See Chapter Four.)

Angry with de Vosjoli for exposing that the KGB had infiltrated both NATO and de Gaulle's cabinet, creating the potential for a damaging scandal that would redound against De Gaulle, the French had assigned him to "organize a clandestine intelligence network in the United States for the specific purpose of collecting information about U.S. military installations and U.S. scientific research, including U.S. deployment of ICBM's." So the real life de Vosjoli writes in his memoir, *Lamia*.

Disgusted with de Gaulle for caring more about his reputation than ridding the French services of KGB infiltrators, de Vosjoli rejected this assignment. He resigned, and renounced his French citizenship. By that time he was closer to CIA's Counter Intelligence component than he was to the French services.

Oddly, in *Farewell America* we find de Vosjoli back in France and in the good graces of the French services, from whom he had fled five years earlier in fear of his life. This fictional "Philippe" asserts that "South Texas" people plotted the assassination. His area of expertise is the oil industry, he claims, lending credibility to "Hepburn's" claim that H.L. Hunt was the mastermind of the Kennedy assassination.

"Philippe" tells the young interlocutor sent by Jim Garrison that he went to Mexico City where at the "Hotel Luna" he met some of the "ambush group," Cuban assassins of President Kennedy, even as the real-life de Vosjoli did travel to Mexico after his October 1963 resignation. Then the fictional "Philippe" retreats behind metaphor. The Mexican hotel had a "Cuban band" playing "dangerous instruments," he says. He offers to meet with Mr. Garrison, "if it was desirable," an offer the actual de Vosjoli, a close friend of CIA's James Angleton, was highly unlikely to have made.

It seems as if a faction of French intelligence, furious with de Vosjoli, was taking the opportunity of the Garrison overture to exact revenge on its former employee. On its last page, the author of *Farewell America*, whose real name apparently was Herve Lamarre, thanks a "Philippe" who was "in France."

When he returned to the United States, Garrison's volunteer told a fellow researcher named Steve Burton that he had met "PHILIPPE (LNU), former head of French Intelligence in the United States." The French believe that "H.L. Hunt was the prime mover of the conspiracy," he had concluded. There had been an executive council of five members planning the crime, among them lawyer Roy Cohn.

"Hunt can't be touched," Lamarre had said, adding that "oil killed Kennedy," and that French intelligence had "infiltrated the oil industry."

VI

Mulling over all this, Harold Weisberg identified "Philippe" correctly as the hero of *Topaz*, de Vosjoli's life story as told by Leon Uris, whom de Vosjoli hired as a ghost writer for the purpose. Then, because there were too many contradictions in the story, Weisberg sought a physical description of the man Garrison's volunteer met in Paris. Weisberg's papers do not reveal that he obtained one.

Later, Weisberg speculated that FBI records on *Farewell America* had been withheld by the government owing to CIA's involvement with de Vosjoli, "the doubled head of French intelligence in the U.S. for a period of time that included the Cuban Missile Crisis." Could de Vosjoli himself have been the author of *Farewell America*? Weisberg wondered.

Rothermel promised Weisberg he would "through my sources in Europe…see what we can find about the Lamarocs [sic] and the other people of interest." Pouring fuel onto the smoldering fire of H.L. Hunt's culpability, Rothermel told Weisberg, "Mr. Hunt does know Roy Cohn." Then, he added, "As far as I can determine the last time he saw Cohn was about the time of the death of Joe McCarthy." This was on May 2, 1957, more than a decade earlier.

"I think it [*Farewell America*] is CIA," Weisberg concluded. "It's intelligence, but not French intelligence." Eight years later, Weisberg wrote Rothermel that *Farewell America* was "a department of disinformation operation." Weisberg still had not figured out that the same disinformation as Lamarre had disseminated in *Farewell America* had been perpetrated for years by Rothermel himself. Rothermel called *Farewell America* "extremely derogatory of Mr. Hunt," and said no more.

Meanwhile, Rothermel was cultivating another researcher into the Kennedy assassination named Gary Schoener. "I am in contact with a man formerly with the CIA, and I have suspected this association is still in effect," Rothermel wrote Schoener. Schoener in turn told Rothermel about a source of his own, a Minneapolis lawyer named David Kroman, who had run unsuccessfully for Attorney General of Minnesota.

Kroman had served time at the federal psychiatric prison in Springfield, Illinois alongside CIA renegade Richard Case Nagell, who purported to have been assigned to put Lee Harvey Oswald under surveillance in New Orleans. Kroman had an assassination-related story of his own. He claimed to have met with H.L. Hunt in 1964 and 1965, when Hunt "confided a number of important things to me." Kroman had used a phony name to get in to see Hunt.

"Nobody but nobody gets to interview Hunt!" Kroman had exulted. Kroman said he had uncovered a plan "to hit Kennedy in Miami...it was a right-wing extremist group including the Cuban-Batista Party and financed by H.L. Hunt and other individuals." It was Kroman's persistent refrain: "Mr. Hunt was a major figure behind the assassination." Kroman claimed to possess "documents which would prove the connection of H.L. Hunt to the Dallas plot." No such documents ever surfaced.

Skeptical, Schoener wondered whether Kroman was a "government agent." Unaware that in talking to Rothermel he was talking to a government agent who was himself attempting to frame H.L. Hunt, Schoener promised to send Rothermel his "full file" on Kroman.

Throughout the decade of the 1960's, Rothermel played a double game. He seemed to oppose speculation that H.L. Hunt was behind the Kennedy assassination. Simultaneously, he planted seeds of doubt on that question. Among the arguments that Rothermel occasionally set forth as evidence that H.L. Hunt was *not* behind the Kennedy assassination was that he was very tight with his money. This was a man who brought his lunch to work, and re-used the same brown paper lunch bag every day, Rothermel said.

PART TWO: Paul Rothermel, Draped In Immunity

Have you ever worked for or in any way, directly or indirectly, served the CIA?

      – Harold Weisberg to Paul Rothermel, July 4, 1975

Suspecting that Bill Wood was disloyal, that he was lying, and that he was still working for CIA in some capacity, Jim Garrison fired him in December 1968. Wood immediately telephoned CIA, once more to offer the Agency his services. A Dr. Stephen Aldrich came on the line. He had information he needed to communicate to the Agency, Wood said.

The next day, without waiting for a return call, Wood telephoned CIA yet again. Wary, CIA requested of the FBI that they visit Wood to "request elucidation" in one more example of CIA/FBI collaboration. CIA instructed the FBI to tell Wood that CIA was "prepared to listen" to what he had to say. CIA then disseminated a memorandum. Should Wood appear at a Domestic Contact office, whatever he said "should be noted without comment and reported."

CIA was dubious of their former contact's motives. CIA had fired Wood, and in March 1967 had refused to take him back. His re-surfacing might "result from personal animosity toward the Agency." Or it might reflect an "attempted provocation by Garrison or from both."

CIA had no difficulty keeping Wood under surveillance because, upon leaving New Orleans, he promptly headed straight for Rothermel's door. Hysterical, Wood claimed that "Garrison was determined to either assassinate him or completely ruin him by disclosures out of his office." The story conveyed by Rothermel was that Wood feared that Garrison, or his officers, would shoot him. Rothermel now oozed sympathy for Wood. Wood was, in Rothermel's words, "a former CIA man."

Rothermel then wrote two memoranda on the subject of Wood and Garrison. For the record, he wrote that Wood "in no wise meant to infer that either H.L. Hunt or myself had anything to do with the assassination."

Wood claimed that he was broke. He begged Rothermel for a job, pleading that he "was not antagonistic toward Mr. Hunt." He repeated that "Garrison had never indicated hostility toward Mr. Hunt," which was, of course, not what Rothermel wanted to hear. Rothermel didn't give Wood a job, but he did recommend him to "two people who might need some private detective work."

Rothermel reported on Wood's visit to J. Walton Moore at the Dallas CIA field office. He told Moore that Jim Garrison was so interested in N. B. [Nelson Bunker] Hunt because "one of N. B. Hunt's good friends had made a statement that Hoover was behind the assassination." In fact, Garrison was interested neither in Hoover nor Nelson Bunker Hunt as suspects in the Kennedy assassination.

In May 1969, Washington D. C. lawyer Bernard Fensterwald, who had served as General Counsel for Missouri Senator Edward V. Long's subcommittee on "Administrative Practices and Procedures," focusing on wiretapping and electronic eavesdropping, visited Paul Rothermel. "It may be possible," Rothermel wrote H.L. Hunt, "that Fensterwald is going to write a new book, pointing the finger at the Hunts." Soon Fensterwald's visit was the subject of a Rothermel-authored CIA contact report. Rothermel turned the materials Fensterwald had left with him over to the Dallas police, who in turn shared their files on Harold Weisberg and Fensterwald with Rothermel. These files Rothermel found "highly entertaining and amusing."

Fensterwald had reintroduced the name "Jim Braden," aka "Eugene Hale Brading," about whom Gary Schoener had also talked. Fensterwald confided that Braden had met with his California parole officer a few days before the Kennedy assassination. At that meeting, he mentioned that he was on his way to Dallas...to meet with Lamar Hunt.

On November 22, 1963, famously, Braden had been taken briefly into custody by the Dallas police, who picked him up in the Dal-Tex building at Dealey Plaza. If you wanted to blame the Hunts for the Kennedy assassination, what could be more useful than a connection with Braden!

Like Weisberg, Fensterwald believed he had located in Rothermel an exceptional source on the Kennedy assassination. "I am still hopeful that at some juncture you will permit me to go through the first four volumes of your files," Fensterwald later wrote Rothermel.

Weisberg continued to share his theories with Rothermel. "I am no less convinced that there has been and may still be an Agency operation afoot, and I am without doubt that there is Agency involvement," Weisberg wrote

Rothermel. Rothermel then forwarded this Weisberg letter to CIA, the FBI, and the Dallas police.

II

The two men closest to H.L. Hunt in his operation were Rothermel and Hunt's chief assistant, John Curington. Like Rothermel, Curington was a lawyer. Each was paid less than thirty thousand dollars a year by the notorious skinflint. Among Curington's duties was managing the food division of Hunt Oil (HLH Products), from which Hunt sold products in keeping with his crackpot ideas about nutrition.

A former roustabout, Curington affected the persona of a Westerner: cowboy boots and a black Stetson. He was a plain, balding man who hid behind dark-rimmed coke bottle eyeglasses. Hunt trusted him almost as much as he did Rothermel.

In 1969, Hunt Oil was denied a loan by the First National Bank of Dallas on the ground that the company lacked liquidity, no matter that magazines were claiming that H.L. Hunt was the richest man in the world. In 1968, the food division had lost $7.9 million. It emerged that millions of dollars had been embezzled from the food component of Hunt Oil.

In 1969 as well, Paul Rothermel advised the old man to change his will in favor of his "second family," the children of Ruth Ray Hunt, whom he had married in 1957, two years after the death of his wife Lyda. Ruth had been his mistress for years. Rothermel suggested that Hunt make Ray Hunt, Ruth's son, his executor. Hunt agreed. (Ray Hunt would later serve on the board of Halliburton, and on George W. Bush's Foreign Intelligence Advisory Board; Bush would even attempt to offer him a Kurdish oil concession).

Hunt's nephew, Tom Hunt, investigated the embezzlement only to uncover that the perpetrators were Rothermel, Curington and John Brown, that employee with demonstrable ties to organized crime whom Rothermel had permitted to continue working for H.L. Hunt. Remaining on the job, Rothermel suddenly became H.L. Hunt's defender to the press: Hunt was not "anti-Semitic and very much wants to clear the record where it is inaccurate," Rothermel said. Hunt did not support the John Birch Society, Rothermel added.

Tom Hunt uncovered kickbacks and "side deals" through shadowy brokerage and trading companies. Among the specious entities through which Rothermel, Curington and Brown laundered the money they were stealing from Hunt was Empire Trading, a CIA proprietary run by Henry Klepak and Sidney Schine with offices close to Hunt Oil in the Mercantile Building. We have already met Klepak and Schine as they smuggled airplanes and war materiel into François Duvalier's Haiti.

Other organizations through which the embezzlers filtered the money they stole from Hunt were called "Tri-Point Brokerage" and "Marion Salvage." Rothermel, whose middle name was "Marion," awarded Marion Salvage considerable Hunt business, while skimming off $5 million for himself.

It wasn't easy for Nelson Bunker Hunt, his younger brother W. Herbert Hunt, and their cousin Tom Hunt to pry the octogenarian Hunt away from his security advisor. "I owe my life to Paul Rothermel," the increasingly dotty old man said when he was informed of the embezzling. "There is no way he could be involved!"

Confronted, Rothermel quickly defended his having allowed John Brown to continue working for Hunt. Brown was only a paid FBI informant, Rothermel claimed. He was not "mobbed up."

One day Tom Hunt discovered a wire connecting his office phone to Rothermel's. Even this did not persuade the old man, stubbornly loyal to his betrayers. Bunker and Herbert now hired the Burns Agency to do a private investigation of Rothermel and his confederates.

On November 14, 1969, Paul Rothermel, now forty-three years old, and John Curington resigned from Hunt Oil. It was a Friday. On Saturday morning, before the Hunts could change the office locks, Rothermel and Curington removed what were termed "mountains" of food division files from the offices of Hunt Oil. John Brown resigned a few days later.

After Rothermel's departure, there was a marked decline in the number of threats on the life of H.L. Hunt.

In the absence of the records, Bunker and Herbert decided that the only way to bring Rothermel to justice was to tap his telephone. It was only earlier in 1969 that wiretapping had been made a federal offense. The events that followed, which included the arrest of the wiretappers, and the charging of Bunker and Herbert, are well-chronicled in *Texas Rich* by Harry Hurt III.

Long-time intelligence operative Rothermel was not about to admit to any wrong-doing. With higher authority behind him, he would not go quietly. Seizing the offensive, Rothermel claimed that he had begun "to fear for his life," a strategy echoing William Wood's outlandish charge that the District Attorney of Orleans Parish was about to shoot him. Rothermel claimed that Hunt's sons were framing him out of anger because he had encouraged their father to change his will to benefit his "second family." In fact, by now Bunker and Herbert were richer than the old man.

Rothermel's assassination researcher friends bought his lies. Rothermel had to leave Hunt's employ, Harold Weisberg concluded, because of a "humanitarian thing the monsters could not abide, getting the father to make an arrangement for his bastards...they got my friend." On the Hunt beat for the *New York Times*, Martin Waldron had to enlighten Weisberg: Bunker Hunt had told Waldron that the way the will was newly executed actually cost the second family money.

Rothermel rallied the mainstream press to his cause. He told Texas mogul Jesse Jones' *Houston Chronicle* that Hunt had sanctioned "all our side deals," which was not the truth. When the case came to court, Rothermel stood up and insisted that Hunt "was so fond of him that he wrote a letter approving any transaction that Mr. Rothermel might make." Rothermel held up a sheet of paper.

Philip Hirschkop, representing Bunker and Herbert, then demonstrated that the letter had been typed on a machine that wasn't manufactured until two years after old man Hunt's letter was dated.

Rothermel refused to reply to Hirschkop's question as to "what role I might have played for the U.S. government." The locution, "might have played," is a virtual admission that Rothermel was working for a government agency in some capacity while he was employed by H.L. Hunt. Later, asked why he had resigned from Hunt Oil, Rothermel said, "I couldn't work for a man playing God."

Rothermel's wife then sued Herbert Hunt for $1.5 million for invading her privacy with the wiretaps. A deal was negotiated in which Joyce Rothermel would drop her suit and the perpetrators Rothermel, Curington and

Brown would pay back $100,000 to the Hunts. Rothermel's share was a scant $25,000. In exchange, the Hunts would proffer no criminal charges against the embezzlers. In May 1971, as part of the deal, Rothermel agreed not to write a book about the Hunts, which he had been threatening to do.

The wiretapping case dragged on for years. Having paid off some witnesses, the Hunts were then charged with obstruction of justice. President Richard Nixon, behind the scenes, had granted the Hunts "immunity in exchange for certain (unspecified) favors." The Watergate break-in forced Nixon to renege on this agreement. Bunker concluded that Watergate had to have been a CIA operation. Most of the Watergate burglars bore CIA histories and affiliations, from master "plumber" E. Howard Hunt, James McCord, Frank Sturgis, and Rolando Martinez to Bernard Barker.

Although in the reporting of the Hunt-Rothermel story several Texas newspapers chose not to mention Paul Rothermel's name, the *Dallas Morning News* did note that William Herbert Hunt and Nelson Bunker Hunt attributed "the new federal charges against them" to "a CIA effort to discredit the Hunt Oil empire"; they had "refused on three different occasions to place CIA agents in the Hunt International Petroleum Company."

Paul Rothermel was never indicted for the embezzlement of which he was obviously guilty, or for any other crime. The federal government granted him immunity from prosecution. Its justification was that Rothermel had cooperated with the government by testifying before a federal grand jury. Yet, by the time he did, the Hunt letter sanctioning Rothermel's "side deals" had been exposed as a forgery. Rothermel's grand jury testimony added nothing new to the record.

Fueled by the higher authority protecting him from accountability for his crimes, Rothermel was arrogant. "Certainly I wasn't due to be indicted on anything," Rothermel declared. John Curington and John Brown, convicted of mail fraud, received probated sentences and never spent a day in prison. It was Texas-style justice.

Only in 1971, when Harold Weisberg interviewed H.L. Hunt, did Hunt reveal that he had finally come to his senses about Rothermel. "Rothermel is a crook who was in cahoots with [my] food people," Hunt said. "He stole a little and made possible the theft of millions." Weisberg rushed immediately to tell Rothermel what Hunt had said about him.

Along the way, Rothermel sought revenge on lawyer Hirschkop, who had so humiliated him in court. In January 1973, Rothermel contacted Weisberg with a request. "Can you find out anything about the Hirschkop-Hunt relationship?"

This was going too far. "Hirschkop is able and fearless," Weisberg said, "known for the vigor of his defenses of unpopular clients."

Rothermel inquired whether the Hunts were allowed to view their CIA file. So he acknowledged that he knew that such a file existed.

"They are," Weisberg said. "Others are not."

Finally Weisberg broke his silence to inquire of Rothermel about his own intelligence connections. It had occurred to him, Weisberg wrote Rothermel, that there existed the "possibility that you have more than one interest in this." Rothermel had tantalized Weisberg with tidbits of information about CIA that seemed to originate from inside. One was that "there was a CIA front on Elm [Street in Dallas]."

"Have you ever worked for or in any way, directly or indirectly, in any way served the CIA?" Weisberg said.

Rothermel denied the allegation. Of course, as we have seen in Haiti, it was Agency protocol, no matter who asked, to deny, absolutely and categorically, any Agency connection.

"I have no trouble taking your word when you say you did not work for the CIA," Weisberg backtracked. "And it would make no real difference to me if you did anyway. I used to work for OSS." Still, Weisberg was not done.

As the result of a freedom of information request to the government, Weisberg had received from CIA copies of his own letters to Rothermel. "What I am interested in," Weisberg pleaded, "is how the CIA got what had to have come from you, directly or indirectly...They do have this relating to me and they have lied and said they do not." Weisberg added that "the information is also accurate, so I don't think it was a third or fourth-hand deal."

Then, having cornered Rothermel with irrefutable evidence of his CIA affiliation, Weisberg retreated. "Nothing wrong with that," he says. "Nor, in your position, would there have been anything wrong with contact with someone in a CIA station or basis. They have a perfectly proper interest in oil, for example."

Two months after Weisberg's exchange with Rothermel about his CIA connections, Martin Waldron asked Weisberg whether he thought Rothermel was a CIA employee. Once more, Weisberg covered for Rothermel. "If Rothermel is CIA, I have no reason to believe in the sense of employee," Weisberg said. "I have no doubt he had contact with those who served CIA but no reason to believe he did personally." Then Weisberg termed Bunker, Herbert, and even the gentle Lamar Hunt, beloved for having created the American Football League, "very dangerous." One, Bunker, had a "private army," another slice of Rothermel disinformation that Weisberg had swallowed whole.

At trial that same year, 1975, Hirschkop argued that "the government may have been trying to cover up the infiltration of the Hunt Oil Company by the Central Intelligence Agency." Fifty motions had been filed over the years; the Hunts' legal fees had mounted to over a million dollars.

Hirschkop was unrelenting as he stated that "CIA had opposed the government's dropping the wiretap charges against Nelson Bunker Hunt because he had three times refused the Agency's request that they be permitted to place an agent in his Libyan operation." Hirschkop termed Rothermel "a government agent, possibly attached to the CIA, who had been assigned to watch the Hunts because of their politics." By now, the Hunts had obtained CIA's file on them. So had Martin Waldron, who requested the CIA documents on behalf of the *New York Times*.

On June 13, 1976, Bunker and Herbert Hunt were acquitted of the wiretapping charges. On the obstruction of justice charge, Herbert was acquitted. Bunker pleaded *nolo contendere* and was fined one thousand dollars. Hirschkop had been unable to establish conclusively in a court of law that Rothermel had been a CIA plant embedded in Hunt Oil.

Bunker had to return to court against his fellow oil producers in the matter of Qaddafi's confiscation of the oil fields in Libya. The companies had agreed to support each other in such a circumstance, only for Bunker to have been left out in the cold. A CIA memo, one of twelve, surfaced during this trial.

It acknowledges that the Agency had indeed requested of Nelson Bunker Hunt that they be permitted to utilize his Middle Eastern oil operation to provide its employees with cover. The other eleven documents, CIA insisted, could not be made public because they might jeopardize "intelligence sources and methods."

Already by the late 1970's, the federal courts were susceptible to CIA influence. U.S. District Court Judge Halbert O. Woodward carried Bunker's CIA file into his chambers. Then he ruled that the charge that the Hunts were being persecuted by CIA was groundless. The CIA file was not relevant to Bunker's problem with Qaddafi, Judge Woodward determined. Bunker settled his antitrust suit against the other oil companies for $32 or $34 million, a figure not remotely close to what was owed to him.

III

All the while, Paul Rothermel kept up his campaign to implicate the Hunts in the Kennedy assassination. Any author or reporter who telephoned could gain an interview with Rothermel on the subject. Weisberg too remained available to Rothermel. "If you decide to go ahead with your literary project and want me to do anything, ask it," Weisberg said.

Seizing on the rumor he had from Gary Schoener and Bernard Fensterwald that Jim Braden had visited Hunt the day before the assassination, Rothermel passed on this disinformation as his "distinct impression" to author Pete Noyes, author of *Legacy of Doubt*. In a September 1970 conversation, Rothermel treated Noyes to an attack on Bunker, who was "taking a million dollars out of Libya every three days." Bunker had a member of El Fatah on his payroll, Rothermel confided. Bunker believes Jews are more dangerous than Communists, he said.

Eugene Hale Brading had visited the Hunts "both prior to and after the assassination," Rothermel told author Dick Russell in 1976. For Russell alone, Rothermel produced an even juicier tidbit. On the afternoon of the Kennedy assassination, Rothermel claimed, Hunt had sent him out to purchase the Zapruder film, that eight millimeter home movie of the crime shot by a dress manufacturer.

"With a substantial amount of money," Rothermel said, "and on orders from the Hunts," he had bought "the first copy *as far as I know.*" (Italics added). Frequently Rothermel would add a qualifier to his lies.

Historian of the Zapruder film David Wrone told the author that there is no chance whatsoever that Rothermel bought or even viewed the Zapruder film on November 22nd. One copy had gone to *Life* magazine, two to the Secret Service, and a fourth to the FBI. The Secret Service provided CIA with its copy that evening. Zapruder took one copy and the original home with him. Rothermel had neither sought nor obtained a copy of the Zapruder film.

Rothermel then quickly claimed to Russell that he was certainly not casting suspicion on the Hunts for the crime. "I think certain people wanted to find out who did it," he added. Rothermel repeated the story on the telephone to Russell in 1992, melodramatically claiming, "I'm frightened for my life!"

When Russell printed Rothermel's story about H.L. Hunt and the Zapruder film in *The Man Who Knew Too Much*, his exhaustive study of CIA operative Richard Case Nagell, Rothermel threatened to sue him. "I said no such thing," Rothermel said. He never sued Dick Russell.

Rothermel also regaled Jim Hougan, author of *Spooks*, with these tales. Bunker was "prepared to kill me when I refused to sign up for his 'death squads,'" Rothermel said, referring to a paramilitary group he alleged was financed by Bunker. "I'm frightened of my old boss," Rothermel said. When Hougan went to Bunker to confirm this story, Bunker urged him to investigate Rothermel's government background.

"I think you'll find he's CIA," Bunker said.

During the deliberations of the House Select Committee on Assassinations in the late 1970s, Paul Rothermel was perceived as a person of interest. He was now practicing family law in Dallas and soon would become a family court judge for Dallas County. He would talk only to the FBI, Rothermel informed the HSCA. He refused to testify before either a Senate or a House Investigating Committee.

His ostensible loyalty to his former FBI employers did not inhibit Rothermel from lying to them. To the FBI, he repeated that the underworld figure Eugene Hale Brading had visited the Hunt offices the day before the assassination. He buttressed the story this time by invoking a witness, a receptionist named Bobby Drake, who had told him, he claimed, about Brading/Braden's visit. Or, he reconsidered, he might have learned about the visit from Drake's log book.

Quickly, Rothermel added that the Hunt Oil log books and long distance telephone logs for September and October 1963 had disappeared. (The incident has an eerie double: the John F. Kennedy Presidential Library and Museum informed the author that the log book for 1963 of Bobby Kennedy's secretary, Angela Novello, had disappeared. All of Novello's records were available, but for this one).

Questioned by the FBI, Brading, now sixty-three years old, denied that he knew Nelson Bunker Hunt. He also denied that he had visited the Hunt offices or signed a visitor's "sign-out book."

"Never, any time in my life," Brading said.

In his 1977 conversations with the FBI, Rothermel depicted Nelson Bunker Hunt as a murderous right-wing fanatic who had set up an organization in Europe called "Der Bund," which had "accepted several assignments from the CIA." Bunker had also financed a paramilitary group, possibly called the "American Volunteer Group," and had advocated "violence and illegal activities to deal with the Communist threat and certain liberal world leaders." Bunker had even asked him, Rothermel claimed, to investigate a German-made gas gun that would leave behind only symptoms of a heart attack. The "Hunt family," Rothermel charged, wanted to use such gas guns to "eliminate the Communists in the United States."

"I won't do anything that's illegal," Rothermel claimed he told Bunker. This had earned him a "severe grudge" and even the possibility that Bunker "might arrange to have me killed someday."

Rothermel did admit that he and John Curington had been paid informants for the IRS. Their handler had been a man named Gene Boren; Rothermel had been paid in five separate checks. So the list of government agencies for whom Rothermel had worked while being employed by H.L. Hunt multiplied. Rothermel requested that the FBI protect his identity in the event that any of the information he had offered be disseminated outside the Bureau.

Lee Harvey Oswald had allegedly written a letter addressed to a "Dear Mr. Hunt," suggesting "that we discuss the matter fully before any steps are taken by me or anyone else." There is no evidence that the "Mr. Hunt" was H.L. Hunt, rather than CIA's E. Howard Hunt, or any other Hunt. But Rothermel mailed copies of Oswald's letter to "several individuals." Kennedy's assassination "was not unwelcomed" by the Hunt family, Rothermel said.

At the end of February 1977, distraught, caught in the web of his own lies, Rothermel telephoned Bureau Special Agent Udo Specht, Jr., and requested that the information he had given the Bureau about his having been an Internal Revenue Service informant be "treated as confidential." He was concerned because the agreement he had signed about not publishing a book about the Hunts also "contained certain other conditions concerning his furnishing information about the Hunt family."

When the FBI interviewed Rothermel's embezzling confederate John Curington, Curington followed the same script. He attempted to implicate the Hunts in the Kennedy assassination. He had heard Eugene Hale Brading being introduced in Nelson Bunker Hunt's office, Curington said. He was also aware of "street talk" that Jack Ruby "had been in Lamar Hunt's office on several occasions prior to November 22, 1963."

Curington then added a new wrinkle to the story. It was H.L. Hunt himself who told him he feared that his son, Nelson Bunker Hunt, "would carry through on some type of kill squad theory." Curington then admitted that the term "killing squads" was his own invention!

At this, the FBI requested that Bunker come in for another interview. Bunker was warned in advance. He would be questioned about the assassination of President Kennedy.

"You mean information you got from your old friend, Paul Rothermel?" Bunker said tartly. Rothermel was "a sorry son-of-a-bitch who stole nine million dollars from the company," Bunker said.

"Did you have any knowledge of a 'kill squad' organized to liquidate or kill certain liberal or world leaders prior to the assassination?" the FBI said.

"This is news to me," Bunker said. And no, he had never met Jack Ruby. Bunker suggested that the FBI would do well to investigate Rothermel, rather than Rothermel's accusations.

Three months later, on June 17, 1977, the scandal sheet *National Enquirer* published an interview with John Curington. H.L. Hunt had died in November 1974, but he remained a target of his former employees. Kennedy was assassinated, Curington claimed, "by men who received money from the late billionaire H.L. Hunt…right-wing Hunt followers knew he hated Kennedy and they thought they were doing what he wanted." Like Rothermel, Curington invoked Oswald's "Dear Mr. Hunt" letter as evidence of Hunt's complicity in the assassination.

Curington added two fresh pieces of gossip. He claimed that he had encountered Marina Oswald leaving the executive suite of H.L. Hunt on a Saturday morning several weeks after the assassination. "I have no doubt in my mind," Curington said. It was Marina. Contacted by the *Enquirer*, Marina Oswald denied emphatically that she had ever visited Hunt's offices.

Curington's other bombshell was that Hunt had ordered him to spy on the police security surrounding Oswald on the day after the assassination. After Oswald's arrest was announced, Hunt had requested that Curington visit Dallas Central police headquarters to determine exactly how tight the security was around Oswald.

As the elevator doors had opened in front of him, Curington had found himself face to face with Oswald. Oswald's police escort had even introduced Curington to Oswald. When he returned to the office, Curington said, H.L. Hunt was "very happy" that the security around Oswald was so lax.

It does not seem to have been accidental, given CIA's presence in the attempt to involve the Hunts in the assassination, that Curington's accusations appeared in the *National Enquirer*. CIA was a dominating presence at the tabloid from the moment of its inception in 1952, according to Paul David Pope in a memoir of his father. Gene Pope, the *Enquirer's* publisher, had worked for CIA since his twenties when he served at the Italy desk, psy ops. He left CIA to serve in Korea. After Pope bought the failing New York *Enquirer* with a loan from mobster Frank Costello and transformed it into the *National Enquirer*, CIA hovered as an editorial presence.

In Pope's most telling example, an enterprising *Enquirer* reporter photographed a document in Henry Kissinger's open briefcase. It revealed that CIA was giving Howard Hughes "money to secretly fund with campaign donations twenty-seven congressmen and senators who sat on subcommittees critical to the agency." This document revealed as well that CIA was funding fifty-three international companies named as CIA fronts, including Hughes' own Summa Corp. There was also a list of reporters for mainstream news organizations who were under the sway of the Agency.

With the negative of this document in hand, Gene Pope, who numbered William Colby among his intimates, called CIA. None of the revelations in the Kissinger document ever appeared in the *Enquirer*. But among the *Enquirer's* regular features was a column called "WORLD-WIDE INTELLIGENCE," which was fueled by CIA material.

Along the way the Agency vetoed some articles and planted others, as seems to be the case with the Curington article blaming H.L. Hunt for the Kennedy assassination. So the *National Enquirer* joined *Reader's Digest,*

Conover Mast Publications, to which CIA assigned the cryptonym LP/OVER, and respectable publishing houses like Farrar, Straus & Giroux, as media entities cooperating with CIA.

In 1976 and 1977, it wasn't only Rothermel and Curington who suggested that H.L. Hunt and/or his sons were complicit in the Kennedy assassination. CIA asset and former "friend" of Lee Harvey Oswald, George de Mohrenschildt, began to tell anyone who would listen that "H.L. Hunt and the bunch were behind the assassination," with Hunt bearing a major role "with the conspiracy." It was as if de Mohrenschildt were reading from the text of *Farewell America*.

He had known Hunt for twenty years, de Mohrenschildt told Dutch journalist Willem Oltmans. Hunt's address, and, separately, that of Hunt Oil, do appear in de Mohrenschildt's address book. He had gone to all of Hunt's parties, de Mohrenschildt claimed. The trajectory of the assassination traveled "upwards to Hunt and downwards to Oswald." So he followed the CIA's script.

De Mohrenschildt also invoked the "Dear Mr. Hunt" letter. "Why would Oswald write to Hunt?" de Mohrenschildt said disingenuously. After de Mohrenschildt died, Rothermel sent a clipping to Weisberg referring to de Mohrenschildt's "alleged" suicide.

As if he were attempting to prove that he could not have embezzled the nine million dollars that Bunker calculated that he had pilfered, in 1977 Rothermel wrote to Weisberg that he was broke. "I am making the overhead at the office and am paid little for my time," he complained.

In 1993, Rothermel wrote an angry letter to three people involved in investigations of the Kennedy assassination: Warren Commission lawyer and now Senator Arlen Specter; Representative Louis Stokes, who had served on the House Select Committee on Assassinations; and HSCA chief counsel, G. Robert Blakey. He had sent records to the HSCA on the understanding that he would be called as a witness, Rothermel wrote. Yet he had not been called.

Rothermel accused Bernard Fensterwald of keeping "for his private use all or a portion of my records." Since Fensterwald had died on April 22, 1991, Rothermel demanded his "personal property" from the Fensterwald estate. "Either Fensterwald or his estate had sold my documents," Rothermel said.

He was "receiving numerous calls and threats," Rothermel claimed yet again. These, he said, amounted to "a great personal tragedy for me." Used, and apparently cast off by CIA, Rothermel seems to have ended up bitter, isolated and confused.

No evidence linking H.L. Hunt or any of his sons to the Kennedy assassination ever emerged. H.L. Hunt seemed to be telling the truth when he told an interviewer in August 1966 that he had never had anything against John F. Kennedy. Before the 1960's, Hunt pointed out, the Kennedys had been "in the oil business." All along they had more in common than appearances suggested.

Paul Rothermel fell off the roof of his house and died on October 10, 2002. Like Allen Dulles, Richard Helms, and other CIA employees higher on the chain of command, Rothermel died with his secrets.

NOTES

335: Addendum H.L. HUNT & SONS & CIA
335: PART ONE – Mr. Rothermel, I Presume?

335: H.L. Hunt calls himself a "constructive," and admits he is "a registered Democrat who often votes Republican": *Playboy* Interview: H.L. Hunt," August 1966, p. 51.

335: "supreme American patriot of our time": Hunt editorial, 1951. In papers of Harry Flood Byrd, Special Collections, University of Virginia Library.

336: Mack Rankin: See: Alan Peppard, "Oil In The Family," *Vanity Fair*, June 2008, pp. 100-106, p. 103.

337: Hugh Roy Cullen "was possibly the wealthiest individual in Texas in the decade following World War II": Don E. Carleton, *Red Scare! Right-Wing Hysteria, Fifties Fanaticism And Their Legacy in Texas* (Texas Monthly Press: Austin, 1986), p. 69.

337: "the single largest contributor to McCarthy's Senate re-election campaign": Carleton, p. 91.

337: Lyndon Johnson asked H.L. Hunt to publish a pamphlet attacking John F. Kennedy: Billie Sol Estes, "Billie Sol Estes: A Texas Legend" (BS Productions: Granbury, Texas, 2005), p. 66. Self-published. Billie Sol Estes now resides in the small town of Granbury.

337: "Future historians will praise us....": H.L. Hunt to Lyndon Johnson. This letter, undated and unsigned, but clearly from Hunt, resides in the H.L. Hunt file at the LBJ library in Austin, Texas. It was uncovered by researcher Bruce Adamson.

338: H.L. Hunt writes to President Eisenhower: Adamson, Volume III ("H.L. Hunt Theory"). pp. 17-18; 47-49. Adamson quotes from or reproduces letters from H.L. Hunt to four presidents.

339: "engaged in counterespionage": William F. Billings to John Curington, April 4, 1961. Cited in Adamson, III, p. 23.

340: square Germanic features: See Harry Hurt III, *Texas Rich: The Hunt Dynasty From The Early Oil Days Through The Silver Crash* (Replica Books: Baker & Taylor: Bridgewater, New Jersey, 199), p. 188. *Texas Rich* was originally published in 1981 by W. W. Norton and Company.

341: Hughes had to hire INTERTEL: CIA. 104-10122-10288. FROM: WITHHELD (The memo is in fact signed by John G. Southard). TO: MEMO FOR THE RECORD. TITLE: ROBERT D. PELOQUIN, PRESIDENT, INTERNATIONAL INTELLIGENCE, INC. (INTERTEL). DATE: 05/20/71. PAGES: 6. JFK44:F25 1004.03.25.10:45:15:160005. NARA.

341: "unconfirmed reports of possible violence": Hurt, p. 223.

341: "if an incident were to occur": Hurt, p. 224.

342: Rothermel tells the FBI that he wrote the memorandum to dissuade H.L. Hunt and other Hunt oil employees from becoming involved in anti-Kennedy activities. Ibid. Rothermel Interview with SA David H. Israelson.

343: H.L. Hunt writes a letter to prominent Democratic Party politicians urging a concerted effort to defeat John F. Kennedy in the 1965 general election: See: H.L. Hunt to Senator Harry Byrd. July 11, 1963. Albert and Shirley Small Special Collections Library. University of Virginia at Charlottesville. Harry Flood Byrd, Sr. Papers, Folder: Correspondence, 1961-1965, HOS-K. Box 270. For the FBI's reaction, see: Federal Bureau of Investigation, May 10, 1977, plus 4/26/77. The Parmet interview is heavily redacted. Parmet told the FBI that "in view of recent allegations in the newspapers, H.L. Hunt may have been in some way involved in a plot to assassinate President John F. Kennedy on November 22, 1963...." TO: Director, FBI. (62-109060). FROM: SAC, DALLAS (89-43) (P). 62-107060-7. Available on maryferrell.org website. The Bureau writes that Parmet "conceded that the entire letter bore on the removal of KENNEDY through the electoral process" and "that the entire letter was strictly political in content."

343: "If you're not a free-wheeling outfit....": Quoted in David M. Barrett, *The CIA & Congress: The Untold Story From Truman To Kennedy* (University Press of Kansas, Lawrence, Kansas, 2005), p. 174.

343: "members of the Dallas Police Department Intelligence Division." FBI. 11/3/75. TO: DIRECTOR, FBI. FROM: SAC, DALLAS. 62-107060-7398. Rothermel Interview with SA David H. Israelson.

343: John Richard Salisbury informs the Secret Service that Robert L. Norris, his relative by marriage, was possibly sent by H.L. Hunt to engage Oswald to kill President Kennedy. Report made 12/2/63. SAIC Lane Artreme. Status is marked "Closed-Houston."

344: Rothermel could justify spending his time...a pretext: Interview with Philip Hirschkop, July 1, 2009.

344: On Nelson Bunker Hunt's contribution to the "Welcome, Mr. Kennedy" advertisement: Bunker told the FBI that he contributed "between $200.00 and $300.00 for publication of the advertisement": FBI (DL 100-10461) Interview by Harlan Brown and Edwin D. Kuykendall with Nelson Bunker Hunt. 5/15/1964. NARA. Hurt prints the "Welcome, Mr. Kennedy, To Dallas" advertisement on p. 227 of *Texas Rich*.

344: Rothermel advises Bunker to consider not talking to the FBI: Hurt, p. 236.

347: Jack Ruby admitted that he had never met Lamar Hunt, although he would like to meet him: FBI. 7/10/64. Connie Trammel Penny interview with Will Hayden Griffin, DL 44-1639. NARA.

347: Ruby asked Connie Trammel for Lamar Hunt's telephone number: Ibid.

347: Lamar Hunt tells the FBI that he has never been acquainted with Jack Ruby. FBI telephone interview with Lamar Hunt. SA Lansing P. Logan. December 17, 1963.

347: Rothermel paid Weisberg's airfare and hotel accommodations: Harold Weisberg to Paul Rothermel. 5/6/75. Harold Weisberg Archive. Hood College.

347: Rothermel asks Weisberg to help him prove that Lamar Hunt knew Jack Ruby: Harold Weisberg to Paul Rothermel. 1/13/70. Weisberg Archive. Did Ruby arrange for Connie Trammel to see Lamar Hunt? It wasn't so.

348: "Lyndon B. Johnson is mortally afraid of being assassinated": Hurt, p. 237.

348: Rothermel knows about a CIA-sponsored Manolo Ray invasion of Cuba: Hurt, p. 237.

348: Rothermel knows about an issue of *Life* magazine in advance: Hurt, p. 240.

349: "good cooperation": Quoted in Dick Russell, *The Man Who Knew Too Much* (Carroll & Graf: New York), p. 598. CIA refused to make public the other documents in their Hunt file, hiding behind the boiler plate excuse that by so doing they might jeopardize "intelligence sources and methods." Hunt lawyer Philip Hirschkop notes that one CIA document surfaced at the Hunt wiretapping trial. Interview with Philip Hirschkop, July 7, 2009.

349: For Bunker's "concession agreement with the Libyans": Hurt, pp. 261-262.

349: "so rich he didn't need them": Conversation with Philip Hirschkop, July 1, 2008.

350: Bechtel accepts CIA agents into its Libyan operation: McCartney, *Friends In High Places: The Bechtel Story: The Most Secret Corporation and How It Engineered The World* (Ballantine Books: New York, 1989), p. 118.

350: Rothermel "is CIA": Martin Waldron telephone call to Harold Weisberg from Austin, Texas. 9/23/75. Harold Weisberg archive.

350: Rothermel informs to the CIA field office: See, for example, CIA. ATTN: Director, Domestic Contact Service. Deputy Director, DCS. From: Chief, Houston Office. 26 April 1968. SUBJECT: Bill Wood, Agent for Jim Garrison, Making Inquiries in Dallas.

351: "Harry Blue": MEMORANDUM. November 3, 1967. TO: FILE. FROM: JIM GARRISON, District Attorney. RE: H.L. HUNT. NODA. NARA.

351: Rothermel sends Wood's chart, which names Hunt, to the FBI: Paul Rothermel to J. Gordon Shanklin, January 6, 1969. Rothermel included a note from an Oklahoma man, A. L. Jones, to Shanklin. See: FBI. 9/1/64.TO: SAC, OKLAHOMA CITY. FROM: SAC, DALLAS. RE: LEE HARVEY OSWALD, IS-R-CUBA. Rothermel was still employed by Hunt Oil when he served as an informant to J. Gordon Shanklin at the Dallas FBI field office: See: Paul Rothermel to Mr. J. Gordon Shanklin, May 20, 1968. With Enclosures. FBI. 89-43-8319. Harold Weisberg Archive.

Rothermel also forwarded a Weisberg letter to Shanklin pondering whether Philippe de Vosjoli was the "Philippe" mentioned by Herve Lamarre in *Farewell America*: CIA. 104-10515-10138. FROM: HAROLD WEISBERG. HEADER: JAMES HEPBURN, HERVE LAMARRE. TITLE: I ASK THOSE OF YOU TO WHOM I SEND THIS MEMORANDUM TO PLEASE KEEP IT ENTIRELY TO YOURSELVES, UNLESS SEPARATELY. DATE: 01/09/69.PAGES: 4. SUBJECT: WEISBERG. JFK64-25:F2 1999.05.29.11:19:52:826107. Obviously, Rothermel ignored Weisberg's request for confidentiality.

352: Wood a once and future CIA employee: See: CIA records on its relationship with William C. Wood (aka Bill Boxley): CIA. Memorandum No. 9. Subject: Garrison and the Kennedy Assassination. Reference: CI/R & A.104-10310-10253. CIA-DDP FILES. January 3, 1969. NARA.

See also: CIA. 104-10515-10040. From: Donovan E. Pratt, DC/CI/R & A. Memo: Garrison and the Kennedy Assassination: William Clarens Wood, Jr., Alias William Boxley. January 3, 1969. 7 pages. NARA.

See also: CIA. 104-10189-10241. TO: DIRECTOR, DOMESTIC CONTACT SERVICE. Attn: Deputy Director, DCS. FROM: CHIEF, HOUSTON OFFICE. 26 April 1968.Subject: Bill Wood, Agent for Jim Garrison, Making Inquiries in Dallas. This memo is signed by Ernest A. Rische.

See also: "GARRISON PROBE," MEMO by Paul Rothermel, February 12, 1969. NARA.

352: Wood reapplied for CIA employment in February 1967: See: CIA. Attn: Director, Domestic Contact Service. Ibid., 6 April 1968. A CIA document of 5 June 1968 has CIA acknowledging that Wood had been a "contract instructor" for them: CIA. 104-10310-10253. CIA-DDP FILES.

352: Rothermel vows to "guide" the Garrison investigation: CIA. 104-10515-10129. January 26, 1968. TITLE: REPORT: JIM GARRISON. PAGES: 1. JFK64-25:F2 1999.02.17.08:45:26:606129. NARA.

353: Rothermel reports to CIA about information relating to an "intelligence meeting" attended by H.L. Hunt: Paul Rothermel, THE GARRISON PROBE. April 4, 1968. NARA.

353: *Farewell America*: "James Hepburn," *Farewell America* (Frontiers Publishing Company: Vaduz (Liechtenstein) 1968.

357: "I think it is CIA": Harold Weisberg to Richard A. Sprague. January 10, 1969. Sprague Papers. Georgetown University Library. 5/6/75.

357: "department of disinformation information": Harold Weisberg to Dear Paul. 5/6/75. Weisberg Archive.

357: "extremely derogatory of Mr. Hunt": Hurt, p. 243.

358: David Kroman: Kroman had run for Attorney General of Minnesota: "Fugitive Sends Challenge To DA in New Orleans," *Times Picayune*, March 27, 1968, p. 18. That Kroman had met with Hunt: email to the author from Gary Schoener, July 5, 2009. That Kroman claimed that the assassination was "financed by H.L. Hunt": MEMORANDUM. January 30, 1968. TO: JIM GARRISON, District Attorney. FROM: STEPHEN JAFFE, Investigator. RE: Interview on January 27, 1968 with: DAVID R. KROMAN, Minneapolis, Minn. SUBJECT: RICHARD CASE NAGELL, Federal Prisoner #PMB-A-16606-H. Medical Center for Federal Prisoners, Springfield, Mo. NODA. NARA. The Kroman lead exemplifies the false "leads" sent on a regular basis to Jim Garrison.

358: "Mr. Hunt was a major figure behind the assassination": Gary Richard Schoener to Mr. Paul Rothermel, February 9, 1969. NARA.

358: Schoener speculated whether Kroman was a "government agent": Gary Richard Schoener to Mr. Paul M. Rothermel, February 6, 1969. Rothermel provided CIA with his correspondence with Schoener: CIA. 104-10515-10133. ORIGINATOR: PRIVATE. FROM: GARY RICHARD SCHOENER. TO: PAUL M. ROTHERMEL, JR. TITLE: MANY THANKS FOR FINDING TIME TO ACKNOWLEDGE RECEIPT OF THOSE PAGES FROM FAREWELL AMERICA. DATE: 02/06/69. PAGES: 1. NARA.

358: "trying to frame Mr. Hunt": Gary Richard Schoener to Mr. Paul M. Rothermel, Jr. February 6, 1969. In Gary Richard Schoener to Mr. Paul Rothermel, February 9, 1969, Schoener relates a telephone conversation with a secretary-girlfriend of Kroman's in which the woman quotes Kroman as saying that "Hunt was involved."

359: PART TWO – PAUL ROTHERMEL, DRAPED IN IMMUNITY

359: "Have you ever worked for or in any way...." Harold Weisberg to Mr. Paul Rothermel, Jr. 7/4/75. NARA

360: "former CIA man": Paul Rothermel, "GARRISON PROBE," February 12, 1969. This is Rothermel's second memorandum about the Garrison investigation. In this memo, Rothermel speculates that Garrison was "interested in N. B. [Nelson Bunker] Hunt... because one of N. B. Hunt's good friends had made a statement that Hoover was behind the assassination...which intrigued Garrison." Rothermel also insisted that "Garrison is convinced that the assassination was carried out by General Edwin Walker with the financial support and backing of Herman and George Brown of Houston and H.L. Hunt of Dallas," an avenue Garrison rejected.

360: Wood asked Rothermel for a job, and, although he didn't hire him, Rothermel gave him a few leads. See: RE: GARRISON FILE. January 29, 1969. An unstable individual, Wood told Rothermel that "Garrison is determined to either assassinate me or completely ruin me by disclosures out of his office."

360: Rothermel calls J. Walton Moore of the CIA's Dallas field office and informs him of Wood's visit: CIA. 26 April 1968. TO: DIRECTOR, DOMESTIC CONTACT SERVICE. ATTN: DEPUTY DIRECTOR, DCS. FROM: CHIEF, HOUSTON OFFICE. RE: BILL WOOD, AGENT FOR JIM GARRISON, MAKING INQUIRIES IN DALLAS. This document was signed by Ernest A. Rische, the CIA officer who was handling the surfacing of the name "George R. Brown" in the Garrison investigation.

361: Fensterwald visits Rothermel in May 1969: Paul M. Rothermel, Jr. to Mr. Harold Weisberg, June 2, 1969.

361: Jim Braden was going to Dallas to see Lamar Hunt: Bernard Fensterwald, Jr. to Mr. Paul Rothermel, c/o H.L. Hunt. July 23, 1969. Fensterwald wrote on the stationery of the Committee To Investigate Assassinations.

361: "there is agency involvement": Harold Weisberg to Mr. Paul Rothermel, 2/22/69. 1 pages. Weisberg Archive.

362: for the description of John Curington, see: Harrison Edward Livingstone, *Killing The Truth: Deceit and Deception in the JFK Case* (Carroll & Graf Publishers, Inc.: New York, 1993), p. 500.

363: "side-deals with shadowy brokerage....": Hurt, pp. 280-282.

363: skimming off $5,000,000 for himself: Martin Waldron call from Austin, Texas. 9/23/75. Weisberg Archives.

363: "I owe my life to Paul Rothermel": Hurt, p. 282.

364: with the departure of Rothermel, there was a marked decline in the number of threats: Hurt, p. 311.

364: Rothermel claims that when he learned that his phones were wiretapped, he "began to fear for his life': Jim Hougan, *Spooks: The Haunting of America – The Private Use of Secret Agents* (William Morrow and Company, Inc.: New York, 1978), p. 78. Hougan writes: "Paul Rothermel, for instance, a former FBI agent hired by the ultra-rightist Hunt family in Texas, is convinced that Nelson Bunker Hunt was prepared to kill him after Rothermel refused to participate in what he says was Hunt's intention to establish an American version of the Brazilian death squads," p. 52.

365: "humanitarian thing...friend": Harold Weisberg to Dear Walter, 12/13/71. Weisberg Archive. "Walter" is apparently Walter "Tabaka," who had a claim against H.L. Hunt regarding money and claimed to have represented H.L. Hunt in Washington from about 1965 to 1974. See: Harold Weisberg to Paul M. Rothermel, Jr. 5/15/77. Weisberg was asking for Rothermel's help in deciphering the Tabaka claim.

365: "approving any transaction that Mr. Rothermel might make": Martin Waldron, "Wiretapping Trial of Two Sons of H.L. Hunt Is Postponed When Supreme Court Does Not Act On Case," *New York Times*, April 15, 1975.

365: On what role I might have played": Hurt, p. 333.

365: "I couldn't work for a man playing God": Hurt, p. 346.

366: Rothermel's share was $25,000. Martin Waldron call to Harold Weisberg, 9/23/75.

366: Newspapers chose not to mention Rothermel's name: See, for example, Karen Deike and Hugh Aynesworth, "Indictments Name Hunts, Five Others," *Dallas Times Herald*, July 22, 1975. Buried in Aynesworth's "Hunt Case Born In Midnight Burglary," *Dallas Times Herald*, July 23, 1975, is one mention of the countersuits by "ex-employees, Paul M. Rothermel, Jr., John H. Brown and John W. Curington," suits that were "later dropped after a secret meeting." Aynesworth mentions that Curington and Brown were charged and convicted of embezzlement. He says nothing about the fate of Rothermel, or how or why he escaped the same charges.

366: "refused on three different occasions to place CIA agents in the Hunt International Petroleum Company": Rena Pederson, "Hunts Protest Charges," *Dallas Morning News*, July 23, 1975.

367: Curington and Brown, convicted of mail fraud, received probated sentences, and never spent a day in prison: Hurt, p. 355.

367: Weisberg interviews Hunt: Weisberg's memorandum is headed: "Placid Oil Co.; Ray Leads; Hunt?" 12/7/71. Dallas. Harold Weisberg. Weisberg Archive. Hunt told Weisberg that Rothermel "is a crook": Harold Weisberg to dear Paul. 5/6/75. Weisberg Archive. Weisberg wrote Rothermel that Hunt "appeared to be reluctant to call you a crook." Hunt told Weisberg that he had given Rothermel "a small settlement," which seemed to Weisberg to contradict Hunt's having called Rothermel a "crook."

368: Rothermel asks Harold Weisberg to see what he can find out about the Hirschkop-Hunt relationship: Harold Weisberg to Paul M. Rothermel, Jr., January 28, 1973. Weisberg Archive.

367: "They are": Harold Weisberg to Paul Rothermel. 7/18/75. Weisberg Archive.

367: "more than one interest in this…have you ever worked for or in any way, directly or indirectly, in any way served the CIA?": Ibid., Harold Weisberg to Mr. Paul Rothermel, Jr., 7/4/75.

368: "There was a CIA front": Notes of Harold Weisberg. 12/1/71.

368: "how the CIA got what had to have come from you": Harold Weisberg to Mr. Paul Rothermel, Jr.: 2/3/76.

368: "they have lied and said they do not": Ibid.

369: at trial: Hirschkop says, "the Government may have been trying to cover up the infiltration of the Hunt Oil company by the Central Intelligence Agency": See: Martin Waldron, "Wiretapping Trial of Two Sons of H.L. Hunt Is Postponed When Supreme Court Does Not Act On Case," *New York Times*, April 15, 1975, p. 19.

369: fifty motions had been filed. See, for example, The United States of America, Plaintiff-Appellant v. Nelson Bunker Hunt and W. Herbert Hunt, Defendant-Appellees, United States Court Of Appeals for the Fifth Circuit, December 23, 1974. 505 F2d 931. See also: Waldron, "Wiretapping Trial of Two Sons of H.L. Hunt Is Postponed…."

369: Martin Waldron views the CIA file on the Hunts. Ibid., Waldron call to Weisberg.

369: CIA document that surfaced: Conversation with Philip Hirschkop, July 7, 2009.

370: Judge Woodward rules that the charge made by the Hunts that they were persecuted by CIA was groundless: Adamson, III, p. 43.

370: remotely what he was owed: Conversation with Philip Hirschkop, July 7, 2009.

370: Rothermel tells Pete Noyes that Eugene Hale Brading visited the Hunts. In his book Noyes leaves the issue of Eugene Hale Brading's visiting the Hunts as an open question: "What, if anything, did Eugene Hale Brading have to hide?" See: Noyes, *Legacy of Doubt* (Pinnacle Books: New York, 1973), p. 224.

370: Bunker takes a million dollars out of Libya every three days, and has a member of El Fatah on his payroll: Date: 5/1/87. "Conversation with Rothermel," Hand written notes. AARC, Gift of Pete Noyes.

371: Rothermel tells Dick Russell that Eugene Hale Brading had visited the Hunts: Russell, *The Man Who Knew Too Much*, p. 593.

371: "the first copy": Dick Russell, Updated version of *The Man Who Knew Too Much*, (Carroll & Graf: New York, 2003), p. 585.

371: Historian David Wrone is certain that Paul Rothermel did not purchase a copy of the Zapruder film on 11/22/1963: email from David Wrone, 12/30/09. Wrone's book on the subject is *The Zapruder Film: Reframing JFK's Assassination* (University Press of Kansas, 2003).

371: "frightened for my life": Russell, p. 599.

371: Rothermel threatens to sue Dick Russell: email from Dick Russell, July 3, 2009. Russell deleted all references to his interviews with Rothermel from the revised edition of his book.

372: "I think you'll find he's CIA": Conversation with Jim Hougan.

372: Rothermel says he will talk only to the FBI, and not to any U.S. Senate or House Investigating Committee: See: FBI interview with Paul Rothermel, 2/1/77. Interview by SA Udo H. Specht, Jr. in Richardson, Texas on 1/29/77.

372: Rothermel contends that the Hunt Oil log books and long distance telephone logs for September and October 1963 had disappeared: FBI interview with Rothermel, 1/29/77.

374: "sorry son-of-a-bitch": Nelson Bunker Hunt FBI interview, 3/7/77, with Special Agents Nile A. Duke, Jr., and Udo H. Specht, Jr. in Dallas, Texas.

374: Rothermel "stole nine million dollars": Nelson Bunker Hunt interview with FBI. 3/7/77. See also: HSCA interviews with Rothermel and Curington: ADMIN FOLDER – N2: HSCA ADMINSITRATIVE FOLDER, 1/27/77. MICHAEL M. UHLMANN'S CORRESPONDENCE TO THE SSCIA.

375: "This is news to me": FBI interview with Nelson Bunker Hunt, March 1, 1977.

375: "men who received money from the late billionaire H.L. Hunt…right-wing Hunt followers knew he hated Kennedy and they thought they were doing what Hunt wanted": William Dick and Ken Potter, "JFK Assassins Got $$ From Kennedy-Hating Billionaire," *National Enquirer,* June 14, 1977, p. 16. Curington told author Harrison Livingstone that Hunt sent him to the Dallas police station where Oswald was being held": Livingstone, "Killing The Truth," p. 502.

376: "money to secretly fund with campaign donations": Paul David Pope, *The Deeds Of My Fathers: How My Grandfather and Father Built New York And Created The Tabloid World of Today,* p. 309.

376: Summa Corp: Ibid., p. 309. For CIA's connections with Howard Hughes: CIA released only the second page of this document: SUBJECT: DCD Response to the Agency-Watergate File Review. Numbers (f) through (k) of the original document are available. The documents admits that DCD has had [ ] relationships with the Hughes Tool Company and the Hughes Aircraft Company [ ].

377: Farrar, Straus and Giroux: Roger Straus Jr. himself admitted openly to the author that he had served CIA, making his publishing house available to the Agency beginning in the post-war period after he completed his service to the U.S. Navy.

377: George de Mohrenschildt spreads rumors that H.L. Hunt was behind the Kennedy assassination: Adamson, III, p. 47.

377: Oltmans: For a description of Oltmans' interviews with George de Mohrenschildt, see: HSCA. RECORD NUMBER: 180-10105-10250. AGENCY FILE NUMBER: 014316. FROM: OLTMANS, WILLEM. TITLE: TESTIMONY OF WILLEM OLTMANS. DATE: 04/01/77. PAGES: 146. TRANSCRIPT. NARA.

377: "to all his parties": Ibid. Oltmans testimony, p. 42.

377: "alleged" suicide of George de Mohrenschildt; Paul Rothermel, Jr. to Mr. Harold Weisberg, March 31, 1977.

377: "I am making the overhead": Paul M. Rothermel to Harold Weisberg, February 2, 1977.

378: "kept for his private use": Paul M. Rothermel, Jr. to Senator Arlen Specter, Representative Louis Stokes, G. Robert Blakey, Jim Lesar and Mark Flannigan. RE: House Select Committee On Assassinations. February 10, 1993.

378: "a great personal tragedy for me": Ibid. Paul M. Rothermel, Jr. to Senator Arlen Specter, etc.

378: "in the oil business": *Playboy* interview with H.L. Hunt. August 1966, p. 60.

Documents of Interest

Our Man in Haiti:

Addendum – H.L.Hunt & Sons and CIA:

SECRET

O
P
Y

14 September 1948

MEMORANDUM FOR: THE EXECUTIVE SECRETARY
NATIONAL SECURITY COUNCIL

SUBJECT: Office of Policy Coordination Cooperation with
Federal Bureau of Investigation

Reference: Memorandum, 13 September 1948 to Admiral
Souers from Frank G. Wisner

The reference memorandum is approved and forwarded
herewith.

(Signed & Dispatched 9/14)

R. H. HILLENKOETTER
Rear Admiral, USN
Director of Central
Intelligence

Encl
Ref Memo in dup

ALL FBI INFORMATION CONTAINED
HEREIN IS UNCLASSIFIED
DATE 5/14/98 BY _____

SECRET

CIA HAS NO OBJECTION TO
DECLASSIFICATION AND/OR
RELEASE OF THIS DOCUMENT

The next 15 pages (pp 389-403) are CIA documents
that reveal a CIA liaison agreement with the FBI.

Y

13 September 1948

MEMORANDUM FOR: ADMIRAL SIDNEY W. SOUERS
                       Executive Secretary, NSC

VIA: Admiral R. H. Hillonkoetter
                       Director of Central Intelligence

FROM: Frank G. Wisner
                       Assistant Director, CIA

SUBJECT: Cooperation with FBI

     1.   This memorandum is submitted pursuant to our telephone conversation of this morning in order to provide you with additional background in connection with my request that you arrange for a White House introduction of myself to Mr. J. Edgar Hoover, Director of the Federal Bureau of Investigation.

     2.   Certain important activities of the Office of Policy Coordination will involve the establishment and maintenance of liaison with foreign nationality groups within the United States and the movement of limited numbers of individuals, both American and foreign, within the United States as well as between this country and foreign countries. It is considered essential that Mr. Hoover be informed of such of our activities as will touch upon his area of responsibility, and also that the cooperation and assistance of the FBI will be available to this Office. In order to insure the fullest possible understanding and to make certain that Mr. Hoover's organization will lend the amount and kind of coopera-tion which will be necessary for the successful functioning of certain of our operations, it is believed that a White House introduction to Mr. Hoover is warranted. I have discussed this matter with Mr. George Kennan who agrees that the initial approach to Mr. Hoover should be made on the highest possible level. I, therefore, request that you undertake the arrangements which are required in order to obtain a White House introduction. It would be desirable if the introduction could stress the importance which is attached by the National Security Council to the new activity and could indicate that I am prepared to discuss with Mr. Hoover the features of the activity which will be of concern to him.

     3.   If you require fuller particulars or a different form of presentation of this request, please advise me so that I may provide that which is needed.

                                      FRANK G. WISNER

ALL FBI INFORMATION CONTAINED
HEREIN IS UNCLASSIFIED
DATE 5/14/98 BY 56LS-S
(JFK)

SECRET

CIA HAS NO OBJECTION TO
... ASSIFICATION AND/OF ...

TOTAL DENIAL

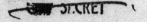

22 September 1948

Mr. D. Milton Ladd
Assistant to the Director
Federal Bureau of Investigation
Washington 25, D. C.

Dear Mr. Ladd:

Confirming our telephone conversation of today, I am enclosing a draft of a proposed memorandum which I have prepared for the purpose of recording the understanding which has been arrived at between us in regard to the cooperation and liaison between my office and the Bureau. I have endeavored in this draft to set out the essential features of our conversation of yesterday afternoon and I should appreciate your indicating to me any modifications or changes which you may deem necessary or advisable to reflect your recollection and understanding of our conversation. Upon my receipt of your suggested changes, if any, and following any further discussion between us which may be indicated as desirable, I shall prepare this memorandum in final form and furnish to you the original and a copy thereof, with the request that you initial and return to me the copy.

In accordance with the terms of our understanding, I should like to submit to you herewith the names of certain of the individuals and groups with whom it is proposed that my office will have dealings in connection with our authorized activities. From time to time in the future I shall furnish you with additional names. The following are the names:

I - Individuals:

George M. Dimitrov, Exiled Secretary General of
    Bulgarian Agrarian Party

Stefan Osusky, prominent Czech Refugee leader

Ferenc Nagy, head of Hungarian Small Holders Party

Dr. Vladko Macek, representative of Croatian
    Peasant Party

Stanislas Mikolajczyk, former Polish Vice Premier

Andre Cretzianu, former Rumanian Cabinet Minister

Downgraded to SECRET per
Paul J. Burns, 019210

ALL FBI INFORMATION CONTAINED
HEREIN IS UNCLASSIFIED
DATE 5/10/90 BY

CIA HAS NO OBJECTION T

Series B.

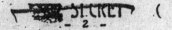

SECRET
- 2 -

II - Groups and Organizations:

International Peasant Union which is made up of
representatives of Polish Agrarian Party; Bulgarian
Agrarian Party; Croatian Peasant Party; Hungarian
Small Holders Party; Rumanian National Peasant Party;
Serbian Agrarian Union and a number of recognized
Czochoslovak political leaders.

In view of the highly classified character of our activities,
I am sure that you will appreciate the importance of maintaining the
maximum security precautions.

Sincerely yours,

FRANK G. WISNER
Assistant Director for
Policy Coordination

Enclosure - 1

D R A F T

Y

22 September 1948

MEMORANDUM FOR THE RECORD:

SUBJECT: Cooperation and Liaison Between Federal Bureau of
Investigation and Office of Policy Coordination, CIA

1. This memorandum records an understanding which has been
arrived at in conversations between Mr. D. Milton Ladd, Assistant
to the Director, Federal Bureau of Investigation, and Mr. Frank G.
Wisner, Assistant Director, and Chief of the Office of Policy
Coordination, of CIA. The conversations in question were duly
authorized by the Associate Director of the Federal Bureau of
Investigation and by the Director and Deputy Director of CIA and
were arranged by the Executive Secretary of the National Security
Council on behalf of the White House. The purpose of the understanding is to provide a basis for cooperation and liaison between
the FBI and the Office of Policy Coordination, CIA, and the following
points summarize the essential elements of the understanding:

a. In view of the distinctive character of the activities of the Office of Policy Coordination, it is considered
advisable that separate and direct liaison be established
between that office and the FBI. For this purpose the FBI
will provide a special liaison officer who will be nominated
by the FBI within the near future. (This arrangement has
been specifically approved by the Deputy Director, CIA, in
the absence of the Director.)

b. It is understood that in the discharge of the duties
and obligations laid upon the Office of Policy Coordination by
the National Security Council, it is necessary for this
Office to have dealings with individuals and groups of foreign
nationalities within and without the United States and to
sponsor the movement from time to time of such individuals
and representatives of such groups between the United States
and foreign countries. The Office of Policy Coordination
recognizes the primary responsibility of the FBI in the field
of United States domestic security, and the FBI acknowledges
that it is essential for the Office of Policy Coordination
to have direct dealings with the individuals and groups aforementioned.

c. In order that the interests of both parties to this
understanding shall be served, it is understood that the
Office of Policy Coordination keep the FBI generally informed
concerning the extent and character of its dealings with

owngraded to SECRET per
aut. J. Burns 019210

SECRET

COPY _1_ OF _1_ C

ALL FBI INFORMATION CONTAINED
HEREIN IS UNCLASSIFIED
DATE 5/14/98 BY 5668 SLD/ude

CIA HAS NO OBJECTION
CLASSIFICATION AND

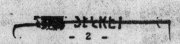

- 2 -

foreign individuals and groups within the United States.
More specifically the Office of Policy Coordination will,
in so far as possible, inform the FBI sufficiently in
advance of its proposed dealings with such individuals
and groups to enable the FBI to advise the Office of
Policy Coordination of any security risks which may be
involved in dealing with such individuals and groups
and in order to provide the FBI with adequate opportunity
to indicate individuals which it is employing for its own
purposes in connection with the penetration of foreign
groups.

d. There shall be an exchange of information between
the FBI and the Office of Policy Coordination concerning
the significance, activities, and reliability of such
individuals and groups of foreign nationalities within the
United States as may be of interest to the Office of Policy
Coordination.

_____
F. G. W.

_____
D. M. L.

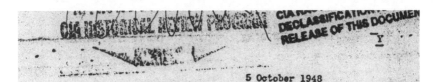

5 October 1948

MEMORANDUM FOR: DEPUTY DIRECTOR, CIA

SUBJECT: Cooperation and Liaison Between FBI and OPC, CIA

1. Pursuant to our recent conversations with regard to the subject above mentioned, I am submitting to you herewith a copy of the memorandum which records the understanding arrived at in conversations between Mr. Ladd and myself governing the relationship between my office and the FBI. I have been informed by a letter signed by J. Edgard Hoover, which has just been delivered to me, that the arrangement set forth in the memorandum is satisfactory to the Bureau and that Special Agent Richard W. Lawrence has been designated to handle the liaison with my office.

2. I believe that this agreement, although quite brief, should provide the basis for a satisfactory relationship between my office and the FBI, and I am very glad that Mr. Hoover has given it his approval.

FRANK G. WISNER
Assistant Director for
Policy Coordination

Encl:
Record Memo of 22 Sept. 48

ded to SECRET per
Burns, 019210

REVIEWED BY FBI/JFK TASK FOR
ON 6/14/98

☑ RELEASE IN FULL
☐ RELEASE IN PART
☐ TOTAL DENIAL

SECRET

~~SECRET~~

14 November 1949

MEMORANDUM FOR: DIRECTOR OF CENTRAL INTELLIGENCE

SUBJECT: Liaison With the Federal Bureau of Investigation

Reference: (a) CIA Administrative Instruction No. 50-19, Subject as above, 5 October 1949

Enclosures: (a) CIA Administrative Instruction No. 50-19, Subject as above, 5 October 1949 (TAB A) S.

(b) Memorandum for Executive Secretary, NSC, from DCI, Subject: "OPC Cooperation With the FBI", 14 September 1948 (TAB B) S

(c) Letter to Assistant to the Director, FBI, from ADPC, 22 September 1948 (TAB C) FC7S 4S

(d) Letter to ADPC from Director, FBI, 2 October 1948 (TAB D) C

(e) Memorandum for Deputy Director, CIA, from ADPC, Subject: "Cooperation and Liaison Between FBI and OPC", 5 October 1948 (TAB E) FC7S 413

JFK TASK FORCE

1. There has just been brought to my attention the fact that the reference memorandum contravenes the agreement between OPC and the Federal Bureau of Investigation, which was entered into on 2 October 1948 with your express approval. (TAB B) I understand that the reference memorandum (which I am told was promulgated for your signature by the Deputy Executive) was issued without either the concurrence of this office or notice to this office that it would be issued in the face of our nonconcurrence.

2. The agreement between OPC and the Federal Bureau of Investigation (TABS C & D) represents an exceptionally advantageous arrangement which was negotiated with great care. In your absence the Deputy Director was advised of its consummation on 5 October 1948. (TAB E)

3. The reference memorandum would appear to completely nullify this agreement which has proved to be highly effective in our operations, and which I consider to be essential to the efficient performance

graded to SECRET per ty of Paul J. Burns, 19210

~~SECRET~~

COPY 1 OF 5 COPIES

HISTORICAL DOCUMENT

ALL FBI INFORMATION CONTAINED HEREIN IS UNCLASSIFIED DATE 5/14/98 BY 5668-SL/jrdk (JFK)

CIA HAS NO OBJECTION TO DECLASSIFICATION AND/OR RELEASE OF THIS DOCUMENT

of our mission.

4. Accordingly, I request the opportunity to discuss this matter with you in greater detail and I recommend that the reference memorandum be amended to provide for separate and direct liaison between OPC and the Federal Bureau of Investigation on all matters prescribed in the Memorandum for the Record, 22 September 1948. (Enclosure to TAB C)

FRANK G. WISNER
Assistant Director for
Policy Coordination

Enclosures: 5
(As described above)

Endorsement   16 November 1949

To: Assistant Director for Policy Coordination

1. Returned.

2. OPC will continue to maintain liaison with the FBI for all matters relating to operational support of OPC.

Enclosures: 5
(As described above)
OPC 01/13/49
CVH/dr

cc: Mr. Hulick (#3)
DCI (#1-2)
Enclos. OPC Reg. (#4)
OPC Chrono (#5)

R. H. HILLENKOETTER
Rear Admiral, USN
Director of Central
Intelligence

397

SECRET

CENTRAL INTELLIGENCE AGENCY
Washington, D. C.

ADMINISTRATIVE INSTRUCTION
NO.   50-19

5 October 1949

SUBJECT: Liaison with the Federal Bureau of Investigation

    1. In order to facilitate the exchange of information with the Federal Bureau of Investigation, to eliminate duplication in requests to and from the FBI, and to insure the establishment and maintenance of efficient, orderly and controllable liaison channels, all liaison between the Central Intelligence Agency and the Federal Bureau of Investigation will be governed by the following policy:

    a. The Chief of the Inspection and Security Staff is designated as the sole liaison channel for all matters pertaining to the security of the personnel and installations of CIA, including:

    (1) Information concerning investigations of all personnel;

    (2) Physical security investigative information;

    (3) Information of a necessary operational support nature;

    (4) Any additional special information falling within the scope of the functions and jurisdiction of the Chief, I&S.

    b. The Assistant Director for Special Operations is designated as the sole liaison channel between CIA and FBI for all other matters except those covered by paragraph 4 hereunder. The Assistant Director for Special Operations is responsible for:

    (1) Servicing the needs of all other Offices and Staffs;

    (2) Transmitting to the Office of Collection and Dissemination for appropriate dissemination information received from the FBI which is of value to the overt Offices:

    (3) Transmitting to the Office of Collection and Dissemination all requests from the FBI for intelligence produced or to be produced by the overt Offices;

    (4) Transmitting to the FBI all requests from the overt Offices for information to be supplied by the FBI.

    2. Inasmuch as the intelligence product of the Federal Bureau of Investigation under its internal security mission is largely in the

SECRET

ALL FBI INFORMATION CONTAINED
HEREIN IS UNCLASSIFIED
DATE 5/4/98 BY 5668 SD/vde
(JFK)

CIA HAS NO OBJECTION TO
DECLASSIFICATION AND/OR
RELEASE OF THIS DOCUMENT

JFK TASK FORCE

counter-espionage and related fields, and inasmuch as the Assistant
Director for Special Operations has primary operational responsibilities
in counter-espionage matters, all collection requests made by the Central
Intelligence Agency of the Federal Bureau of Investigation will be routed
through the Assistant Director for Special Operations.

3. No request will be made to the FBI by CIA personnel for any
information except through the two channels prescribed above.

4. Nothing in this Instruction is intended to interfere with the
working relationship between co-members of the Intelligence Advisory
Committee or other committees upon which both CIA and FBI are represented. In the event, however, that such working relationships involve
requests for information or operational assistance, such requests must,
in all cases, be coordinated in advance with the Chief, IAS, or the
Assistant Director for Special Operations, depending upon the nature
of the request.

5. Any discussions or relationships with the FBI at the working
level which are considered necessary or advisable must be arranged
through the channels prescribed above.

R.H. Hillenkoetter

R. H. HILLENKOETTER
Rear Admiral, USN
Director of Central Intelligence

DISTRIBUTION: A

Oct 12 3 29 PM '49

MEMORANDA ON LOAN TO EAD   18 OCTOBER 1949
Via Cornelius

(a) 30 August 1948

    Memorandum for the Record

    FROM Merritt K. Ruddock

    SUBJECT: Proposed Discussion with J. Edgar Hoover
    (No TS No.)

(b) 21 September 1948

    Memorandum for the Files

    FROM Frank G. Wisner

    SUBJECT: FBI Cooperation and Liaison
    (No TS No.)

(c) 22 September 1948

    Memorandum for the Record

    SUBJECT: Cooperation and Liaison between Federal Bureau of Investigation
           and Office of Policy Coordination, CIA

    Written by Frank G. Wisner

(d) 22 September 1948

    Letter to Mr. D. Milton Ladd

    From FGWisner

(e) 5 October 1948

    Memorandum For: Deputy Director, CIA

    SUBJECT: Cooperation and Liaison between FBI and OPC, CIA

    FROM: FGWisner

(f) 5 October 1948

    Memorandum for the Files

    SUBJECT: FBI Liaison

    FROM: FGWisner

REVIEWED BY FBI/JFK TASK FORCE

ON. 6/14/78

document is incomplete

clear from the record. In any event, the results
were salutary and he did see Mr. D. Milton Ladd,
Assistant to the FBI Director, on 22 September 1948.
A memorandum for the record *dated 22 Spt 48* was duly drawn entitled:
"Cooperation and Liaison Between the Federal Bureau
of Investigation and Office of Policy Coordination,
CIA." It was initialed by Wisner and Ladd and it
made the following points: (a) a special liaison
officer was to be nominated by the FBI as a separate and direct channel to OPC apart from the established CIA liaison (Wisner noted that this arrangement had been specifically approved by the DD-
CI in the absence of the DCI.); (b) OPC recognized
the primary responsibility of the FBI for domestic
security and the FBI acknowledged that OPC would
have direct dealings with individuals and groups of
foreign nationalities within and without the United
States and would sponsor the movement from time to
time of such individuals and representatives of
such groups between the United States and foreign
countries; (c) OPC would keep the FBI generally informed concerning the extent and character of its
dealings with these foreign individuals and groups

EWED BY FBI/JFK TASK FORCE
6/14/98 *dal*

- 571 -

RELEASE IN FULL
RELEASE IN PART
TOTAL DENIAL

SECRET

ALL FBI INFORMATION CONTAINED
HEREIN IS UNCLASSIFIED
DATE 5/14/98 BY 5608 SUB/nde
(JFK)

401

within the United States in time for the FBI to inform OPC of any security risks and in order to provide the FBI with an opportunity to indicate those
individuals which it might be employing for its own
purposes; and (d) there would be an exchange of information between the FBI and OPC concerning the
significance, activities and reliability of such
individuals and groups. Ladd's copy of this memorandum was accompanied by a letter from the ADPC
identifying the individuals and groups of current
interest to OPC.

On 2 October 1948 Wisner received a letter from Hoover approving the memorandum regarding
cooperation of liaison and appointing Special Agent
Richard W. Lawrence as the FBI liaison representative to OPC. On 5 October Wisner sent a copy of
this correspondence to the DDCI.

One year later it came to Wisner's attention that on 5 October 1949 CIA Administrative Instruction No. 50-19 had been issued on the subject
of liaison with the FBI, signed by Hillenkoetter
and stating that the chief of the Inspection and
Security Staff was designated as the sole channel

- 572 -

SECRET

for all matters pertaining to the security of the
personnel and installations of CIA and that the
ADSO was designated as the sole liaison for all
other matters. Wisner directed a rather frosty
memorandum to the DCI on 14 November 1949, enclosing the full file of previous memoranda and pointing out the Instruction was issued without the concurrence of his office or without notice that it
would be issued in the face of OPC's nonconcurrence.
He recommended that the Instruction be amended to
provide for separate and direct liaison between
OPC and the FBI. The file was returned to the ADPC
on 16 November 1949, with the following endorsement:
"OPC will continue to maintain liaison with the FBI
for all matters relating to operational support of
OPC."

By OPC regulation the ADPC restricted all
OPC liaison with the FBI to himself. This is the
way the matter rested until shortly after the creation of the Clandestine Service. On 8 August 1952
CSN 70-4 placed the responsibility for sole liaison
with the FBI in the Foreign Intelligence Staff C
for all CS activities under the DDP.

. - .573 -

SECRET

SECRET

CIA SPECIAL COLL
RELEASE AS SANIT

Declassified and Approved for Release
by the Central Intelligence Agency
Date: 6/25/03

OTE 92-1403
10 February 1992

MEMORANDUM FOR: Director of Central Intelligence

VIA: Director of Training and Education
Director, Center for the Study of Intelligence

FROM: J. Kenneth McDonald
Chief, CIA History Staff

SUBJECT: Survey of CIA's Records from House Select
Committee on Assassinations Investigation

1. As you requested on 16 January, the History Staff has
now surveyed CIA's records from the House Select Committee on
Assassinations (HSCA) investigation into the assassination of
President John F. Kennedy. As promised in my 30 January
interim report, I can now give you a full account of our
findings, and of my recommendation for transferring this HSCA
collection at its existing classification to the National
Archives through CIA's Historical Review Program.

2. After the Office of Congressional Affairs arranged
permission from Congress for History Staff access to the
sequestered 64 boxes of this collection, we examined these and
other related holdings at Headquarters and the [/O
]. As a result of careful, persistent, and
determined inquiries, we are fairly confident--although by no
means certain--that we have seen all the documents that CIA
collected for the HSCA investigation of 1977-1979. The summary
of our findings which follows is documented in more detail in
attachments A and B.

3. General Description: The HSCA collection (defined as
all records that the CIA provided to that Committee for its
1977-1979 investigation) is a large and chaotic collection.
Beyond the 64 boxes sequestered by Congress that have been
involved in FOIA litigation, there are 16 boxes of Oswald's 201
file and numerous loose folders (mainly from Mexico City
Station records) that were collected for the Warren Commission
investigation. Most of this material can be found on microfilm
in the sequestered collection. Of the 64 boxes, 34 have
material collected by the Directorate of Operations, while

CL BY [03
DECL OADR

SECRET

The next 5 pages (pp. 404-408) are from CIA's history component, acknowledging that
Clay Shaw was in fact a "highly paid" CIA employee, as Jim Garrison had suspected.

SECRET

29 contain records from the Office of Legislative Counsel (now
OCA), Inspector General, Office of the General Counsel,
Directorate of Science and Technology, Office of Security, as
well as several boxes of HSCA staff notes and records. Box No.
64 contains 72 microfilm reels (each equivalent to a box of
records), which include the Oswald 201 file and Mexico City
Station records, as well as other 201 files and information
about Cuban exile groups.

4. Organization: The collection is arranged haphazardly,
having been gathered in response to a series of HSCA and (in
the case of the Oswald 201 file) Warren Commission requests.
Although portions of the collection are organized by a variety
of systems, there is no overall intellectual control of the
entire body of records. We found fifteen indexes to the
collection, none of which is adequate for control or retrieval.

5. Sensitivity: Although the collection is almost
entirely at SECRET or lower classification, there is a
scattering of TOP SECRET and codeword documentation. Materials
we consider especially sensitive--more for privacy than
national security reasons--include 201 files, phone taps, mail
intercepts, security files, photo surveillance, names of
sources, watch lists, and MHCHAOS documentation. Such material
occurs throughout the collection, usually in response to HSCA
requests for name traces. There are 22 microfilm reels of 201
files in addition to the Oswald file, while eight boxes contain
security records, including, for example, files on David Atlee
Phillips, Martin Luther King, and Clay Shaw.

6. Non-CIA Material: The collection includes a lot of
third-agency material, mostly from the FBI. FBI reports
dominate the 16 boxes of Oswald's 201 file, and nearly half of
the 34 boxes of DO-collected material consists of third-agency
material. The collection's remaining 29 boxes contain mostly
CIA records, as does the box of microfilm, except for Oswald's
201 file. There is also some documentation of foreign liaison,
mainly with the Mexican government.

7. CIA Complicity? Our survey found nothing in these
records that indicates any CIA role in the Kennedy
assassination or assassination conspiracy (if there was one),
or any CIA involvement with Oswald. These records do reveal,
however, that Clay Shaw was a highly paid CIA contract source
until 1956. While nothing surfaced on Carlos Marcello in the
collection, we found substantial documentation on other members
of the mob, including Santos Trafficante.

8. Although the results of our survey fully support my
earlier recommendation against inviting a panel of historians

SECRET

into CIA to examine and report on this collection, the problem
that this proposal addressed remains—the widespread
allegations, given new impetus by Oliver Stone's "JFK," that
CIA was part of a conspiracy to assassinate President Kennedy.
That CIA has a closed collection of records concerning the
Kennedy assassination is well known, both because it is part of
over 800 cubic feet of HSCA investigation records that Congress
has closed until 2029, and because our 64 boxes of these
records have been the subject of FOIA requests, litigation, and
court orders. Since opening all US Government records on the
Kennedy assassination has been proposed by former President
Ford, Congressman Louis Stokes, and others, many observers will
consider your decision on this question a test of your new
openness policy.

9. Options: CIA's three principal options are to keep the
Agency's HSCA records closed and in our hands, to open them
entirely, or to transfer them to the National Archives. Before
making my case for the third option, I should note the
following considerations with respect to the first two:

a. Closed: To maintain the status quo would keep the
collection classified, closed and in CIA's hands,
sequestered by Congress until 2029. CIA would, however,
remain subject to the 1988 court order to review portions
of it in response to FOIA litigation. While putting the
collection into Historical Review Program processing would
speed and broaden its declassification review (which would
nevertheless take several years), such an internal shift
would probably not change the public perception of our
closed position. Although keeping these records closed
remains a viable option, it tends both to encourage
suspicion that CIA is part of a cover-up, and to undermine
the credibility of CIA's openness policy. If Congress
should decide to open all HSCA records, however, CIA would
be hard put to keep its HSCA collection closed.

b. Opened: To open the HSCA collection would require the
permission of Congress. Indeed, CIA would presumably not
consider this option except in response to congressional
action or pressure, or in order not to be the last hold-out
in a Government-wide opening of Kennedy assassination
records. While opening the collection would disclose a
good deal of information that deserves continued protection
for privacy or national security reasons, a total release
would dramatically demonstrate CIA's new openness, and
rapidly reveal that these records contain nothing pointing
to a CIA role in the Kennedy assassination.

SECRET

10. Recommendation: I recommend that CIA transfer its entire HSCA collection (as defined and identified in this report) at its existing classification to the National Archives and Records Administration (NARA), for continuing declassification review by Archives staff, in accordance with the relevant laws, regulations and CIA guidelines. This transfer should be carried out under the auspices of CIA's Historical Review Program. To retire this HSCA collection to the National Archives offers some significant advantages:

a. It would get the collection off our hands. Retiring the records to the National Archives, which is by law the eventual repository for all permanent US Government records, should reduce public suspicion of a CIA cover-up. Such a transfer would not set a new precedent, since CIA has previously retired over 4000 cubic feet of Office of Strategic Services operational records to NARA, as well as all CIA records so far declassified under the Agency's Historical Review Program. Although CIA has not previously transferred classified records to NARA, the transfer of this HSCA collection, resulting from a congressional investigation, follows the special precedent of the classified CIA documents retired to NARA's vaults as part of the records of the Watergate and Iran-Contra investigations.

b. Transferring these HSCA records to the National Archives will protect their existing classification. The Departments of State and Defense have routinely retired classified records to NARA for years. In accordance with statutory guidelines, NARA must ensure the confidentiality of investigatory sources and the proper protection of personal privacy and national security information, including intelligence sources and methods. NARA would continue the court-ordered declassification review according to CIA guidelines. CIA can accelerate the declassification of this collection by funding review positions at NARA, as the Department of State and other agencies have done in the past. (Attachment C outlines declassification procedures for classified records retired to the National Archives.)

c. NARA's professional archivists will bring this collection under control (as they have done with the 4000 cubic feet of disorganized OSS records that CIA has retired since 1984), so that it can be usefully researched as it is declassified. Moreover, many of the records in this collection (especially photographs, carbon flimsies, and Thermofax) need expert preservation, which NARA is organized to provide.

SECRET

d. If Congress should eventually undertake to open this entire collection without regard to classification, the National Archives will be in a stronger position to protect its national security and privacy information than the CIA, whose motives would appear self-serving, if not sinister.

11. Action: If you wish to retire the Agency's House Select Committee on Assassinations collection to the National Archives, the following actions (from the offices noted) will be needed:

a. Request permission from Congress. (Office of Congressional Affairs)

b. Transfer responsibility for court-ordered FOIA declassification review from CIA to the National Archives. (Office of the General Counsel, with Information Management Staff, DO)

c. Prepare CIA guidelines for NARA's declassification review. (Office of Information Technology, DA)

d. Prepare the appropriate Historical Review Program documentation and NARA forms, and deliver the records. (Office of Information Technology, DA)

e. Announce the transfer jointly with Dr. Don Wilson, Archivist of the United States, and Congressman Louis Stokes. (Public Affairs Office)

/s/ J. Kenneth McDonald

J. Kenneth McDonald

Attachments

SECRET

9 May 1963

CHRONOLOGY OF DATA CONCERNING MR. CLEMARD JOSEPH CHARLES (HAITIAN)

29 April 1963	General Fitch advised Mrs. Matlack of potential source on Haiti, a Mr. Clemard Joseph Charles (Haitian). Referral was made by Major General Del Mar, Director, Inter-American Defense College. Del Mar had received information as a result of a letter from Mr. Joseph D. F. Dryer, West Palm Beach, Florida (business associate of Charles) to "Jackie" Del Mar, stepmother of General Del Mar.
30 April 1963	General Fitch authorized Mrs. Matlack direct contact with General Del Mar for purpose of developing background information and direct contact with Mr. Dryer. This action was necessary as Charles had failed to make telephone contact with Mrs. Matlack on 29 April. Colonel Samuel Kail, Deputy Chief, CAC, was requested to contact Dryer to get background information on Charles and establish a channel for contact by Mrs. Matlack. Charles had departed for New York City the evening of 29 April - address unknown to General Del Mar. Colonel Kail had previously known Dryer in Cuba, when Dryer opened Cuban element of his North Atlantic Kenef Int.
1 May 1963	Colonel Kail telephonically reported that Dryer stated Charles was President of Blauque Commercial D'Haiti, also Director of Dryer's firm in Haiti, as well as part or sole owner of some eight or more enterprises in Haiti. Dryer's estimate of Charles was that he was honest, highly regarded in Haiti and had a good potential to be President of Haiti. Dryer stated he had fully investigated Charles prior to making him Director of Dryer's Company and was impressed by his honesty and his adroitness in being in everybody's good graces in Haiti. Charles had always been apolitical until recently, when he developed ambition to be the President. Dryer said he was cousin of former Haitian Ambassador to U.S. Dorceous (sp?) Joseph Charles. Dryer telephoned Charles in New York City and introduced ~~Colonel Kail, who asked that~~ he talk to Mrs. Matlack.
May 1963	Coordination on Charles' case and invitation for CIA participation effected by Mrs. Matlack with Mr. Tony Czajkowski, CIA/OO at 0815 hours. Arrangement reached to send Captain Rogers, DIA Desk Officer, to New York to meet with Mr. James Balog, CIA New York Field Office representative, for interview with Charles at 1330 hours 2 May. Balog to use OACSI cover for

The next 4 pages (pp. 409-412) are from a document of the 902nd Military Intelligence Group. Inscom: U.S. Army Intelligence and Security Command – Chronology of data concerning Mr. Clémard Joseph Charles (Haitian).

interview. All available information on Charles was given
Czajkowski for transmittal to Balog and M/R on last-minute
information was given to Captain Rogers to pass to Balog
prior to interview. Interview lasted four hours. Charles
then introduced his business associate and traveling companion, Mr. George de Mohrenschildt and Mrs. de Mohrenschildt,
who stated he has a Haitian holding company which "cooperates
with Charles' Bank" in an effort to rework and create certain
industries and enterprises. He stated he has absolute confidence in the honesty and ability of Charles, whom he considers
potential leader in democratic Haiti. (de Mohrenschildt also
acts as interpreter for Charles, has been in and out of Haiti
for past two years, most recently left Haiti approximately 18
April, and plans to return to Haiti on 24 May, if feasible.)
Rogers returned night of 2 May 1963.

3 May 1963

Czajkowski reported Balog (CIA) very pleased with interview,
reporting results by TWX. Balog was continuing contact with
Charles. Czajkowski stated CIA had long range interest in
Charles. Mrs. Matlack agreed he looked like a CIA source,
but requested that as long as Charles remained in U.S., Army
continue their contact if intelligence interest so dictated.
Further, suggested that Kail could pick up contact in Miami
when Charles arrived there to stay with Dryer prior to return
to Haiti. Mrs. Matlack suggested further CIA contact, if
desired, in the Miami area through Colonel Kail with both
Dryer and Charles. Czajkowski said he would advise on this
action later.

6 May 1963

TWX reporting by Balog and Rogers (all advance copies) given
to Current Intelligence, DIA and Production Division, DIA.
Current Intelligence had several general questions to be.
asked of Charles. Approximately 1630 hours, Captain Rogers
had a long distance call from Mrs. de Mohrenschildt stating
they and Charles would meet him at 1200 hours 7 May and would
he get them a hotel. He transferred the call to Mrs. Matlack
as he unaware of any appointment. Mrs. Matlack was completely
in the dark but accepted the request for meeting and hotel
reservation. Mrs. de Mohrenschildt asked that she or Mr.
Charles have confirmation of arrangement NLT 1830 hours.
Mrs. Matlack immediately contacted Czajkowski for information.
Czajkowski was also in the dark. Mrs. Matlack recommended that
CIA make the arrangements in view of the color problem and their
long range interest. Czajkowski claimed inability to handle and
urged that she carry it through. Mrs. Matlack requested he determine the situation from Balog. Mrs. Matlack requested guidance through Intelligence Division, State, on setting up suitable hotel accommodations for Mr. Charles in view of color
problem. Upon obtaining advice from Deputy Chief of Protocol

402

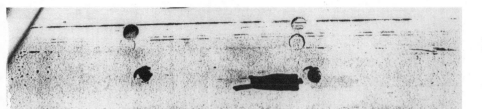

Mr. William Tonesk, Mrs. Matlack made two different and
tentative reservations - Mayflower and Albon Towers Hotels.
She then called Mr. Charles, who put Mrs. de Mohrenschildt
on the phone. Albon Towers was agreed upon, luncheon meeting reconfirmed for Williard Hotel lobby at 1200 hours on
7 May.

7 May 1963

0840 hours, Mr. Czajkowski left message that Mr. Balog informed him by phone 1930 hours 6 May, that CIA Ops people
are interested in seeing Charles and had arranged meeting
at Williard Hotel for 07/1200 hours May. Czajkowski was
still in the dark as to whether this was the same luncheon
date Mrs. Matlack had advised him of on 6 May, but indicated
CIA wanted Charles alone and he was to iron out any conflict.
He stated he tried to reach Mrs. Matlack after the call from
Balog. Mrs. Matlack immediately contacted Czajkowski stating
she felt she had to follow through for-the meeting for several
reasons -

    a. Mrs. Matlack had been established as Mr. Charles'
point of contact and he had expressed initial reluctance to
be "interviewed" unless she was present and/or vouched for
the personnel.

    b. He obviously believed the "someone" for the luncheon
appointment was Mrs. Matlack and, in view of her previous non-
appearance at the 2 May New York meeting, might be wary. Mrs.
Matlack recommended that she meet Charles, introduce the CIA
Ops man, have an excuse of prior commitment, and leave.
Czajkowski agreed and said he would call back the identity
(real or otherwise) of the interested CIA man. Czajkowski
called back stating DDP would not show if Mrs. Matlack were
there - they would make other arrangements. Mrs. Matlack
demanded that a CIA representative be there as she had absolutely nothing to see Mr. Charles about. After checking
out further, Czajkowski called saying he would be there as
a Dr. Professor of George Washington University. The meeting
took place. During luncheon it was obvious that Charles
looked to Mrs. Matlack as his point of contact. He asked
that she arrange for an appointment for him with Mr. Edmund
Wise, AID, and that she reproduce for him a letter of introduction to Senator Humphrey from a Mr. Wasserman, 40 Wall
Street, New York City. He invited her and Mr. Czajkowski
to dinner for 9 May. Both were non-committal. Immediately
upon returning to the office, Mrs. Matlack requested assistance from Intelligence Division, State, for contact with
Mr. Wise, AID. She was later advised that Mr. Abbuhl, Haitian
Desk Officer, Department of State, said Charles was "bad medicine", "a cheap two-bit crook", "unreliable", and "mixed up in
a variety of unsavory business deals". Mr. Zagorsky, State,

warned Mrs. Matlack - "as a friend" - not to sponsor
Charles in an appointment with AID. He added, however,
that Abbuhl was anxious to get more intelligence information
from Charles as Charles had "a pipeline to the Palace". At
approximately 1645 hours, Mr. Czajkowski left word that CIA
had no further interest in Charles.

8 May 1963

Mr. Czajkowski was unable to determine why CIA dropped Charles
and stated he had received no guidance as to course of action.
He agreed that it appears undesirable to drop him without eas-
ing out of the picture. This in reference to Mrs. Matlack, as
he did not feel he was involved. Colonel Roth, Operations
Branch, attempted to obtain from CIA/DDP the reason for their
abrupt dropping of Charles. Their position is that they were
interested only in listening and, after their contact of 7 May,
had satisfied their interest. This does not appear to be
realistic as their New York representative has been "listening"
since 2 May on a daily basis. CIA/DDP stated they had no reason
to drop him because of derogatory information. Colonel Roth is
requesting an SRI for further information. Colonel Reinhard
and Colonel Albro were briefed at 1400 hours and agreed that
in view of the urgent phone messages being left for Mrs. Matlack
by Charles, she should call him with the explanation that she
had not been able to set up an appointment with Mr. Wise due to
press of business. Mr. Charles was contacted by phone, he
accepted the explanation and her regrets for dinner tonight in
a gracious manner. He is on his way to Chicago and will call
Mrs. Matlack at 1730 hours on 13 May to determine if she has
an appointment for him with Mr. Wise or another appropriate
representative in AID. He has an appointment with Senator
Keating at 1600 hours, 14 May.

104

~~SECRET~~

Reports received from George de MOHRENSCHILDT

R. S. Travis
Support Branch
Contact Division, OO

CD/OO Case 43259

20 Apr 64

Paul Hartman
CI Staff
2-C-42 HQS
29

Attached are numbers of
reports received from
George de MOHRENSCHILDT.

APPROVED FOR RELEASE 1994
CIA HISTORICAL REVIEW PROGRAM

RST:wh

~~SECRET~~

The next 2 pages (pp. 413-414) are from a CIA document indicating reports received
from George de Mohrenschildt.

SECRET

Reports from George de Mohrenschildt: CD/OO Case 43259

00-B-3,094,376

00-A-3,094,428

00-B-3,094,429

00-A-3,094,857

00-A-3,094,858

00-A-3,095,095

00-B-3,095,096

00-A-3,095,671

00-A-3,103,330

00-B-3,107,668

SECRET

Documents

GEORGE DE MOHRENSCHILDT
PETROLEUM GEOLOGIST AND ENGINEER
DALLAS 1, TEXAS

Haitian Holding Company

Lllr uer- # 7
CO E. 3.260. 813

August 1, 1962

This Holding Company will cooperate with the Banque Commerciale d' Haiti, Port-Au-Prince, Mr. B. Cindine-Tardieu, adviser to the Bank, local Haitian and American enterprises in reworking and creating certain industries and enterprises in Faiti, West Indies.
   1. Personalities involved.
Charles, Clemard Joseph, President of the Banque Commerciale d'Haiti, the only native bank in existence. His references: Irving Trust Company, NYC., Mr. Joseph Welsh, International Division, Manufacturers Trust Company, NYC., Mr. James Greene, vice-president. American Express Company, NYC., Mr. Marshall S. Walker, vice-president overseas banking. Mr. Charles is also a sole representative in Haiti of General Electric Ltd. and of Siemens Schuckert Werke.
B. Cindine-Tardieu, well known in banking circles in France and England, came to Haiti in 1935 on behalf of an English Syndicate of Investment to organize export of precious wood and to build starch factories in the whole Carribean area. At a later date he built up the total export of bananas from Haiti to USA. Mr. Tardieu owns a chocolate paste factory in Port-Au-Prince and has considerable real estate holdings. He has actively contributed for years to the development of cooperatives in Haiti. He is adviser to the Banque Commerciale and is Mr. Charles' spiritual father; this sounds strange but such is the case.
Mr. Tardieu's original investment of $50,000 will be of real estate holdings evaluated by the Court for which he will obtain debentures payable out of the profits of the Holding Company only. He will not be the stockholder.
George de Mohrenschildt familiar with Haiti from many trips and several surveys made by him in the interior, has a tentative agreement with the Haitian Government (Minister of Finance) made through the Banque Commerciale d'Haiti for a complete geological a geophysical survey of the country for the amount of $181,670 and an additional aereal survey for $85,340 - for oil, gas and other minerals - and is apporting into the Holding Company all profits from this Survey and any eventual oil and/or mineral concessions.
   2. The Holding Company.
It will consist of 100 shares of $1,000 each. The money is to be spent on preparing projects, expenses connected with the projects, elaboration of agreements and guarantees in Washington and Haiti. It will bring native and American capital together, working thus along the lines of the Alliance for Progress. It will retain small participations in all industries and enterprises outlined below, will prepare detailed engineering and economic studies for each project and will supervise their completion. Each individual partner in the Holding Company will be given an opportunity to participate to a larger extent in any of the projects and the Banque Commerciale d'Haiti will have a participation of at least 10% in the capitalization of each project.
   3. The projects which the Banque Commerciale is considering at present and in which it will participate are the following: 1. Planting of tobacco on a larger scale and building of a cigar factory. 2. Development of cheap housing. 3. Building of a wharf. 4. Construction of a hydroelectric plant in conjunction with a completed dam (by Brown and Root), following electrification. 5. Lobster tail canning and freezing for export. 6. Plant for dessicated coconut and coconut candy. 7. Building and operation of a cotton wool plant. 8. Organization of a local Insurance Company. 9. Co-operation of a sisal plantation and factories already in existance. 10. The telephone system. 11. Refining of vegecable oil. 12. Manufacture of containers for domestic oil distribution. 13. Manufacture of margerine. 14. Participation in building of small sugar plants near the existing plantations. 15. Building of a casino. 16. Other projects, among them local making of films, which come to the attention of the Banque Commerciale d'Haiti.
   4. This is the first attempt of bringing together the local Bank, capital, American financing and US.Government help together. One should not forget the highly important geographical position of Haiti.

                    Sincerely *G. de Mohrenschildt*

CIA HISTORICAL REVIEW PROGRAM
RELEASE IN FULL
1999

1962 letter from de Mohrenschildt describing the holding company he planned to initiate in Haiti.

Dear Jackie:

Thank you very much for your last letter. Please excuse me for not answering it sooner but I was away on a trip and have only just returned. One of the gentlemen of whom I spoke to you is now in this country and will be travelling to Washington next week. His name is Mr. Leonard Joseph Charles. I have given Mr. Charles your address and telephone number in order for him to make an appointment. He is travelling with a business associate whom I understand is somehow associated with Vice President Johnson. Mr. Charles has an appointment with Mr. Johnson. Mr. Charles is one of the very few businessmen in his country who has had the confidence of the last several Presidents and, at the same time, resisted the temptation to acquire wealth and position by accepting political appointments. I also believe he has kept his assets at home, unlike many. However, as his country is now in a potentially dangerous period he would like to discuss this situation with well informed U.S. sources. Mr. Charles is very cognizant of the present situation and, as he intends to continue in business, he does not wish to run any unnecessary risks.

Although Mr. Charles is not a member of the Government, he is very active in the Chamber of Commerce, local business affairs, and President of the Banke Commerciale (phonetic spelling) and I believe is in President Duvalier's favor. 124

The next 2 pages (pp. 416-417) are a letter from Joseph F. Dryer, Jr. to Cooksey, Jackie. Document of the 902nd Military Intelligence Group (INSCOM/CSF) on the subject of Clémard Joseph Charles.

Thank you again for your greatly appreciated interest. I am sure
that after talking with Mr. Charles you will do what you can to steer him
in the right direction.

With warmest regards and many thanks for that last flying trip to
the airport.

Joe

Above from Mr. Joseph F. Dyer, Jr — North Atlantic Kennels
dictated over telephone by Gen. del Mar   109 Lake View Ave
to Gen. Fitch (Mrs. Cooksey)   West Palm Beach,
                                                  Fla.

125

417

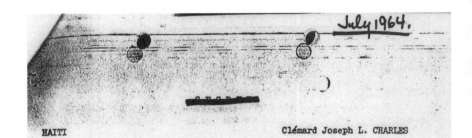

July 1964.

HAITI   Clémard Joseph L. CHARLES

President and General Manager,
Commercial Bank of Haiti

OFFICE OF
CENTRAL REFERENCE

BIOGRAPHIC
REGISTER

President and general manager of the
Commercial Bank of Haiti, Clémard Joseph Charles
is a controversial businessman with political
ambitions and has been known as a confidant of
President François Duvalier. One well-informed
high US official reported in early 1963 that
Charles, a "slippery character," was active on
the Haitian scene; nevertheless, considerable
doubt existed at that time concerning his
importance or political significance, despite
the fact that he appeared to have "a line into
the Palace" and was persona grata with the President. A few months after
this estimate was made, Charles conversed with a US Embassy official.
Throughout their talk he showed an obvious desire to demonstrate his total
political disinterest in the past while simultaneously hinting that he
could become a political figure in the near future. He made guarded
statements concerning the Duvalier regime, unhesitatingly giving the
impression that he was the President's friend, both through desire and
through necessity, but that he definitely did not agree with some of the
government's policies. (He alleged that Duvalier had some years earlier
offered him the commercial portfolio in the Haitian cabinet, but said that
he had declined it.) He attributed his support of the current government
to the fact that it would be dangerous for a Haitian to withhold it. The
following month (May 1963), on a business trip to the United States,
Charles told a former US journalist that he was in a position to become
head of a provisional government after Duvalier was removed from the
scene. He expressed a belief that the President was ready to institute
a reign of terror and that he was willing to accept Soviet bloc aid. In
the opinion of the journalist, Charles firmly believed that this was the
last chance for the United States to help establish a democratic Haiti,
friendly toward the United States, and save the country from a Castro-type
Communist takeover. Charles said that although he was on good terms
with Duvalier; he now felt that the President had gone crazy and must be
stopped before he liquidated the opposition. He talked freely of his wide
range of support (peasants; forcibly retired, anti-Duvalier army officers;
intellectuals; journalists; and businessmen) and of the prominent
individuals who were anti-Duvalier and ready to back "my government."
He added that if he did not become Provisional President he would be
satisfied with the post of Secretary of Finance and Economic Affairs.
In addition to his having reached the constitutional age requirement for
President (40), Charles gave as another qualification the fact that he was
of "100 per cent black origin," noting that only those in this category
could win the presidency.

**The next 3 pages (pp. 418-420) are from the Central Intelligence Agency, Office of
Central Reference, Biographic Register: CLÉMARD Joseph L. Charles.**

Clémard Joseph L. CHARLES (Cont)

Charles said that if he were to be President he would need the "moral and economic help of the US Government and people" to transform Haiti into a true and prosperous democracy. He noted that he would need about a year to put into effect his "plan for the economic and social development of Haiti," which included the following points: creation of a balanced economy adapted to Haitian conditions; development of industry and exploitation of natural resources; and modernization of agriculture. He said that he would like to present this plan to US officials for their consideration.

In connection with Charles' business interests, a prominent and knowledgeable Haitian reported in March 1963 that the BCH was in bad shape, "holding a worthless portfolio made up of notes guaranteed by political figures," and that Charles himself was dishonest; for example, he had approved a loan for $14,000 on his daughter's signature alone. Furthermore, Charles was alleged by this same source to know nothing about banking and to be a favorite of President Duvalier. This estimate was confirmed by one US official who added that Charles was more accurately described as a "promoter" than as a businessman and that he was a partner in the BCH rather than the sole owner. According to statements which Charles made in conversation with a US Embassy official in April 1963, he did start the bank's operations in partnership with four US citizens, at least one of whom had a lengthy criminal record involving a variety of jail sentences and convictions. Charles claimed to have paid off his partners with $150,000. He emphasized that he owed nothing to anyone and that although he had been slow in making payments, he enjoyed a spotless record. In this conversation and others Charles stated that he had invested approximately $500,000 in various Haitian business enterprises; as a patriot, he has said, he would under no circumstances remove this money from Haiti. Fairly recently he has become involved in the operation of a sisal plantation at Montrouis, on land owned by the Haitian-American Society for Agricultural Development (SHADA).

Charles endeavors to attract US venture capital for various Haitian projects and claims to be thoroughly pro-United States. He allegedly is an honorary citizen of Long Beach, Long Island, New York, having promoted a "sister city" relationship between that town and Port-au-Prince; in 1962 he reportedly received the key to New York City. He has visited the United States, the United Kingdom and Western Europe many times on business trips. In July 1964 Charles traveled to Mexico and the United States, ostensibly to discuss establishment of a sisal cordage factory in Haiti, but in reality to obtain 30 surplus T-28 trainer aircraft. Charles subsequently was reported to be attempting to purchase 24 US surplus naval craft for Haiti's armed forces. The United States, according to the New York Times, is refusing to license exports of military equipment to Haiti on the ground that she is not participating in a regular assistance program. Equally important, however, is believed to be the Johnson

Clémard Joseph L. CHARLES
(Cont)

A dark Negro about 5 feet 7 inches tall, Clémard Joseph L. Charles was born at Gonaives, Haiti, on 21 April 1923; according to Charles himself, his father was a professor and his mother was a "simple peasant." Charles received his primary education at a parochial school and graduated from the Lycée Geffrard in 1939. According to his own account, during his early career Charles taught in rural Haitian schools, and worked as a pathologist, an upholsterer, a time-keeper, a plantation supervisor and a free-lance journalist. In 1947 he was appointed comptroller general of the Haitian Southern Banana Industry and in 1948 he became its general agent. The following year he established himself as a manufacturer's representative and created his own export-import business. He later said that his ventures into the plantain (banana) business and into connections with the General Telephone Company of Coventry, England, were both unsuccessful due to political interferences. His success story, according to a US official, "apparently hinges on the fact that he feels he has achieved stature in the community both socially and politically." Charles states that he created the BCH in 1960 and is now its sole owner. He is also full or part owner of several other industrial and commercial enterprises in Haiti and is sole representative in his country of the General Electric Company, Ltd., of London, England, and of Siemens Schuckert Werke, Germany.

Charles is vice president of the Haitian Chamber of Commerce and also belongs to several other commercial and civic organizations, including the Industrial Association of New York. He and his wife, Sophie, have one adopted son.

JBL:ysb   July 1964

... ONLY. TO BE
... OF ACTION.

ESSAGE

DEPARTMENT OF THE AR
STAFF COMMUNICATIONS DIVISION

ACTION COPY

This record copy will be
disposed of in accordance
with AAIN

PRIORITY
P 120329Z MAY 63

FM USARMA PORT AU PRINCE

TO RUEPCR/DEPTAR FOR ACSI

EXCLUSIVE Postponement
Section 6(3)

EXCLUSIVE NO FOREIGN DISSEM C-31 FROM OUSARMA HAITI SGD WARREN
EXCLUSIVE FOR ALBRO. KNELT (**↔**) REF DA 927919

1. (**✷**) CHARLES IS PRES COMMERCIAL BANK OF HAITI WHICH RATED
POOR THIRD AMOUNG FOUR BANKS PORT AU PRINCE. BORN ▆▆▆▆▆▆▆ OF ▆ [D]
PEASANT PARENTS, WORKED ODD JOBS AFTER HIGH SCHOOL GRADUATION, 1939.
1947 TO 1952 BUSINESS ACTIVITIES HAITI INCLUDING ESTABLISHMENT OWN
EXPORT-IMPORT CONCERN. 1953 TRAVELED LONDON MEMBER GOH ECONOMIC
COMMISSION. 1954 NEGOTIATED CONTRACT FOR GOH WITH GENERAL ELECTRIC
CO LTD COVENTRY, ENGLAND, FOR RENOVATION TELEPHONE SYSTEM, HAITI.
CONTRACT SUBSEQUENTLY FELL THRU. 1957 MEMBER GOH MISSION TO INTERNAT
IONAL CONFERENCE BRUSSELS. 1960 CREATED COMMERCIAL BANK. HAS ENTERE
RECENTLY INTO THREE-WAY CONTRACT BETWEEN DE MOHRENSHILDT--GOH--HIS
TANK FOR OIL AND NATURAL GAS EXPLORATION HAITI. REPORTED AS CLOSE
FRIEND DR ELMER LAUGHLIN AMERICAN ADVISOR DUVALIER. ALTHOUGH
OFFICIAL BALANCE SHEET OF HIS BANK SHOWS FAIRLY HEALTHY CONDITION
PRESIDENT OF NATIONAL BANK OF HAITI, ANTONIO ANDRE, TOLD EMBASSY
OFFICER RECENTLY THAT CHARLES DISHONEST, KNEW NOTHING OF BANKING,
AND THAT ANDRE COULD FORECLOSE CHARLES' BANK BUT PRESIDENT DUVALIER
HAD ASKED HIM TO AVOID SCANDAL. COMMENT: FORMER EMBASSY DCM PHIL
WILLIAMS ONCE STATED CHARLES COMMON CROOK AND SHOULD BE AVOIDED.
DO NOT BELIEVE HE THAT BAD, BUT NEAR CERTAIN HE OPORTUNIST AND
MOTIVES THIS APPROACH DA COULD BE RELATED HIS PERSONAL STATURE
HAITI. ONE GOOD GUESS BEING IN STATES DURING CURRENT CRISIS
FRIGHTENED HIM INTO MAKING APPROACH AS MEANS PERSONALLY BENEFIR
HERE WHEN CHANGE OCCURS. WOULD URGE INFORMATION PROVIDED BE EV-
ALUATED WITH DUE ALLOWANCE FOR POSSIBLE SELF SERVING MOTIVES.
2. (**✷**) DE MORENSHILDT SPENT ONLY SHORT TIME HAITI ARRANGING
OIL BUSINESS DEAL THEREFORE NOT WELL KNOWN. INTERVIEW WITH EMBASSY
OFFICER BLAQUE REVALS HE KNEW DE M IN NEW YORK PRIOR WW 11. LATTER'S
AUNT WAS PROMINENT NY SOCIAL FIGURE. BLACQU STATES DE M CAME FROM
VERY PROMINENT BALTIC FAMILY HIGH IN DIPLOMATIC AND MILITARY CIRCLES
DURING TZARIST REGIME. BLAQUE OUT OF CONTACT WITH DE M SINCE BEFORE
W11 AND UNTIL RECENTLY WHEN DE M ARRIVED HAITI. BLAQUE CAN NOT
REPEAT NOT VOUCH FOR CHARACTER, ETC, BUT STATES NO REPEAT NO REASON
TO SUSPECT HIM OF DISHONESTY. BLAQUE ADVISED DE M THAT FORTHCOMING

USAFSG/ 5692/c8
097
DA IN 46459

0000

The next 2 pages (pp. 421-422) are from the 902 Military Intelligence Group – From:
USARMA Port Au Prince To: Deptar for ACSI [Dorothe Matlack]. May 1,1963.

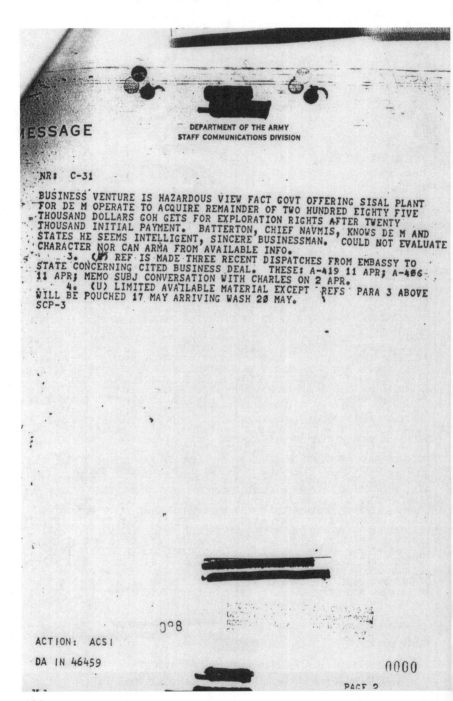

ESSAGE

DEPARTMENT OF THE ARMY
STAFF COMMUNICATIONS DIVISION

NR: C-31

BUSINESS VENTURE IS HAZARDOUS VIEW FACT GOVT OFFERING SISAL PLANT
FOR DE M OPERATE TO ACQUIRE REMAINDER OF TWO HUNDRED EIGHTY FIVE
THOUSAND DOLLARS GOH GETS FOR EXPLORATION RIGHTS AFTER TWENTY
THOUSAND INITIAL PAYMENT. BATTERTON, CHIEF NAVMIS, KNOWS DE M AND
STATES HE SEEMS INTELLIGENT, SINCERE BUSINESSMAN. COULD NOT EVALUATE
CHARACTER NOR CAN ARMA FROM AVAILABLE INFO.
    3. (U) REF IS MADE THREE RECENT DISPATCHES FROM EMBASSY TO
STATE CONCERNING CITED BUSINESS DEAL. THESE: A-419 11 APR; A-406
11 APR; MEMO SUBJ CONVERSATION WITH CHARLES ON 2 APR.
    4. (U) LIMITED AVAILABLE MATERIAL EXCEPT REFS PARA 3 ABOVE
WILL BE POUCHED 17 MAY ARRIVING WASH 20 MAY.
SCP-3

008

ACTION: ACSI

DA IN 46459

0000

PAGE 2

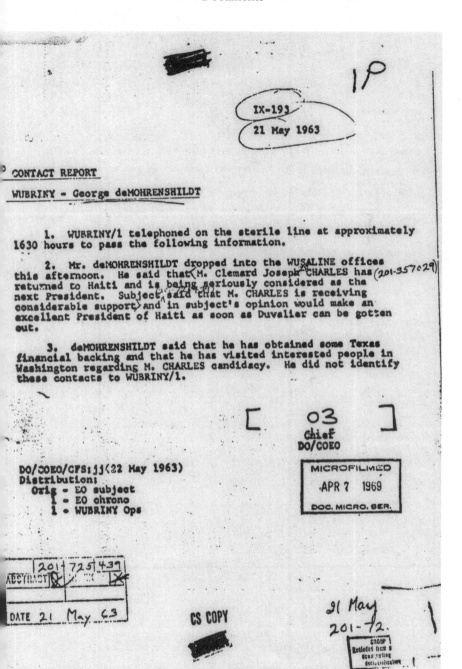

IX-193
21 May 1963

CONTACT REPORT

WUBRINY - George deMOHRENSHILDT

1. WUBRINY/1 telephoned on the sterile line at approximately 1630 hours to pass the following information.

2. Mr. deMOHRENSHILDT dropped into the WUSALINE offices this afternoon. He said that M. Clemard Joseph CHARLES has (201-357029) returned to Haiti and is being seriously considered as the next President. Subject said that M. CHARLES is receiving considerable support and in subject's opinion would make an excellent President of Haiti as soon as Duvalier can be gotten out.

3. deMOHRENSHILDT said that he has obtained some Texas financial backing and that he has visited interested people in Washington regarding M. CHARLES candidacy. He did not identify these contacts to WUBRINY/1.

[03   ]
Chief
DO/COEO

DO/COEO/CFS:jj(22 May 1963)
Distribution:
    Orig - EO subject
       1 - EO chrono
       1 - WUBRINY Ops

MICROFILMED
APR 7 1969
DOC. MICRO. SER.

201 725 439
ABSTRACT

DATE 21 May 63

CS COPY

21 May
201-72.

GROUP
Excluded from 8
downgrading
declassification

CIA Contact Report. WUBRINY-George M de Mohrenschildt. 21 May 1963. Ix-193.

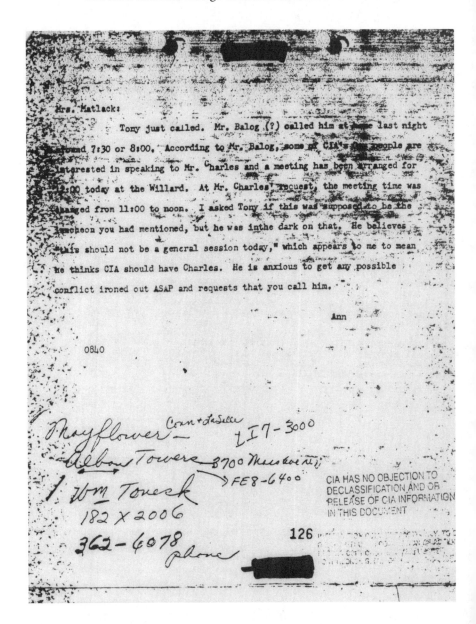

Mrs. Matlack:

Tony just called. Mr. Balog (?) called him at ▓▓▓ last night around 7:30 or 8:00. According to Mr. Balog, some of CIA's ▓▓ people are interested in speaking to Mr. Charles and a meeting has been arranged for 12:00 today at the Willard. At Mr. Charles' request, the meeting time was changed from 11:00 to noon. I asked Tony if this was supposed to be the luncheon you had mentioned, but he was in the dark on that. He believes "this should not be a general session today," which appears to me to mean he thinks CIA should have Charles. He is anxious to get any possible conflict ironed out ASAP and requests that you call him.

Ann

0840

Mayflower — Conn + LaSalle $LI7-3000$

Albon Towers — 3700 Mass Ave N,

Wm Toneck $FE8-6400$

182 X 2006

362-6078 *phone*

126

CIA HAS NO OBJECTION TO DECLASSIFICATION AND OR RELEASE OF CIA INFORMATION IN THIS DOCUMENT

902nd Military Intelligence Group – Message From Dorothe Matlack indicating CIA interest in Clémard Joseph Charles.

Documents

DISPATCH

TO: Chief, KUDESK

INFO: Chief, WH Division
Chief, EE Division

FROM: Chief of Station, [16-8]

SUBJECT: George de MOHRENSCHILDT's Contacts with Polish Commercial Delegation in Port-au-Prince.

Reference: [33]-1419, dated 6 October 1964

1. Following information concerning George de MOHRENSCHILDT's contacts with the Polish Commercial Delegation in Port-au-Prince was provided by KWIMOR-1. This report covers the period 16 September to 31 December 1964. de MOHRENSCHILDT's past contact with the delegation has been reported in reference and several other reports.

2. Station notes that George de MOHRENSCHILDT or his wife Jeanne visited the delegation but once during the Polish Commercial Attache, Wlodzimiers GALICKI's (201-314948), absence from Port-au-Prince. This one occasion was on 27 October, two days before GALICKI and his family returned to Port-au-Prince. On that one visit, Mr. de MOHRENSCHILDT was accompanied by an unidentified American, De MOHRENSCHILDT, the American, and the acting Commercial Attache, Caslair SALACINSKI, (201-752851), stood together in the courtyard for about half an hour. The American was short, fat with greying hair.

3. 30 October: (Day after GALICKI's return to Port-au-Prince.) Mrs. de MOHRENSCHILDT visit the GALICKI's for an hour during the day. Mr. and Mrs. de MOHRENSCHILDT have dinner with GALICKI's later that evening.

   3 November: GALICKI's have dinner at de MOHRENSCHILDT's.

   5 November: Mr. and Mrs. de MOHRENSCHILDT stop by for one hour and a half. They drink and talk with GALICKI's.

   10 November: Mr. and Mrs. de MOHRENSCHILDT and unknown American stop by for an hour. All speak Polish.

Distribution:
2-Chief, KUDESK
2-Chief, WH Division
2-Chief, EE Division

201-725439

29 January 1965

SECRET   201-725439   [33] 1506   OPS CONTACTS
                                                  FOL CA

CIA SPECIAL COLLECTIONS
RELEASE AS SANITIZED

Declassified and Approved for Release
by the Central Intelligence Agency
Date: 2/2003

The next 2 pages (pp. 425-426) are CIA surveillance documents of George de Mohrenschildt in Haiti: 01/29/1965

CONTINUATION OF DISPATCH [22]

12 November: Mr. and Mrs. de MOHRENSCHILDT stay by office but GALICKI's are out so they leave.

14 November: Mr. and Mrs. de MOHRENSCHILDT have dinner with GALICKI's. Stay for 1½ hours.

16 November: Mr. and Mrs. de MOHRENSCHILDT have dinner with GALICKI's. Stay for two hours.

19 November: Mr. and Mrs. de MOHRENSCHILDT have dinner with GALICKI's to celebrate Mrs. GALICKI's birthday. Mr. and Mrs. SALAZINSKI also present.

24 November: Mr. and Mrs. de MOHRENSCHILDT have dinner with GALICKI's. Stay for 2½ hours.

29 November: Mr. de MOHRENSCHILDT brings unknown woman to GALICKI's at eight o'clock in the morning. They have tea for ½ hour and leave.

1 December: Mr. de MOHRENSCHILDT and GALICKI chat for ½ hour.

3 December: Mr. and Mrs. de MOHRENSCHILDT have dinner with GALICKI's.

7 December: Mr. and Mrs. de MOHRENSCHILDT arrive with unknown woman, have tea and chat for two hours. Woman speaks French, is white, tall thin, long hair and long face.

8 December: Mr. and Mrs. de MOHRENSCHILDT dine with GALICKI's. Stay for 3/4 hour.

15 December: Mr. and Mrs. de MOHRENSCHILDT have two o'clock lunch with GALICKIs. Stay 3/4 hour.

19 December: Mr. and Mrs. de MOHRENSCHILDT have rum, tea and cakes with GALICKIs. Stay 1½ hours.

21 December: Mr. and Mrs. George de MOHRENSCHILDT have tea and drinks with GALICKIs. Stay 1½ hours.

24 December: Mr. de MOHRENSCHILDT bring an American couple with two daughters to see GALICKI. Both husband and wife are tall and thin. Party stays for 15 minutes.

26 December: Mr. de MOHRENSCHILDT brings two American men and a baby all of them wearing bathing suits. One of the men is bald, the other has short hair. Party leaves without GALICKIs after 10 minute stay.

29 December: Mr. and Mrs. de MOHRENSCHILDT stop by with friends and stay for 3/4 hour.

4. EVMINOR-1 cannot identify by name the Americans with whom the de MOHRENSCHILDT's have frequent contact and may introduce to GALICKI. However, _____. The identity of the two American men who visited GALICKI on 26 December maybe associated with the "Sam" reported in [22]-1463. The unknown woman noted on 7 December maybe the "Alex" noted [22]-1461 paragraph k. The unknown woman visitor of 29 November maybe Verna SOMOFF noted in [22]-1449. According to Pan American manifests Miss SOMOFF left Port-au-Prince at about 9 pm on the 29th of December.

Joseph G. HENSON

FORM 83a — USE PREVIOUS EDITION.

CLASSIFICATION SECRET   ☐ CONTINUED   PAGE NO. 2

BANQUE COMMERCIALE D'HAITI

SOCIETE ANONYME DE BANQUE

AU CAPITAL AUTORISE DE UN MILLION DEUX CENT CINQUANTE MILLE GOURDES

ADRESSE TELEGRAPHIQUE
COMBANK

P. O. BOX 1007

CLÉMARD JOSEPH CHARLES
PRESIDENT ET DIRECTEUR

SIEGE SOCIAL ET BUREAU PRINCIPAL
RUE DU CENTRE
PORT-AU-PRINCE, HAITI

PORT-AU-PRINCE June 6, 1967

REFERENCE

Miss D. K. Matlack
CACSI/DA
Washington 25, D.C.

Dear Miss Matlack:

       May I recall the kind-reception you
gave me in May 1963, when I was in Washington, also
your courtesy in recommending me the Alban Towers
Hotel, 3700 Massachusetts Avenue, where I lodged in
Room 522. You will remember the conversation I had
with you regarding the future of my country, and the
hope I expressed that the assistance of the U. S.
would not fail us.

       I have earnestly worked since in
order that Haiti may be relieved from the tyranny
and misery in which has been inconsiderately thrown,
and have succeeded in securing the sympathy and support of a great majority of the populations all over
the Republic, including religious people, businessmen,
professionals, intellectuals, etc. A plan has been
prepared and will be executed by a military man who
has with him most of the officers in the Army. These
people are ready and eager to begin operations and
are only awaiting word from me.

       I would have already given them
order to strike, through the Chief who is the only
one in contact with me, were it not for my apprehens-
ion that the turmoil that will necessarily follow
might serve Castro's plan to introduce communist agitators in the country. I also have reason to wonder
about Balaguer's position on account of his friendly
feelings for Duvalier. Therefore, before going any
further, I feel that it would be wise for me to have
the U.S. assurance that these two forces will be
properly neutralized, and I am requesting your kind
cooperation so that this assurance may be given to me.

The next 2 pages (pp. 427-428) are from the 902nd Military Intelligence Group, a letter from Clémard Joseph Charles to D. K. Matlack. 06/06/67.

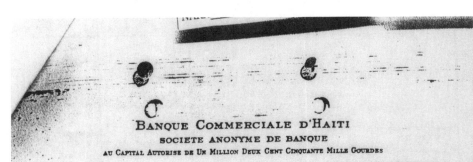

BANQUE COMMERCIALE D'HAITI
SOCIETE ANONYME DE BANQUE
AU CAPITAL AUTORISE DE UN MILLION DEUX CENT CINQUANTE MILLE GOURDES

ADRESSE TELEGRAPHIQUE
COMBANK

P. O. BOX 1007

CLÉMARD JOSEPH CHARLES
PRÉSIDENT ET DIRECTEUR

SIEGE SOCIAL ET BUREAU PRINCIPAL
RUE DU CENTRE
PORT-AU-PRINCE, HAITI

PORT-AU-PRINCE June 6, 67.

REFERENCE

Page 2.-

I have requested my friend and associate in New York, Mr. Louis A. Brun, to turn personally this letter over to you, also to give you all the details that it would not be proper for me to write. You may feel free to talk at length with Mr. Brun on all matters relating to my project. You will also be kind to give him any reply you may have for me, which he will keep in New York until my next visit to the U. S. shortly.

Permit me to thank you in advance for your contribution to the relief of my country, and to assure you that your cooperation will ever live in my memory.

Respectfully yours,

Clémard JOSEPH CHARLES.-

069

Documents

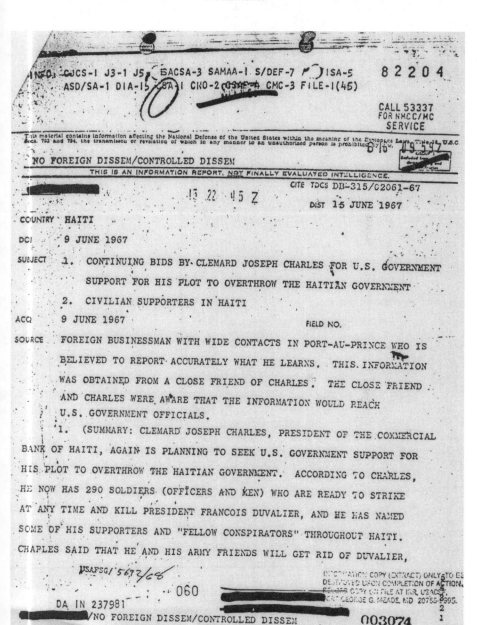

INFO: CJCS-1 J3-1 J5, SACSA-3 SAMAA-1 S/DEF-7 ISA-5
ASD/SA-1 DIA-15 8A-1 CNO-2 CMC-3 FILE-1(45)

82204

CALL 53337
FOR NMCC/MC
SERVICE

This material contains information affecting the National Defense of the United States within the meaning of the Espionage Laws, Title 18, U.S.C. Secs. 793 and 794, the transmission or revelation of which in any manner to an unauthorized person is prohibited by law.

NO FOREIGN DISSEM/CONTROLLED DISSEM

THIS IS AN INFORMATION REPORT, NOT FINALLY EVALUATED INTELLIGENCE.

CITE TDCS DB-315/02061-67

15 22 45 Z

DIST 15 JUNE 1967

COUNTRY HAITI

DCI   9 JUNE 1967

SUBJECT 1. CONTINUING BIDS BY CLEMARD JOSEPH CHARLES FOR U.S. GOVERNMENT
             SUPPORT FOR HIS PLOT TO OVERTHROW THE HAITIAN GOVERNMENT
         2. CIVILIAN SUPPORTERS IN HAITI

ACQ   9 JUNE 1967   FIELD NO.

SOURCE   FOREIGN BUSINESSMAN WITH WIDE CONTACTS IN PORT-AU-PRINCE WHO IS
         BELIEVED TO REPORT ACCURATELY WHAT HE LEARNS. THIS INFORMATION
         WAS OBTAINED FROM A CLOSE FRIEND OF CHARLES. THE CLOSE FRIEND
         AND CHARLES WERE AWARE THAT THE INFORMATION WOULD REACH
         U.S. GOVERNMENT OFFICIALS.

         1. (SUMMARY: CLEMARD JOSEPH CHARLES, PRESIDENT OF THE COMMERCIAL
BANK OF HAITI, AGAIN IS PLANNING TO SEEK U.S. GOVERNMENT SUPPORT FOR
HIS PLOT TO OVERTHROW THE HAITIAN GOVERNMENT. ACCORDING TO CHARLES,
HE NOW HAS 290 SOLDIERS (OFFICERS AND MEN) WHO ARE READY TO STRIKE
AT ANY TIME AND KILL PRESIDENT FRANCOIS DUVALIER, AND HE HAS NAMED
SOME OF HIS SUPPORTERS AND "FELLOW CONSPIRATORS" THROUGHOUT HAITI.
CHARLES SAID THAT HE AND HIS ARMY FRIENDS WILL GET RID OF DUVALIER,

USAFSG/5672/68

060

DA IN 237981

INFORMATION COPY (EXTRACT) ONLY, TO BE
DESTROYED UPON COMPLETION OF ACTION.
RECORD COPY ON FILE AT HR, USACS,
CRT GEORGE G. MEADE, MD 20755-8295.

/NO FOREIGN DISSEM/CONTROLLED DISSEM

003074

2
1

(classification)   (dissem controls)

The first page of a seven-page document from the 902nd Military Intelligence Group. Information Report. 06/15/67. Subjects: Charles, CLÉMARD J, US Government support for plot to overthrow the Haitian government.

THE NATIONAL ARCHIVES

NARA VHK _____ DATE 3-6·06

SURELL BRADY
CIA FILE REVIEW
8/24/78

Central Intelligence Agency
has no Objection to Release
Date: 2003

DOROTHE K. MATLACK

DDO

THIRD AGENCY DOC:

    DEPT. OF ARMY DOC

    12 AUG 1955

    MEMO FOR: DIR, CIA, FM: COLLECTION D·V, G-2

    SUBJ: INTERAGENCY DEFECTOR COMM

    CLASS: SECRET

    REFER TO G2-CDDA

[ENTIRE FILE CONSISTED OF CABLES AND MEMOS 1951, 1952
ABOUT CONDITIONS IN CHILE AND POLISH DEFECTOR
TO CHILE, BOROWIEZ]

The next 4 pages (pp. 430-433) are from HSCA researcher Surrell Brady's notes from
CIA files reporting on CLÉMARD Joseph Charles' CIA handler, Francis D. Rachfield indicating that CIA retained an interest in Charles in 1967. CIA document made available
to HSCA: 08/24/78

8/24/18

'N

CLEMARD JOSEPH CHARLES

DDO   201-357 029

VOL. II   FEB. 1966 - DEC. 1968

[FIRST DOC ON BOTTOM IS DATED 2/2/67]

INS DOC 5/3/67
    ENTERED MIAMI 4/30/67
    US ADDRESS WALDORF ASTORIA, NYC
    DOB 4/21/23 CONAIVES, HAITI

MESSAGE 3/15/67
    CHARLES ASKED RACHFIELD IF POSSIBLE TO PASS A
    MSG OUT OF CHANNELS DIRECTLY TO CHIEF LNPURE

    HE VERY PRO-WOLADY
    WELL KNOWN HIGH LEVELS LNHARP

MESSAGE 3/22/67
    SEE BIOGRAPHIC TRACES REGISTER REPORT OF JULY 1964 FOR
    SUMMARY EMBASSY TRACES

SUMMARY OF LNPURE TRACES ON CLEMARD JOSEPH CHARLES

- CIALE D'HAITE (CN) IN 1960 AND IS NOW SOLE OWNER
BY HIS OWN ACCT HE TAUGHT IN RURAL SCHOOLS,
WORKED AS PATHOLOGIST, UPHOLSTERER, TIME-KEEPER,
PLANTATION SUPERVISOR + FREE LANCE JOURNALIST

ONE ORIG PARTNER OF BANK WAS GERALD P. CONNOLLY,
ALLEGEDLY FROM CHICAGO; CRIM. RECORD +
SENTENCES + CONVICTIONS

IS SOLE REP IN HAITI OF GEN. ELEC CO., LTD, LONDON
AND SIEMENS SCHUKERT WERKE, GERMANY
DIR. OF PORT CONCESSION + TOOK OVER OIL REFINERY
CONCESSION

IN JULY 1964 CHARLES TRAVELLED TO MEXICO AND THE
US, OSTENSIBLY TO DISCUSS EST. OF A SISAL CORDAGE
FACTORY IN HAITI, BUT IN REALITY TO OBTAIN 30
SURPLUS T-28 TRAINER AIRCRAFT. C. SUBSEQUENTLY
WAS REPORTED TO BE ATTEMPTING TO PURCHASE
24 US SURPLUS NAVAL CRAFT FOR HAITI'S ARMED
FORCES

FRANCIS D. RACHFIELD = MATTHEW N. CHUBB
CASE OFFICER

432

CONFIDENTIAL TELETYPE 5/20/68

CHARLES USES PSEUDONYM "JACOBY" IN HIS CONFI-
DENTIAL CORRESPONDENCE

MEMO 6/12/67

FROM: KENNETH T. RIPLEY
ASSESSMENT OF CLEMARD JOSEPH CHARLES

HE HAS PLAYED DUVALIER'S GAME TO THE HILT, OFTEN
ENTRUSTED W/ MISSIONS ABROAD WHICH WERE, IN
EFFECT CONTRARY TO US GOVT. INTERESTS. (HE PLAYED
A PRINCIPAL ROLE IN THE ATTEMPT TO SMUGGLE
B-26 AIRCRAFT OUT OF THE US FOR DUVALIER'S USE.
IN THAT CONNECTION HE WENT TO ARIZONA TO TRY
TO PURCHASE US AIR FORCE SURPLUS PLANES, USING
US CITIZENS OF SUSPICIOUS NATURE AS HIS AGENTS.)

charles

LAW OFFICES
FENSTERWALD & ASSOCIATES
SUITE 900, TWIN TOWERS BLDG.
1000 WILSON BOULEVARD
ARLINGTON, VIRGINIA 22209

(703) 276-9297

BERNARD FENSTERWALD, JR.
BERNARD FENSTERWALD, III
JAMES H. LESAR (D.C. ONLY)

GORDON P. HARRISON (D.C. ONLY)
OF COUNSEL

NEW YORK ASSOCIATES
BASS, ULLMAN & LUSTIGMAN
747 THIRD AVENUE
NEW YORK, NEW YORK 10017

(212) 751-9494

June 30, 1983

MEMORANDUM

TO: Gary Shaw   FROM: Bernard Fensterwald, Jr.
    Mary Ferrell

RE: Clemard Joseph Charles

Today I had a meeting at the Pentagon with representatives of both DIA and
Army Intelligence. The meeting was arranged by Nate Dodell, the Assistant
U.S. Attorney dealing with the Shaw/Allen FOIA cases. By far the most
knowledgeable government person was Mr. Roger Pierce of Army Intelligence,
who had been on active duty with Army Intelligence for 20-odd years and
is now a civilian with Army Intelligence. It is quite obvious that he is
the Department of the Army's "man" with respect to the Kennedy assassination.
He was not only very knowledgeable about Charles and his activities, but had
known Richard Nagell and his activities quite well, as well as the activities
of Tommy Davis.

To get to the easy part first, there were only three DIA records with respect
to Charles. Before today's meeting, DIA decided in effect to declassify them
and make them available, without revealing the forms on which they existed.
The three documents are summarized in DIA's memorandum of June 30, 1983,
attached hereto. The most interesting thing to note is that the first two
documents are from the Army Attache in Haiti and he got Charles' name all
mixed up. Despite that Army Intelligence was able to locate information
on Charles. Presuming that I can get nothing further from DIA, I agreed to
dismiss one count in the lawsuit.

Much more interesting was the conversation with Pierce about 9 Army Intelligence
records (see attached affidavit of General Odom). We went through an "oral
Vaughn" with respect to these documents. And during this conversation I
learned the following about Charles.

1. Charles is now deceased. He died in Haiti in 1981. His death was under
    "bizarre circumstances" but the details, according to Pierce, are unknown
    to the U.S. Government. Apparently the government has made a number of
    inquiries, but the Haitian Government will not divulge the details.
    We do know that the death was violent.

2. Charles and George de Mohrenschildt spent most of the month of May, 1963,
    in Washington. Document "d" sets forth the chronology of the itinerary
    of this visit. Although Pierce would not reveal the details of this

The next 2 pages (pp. 434-435) are a memorandum from: Bernard Fensterwald, Jr.
to: Gary Shaw, Mary Ferrell. Re: CLÉMARD Joseph Charles. Report of a meeting Fensterwald had with Army Intelligence who reported to him in 1983 that CLÉMARD
Joseph Charles had died.

434

MEMORANDUM
RE: CLEMARD, Joseph Charles
June 30, 1983
Page Two

itinerary, he stated that Charles was here for approximately three weeks.

3. Charles had two distinct objectives: (a) he came with an unspecified amount of money which he wanted to invest in the U.S.; (b) he had a much broader non-commercial objective which would require cooperation from many departments and agencies of the U.S. Government. He wished to meet with various high officials, but he was shuffled off onto medium-rank U.S. officials. No meetings were physically held at the Pentagon.

4. According to Pierce, George de Mohrenschildt acted as introducer, interpreter, and general foot-rubber. He did not appear to have a substantive role in Charles' project, whatever it was.

5. Pierce would not reveal the nature of Charles' objective but said that revelation of it publicly would still raise all sorts of hell in the Caribbean. It is my hunch, totally unconfirmed by Pierce, that Charles was fomenting some type of overthrow of the Duvalier government. Whatever his objective, he received little or no symphathy or help from the U.S. Government.

6. I reminded Pierce that during May, 1963, Tommy Davis was recruiting a mercenary force in Los Angeles to overthrow the Duvalier government. He was well aware of this fact but would make no comment about it.

7. Pierce had known Richard Nagell and knew of his involvement in the case. He was non-committal when I said that Nagell had known Oswald in Japan and Mexico. He was also non-committal about Nagell's monthly check from the U.S. Government.

I told Dodell and Pierce that I thought that we would ask Judge Pratt to look at the 9 Army records as they were all being withheld in toto. We will probably proceed on this basis.

435

DISPOSITION FORM
(AR 340-15)

REFERENCE OR OFFICE SYMBOL	SUBJECT
ODLA	Security Considerations re Clemard Joseph CHARLES, SD 11612

TO	FROM	DATE	CMT 1
OD	Ch, ODLA	5 Sep 68 MAJ Gauer/sh/48441	

1. (S) BACKGROUND: Clemard J. CHARLES came to the attention of USI in April 1963 when General Fitch, then Assistant Chief of Staff for Intelligence, advised Mrs. Matlack, Chief, Exploitations Branch, Resources Division, DFI, of Subject's apparent long range potential for the U. S. Intelligence community. Referral was made by Major General Del Mar, Director, Inter-American Defense College. Major General Del Mar has received information on Subject as a result of a letter from CHARLES's business associate, Mr. Joseph D. F. Dryer, Jr., West Palm Beach, Fla, to "Jackie" Del Mar, stepmother of General Del Mar. CHARLES came to the U. S. in 1963 in an apparent attempt to obtain support from the U. S. government of his determination to overthrow the Duvalier regime.

2. (S) PERTINENT SECURITY DATA:

    a. Mrs. Matlack, coordinating with CIA(W) and DIA, began assessment of Subject to determine His usability as a clandestine agent in Haiti. During the months in which personal contacts were being conducted, April and May 1963, Subject had personal contact with the following USI individuals:

    (1) Mrs. Dorothy MATLACK, Chief, Exploitations Br, Resources Div, DFI, OACSI.

    (2) Mr. Tony CZALJKOWSKI, CIA/00, Washington, D. C.

    (3) "Major" BALOG, CIA Rep, New York, N. Y.

    (4) Mr. Louis A. BRUN, CIA Source, New York, N. Y.

    (5) COL Samuel KAIL, Military Chief, CAC, Miami, Fla.

    (6) Major ROGERS, U.S. Army Debriefer, DIA, Washington, D. C.

    b. Another of CHARLES's business associates and political advocates, Mr. George De Morenschildt, a business associate of Vice President L. B. Johnson, traveled with Charles in 1963 when he visited various U. S. government officers, both in Washington and in New York. It was De Morenschildt, allegedly a French espionage agent during World War II and now a prominent business financier in Texas, who appeared to have the close personal contacts that provided CHARLES the opportunity to air his views and intentions to the higher echelons of USI and the

008

S NO OBJECTION TO
SSIFICATION
SE OF CIA IN
DOCUMENT
A FORM 1 FEB 62 2

The next 3 pages (pp. 436-438) — AGENCY: INSCOM/CSF; AGENCY FILE NUMBER: AC85140WJ-PAGES 8-10 – DATE: 09/05/68. Note in this document the description of George de Mohrenschildt as "a business associate of Vice President L. B. Johnson." On p. 3, military intelligence acknowledges that CLÉMARD Joseph Charles "and many of his personal acquaintants have many overt and covert contacts within various U.S. Intelligence agencies ...."

ODLA   ·5 Sep 68
SUBJECT: Security Considerations re Clemard Joseph CHARLES

U.S. Government; on occasions, it was either De Morenschildt or CHARLES who made direct telephone contact with USI, rather than vice versa. How these telephone numbers were obtained is not known.

    c. On 7 May 1963 CIA(W) informed Mrs. Matlack that CHARLES was of no further interest to them. No explanation for this decision was given. This incident left Mrs. Matlack with the task of deciding the final disposition of CHARLES's intelligence potential. From all evidence available in CHARLES's file, it is not clear as to Mrs. Matlack's final decision, from 1963 to 1968, when the case was made available to USAFSG. However, when Mrs. Matlack briefed MAJ Gauer and Mr. Barbella, ODLA, USAFSG, at the direction of COL Rolfe, Mrs. Matlack revealed that CHARLES had mailed correspondence to a CIA controlled A/A in New York during the period 1963 - 1968. The correspondence received at the A/A was forwarded to Mrs. Matlack for disposition. The most recent correspondence from CHARLES, dtd 12 Jun 68, were letters addressed to Mrs. Jacqueline Del Mar requesting her financial assistance to obtain CHARLES's release from prison (see para 2d). During her briefing Mrs. Matlack revealed that she did not want to forward the letters to Jacqueline Del Mar, who, subsequent to 1963, married the Panamanian ambassador to the US. Mrs. Matlack was anxious to receive guidance on the course of action to pursue with the letters and asked what FSG proposed to do with CHARLES. On 1 August 1968, Mrs Matlack was advised that nothing would be done about the most recent letters received and addressed to Mrs. Del Mar. Time had, by that time, overtaken any need to respond to these letters. Mrs. Matlack was further advised that FSG was conducting a security review of the CHARLES file and would advise her of the results.

    d. CHARLES's political intentions, during the period 1963-1968, were not confined to a small group of HIS elite associates, but, in fact, were widely spread throughout all levels of the Haitian citizenry, to include the Haitian exile community. This fact was made evident in a letter from CHARLES, dated 6 June 1967, sent directly to Mrs. Matlack, OACSI/DA, Washington, D.C. CHARLES also made it known in this letter that his plans to overthrow Duvalier had culminated to the extent that his vast number of supporters in this effort were "ready and eager to begin operations" and were only awaiting word from CHARLES. The month in which this letter was written, June 1967, began the succession of events that impeded CHARLES's hope of becoming President and reduced his political and economic power. CHARLES was later imprisoned and many of his collaborators were executed. This otherwise unprovoked 'purge' of national officials presumably arose as a result of Duvalier's awareness of the planned coup.

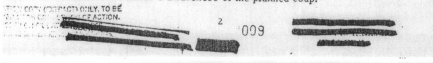

2   009

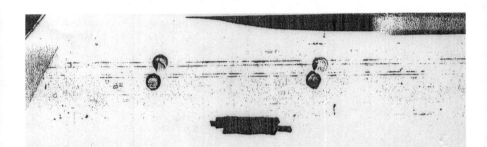

ODLA   5 Sep 68
SUBJECT: Security Considerations re; Clemard Joseph **CHARLES**

3. (U) CONCLUSIONS: All available evidence in the case of Clemard Joseph
CHARLES indicates that he and many of his personal acquaintances have many
overt and covert contacts within various U.S. Intelligence agencies and that
any attempt to control this individual involves the risk of a compromise of very
sensitive information, to include identification of numerous USI personalities.
As indicated in paragraph 2a, CHARLES already has had contact with various
USI personalities; any additional contact will only further the risk of compromise
of USAFSG. As indicated in paragraph 2d, CHARLES's anti-GOH activities have
become well known throughout Haiti and there is now reason to believe that He
is under strong suspicion by Duvalier. Consequently, it may be concluded that
all His activities will be closely monitored in the future and that any attempt on
the part of USI to contact CHARLES would be highly subject to detection by the
Government of Haiti.

4. (U) RECOMMENDATIONS: Recommend that USAFSG take no action to attempt
to contact subject and that Mrs. Matlack be informed that this Headquarters has
taken action to terminate OI in him.

RALPH C. GAUER
Major, MI
Chief, ODLA

3

Documents

PUBLIC RELATIONS • ADVERTISING
321 SOUTH HENDERSON • P. O. BOX 2737 • FORT WORTH, TEXAS 76101 • EDison 5-1373

April 26, 1968

Mr. Paul M. Rothermel, Jr.
Hunt Oil Company
1401 Elm Street
Dallas, Texas 75202

Dear Mr. Rothermel:

I am flattered that my brief letter to Mr. Hunt regarding the
Kennedy assassination prompts you to inquire whether I would be
interested in a writing job for Mr. Hunt's varied interests.

Indeed, I did major in journalism at TCU, was editor of the
campus newspaper, and graduated with honors in 1949. However,
since 1949 I have been in the advertising business. I am vice-
president and executive art director of the largest (and best!)
public relations and advertising agency in Fort Worth. My associates
and myself are all owners of our business and are quite pleased
with what we have built over the past 20 years. It would take a
most lucrative and pleasant opportunity to lure me away from my
present job.

Certainly Mr. Hunt could make anyone a very lucrative offer.
And since my political beliefs are very similar to his, I'm
sure we'd get along well. (I agreed with his letter published
in the Star-Telegram yesterday about Hubert Humphrey. Also,
I think Bobby Kennedy is one of the greatest menaces to our
country today. The only politicians on the scene right now
who seem to be talking sense are 1. John Tower, 2. Ronald Regan,
3. Richard Nixon, and 4. George Wallace.)

I admire Mr. Hunt's individualism, patriotism, beliefs, success,
and constant search for truth, and I'm sure that writing for him
would be both pleasant and rewarding. However, I believe that
for the present it is better for me to confine my writing to
"Letters to the Editor" columns.

I don't know for sure what type of writer you're looking for,
but I would like to suggest to you the name of Harold Weisberg,
Route 8, Box 304, Frederick, Maryland 21701. Although he is
probably a liberal of sorts, his search for truth rates him as
an outstanding patriot. He has diligently and at great personal
expense investigated the Warren Report and written 4 books about
its errors. Because of the controversial nature of his books

GUY WITHERSPOON, President • IRVIN A. FARMAN, Executive Vice-President • FRANK BURKETT, Vice-President
EUGENE R. MILLER, Vice-President • JACK WHITE, Vice-President • JOHN G. WITHERSPOON, Secretary-Treasurer

The next 2 pages (pp. 439-440) are a 1968 letter from Jack White to Paul Rothermel.

2

he had to publish them personally at great loss to himself. Despite this, he continues his search for the truth, because he believes the country is in grave danger as long as the truth about the CIA role in the assassination continues to be suppressed by those who are withholding it from us.

I noticed your letter stated that you had done some research into the assassination on your own, and that you also believe the truth should be told. I'd be interested in any facts or conclusions you have reached, and I'm sure Mr. Weisberg would too.

Also, if someone with sufficient finances could be found to back it, I'm sure that a dignified and proper "Assassination Museum" in Dallas near Dealey Plaza would be a very desirable historical site for visitors to Dallas. Every time I visit Dallas, I see dozens of persons, obviously visitors to the city, looking at the place where "it happened". If such a Museum were to be a commercial venture, and if it were extremely well done and very tasteful, I believe it would be very profitable. I believe that easily 1000 persons a day would pay at least a dollar each to visit it. I base this on having stood in Dealey Plaza one afternoon recently for about two hours, during which time at least 200 persons came and read the plaque, looked up to the sixth floor window, and walked over to look at the middle of Elm Street where the shots struck the president.

I had great dislike for the policies of John Kennedy, especially The Bay of Pigs fiasco. But regardless of that, I think our country is in serious shape when the president himself can be gunned down in the street of one of our great cities. And it is even worse to consider that his true assassins are probably still at large, and that for some reason our own government is hiding the real truth from the people.

I hope that you and Mr. Hunt can help contribute to this search for truth in some way.

Sincerely yours,

Jack White

Jack White

P.S. Should Mr. Hunt ever be looking for a good public relations or advertising firm to help his many varied enterprises, I'd be glad to recommend to him one of the best.

BIBLIOGRAPHY

Abbott, Elizabeth. *Haiti: The Duvaliers and Their Legacy*. McGraw-Hill: New York. 1989.

Adamson, Bruce Campbell. *Oswald's Closest Friend: The George de Mohrenschildt Story*. Volumes I-IX. Santa Cruz, California, 1993, 1995, 1997.

Agee, Philip. *Inside The Company: CIA Diary*. Penguin Books: Harmondsworth, Middlesex, England. 1975.

Arévalo, Juan José. *The Shark and The Sardines*. Translated by June Cobb and Dr. Raul Osegueda. Lyle Stuart: New York. 2009. Originally published in 1961.

Avril, Prosper. *From Glory To Disgrace: The Haitian Army, 1804-1994*. Universal Publishers: Boca Raton, Florida. 1999.

Baker, Russ. *Family of Secrets: The Bush Dynasty, The Powerful Forces That Put It In The White House, And What Their Influence Means For America*. Bloomsbury Press: New York. 2009.

Bancroft, Mary. *Autobiography of a Spy: Debutante, Writer, Confidante, Secret Agent: The True Story Of Her Extraordinary Life*. William Morrow and Company, Inc.: New York, 1983.

Blum, William. *Killing Hope: U.S. Military and C.I.A. Interventions Since World War II*. Common Courage Press: Monroe, Maine. 2004.

Bonanno, Bill. *Bound By Honor: A Mafioso's Story*. St. Martin's Press: New York. 1999.

Brewton, Pete. *The Mafia, CIA & George Bush: The Untold Story of America's Greatest Financial Debacle*. Spi Books (Shapolsky Publishers, Inc.: New York. 1992.

Bush, George (with Victor Gold). *Looking Forward: An Autobiography*. Bantam Books: New York. 1988.

--. : *All The Best, George Bush: My Life In Letters And Other Writings*. Scribner: New York. 1999.

Canning, Peter. *American Dreamers: The Wallaces and Reader's Digest: An Insider's Story*. Simon & Schuster: New York. 1996.

Caro, Robert A. *The Years of Lyndon Johnson: Master of the Senate.* Alfred A. Knopf: New York. 2002.

--------------------------. *Means Of Ascent.* Alfred A. Knopf: New York, 1990.

--------------------------. *The Path To Power.* Alfred A. Knopf: New York. 1982.

Cline, Ray S. *Secrets, Spies and Scholars: Blueprint of the Essential CIA.* Acropolis Books, Ltd.: Washington, D. C. 2009. Originally published in 1976.

Danner, Mark. *Stripping Bare The Body: Politics Violence War.* Nation Books: New York. 2009.

Davis, John H. *Mafia Kingfish: Carlos Marcello and the Assassination of John F. Kennedy.* Mc-Graw Hill Publishing Company: New York. 1989.

DeLillo, Don. *Libra.* Simon & Schuster: New York. 1981.

De Vosjoli, P. L. Thyraud. *Lamia* [CODE NAME LAMIA]. Little, Brown and Company: Boston. 1970.

Diederich, Bernard and Burt, AI. *Papa Doc: The Truth About Haiti Today.* Avon: New York. 1969.

Dubois, Laurent. *Haiti: The Aftershocks of History.* Metropolitan Books: New York. 2012.

Dugger, Ronnie. *The Politician: The Life and Times of Lyndon Johnson.* W. W. Norton & Company: New York. 1982.

Epstein, Edward Jay. *The Assassination Chronicles: Inquest, Counterplot, and Legend.* Carroll & Graf: New York. 1992.

Ferguson, James. *Papa Doc Baby Doc: Haiti and the Duvaliers.* Basil Blackwell: Oxford and New York. 1987.

Flammonde, Paris. *The Kennedy Conspiracy: An Uncommissioned Report On The Garrison Investigation.* Meredith Press: New York. 1969.

Fonzi, Gaeton. *The Last Investigation.* Thunder's Mouth Press: New York. 1994.

Frazier, Howard, ed. *Uncloaking the CIA.* The Free Press: New York. 1978.

Girard, Philippe. *Haiti: The Tumultuous History: From Pearl of the Caribbean to Broken Nation.* Palgrave Macmillan: New York. 2010.

Goodwin, Doris Kearns. *Lyndon Johnson And The American Dream*. St. Martin's Press: New York. 1991.

Greene, Graham. *The Comedians: A Novel*. The Viking Press: New York. 1966.

Grose, Peter. *Gentleman Spy: The Life of Allen Dulles*. The University of Massachusetts Press: Amherst. 1994.

Heidenry, John. *Theirs Was The Kingdom: Lila and DeWitt Wallace: The Story Of The Reader's Digest*. W. W. Norton & Company: New York. 1993.

Heinl, Robert Debs and Heinl, Nancy Gordon. *Written In Blood: The Story of the Haitian People 1492-1995*. University Press of America, Inc.: Lanham, Maryland. 2005.

Hersh, Burton. *The Old Boys: The American Elite And The Origins Of The CIA*. Charles Scribner's Sons: New York. 1992).

Hougan, Jim. *Spooks: the Haunting of America – The Private Use of Secret Agents*. William Morrow and Company, Inc.: New York. 1978.

Hurt, III, Harry. *Texas Rich: The Hunt Dynasty From The Early Oil Days Through The Silver Crash*. Replica books: Bridgewater, New Jersey. 1999.

James, C.L.R. *The Black Jacobins: Toussaint L'Ouverture and the San Domingo Revolution*. Vintage Books: New York. 1989.

Josephson, Matthew. *The Robber Barons: The Great American Capitalists, 1861-1901*. A Harvest Book: Harcourt, Brace & World, Inc.: New York. 1963. First published in 1934.

Karalekas, Anne. *History of the Central Intelligence Agency*. Aegean Park Press: Laguna Hills, California. 1977.

Karnow, Stanley. *Vietnam: A History*. Penguin Books: New York. 1991.

Kwitny, Jonathan. *Endless Enemies: The Making Of An Unfriendly World*. Congdon & Weed, Inc.: New York. 1984.

Lane, Mark. *Plausible Denial: Was The CIA Involved In The Assassination Of JFK?* Thunder's Mouth Press: New York. 1991.

Lemoine, Patrick. *Fort-Dimanche, DUNGEON OF DEATH*. Translated from the French with the collaboration of Frantz Haspil. Revised and Edited by Patrick Lemoine and Mayse Prezeau. Trafford Publishing: Uniondale, New York. 2011.

443

LeSueur, James D. *Uncivil War: Intellectuals and Identity Politics During the Decolonization of Algeria.* The University of Pennsylvania Press: Philadelphia. 2001.

Livingstone, Harrison Edward. *Killing The Truth: Deceit and Deception In The JFK Case.* Carroll & Graf Publishers, Inc.: New York. 1993.

Loftus, John and Mark Aarons. *The Secret War Against The Jews: How Western Espionage Betrayed The Jewish People.* St. Martin's Press: New York. 1994. See also: Mark Aarons and John Loftus, *Unholy Trinity: How The Vatican's Nazi Networks Betrayed Western Intelligence to the Soviets.* St. Martin's Press: New York. 1991.

Loftus, John J. *America's Nazi Secret.* TrineDay: Waterville, Oregon. 2010.

Mangold, Tom. *Cold Warrior: James Jesus Angleton: The CIA's Master Spy Hunter.* Simon & Schuster: New York. 1991.

Mellen, Joan. *A Farewell To Justice: Jim Garrison, JFK's Assassination And The Case That Should Have Changed History.* Potomac Books: Dulles, Virginia. 2005.

McCartney, Laton. *Friends In High Places: The Bechtel Story: The Most Secret Corporation and How It Engineered the World.* Ballantine Books: New York. 1989.

McMillan, Priscilla Johnson. *Marina and Lee.* Harper & Row: New York. 1977.

Mosley, Leonard. *Dulles: A Biography Of Eleanor, Allen, And John Foster Dulles And Their Family Network.* The Dial Press/James Wade: New York, 1978.

Nicholls, David. *From Dessalines to Duvalier: Race, Colour and National Independence in Haiti.* Rutgers University Press: New Brunswick, New Jersey. 1996.

Phillips, Kevin. *American Dynasty: Aristocracy, Fortune, and the Politics of Deceit in the House of Bush.* The Viking Press: New York. 2004.

Pope, Paul David. *The Deeds Of My Fathers: How My Grandfather and Father Built New York and Created The Tabloid World of Today.* A Philip Turner Book: Rowman & Littlefield Publishers, Inc. 2010.

Powers, Thomas. *The Man Who Kept The Secrets: Richard Helms And The CIA.* Alfred A. Knopf: New York. 1979.

Pratt, Joseph A. & Christopher J. Castaneda. *Builders: Herman and George Brown.* Texas A & M University Press: College Station, Texas. 1999.

Prouty, L. Fletcher. *The Secret Team: The CIA And Its Allies In Control of the United States And The World.* Skyhorse Publishing: New York. 2008.

Quirk, Robert E. *Fidel Castro.* W. W. Norton & Company: New York. 1993.

Ranelagh, John. *The Agency: The Rise and Decline of the CIA.* A Touchstone Book: Simon & Schuster: New York. 1987.

Reeves, Richard. *President Kennedy: Profile Of Power.* Simon & Schuster: New York. 1993.

Rotberg, Robert I. (with Christopher K. Clague). *Haiti: The Politics of Squalor.* Houghton Mifflin Company: Boston. 1971.

Russell, Dick. *On The Trail Of The JFK Assassins.* A Herman Graf Book: Skyhorse Publishing: New York. 2008.

------------------.*The Man Who Knew Too Much.* Carroll & Graf: New York. 1992.

Revised Edition: Carroll & Graf: New York. 2003.

Saunders, Frances Stoner. *Who Paid The Piper? The CIA and The Cultural Cold War.* Granta Books: London. 2000.

Schlesinger, Jr., Arthur M. *Robert Kennedy And His Times.* Ballantine Books: New York. 1978.

Schreiber, G. R. *The Bobby Baker Affair: How To Make Millions In Washington.* Henry Regnery Company: Chicago. 1964.

Summers, Anthony. *Not In Your Lifetime.* Marlowe & Company: New York. 1998.

Thomas, Evan. *The Very Best Men: Four Who Dared: The Early Years Of The CIA.* Simon & Schuster: New York. 1995.

Trento, Joseph J. *Prelude To Terror: The Rogue CIA and the Legacy of America's Intelligence Network.* Carroll & Graf Publishers: New York. 2005.

-----------------------. *The Secret History Of The CIA.* Forum: Prima Publishing: Roseville, California. 2001.

Tully, Andrew. *CIA: The Inside Story.* William Morrow and Company: New York. 1962.

445

Unger, Craig. *House Of Bush, House Of Saud: The Secret Relationship Between The World's Two Most Powerful Dynasties*. Scribner: New York. 2004.

Uris, Leon. *Topaz: A Novel*. McGraw-Hill Book Company: New York. 1967.

Valentine, Douglas. *The Strength of the Wolf: The Secret History of America's War On Drugs*. Verso: New York. 2004.

Van Buren, Ernestine Orrick. *Clint: Clinton Williams Murchison: A Biography*. Eakin Press: Austin, Texas. 1986.

Weiner, Tim. *Legacy of Ashes: The History of the CIA*. Doubleday: New York. 2007.

Wilford, Hugh. *The Mighty Wurlitzer: How The CIA Played America*. Harvard University Press: Cambridge, Massachusetts. 2008.

Wolfe, Jane. *The Murchisons: The Rise and Fall of a Texas Dynasty*. St. Martin's Paperbacks: New York. 1989.

Index

Index

Sharples Oil Corporation, 35
Shaw, Clay, 54–55, 56, 210, 353
Sigurd, Inc., 16
Smith, Walter Bedell, 147
Snyder, Richard E., 84–85
soldiers of fortune, 26, 119, 201–203,
    236, 271, 285–286, 353
Somoza, Anastasio, 127
Soukar, Michel, 232
Soustelle, Jacques, 148–149, 151, 232
Soviet Realities (SR6), 84, 155
Soviet Union, 11, 45, 152, 315n146
Spain in Arms (film), 26
Specht, Udo H., Jr., 374
Specter, Arlen, 378
SR6, 84, 155
St. Charles Pacific Peace Organiza-
    tion, 285
St. George, Andrew, 237
State Department, 23, 45, 110, 122
Stawinski, Wojciech, 190, 192
Stockman, Father, 178
Stokes, Louis, 378
Stone, C. Frank, III, 83, 86–88, 93, 99,
    113–116
Strength of the Wolf, 150
Stuntz, Mayo, 101–102, 105, 111, 265
Sturgis, Frank (Fiorini), 285–286
Sullivan, Geoffrey, 286
Super Constellation, 244–246

T

T-28 fighter aircraft, 169, 181–184, 184,
    188–189, 199, 201, 205, 248
Tanenbaum, Robert, 271, 273
Taylor, Gary, 44, 121
Taylor, Maxwell, 74
Taylor, Robert, 183
Texas Eastern, 43
Thomas, David R., 76
Thomas, Hugh, 137
Thurn, Elizabeth von, 175
Thurston, Raymond, 116–117, 124
Tilford, James B., Jr., 204
Tilton, Nancy, 274–276

Time, 150, 181, 199
    see also *Life*
Timmons, Benson E. L. (Ellison Lane)
    AID and, 229
    Davidson and, 125
    on de Mohrenschildt, 172, 207–208
    de Mohrenschildt and, 174
    de Mohrenschildt (Jeanne) and, 223
    Duvalier and, 131, 180–181, 211, 229
Tito, Marshal, 41
Tolson, Clyde, 260
Tolstoy, Leo, 34
Tonesk, William, 103
Tontons Macoutes
    actions following invasion, 119
    Charles and, 98
    CIA and, 74
    leader of, former, 196
    members of, 222
    opposing CIA, 74
    power of, 165–166, 251
    as private militia, 7
Topaz, 158–159, 357
Toussaint L'Ouverture, 2, 6
Trafficante, Santos, 281
Train, John, 83, 87
Trammel, Connie, 346–347
Trujillo, Rafael, 119, 131, 137, 202,
    209
    see also Dominican Republic
Tully, Andrew, 151
Turks and Caicos Islands, 244
2010 earthquake, 321n208

U

UN Stabilization Mission, 293–294
Union des Banques Suisses, 232
United States Customs Service, 22,
    236, 239
United States Department of State, 15
Unlawful Killing (film), 213
Uris, Leon, 158–159, 357
U.S. Embassy, 75–76, 122–123
U.S. government
    aid to Haiti, 8–9, 229

461